Know That You Are Worthy

Experiences from First-Generation College Graduates

Edited by
ADAM J. RODRÍGUEZ

Foreword by
YOLANDA NORMAN
FirstGenCollege Consulting

ROWMAN & LITTLEFIELD
Lanham • Boulder • New York • London

Executive Acquisitions Editor: Mark Kerr
Assistant Acquisitions Editor: Sarah Rinehart
Sales and Marketing Inquiries: textbooks@rowman.com

Published by Rowman & Littlefield
An imprint of The Rowman & Littlefield Publishing Group, Inc.
4501 Forbes Boulevard, Suite 200, Lanham, Maryland 20706
www.rowman.com

86-90 Paul Street, London EC2A 4NE

Copyright © 2023 by The Rowman & Littlefield Publishing Group, Inc.

Excerpt from *The Inequality Machine* by Paul Tough, copyright © 2019 by Paul Tough, used by permission of HarperCollins Publishers.

Excerpt from *Moving Up Without Losing Your Way: The Ethical Costs of Upward Mobility* by Jennifer M. Morton, copyright © 2021 by Princeton University Press, used by permission.

Excerpts from *The Privileged Poor: How Elite Colleges Are Failing Disadvantaged Students* by Anthony Abraham Jack, copyright © 2019 by Anthony Abraham Jack. Cambridge, Mass.: Harvard University Press. Used by permission. All rights reserved.

All rights reserved. No part of this book may be reproduced in any form or by any electronic or mechanical means, including information storage and retrieval systems, without written permission from the publisher, except by a reviewer who may quote passages in a review.

British Library Cataloguing in Publication Information Available

Library of Congress Cataloging-in-Publication Data
Names: Rodriguez, Adam J., 1975– editor.
Title: Know that you are worthy : experiences from first generation college graduates / Edited by Adam J. Rodriguez ; Foreword by Yolanda Norman, Concordia University Texas and FirstGenCollege Consulting.
Description: Lanham, Maryland : Rowman & Littlefield, [2023] | Includes bibliographical references and index.
Identifiers: LCCN 2022049177 (print) | LCCN 2022049178 (ebook) | ISBN 9781538162408 (cloth) | ISBN 9781538162415 (paperback) | ISBN 9781538162422 (ebook)
Subjects: LCSH: First-generation college students—United States. | College graduates—United States. | People with social disabilities—Education (Higher)—United States. | Motivation in education—United States.
Classification: LCC LC4069.6 .K56 2023 (print) | LCC LC4069.6 (ebook) | DDC 378.1/9820973—dc23/eng/20221028
LC record available at https://lccn.loc.gov/2022049177
LC ebook record available at https://lccn.loc.gov/2022049178

PRAISE FOR *KNOW THAT YOU ARE WORTHY: EXPERIENCES FROM FIRST-GENERATION COLLEGE GRADUATES*

"*Know That You Are Worthy* will be a gift to the field ranging from high school and college access programs to colleges/universities and beyond. This text is practical but also research-driven. I would strongly encourage that programs like AVID (Advancement Via Individual Determination) and TRIO (programs under Title IV of the Higher Education Act), as well as the many first-generation-only seminars across institutions, incorporate this book into their curriculum. Many first-generation students will see themselves in these narratives and will feel empowered. Come for the stories but stay for the recommendations!" —**La'Tonya Rease Miles, PhD, Career Launch**

"Using the voices of first-generation graduates to illustrate the academic, social, cultural, and psychological challenges faced by these students, *Know That You Are Worthy* provides shared common experiences and advice for incoming first-generation students, as well as recommendations for colleges, faculty, and staff for ways to work toward equity in education opportunities. Readers and those working with first-generation students will be able to more fully understand the unique joys and obstacles experienced by this varied group of learners." —**Mo Cuevas, PhD, LCSW, Worden School of Social Service, Our Lady of the Lake University**

"This book is quite impressive; it is organized around themes that have been central to the discussion of first-generation students." —**Amy Baldwin, EdD, Department of Student Transitions, University of Central Arkansas**

"This book unpacks the diverse and multifaceted experiences of 'being a first-generation student.' It is inspiring for both students and practitioners to normalize being first-generation and better support first-generation students in college." —**Xiaodan Hu, Department of Counseling and Higher Education, Northern Illinois University**

"The stories from *Know That You Are Worthy: Experiences from First-Generation College Graduates* speak from the heart and contain critical insights and guidance. A must-read for students so that they know they are not alone in their own pursuit of success." —**Valerie De Cruz, director, Greenfield Intercultural Center, University of Pennsylvania**

"As access to higher education has increased, first-generation students have become a growing and distinctive population at U.S. colleges and universities. Ensuring student success for first-gens requires that college and university leaders, faculty, and staff understand the unique challenges of this student population, in order to best design programs and curriculum that meet their needs. *Know That You Are Worthy* offers important insights into the experiences of first-generation college graduates, helping to humanize first-gen students' experiences and providing recommendations for colleges that aim to improve first-generation student success." —**Teniell L. Trolian, University at Albany, State University of New York**

To all past, current, and future who were, are, or will be first

Brief Contents

Foreword	xix
Acknowledgments	xxi
Introduction by *Adam J. Rodríguez*	1

SECTION I • STORIES FEATURING ACADEMIC EXPERIENCES   17
Adam J. Rodríguez

Chapter 1   21
Anthony Vargas, Student Affairs, Campus Living University at Buffalo

Chapter 2   **Mapping Out College to Career Goals in Real Time**   26
Jeremy Edwards, PhD, Lecturer for the Program in Writing and Rhetoric at Stanford University

Chapter 3   **Success Is Not a Linear Path**   33
Ivonne Martinez, Pursuing Master's in Data Science

Chapter 4   39
Desireé Vega, PhD, Associate Professor, School Psychology

Chapter 5   44
Yvonne M. Luna, PhD, Associate Vice Provost and Professor of Sociology

Chapter 6   50
Maria Dykema Erb, MEd, Director of the Newbury Center, Boston University

Chapter 7   57
David Winston, MD, PhD, Forensic Pathologist

Chapter 8   62
Mike Santaniello, Professor of Sociology

Chapter 9   67
Lynn Pepin, BSE, Completing PhD in Computer Science

Chapter 10   From North Philly to Faculty: *Testimonio* of a First-Generation Latinx College Student Surviving and Thriving at a Historically White University   72
Stephen Santa-Ramirez, PhD, Assistant Professor of Higher Education, Department of Educational Leadership and Policy, University at Buffalo

Critical Self-Reflection 1   79
Adam J. Rodríguez

SECTION II · STORIES FEATURING SOCIAL EXPERIENCES   83
Adam J. Rodríguez

Chapter 11   The Little Girl from Gay, Georgia   87
Patricia Harris, MA, Senior Director of Education, Operations, and Initiatives, University of North Carolina at Chapel Hill

Chapter 12   In My Own Way   93
David Hernández, Associate Professor, Latina/o Studies Faculty Director of Community Engagement, Mount Holyoke College

Chapter 13   98
Jenny Lieurance, First-Generation Specialist

Chapter 14   103
Glynis Boyd Hughes, Grant Writer and Storyteller

Chapter 15   109
T. Mark Montoya, PhD, Associate Professor of Ethnic Studies

Chapter 16   114
Joyce Stewart, Senior Academic Lecturer, English Department

Chapter 17   120
Kevin L. Wright, EdD, Senior Equity Facilitator/Consultant at the Center for Equity and Inclusion

Chapter 18   **125**
Sonja Ardoin, PhD, Associate Professor and Program Director,
Student Affairs Administration

Chapter 19   **131**
Kamina P. Richardson, Assistant Program Director and Pre-Law Advisor
for Legal Studies Program at Temple University's Fox School of Business

Chapter 20   **136**
Emilee Claire Inez, Admissions Representative, University of Wyoming

Critical Self-Reflection 2   **140**
Adam J. Rodríguez

SECTION III • STORIES FEATURING PSYCHOLOGICAL EXPERIENCES   143
Adam J. Rodríguez

Chapter 21   **To the Garden That Blossomed Seeds of Dreams**   **147**
Ulises Morales, Executive Assistant

Chapter 22   **152**
Mayra González Menjívar, Communications Associate

Chapter 23   **160**
Kallie Clark, MSW, PhD, Educator and Researcher

Chapter 24   **166**
Dawna Jones, MEd, MSW, Director, Mary Lou Williams Center
for Black Culture at Duke University

Chapter 25   **The Paths We Pave**   **172**
Mytien Nguyen, MD-PhD Student

Chapter 26   **178**
Sean Richardson, Pursuing Master's in Higher Education Administration

Chapter 27   **Navigating Uncharted Waters**   **183**
Adj Marshall, Families Program and Policy Administrator
Massachusetts Institute of Technology

Chapter 28   189
Clifton E. Shambry Jr., Assistant Director of Life Design for Diversity and Inclusion

Chapter 29   194
Raquel Gutierrez Cortez, MSCP, Associate Marriage and Family Therapist, Associate Professional Clinical Counselor

Chapter 30   199
Karen Hill, BA, Completing Master of Science in Counseling

Chapter 31   205
Henry Rosas Ibarra, Political Consultant

Critical Self-Reflection 3   211
Adam J. Rodríguez

Chapter 32   Discussion   214
Adam J. Rodríguez

Chapter 33   Tips and Advice for First-Generation College Students and Their Families   223
Adam J. Rodríguez

Chapter 34   Creating Equity and Justice: Recommendations for Colleges, Faculty, and Staff   230
Adam J. Rodríguez

Glossary of Select College Terms   249
Appendix: Resources   259
References   261
Index   265
About the Contributors   275

Contents

Foreword	xix
Acknowledgments	xxi
Introduction by *Adam J. Rodríguez*	1
First-Generation Students Defined	2
College Culture	4
Structure and Content of the Book	7
Contributors	8
Emergence of Themes	10
Sections	12
Critical Self-Reflection	14
The Strengths of First-Generation Students	14

SECTION I · STORIES FEATURING ACADEMIC EXPERIENCES   17
Adam J. Rodríguez

Chapter 1   21
Anthony Vargas, Student Affairs, Campus Living University at Buffalo

Applying to and Preparing for College	21
Experiences in College	22
Contributors to My Success	23
Role of Family	24
Tips and Advice	24

Chapter 2   Mapping Out College to Career Goals in Real Time   26
Jeremy Edwards, PhD, Lecturer for the Program in Writing and Rhetoric at Stanford University

Applying to and Preparing for College	27
Experiences in College	28
Contributors to My Success	30
Role of Family	30
Tips and Advice	31

Chapter 3   Success Is Not a Linear Path   33
Ivonne Martinez, Pursuing Master's in Data Science

    Applying to and Preparing for College   33
    Experiences in College   34
    Contributors to My Success   37
    Role of Family   37
    Tips and Advice   38

Chapter 4   39
Desireé Vega, PhD, Associate Professor, School Psychology

    Applying to and Preparing for College   40
    Experiences in College   40
    Contributors to My Success   41
    Role of Family   42
    Tips and Advice   42

Chapter 5   44
Yvonne M. Luna, PhD, Associate Vice Provost and Professor of Sociology

    Applying to and Preparing for College   44
    Experiences in College   45
    Contributors to My Success: I Didn't Do It Alone   47
    Role of *Mi Familia*   48
    Tips and Advice   48

Chapter 6   50
Maria Dykema Erb, MEd, Director of the Newbury Center, Boston University

    Applying to and Preparing for College   50
    Experiences in College   51
    Contributors to My Success   53
    Role of Family   54
    Tips and Advice   55

Chapter 7   57
David Winston, MD, PhD, Forensic Pathologist

    Applying to and Preparing for College   57
    Experiences in College   58
    Contributors to My Success   59
    Role of Family   60
    Tips and Advice   60

Chapter 8   62
Mike Santaniello, Professor of Sociology

    Applying to and Preparing for College   62
    Experiences in College   63

Contributors to My Success	65
Role of Family	66
Tips and Advice	66

Chapter 9   67

Lynn Pepin, BSE, Completing PhD in Computer Science

Applying to and Preparing for College	67
Experiences in College	68
Contributors to My Success	69
Role of Family	70
Tips and Advice	70

Chapter 10   From North Philly to Faculty: *Testimonio* of a First-Generation Latinx College Student Surviving and Thriving at a Historically White University   72

Stephen Santa-Ramirez, PhD, Assistant Professor of Higher Education, Department of Educational Leadership and Policy, University at Buffalo

Applying to and Preparing for College	73
Experiences in College	74
Contributors to My Success	76
Role of Family	77
Tips and Advice	77

Critical Self-Reflection 1   79

Adam J. Rodríguez

Two Primary Questions	79
Further Discussion Questions	80

SECTION II · STORIES FEATURING SOCIAL EXPERIENCES   83

Adam J. Rodríguez

Chapter 11   The Little Girl from Gay, Georgia   87

Patricia Harris, MA, Senior Director of Education, Operations, and Initiatives, University of North Carolina at Chapel Hill

Applying to and Preparing for College	88
Experiences in College: I Love My SSU	89
Contributors to My Success: Tell Them We Are Rising	90
Role of Family	91
Tips and Advice	92

Chapter 12   In My Own Way   93

David Hernández, Associate Professor, Latina/o Studies Faculty Director of Community Engagement, Mount Holyoke College

Applying to and Preparing for College	93
Experiences in College	94

Contributors to My Success	95
Role of Family	96
Tips and Advice	96

Chapter 13 — 98
Jenny Lieurance, First-Generation Specialist

Applying to and Preparing for College	98
Experiences in College	99
Contributors to My Success	100
Role of Family	101
Tips and Advice	101

Chapter 14 — 103
Glynis Boyd Hughes, Grant Writer and Storyteller

Applying to and Preparing for College	104
Experiences in College	105
Contributors to My Success	106
Role of Family	106
Tips and Advice	107

Chapter 15 — 109
T. Mark Montoya, PhD, Associate Professor of Ethnic Studies

Applying to and Preparing for College	109
Experiences in College	110
Contributors to My Success	111
Role of Family	112
Tips and Advice	112

Chapter 16 — 114
Joyce Stewart, Senior Academic Lecturer, English Department

Applying to and Preparing for College	114
Experiences in College: The Enjoyable and Annoying	115
Contributors to My Success: What Worked for Me	117
Role of Family	118
Tips and Advice	118

Chapter 17 — 120
Kevin L. Wright, EdD, Senior Equity Facilitator/Consultant at the Center for Equity and Inclusion

Applying to and Preparing for College	120
Experiences in College	121
The Classroom	121
Reslife	122
Campus Involvement	122

Contributors to My Success	123
Role of Family	123
Tips and Advice	124

Chapter 18 — 125
Sonja Ardoin, PhD, Associate Professor and Program Director, Student Affairs Administration

Applying to and Preparing for College: LSU Was My Harvard	126
Experiences in College: Finding My Tiger Stripes	127
Contributors to My Serendipitous Success	128
Role of Family: It's Not My Degree, It's Ours	129
Tips and Advice: "My Two Cents" Offering	129

Chapter 19 — 131
Kamina P. Richardson, Assistant Program Director and Pre-Law Advisor for Legal Studies Program at Temple University's Fox School of Business

Applying to and Preparing for College	131
Experiences in College	132
Contributors to My Success	133
Role of Family	134
Tips and Advice	134

Chapter 20 — 136
Emilee Claire Inez, Admissions Representative, University of Wyoming

Applying to and Preparing for College: Before the Bachelor's	136
Experiences in College: Growth in Undergrad	137
Contributors to My Success	138
Role of Family	138
Tips and Advice	139

Critical Self-Reflection 2 — 140
Adam J. Rodríguez

Two Primary Questions	140
Further Discussion Questions	141

SECTION III · STORIES FEATURING PSYCHOLOGICAL EXPERIENCES — 143
Adam J. Rodríguez

Chapter 21 To the Garden That Blossomed Seeds of Dreams — 147
Ulises Morales, Executive Assistant

Applying to and Preparing for College	147
Experiences in College	148

    Contributors to My Success   149
    Role of Family   150
    Tips and Advice   150

Chapter 22   152

Mayra González Menjívar, Communications Associate

    Applying to and Preparing for College   153
    Experiences in College   154
    Contributors to My Success   156
    Role of Family   157
    Tips and Advice   158

Chapter 23   160

Kallie Clark, MSW, PhD, Educator and Researcher

    Applying to and Preparing for College   161
    Experiences in College   161
    Contributors to My Success   162
    Role of Family   163
    Tips and Advice   164

Chapter 24   166

Dawna Jones, MEd, MSW, Director, Mary Lou Williams Center for Black Culture at Duke University

    Applying to and Preparing for College   167
    Experiences in College   168
    Contributors to My Success   169
    Role of Family   170
    Tips and Advice   171

Chapter 25   The Paths We Pave   172

Mytien Nguyen, MD-PhD Student

    Applying to and Preparing for College   172
    Experiences in College   174
    Contributors to My Success   175
    Role of Family   176
    Tips and Advice   176

Chapter 26   178

Sean Richardson, Pursuing Master's in Higher Education Administration

    Applying to and Preparing for College   178
    Experiences in College   179
    Contributors to My Success   180
    Role of Family   181
    Tips and Advice   182

Chapter 27   Navigating Uncharted Waters   **183**
Adj Marshall, Families Program and Policy Administrator
Massachusetts Institute of Technology

    Applying to and Preparing for College   184
    Experiences in College: Assets and Drawbacks   184
    Contributions to My Success   186
    Role of Family   186
    Tips and Advice   187

Chapter 28   **189**
Clifton E. Shambry Jr., Assistant Director of Life Design for Diversity and Inclusion

    The Beginning: Why College   189
    Applying to and Preparing for College   190
    Experiences in College   190
    Contributors to My Success   191
    Role of the Family   192
    Tips and Advice   192

Chapter 29   **194**
Raquel Gutierrez Cortez, MSCP, Associate Marriage and Family Therapist,
Associate Professional Clinical Counselor

    Applying to and Preparing for College   194
    Experiences in College   196
    Contributors to My Success   196
    Role of Family   197
    Tips and Advice   197

Chapter 30   **199**
Karen Hill, BA, Completing Master of Science in Counseling

    Applying to and Preparing for College   199
    Experiences in College   200
    Contributors to My Success   202
    Role of Family   203
    Tips and Advice   203

Chapter 31   **205**
Henry Rosas Ibarra, Political Consultant

    Applying to and Preparing for College   205
    Experiences in College   207
    Contributors to My Success   208
    Role of Family   209
    Tips and Advice   209

Critical Self-Reflection 3 — 211
Adam J. Rodríguez

    Two Primary Questions — 212
    Further Discussion Questions — 212

Chapter 32   Discussion — 214
Adam J. Rodríguez

    Applying to and Preparing for College — 215
    Experiences in College — 217
    Contributors to Success — 218
    Role of Family — 220
    The Costs of Upward Mobility — 221
    Conclusion — 221

Chapter 33   Tips and Advice for First-Generation College Students and Their Families — 223
Adam J. Rodríguez

    College Counseling Services — 226
    Advice for Parents — 227
    Conclusion — 228

Chapter 34   Creating Equity and Justice: Recommendations for Colleges, Faculty, and Staff — 230
Adam J. Rodríguez

    Laying the Groundwork — 231
    Institutional Changes — 233
        Early Intervention — 233
        Admissions Process — 234
        Financial Aid Assistance — 235
        Tutoring Services — 236
        Residence Halls — 236
        Academic Advising — 237
        Mentorship Programs — 237
        Counseling/Mental Health Services — 238
        Increased Representation — 239
    Classroom Level — 241
        Normalizing Adjustment Difficulties — 245
        David Laude and the Texas Interdisciplinary Plan — 246
    Conclusion — 247

Glossary of Select College Terms — 249
Appendix: Resources — 259
    National Organizations — 259
    Books — 259
References — 261
Index — 265
About the Contributors — 275

Foreword

It was the summer of 1998, and I still remember the scenery outside my mother's boyfriend's truck as city buildings and streetlights shifted to stretches of green trees and open fields. I was making my way from Memphis, Tennessee, to Hattiesburg, Mississippi, to begin this new journey in my life called college. Here I was thinking I understood my multiple identities of being a Black, Latina, female, low-income student-athlete who was prepared to figure it all out on my own and get this "college thing" done. Little did I know or anticipate what was involved in the task I had in front of me—navigating through college without having parents who had done the same. You see, it was not until my junior year of college (I still cannot believe it took that long) that I learned about the term "first-generation college student." Despite not learning the term until later, I had felt the "first-gen" identity every step of the way, beginning long before I sat in the truck with my mom that day on the four-hour trip to begin college. During my senior year in high school, I remember signing whatever college application, interest form, and student-athlete questionnaire my track coach gave me. No questions were asked. I had no idea what anything said, but I had total trust in my coach, who told me, "We are going to get you to college, and you don't need to worry about paying for anything."

Throughout my undergraduate years, I navigated through various feelings, from wondering whether I belonged at college, to feeling shame about coming from a low-income neighborhood, to constantly questioning whether I had made the right choice in aspiring to a higher education, to doubting I would ever become a college graduate. Along the way, I am thankful for the coaches, professors, staff (shout out to those loving cafeteria workers), administrators, fellow students, friends, and family who took time to believe in me and helped me to develop the confidence to believe in myself, even when the world said I was statistically disadvantaged and likely to drop out without a degree.

Being a first-generation college student was not easy, but it was a tremendous growth experience that taught me about the unique cultural, social, and familial capital I already possessed. I had only needed to recognize this capital as I navigated the new environment of college, with its different norms and expectations. A lot of the work I do in higher education today is focused on creating intentional opportunities for students to recognize their worth and the strengths they bring to college, especially for my fellow first-generation college students. I attribute a great deal of the inspiration and motivation for my work to my experiences as a first-generation student.

I was humbled when I received the request from Dr. Rodríguez to write the foreword for this book. It captures the lived experiences of first-generation college graduates who tell their stories. As the reader, you are able to witness how each contributor's story adds to the knowledge and themes of what it means to be first-gen and how each voice adds to the diversity within this important student group. I often put out a reminder on Twitter (@FirstGenCollege) that first-generation college students, like all other groups, are not a monolith. As is evidenced in this book, first-generation college graduates come from all types of backgrounds, attend various colleges and universities, and navigate through higher education with multiple identities that highlight the wide-ranging experiences of what it means to be first-gen.

As you dive into this work and hear the different voices from college graduates who each experienced their own version of what it means to be first-gen, continue to pause, reflect, and recognize how the diversity within this group contains both similarities and distinctions that add to the riches of this college student identity known as "first-generation." For faculty, staff, and administrators, how does it challenge or affirm your thinking about how to serve, amplify, and support these students? If you yourself are a current first-generation college student or a graduate, are there situations or feelings here that you are currently experiencing or have experienced in the past? With the help of Dr. Rodríguez's keen eye in the structuring of this book, also notice the common themes that present themselves while you begin to unpack what you can take away from these stories and how they can make an impact on your own college success or the success of others.

To those of you who are current first-generation college students, use this book as motivation, encouragement, and an example of what you are on the path to achieving. To my fellow first-generation college graduates, use this book to affirm, inspire, and learn about others just like you (or different from you) as you continue on in your next chapter. To my fellow university faculty, staff, and administrators, let *us* use this book to recognize, celebrate, and honor the first-gen students on our campuses, share the stories in this book intentionally in our campus conversations, and have critical discussions around the tips and advice the contributors and Dr. Rodríguez offer in this work to help us all acknowledge and remove barriers to college persistence and success.

Dr. Rodríguez, thank you for highlighting the voices and experiences of first-generation college graduates and giving each reader space to do the same in their own communities. First-gen for the win. *Adelante!*

Dr. Yolanda Norman
Proud First-Generation College Graduate (×4)

Acknowledgments

My family is from humble beginnings. My father wore the term *jíbaro* (a Puerto Rican laborer from the hills/country) with pride. I appreciated his affirmation but have also felt *al jíbaro nunca se le quita la mancha de plátano* (a *jíbaro* can never wash away the stain of the plantain). This fear has both haunted me and propelled me forward in life. With time, experience, and perspective, I have come to embrace *la mancha* (the stain). It is mine, and although it has sometimes been a heavy burden to bear, I would not change it.

As the contributors to this book repeatedly point out, it takes a village. So did this book. I am grateful to so many people who made it possible. The heart and soul of it belongs to the 31 brave souls who put their stories onto paper. They allowed themselves to be vulnerable as they revealed their pain and strife, joy and success. I love and admire them. This book, quite simply, would not exist without their courage and tenacity. It would not exist without their stories and their wisdom. They trusted me to help give them a voice, and I hope that I have honored their trust. Anything in this book that is good belongs to them and their efforts. The stains are mine.

Thank you, Amy Backos, for guiding me and tolerating my naivete and shortcomings in this process. You always made me feel like I could do it, and you illuminated the path. You have been not only guide and mentor but also cheerleader. Sara Levley, Roberto González, Maryam Eskandari, and Kristian Kemptrup, among others, all offered valuable feedback, support, and guidance. I am indebted to you all. Thank you to Darcy Crosman. You took my clumsy and awkward words and made them poetry. I dumped hundreds of pages onto your desk, and your only reply was "I got this." You helped make this possible. To Laurie Terzo, who gave me permission to celebrate when otherwise I would have forgotten and stood by me through it all. Thank you to Stephen Santa-Ramirez, whose poetry in his chapter became the title of the book.

Mark Kerr, I am deeply indebted to you for your enthusiastic celebration of this book. I have always been in awe of your unbridled, infectious passion for this project. Each interaction with you was inspiring and motivating. You nudged me along, encouraged me, and guided me in finding the vision and direction of this book. I presented to you a raw clump of clay. It was good clay, but unformed and messy. I am so honored to have had your wisdom and guidance.

Thank you to Joseph and Treasa, my dad and mom. My parents did not get the opportunity to go to college. They sacrificed so much and worked so hard to help get me to where I am now. Although I spend my days, as odd as it remains to me, among

PhDs and accomplished authors, speakers, and presenters, my parents are absolutely the smartest people I know. I shudder when I think of what they would have done with the opportunities that they made for me.

I am music. It is always playing when I write. Therefore, as is true of anything I write, this book has a soundtrack. Music constantly played in the background, infusing the words on the page with their rhythm and melody in ways known and unknown. Thank you to the brilliance of the artists of the main albums I spun while putting pen to paper: Raphael Saadiq's *Jimmy Lee*, Nuyorican Soul's *Self-Titled*, Stevie Wonder's *Innervisions*, Skyzoo's *Milestones*, Anderson .Paak's *Oxnard*, Jon Batiste's *WE ARE*, Tracy Chapman's *Telling Stories*, and Sonny Rollins's *Saxophone Colossus*.

Introduction

Adam J. Rodríguez

I am a clinical psychologist in private practice and an adjunct professor at Lewis & Clark College in Portland, Oregon. I was also a tenure-track assistant professor and the director of clinical training at Notre Dame de Namur University in Belmont, California. I began this journey, however, as a first-generation undergraduate and graduate college student. Along the way, I was a corporate trainer for Bank of America, a bartender, waiter, working musician, telemarketer, ice cream server, personal assistant, fast food worker, retail employee, paperboy, and much more. Four years after completing my bachelor's degree in psychology at San Francisco State University in 2007 at the age of 32, I obtained my doctoral degree at the Wright Institute in Berkeley, California. I am in a professional position that I never envisioned as a young man: I am financially stable and successful in a career that I love and find deeply enriching. As a multiracial boy who grew up in poverty with parents and grandparents who had not attended college, I am my parents' wildest dreams.

As a first-generation student, I am deeply familiar with the pressures, expectations, and struggles associated with being a member of the first generation in one's family to attend college. When I reflect on my past, it sometimes feels like a miracle that I have made it as far as I have. Generally speaking, first-generation college students are a unique group who possess the aptitude, ingenuity, and superlative work ethic necessary to be highly successful in college. At the same time, they face hurdles and challenges that their continuing-generation counterparts do not, which can result in overall lower academic performance, increased isolation, and greater psychological distress. This book is a collection of essays from numerous first-generation alumni who give voice and expression to those hardships and strengths. It is my hope that shedding light on the experiences of first-generation students will help to normalize them, while allowing us to see that the challenges that first-generation students face have far less to do with their abilities or limitations and far more to do with structural and institutional systems at colleges and universities that work to make postsecondary education an inhospitable environment for first-generation students. While these stories are intended to serve as a source of inspiration, to provide you with a supportive community, and to illuminate paths to success in the mysterious new terrain of college, they are also told in the hope that they will help faculty and administrators better understand the students they serve and critically examine and redress the problematic systemic issues within and outside of their institutions that create the hardships that first-generation students face.

FIRST-GENERATION STUDENTS DEFINED

The study of first-generation students is relatively new, which also means that most colleges or universities do not agree on a definition, and many schools do not even track this information. For the most part, college students' generational status may be divided into three categories: (a) students whose parents never attended college, (b) students whose parents attended some college but did not complete a 4-year degree, and (c) students whose parents have a bachelor's degree or higher. Definitions of what makes one a first-generation student versus a continuing-generation student vary. This creates several problems: it makes it difficult for researchers to thoroughly study the experiences of first-generation students, and it makes it difficult for students to adequately appreciate their status and what services may be available to them. *For the purposes of this book, whether your parents never attended college or only attended some college, you are a first-generation student* (Davis, 2010). As Davis (2010) notes, "First-generation student status is not about the number of years a parent attended college or the number of academic units that a parent accumulated"; the primary differences between first-generation students and continuing-generation students is whether or not you grew up in "a home environment that promotes the college and university culture" and is able to provide advice, support, and mentorship based on an understanding of the cultural demands associated with higher education. That kind of environment is critical to feeling "competent and comfortable navigating the higher-education landscape" (p. 4) and gives continuing-generation students a greater sense of ease when they enter college.

Understanding the experiences of first-generation students is important. Growing up in a home environment that does not promote college culture contributes to the numerous challenges first-generation students face. First-generation students tend to attend high schools with less academically rigorous courses and therefore tend to enter college with lower grade point averages, lower scores on standardized tests, and lower confidence in their abilities (Atherton, 2014). We are not only less likely to apply to college (Barry et al., 2009), but when we do apply, we are more likely to apply to less prestigious colleges (Massey et al., 2003; Pascarella et al., 2004). Once there, we are more likely to work longer hours; have a lower family income; have greater family responsibilities, including more financial dependents; and receive less family support connected with pursuing our college degree (Raque-Bogdan & Lucas, 2016). Demands experienced by ethnic minority first-generation students may be even greater (Covarrubias et al., 2018; Vasquez-Salgado et al., 2015). Further, we tend to be less successful in our courses, are more likely to have a lower grade point average, and are less likely to persist and earn our degree (DeAngelo et al., 2011; Ishitani, 2003, 2006).

First-generation students are more likely than continuing-generation students to be from working-class families (Redford & Hoyer, 2017).[1] Longwell-Grice (2021) notes that "one of the largest gaps between first-gen and continuing-gen students is household income" (p. 15). Most first-generation students are from racial/ethnic minority populations (U.S. Department of Education, 2012), with recent data revealing that "49% of first-gen college students were White, 14% were Black, and 27% were Hispanic. An additional 5% of first-gen college students were Asian, and 5% were classified as 'Other'" (Longwell-Grice, 2021, p. 15). In addition to the problems just listed, first-generation students also face interpersonal and institutional classism (Allan et al., 2016; Goward, 2018) and racism (Brown et al., 2007; Ross, 2016). We can experience feelings of guilt related to having opportunities that other members of our family have not had (Covarrubias & Fryberg, 2015).

First-generation students often do not have personally relevant models of success or parental support when encountering college-related experiences. As a first-generation student, you may be more apt to judge your own abilities and potential as inferior to others', which may make it more difficult to be successful. It is typical to feel socially isolated, without sufficient support and opportunities to discuss stressful life events (Stebleton et al., 2014). You may feel like you do not belong, that your obstacles are too great, and that you lack self-efficacy to succeed. You may feel like the struggles are your fault, and you may not realize that college is designed for "those whose families have resources that allow them to devote their time and attention to being a student, do not need or require them to continue to help at home, and can graduate with little or no debt" (Nichols, 2020, p. 6). These factors, and more, create a stressful experience, which can lead to a host of psychological problems, including feelings of demoralization, alienation, isolation, depression, and anxiety, as well as increased substance abuse.

Reading these numerous challenges, it can be easy to feel overwhelmed or discouraged. You might even see these data as an indication that you, as a first-generation student, are not qualified to be successful in college. You may, from time to time, feel inadequate, like an imposter, and maybe even hopeless. This is a normal response to finding yourself in a system that was designed for people from different backgrounds and experiences than yours. It reflects a deeply problematic social, economic, and academic system that favors certain groups of individuals over others.

Some colleges and universities attempt to embrace a "strength-based" perspective that deemphasizes the challenges and highlights your strengths and the strengths of other first-generation students. This approach is commendable but limited. As the stories in this book indicate, as a first-generation student, you cannot ignore the challenges that you will face, and you may have moments when you feel those challenges are evidence of your inadequacies. The field of clinical psychology reminds us that experiences usually contain both good and bad aspects and that to ignore one in favor of the

---

1. For a detailed analysis of the demographics of first-generation college students, see Longwell-Grice, R. (2021). A review of the data. In R. Longwell-Grice & H. Longwell-Grice (Eds.), *At the intersection: Understanding and supporting first-generation students* (pp. 13–24). Stylus.

other is problematic. College is hard, and research demonstrates that first-generation students often do not perform as well as continuing-generation students. As a first-generation student, it is important that you recognize the abilities, talents, and aptitudes that helped you get to where you are. It is important to recognize the strengths you bring to the college campus, but you also cannot ignore the challenges you will face. In fact, it is an advantage to know something about the challenges you may face in college from the outset, similar to the advantages that continuing-generation students benefit from. This book avoids examining the experiences of first-generation students through the lens of only our challenges or only our strengths, but rather attempts to understand how first-generation students, a group of earnest, hard-working, and intelligent individuals, experience more hardships than their continuing-generation counterparts. We confront those challenges, acknowledge our strengths, understand what makes cultural capital critical in college success, and examine college and university systems and structures, which are often inhospitable to first-generation students and designed for continuing-generation students.

COLLEGE CULTURE

Although college has some similarities to high school, it is strikingly different. Colleges and universities have characteristic features, including shared customs, beliefs, values, norms, and "behavioral expectations that define a common academic culture and differentiate them from other kinds of institutions" (Jenkins et al., 2011, p. 130). These vary from campus to campus, but there is much more that unifies the postsecondary education experience than divides it. Consider traveling to a foreign country where you do not speak the language. Maybe it is a country with a language similar to yours, so much of the time you can get by, but you also find yourself grappling with things that you do not fully understand. There will be many words, phrases, and idioms that are incomprehensible to you. With some struggle and discomfort, you may be able to order from a menu, read a map, or visit a museum. You will be able to survive, but if you spend any significant amount of time there—say 4 years, for example—you will likely feel deeply uncomfortable and may never truly adjust. You may even decide to leave early because these feelings are unbearable. To really thrive, you need greater familiarity with the local customs, language, nomenclature, and expectations. You also need to build a community and relationships with others.

In the education setting, "cultural capital," a term first coined by French sociologist Pierre Bourdieu, refers to the necessary information, beliefs, and customs that "students gain from their parents that supports and assists them as they navigate the college experience" (Ward et al., 2012, p. 6). Cultural capital is passed on from very early in a child's life, in ways that are both explicit and implicit. First-generation students enter college armed largely only with our experiences of high school and what we understand from representations of college life we see in the media. Without the benefit of the cultural capital that continuing-generation peers enjoy, first-generation students can be overwhelmed at the differences between high school and college. Colleges are considerably larger than high schools. A college that is considered small will have up to

5,000 attending students. Medium-sized colleges have between 5,000 and 15,000 active students, and a large university will have more than 15,000. In comparison, the average public high school has around 500 students (Public School Review, 2021). In college, class sizes are often much larger, sometimes encompassing hundreds of students in large lecture halls. The classwork is more rigorous and requires more extensive reading as well as more sophisticated critical thinking, analytic, and writing skills. Students are expected to operate in this atmosphere with a great deal of independence. Students must find their classroom on a large campus; review syllabi and create a personal schedule to monitor assignment due dates and tests; acquire necessary textbooks, articles, readers, and other materials for the class; access online portals; use a complex library system in a sophisticated manner; manage financial aid or other sources of income; meet with advisors to determine which classes to take and when; navigate relationships with roommates, peers, professors, and department chairs; and much more. Although you can meet with advisors, doing so requires you to be proactive in arranging these meetings, to have an awareness that these meetings are important, to know which questions to ask, and to have the courage and time available to meet. First-generation students arrive at school without this cultural capital, which leaves us without the knowledge of what it takes to be successful and which "is often a precursor to lower academic achievement and failure to obtain a degree" (Ward et al., 2012, p. 7).

What I have described is the bare minimum of what is required to complete a college degree. This is not necessarily what you must do to either carve out a successful career path after college or be prepared and competitive for graduate school. It also does not describe the things that will help you enjoy college and thrive as an individual. There are also social clubs and organizations, work, managing housing and diet, finding internships, considering graduate school, building professional networks, utilizing campus resources for academic and health purposes, pursuing research and publication, understanding post-college options, and more. Success in college is not necessarily an indication of intelligence or even hard work, although we often think of it that way. Largely, it is an indication of your ability to understand the culture of college and meet its unique demands. Many programs and books focus on improving the cultural capital of first-generation students. This book can also increase the cultural capital of its readers. However, we can, and we need to, do more than simply bridge the cultural gap. We need to more rigorously examine the systems at colleges and universities that make them inhospitable to so many first-generation students, and we need to make significant changes to those systems.

Why do colleges maintain these customs in the first place? Postsecondary education has come to increasingly embrace a neoliberal ideology, which stresses the importance of individual economic achievement and proactive engagement while supporting the myth of the institution as purely meritocratic. College customs are steeped in institutional racism, sexism, and classism. The norms and standards of college culture are "white male, middle- and upper-class, [and] heterosexual" (Harris & Gonzalez, 2012, p. 8); its institutions are entrenched in traditions that have been in place for generations. Remarking on this restrictive culture, Harris and Gonzalez (2012) note that "the nation's most prestigious universities were not established to educate women, people of color, or the working class." In contrast, they were "designed to serve the interests of wealthy men." Universities only opened their doors to more diverse populations through the ongoing efforts of "social movements, federal legislation, judicial decisions, and presidential decrees." Moreover, even after many of the barriers to other populations were raised, "at their core, [these institutions remain] profoundly inhospitable to the experiences and points of view of those formerly excluded" (p. 6).

Following this history, colleges often still adhere to ingrained pedagogical and behavioral standards and practices, even when they have little to no value, are not easily intuited, or are even counterproductive. Postsecondary education remains firmly ensconced in these reified traditions; those in positions to carry out their educational mandates complacently uphold these patterns, unaware not only of their pedagogical limitations but also of their institutionalized classism, racism, and sexism. This system maintains exclusivity by reconstructing "an old and established aristocracy, one in which money begets money, wealthy families remain wealthy for generations, and young people . . . born without privilege and power, stay stuck at the bottom" (Tough, 2019, p. 20).

Let us examine a few ways in which colleges continue to cater to white middle- and upper-class men. Opaque attendance policies, curved grading, class participation points, class rankings, publishing, textbook costs, and access to technologies and professors' office hours are just a few examples. These are standards that universities maintain and that many first-generation students are not familiar with, cannot access, or are unable to participate in due to work or family commitments. Consider the example of the unpaid internship. Within academia, there are many unpaid positions, which students and postgraduates are encouraged to accept to gain experience and expand their network. These positions are not only susceptible to unconscious bias and discrimination in hiring, but even further, they are often inaccessible to first-generation students who frequently have work or family demands or are financially limited and unable to accept unpaid positions.

The experience of a student named Amalia whom I taught helps to exemplify these biases.[2] Amalia was a hard-working, inquisitive, and talented woman who aspired to become a psychotherapist. She had two young children at home and a husband who worked long hours in the evening. Completing her degree offered her a chance to transcend her class status. From my perspective as an instructor, Amalia was a pleasure to have in class. She was enthusiastic, exceptionally bright and talented, and came to each class well prepared. Although she did well in her courses, her schedule did not permit her to be on campus beyond the hours of her classes. She missed out on study groups and was not able to take advantage of office hours, but she was the most discouraged when it came time to apply for a practicum. Practicum is an unpaid position of approximately 12 to 20 hours per week, completed concurrent to coursework, that is required to complete one's degree. She missed the practicum information seminar the department held because she had to be home with her kids; she was unable to attend a feedback session to review her application materials; and she missed the Practicum Fair, where she could have met representatives from hiring agencies. Although these were major hurdles, we could overcome most of them using creativity and flexibility. What we

---

2. Throughout the book, I use pseudonyms to refer to past students or patients whom I have worked with.

could not overcome, however, was the realization that Amalia did not have the hours available to commit to a practicum while taking classes. Raising two children, working to support her family, and completing her coursework, Amalia simply did not have the time required for a practicum. She was frustrated and exhausted and was coming to the realization that she could not find a way to complete the degree's requirements, which meant that her dream of becoming a psychotherapist was threatened.

As colleges and universities become increasingly influenced by neoliberal ideology, imbalanced pay between executives and faculty, and the embrace of corporatization (Harris & Gonzalez, 2012), these deeply set pedagogical structures become harder and harder to critically evaluate and change.

STRUCTURE AND CONTENT OF THE BOOK

What follows is a collection of personal essays from first-generation college graduates. Each contributor is from the first generation in their family to obtain a college degree. There are several intended audiences for this book. College and high school administrators, advisors, and counselors are one important audience. Students studying education and social justice related to education are another audience. Ultimately, though, this book belongs to the current and future first-generation students.

As editor, I will help guide you through stories written by first-generation students for first-generation students. You will hear about what made their college experiences challenging and what made them rewarding. You may strongly identify with some of the authors, and with others perhaps less so, but there is enough variety that every reader can find something of value. The writers share their stories to speak to fellow first-generation students, to help them understand that their challenges and hardships are not a result of their inadequacies but are a consequence of their attempt to navigate a system as an "outsider within" (Collins, 1998). They share their stories because we understand that the life of a first-generation student can feel lonely and isolating, and we know that community is healing. Their stories are told with the hope that you may feel their support and kinship, because they have been where you are now and they are telling their story for you. They share these stories to help you understand that you are not alone and that the hardships you encounter are not because of a personal deficit but largely because of external, systemic issues that often work against the talents of first-generation students. These stories are sometimes painful ones of overcoming a system that was not designed for first-gen students, but they can be powerfully uplifting for others who share these experiences. They are also told in service of turning the mirror onto the institution of postsecondary education, imploring colleges and universities to confront the reality that the old model is no longer appropriate. It serves only a minority of students, and in many ways, it does not even serve them very well.

This leads to the second, equally important, audience for this book. Faculty and administrators need to hear and internalize these stories. Although faculty and administrators have access to academic information and data that can provide them with knowledge of first-generation students, hearing their personal narratives brings depth and breadth to those experiences, making them more relatable and understandable while deconstructing the tendency to regard first-generation students as a monolith. Listening to their stories also has the power to shift perspectives so that faculty and administrators may be more apt to change oppressive models. There are likely many people at colleges and universities who recognize that the current models do not serve all their students well and who are searching for ways to redress these issues. Personal narratives carry great power. As Harris and Gonzalez (2012) state, "Storytelling by individuals, when done well, packs an emotional punch and provides the psychological detail necessary to understand a person with very different life experiences." It is my hope that these stories will help to "bridge the epistemological gap that frequently appears between the lives of people with a particular privilege and those that lack that privilege" (p. 2). Faculty and administrators can transmit their knowledge to students who will benefit from their experiences of being seen and normalized while also receiving a form of mentorship that continuing-generation students normally receive. Two ideas emerge repeatedly throughout this book. First, first-generation students are not a homogenous group. They represent a wide array of individual characteristics influenced by the intersection of many aspects of identity, including race, ethnicity, gender, sexual orientation, socioeconomic status and background, and much more. Second, the struggles associated with first-generation college status are multidetermined, influenced by numerous social factors.

CONTRIBUTORS

Each essay in this book is unique. A disparate group of former first-generation students was compiled, including individuals who obtained degrees in science, technology, engineering, math, the humanities and liberal arts, the social sciences, business, and other fields. It also includes people who went on to obtain a master's degree, PhD, or other graduate degrees. Contributors have graduated from large state schools, small private schools, historically Black colleges and universities, and Ivy League schools. Some attended a community college prior to transferring to a 4-year school, some went straight to 4-year schools, and some contributors took long breaks before completing their degree (as "nontraditional" students). Some contributors completed their 4-year degree recently, within the last 10 years, while some graduated decades ago. Despite this difference, and the differences in college culture now versus 20 years ago or more, many of the challenges of being a first-generation college student are similar, regardless of how recently the writer graduated.

Every chapter in this book is organized in the same manner. Contributors were asked to tell their own story but to follow a format in which they address six specific questions. The questions were developed to address the primary academic, social, and psychological experiences common to first-generation students. There are differences in what one student in one discipline versus another may find beneficial; however, there is a broader cultural element to the college experience that can be conveyed across varying majors and fields of study. The hope is that organizing chapter content to respond to specific questions will make it easier to find the information that is helpful to you, even if the author's field of study is markedly different from your own.

Each chapter begins with a brief introduction of the writer, including their current work and how their experience in college contributed to it.[3] Each of the writers feels as though their college degree was important, if not essential, to the position(s) that they have obtained. Some are working directly in the field of their study; others are in a somewhat different or tangentially related field but acknowledge the importance of their degree in acquiring their job and being successful at it.

The authors then describe their experience of applying to and preparing for college. The path to college can begin incredibly early for some and much later for others. The disadvantages that first-generation students face begin early. Many students find themselves confused or overwhelmed by the process. They may feel as though they are playing catch-up for certain parts of the application process, or they may miss or not be aware of other aspects. Continuing-generation students may receive guidance from family, peers, or school administrators. First-generation students face many challenges, including not seeking out school services because they do not know about them or because they do not believe that college is "right for them." Further, school administrators may not proactively reach out to these students due to racial or class biases. First-generation students may be geographically limited to schools near their family. They may be financially limited and choose not to apply to certain schools because of cost. They may also believe that they are unable to compete for a position in more prestigious universities.

Once students have completed their college application and have been accepted, there are still numerous tasks that may confront the student, including decisions about how to pay for college; whether to live on or off campus; whether to work while in school and what type of job to look for if they do have to work; and numerous social decisions, including how to orient to school and which, if any, activities to participate in. Continuing-generation students are likely to receive some guidance and support when facing these decisions, or they may be in a more stable financial situation and not have to work, or need to work fewer hours, during school. In addition, they often do not have the same family obligations that first-generation students face.

The authors then describe their experience in college, including aspects that were enjoyable as well as those that were arduous, challenging, or unpleasant. As stated above, the academic and psychosocial elements of college both, interactively, play an important role in one's success. Each author, therefore, chose to highlight what felt important to them. For some, academics were at the center of their experience. For others, it was the social elements. For some, they were somewhat equal. Like most significant endeavors, college for first-generation students is usually a combination of positive and challenging experiences.

The authors were also asked to write about what contributed to their success in school. Each of the authors included in this volume was successful in school, based on the metric that each author graduated, even if with interruptions or delays, and is

---

3. This book is primarily focused on the undergraduate college experiences of first-generation students. Although contributors do discuss applying to and preparing for college, most of the content focuses on college experiences. For an excellent read on the path to college and academic pipeline beginning in elementary and middle school, see Nichols, L. (2020). *The journey before us: First-generation pathways from middle school to college.* Rutgers University Press.

currently in a career that is either directly or indirectly related to their field of study. It is true that we can learn much from those who were not "successful" in college. As the editor of this text, however, I have chosen to limit the stories to those of people who have completed their degree. The authors describe tangible, external elements that played a role in helping them while in school. They also describe internal factors that were helpful. In the end, it is generally a combination of both forces that helped students through difficult times.

The authors also tell you about the role that their family played in the process, the type of supports they were able to provide, and the potential hardships they created. First-generation students commonly have family obligations that differ from their continuing-generation counterparts'. Sometimes family members are beneficial and supportive, sometimes they are a burden, often they are some combination of both. The role of family in the experiences and lives of first-generation students is important and influences the student's ability to navigate school and all of its accompanying challenges. In this section, the authors discuss to what extent their relationship to their family played a role in their experiences at school. It was important to include this section because of the differences in family dynamics for first-generation students. The critical role of family is an often ignored or forgotten aspect of their lives.

Finally, the authors present information and advice that they feel was central to their success in college. You will have an opportunity to hear from those who have come before you, who have been successful in college, and who have sometimes had to learn these lessons "the hard way." College difficulties can feel overwhelming and impossible to overcome without support or direct advice. The authors fill that gap in identifying what they feel is essential to finishing college. Each author highlights different areas, but you will find consistency in many of their messages.

EMERGENCE OF THEMES

A series of interconnected themes, which may serve as the underpinnings of the difficulties of being a first-generation student, emerged from the essays of the authors who contributed to this book. Table 0.1 shows the challenges, the upsides or potential outcomes, and the interconnected aspects of these themes. The first theme that emerged is the enormous work ethic of first-generation students. The second theme is the lack of academic preparation many first-generation students enter college with. Among the challenges facing first-generation students are the high schools they typically attend. Nunn (2019) notes that many high schools simply do not prepare students to meet the challenges of college classes. In many of the high schools that first-generation students attend, "academic success is rooted in completing busywork assignments such as copying notes from the board and memorizing without critical thinking." When they enter college, they are still in the process of "building effective study habits of critical thinking and application" (p. 3). The third theme has to do with the financial hardships faced by many first-generation college students, which is often connected to race and class. The fourth theme that emerged concerns the feelings of loneliness and isolation that first-generation students experience. First-generation students often enter college with

TABLE 0.1. Themes from First-Generation Student Stories

Themes	Challenges	Upsides and Potential Outcomes	Interconnectedness with Other Themes
1. Great work ethic	Worked during high school	Working becomes a discipline and a habit	Developed from financial necessity
	Working full time or part time	Greater ability to apply college concepts to life	Lack of time for campus life
	Difficulty with unpaid internship	Greater appreciation for achievement	Lack of cultural capital
	Hours spent applying for scholarships		Devotion to school and its importance as motivating them to push through these hardships
2. Lack of academic preparation	Lack important precollege experiences	Playing catch-up	Lack of cultural capital: Parents can't speak to children about college experience
	Lack of access to academic tutors and testing, exposure to extracurricular activities	Lack of support and understanding of one's true talents	Parents lack college savings and investment accounts
			Lack of financial stability
	High schools tend to be of low academic rigor	Academic struggles and psychological challenges work with each other cyclically, each exacerbating the other	May feel insecure about academic ability
	Students do not develop critical thinking skills		
3. Financial hardship	Often connected to race and class	Financial need creates additional motivation	Invisible barriers of race and class in college institutions
	Older students with dependents, family obligations, and responsibilities		Less time for social aspects of college
	Lower median household income––$38K versus $100K (U.S. Department of Education, 2014)		
	Greater likelihood of attending school part time and attending 2-year schools (U.S. Department of Education, 2014)		
	86.8% identified as people of color (Saenz et al., 2007).		

(continued)

TABLE 0.1. *Continued*

Themes	Challenges	Upsides and Potential Outcomes	Interconnectedness with Other Themes
4. Loneliness and isolation			
	Feeling like an outsider		College culture designed for continuing-generation students
	No formal support services to meet needs of first-generation students	Perceive lack of support from students, faculty, and administrators	Lack of supportive climate for first-generation students
	Values of own community conflict with college community (family belongingness and interdependence vs rugged individualism)	"Alienation, isolation, and invisibility related to . . . social class identity" (Warnock & Hurst, 2016, p. 433).	
	Increased pressure to succeed	Can be overwhelming	

an increased pressure to succeed and may perceive an overall lack of support from other students, faculty, and administration (Hertel, 2002). They may feel stigmatized due to their values or their background.

First-generation students' academic struggles and psychological challenges often compound and exacerbate each other. Their challenges may seem formidable, but they can also be a source of strength. Sometimes the desire to graduate is desperate and born of necessity. First-generation students may feel the burden and weight of carrying the hope and promise of their parents or guilt for having an opportunity that other family members have not had (Nunn, 2019). For many, it can be a choice between successfully completing school or disappointing family, feeling that they poorly represented their race or gender, or facing a life of financial strain. These students are especially motivated and have the experience and habit of working very hard for the things they desire. Simply put, "they want it."

SECTIONS

The themes outlined above organically emerged throughout the essays. For ease of reading, this book has been divided into three sections: stories featuring academic experiences, stories featuring social experiences, and stories featuring psychological experiences. The essays in the first section highlight stories of individuals in which some aspect of their academic experience in college was prominent in their story. The authors discuss the differences in rigor and expectations regarding academic performance and how they met, or sometimes did not meet, those challenges. In some cases, the academic work was central to their challenges, and in other cases, the academic aspect was a strength they could rely on. The essays in the second section highlight stories of individuals for whom the social aspects of college were central to their experience. This includes social challenges, like feelings of isolation or loneliness, as well as strengths, like building community, forming meaningful relationships, and establishing bonds with peers or faculty and relationships with those outside of school and home. The essays contained in the third section highlight stories of individuals in which some aspect of their psychological experience was prominent. By "psychological," I am referring to our internal psychic experience, including our thoughts and feelings, drives and motivations, and internal traits. This includes mental health challenges and psychic distress as well.

After high school, I enrolled in the local community college, where I spent 4 unfocused years, meandering through classes halfheartedly while working long, stressful hours doing customer service for a large bank. My best friend transferred to the University of California (UC) at Davis and encouraged me to do so as well. I had been stuck in a routine in which I was earning a decent income for a 21-year-old, but there were limitations to my job that I was not yet able to see. Stuck in the back of my mind were all the messages my parents had given me throughout my life about the importance of college, so I took my friend's lead and applied to UC Davis and was accepted. I felt immense pride when the acceptance letter arrived in the mail. I found an apartment off campus with my friend and declared a double major in psychology and philosophy. I had no financial support from family, so I kept my job at the bank. This meant that I would be working full time at a job an hour away from school.

Upon transferring, I was immediately overwhelmed. I was not prepared for the greater academic rigor, the faster pace of the quarter system, the vast and immense campus size with huge classrooms, and the 2-hour round trip to a very stressful job. I was confused about which courses I needed to take and had no idea how to get those questions answered. Because of my work schedule, I was rarely on campus and made no friends. I was completely on my own. I instantly fell significantly behind in my classes. Then, 2 months into the quarter and on the day of my father's 50th birthday, my parents separated in a messy and stressful way. My mother moved out of state and we lost contact. My father was deeply stressed. I was already drowning at school, but now it all felt impossible. The coursework was too much, I had no friends or support network, my job was emotionally draining, and I felt alone, stressed, worried, and angry. I stopped attending classes and unceremoniously dropped out of Davis, not even completing one term. I kept my job and returned home, tail tucked firmly between my legs, feeling ashamed and stupid. All my fears that I was not smart enough for college and did not belong there seemed to come true.

Nearly 10 years later, feeling unfulfilled, underappreciated, and trapped in a job that did not suit me, I left my job at the bank. I enrolled at San Francisco State University (SFSU) to finish my bachelor's degree. I started waiting tables, tending bar, and playing music gigs to pay the bills. I had largely healed the wounds from my parents' separation and had a renewed energy and focus to become a psychologist. The same nervous kid who had dropped out of UC Davis finished SFSU with a 3.9 GPA.

In my story, I was overwhelmed by the increased rigor at college, isolated due to my work schedule and long commute, and emotionally distraught by my parents' separation. The complex interaction of the social, academic, and psychological came crashing down all at once. The combination of these forces exacerbated one another and made school untenable.

This book has been divided into sections to help articulate the different dimensions of the college experience, but it must be stressed that they are not strict in the sense that there is tremendous overlap in the narratives and no one story belongs to only one section. As you read the stories, it will become obvious that in various ways all student experiences involve a complex interaction of the academic, social, and psychological. The distinction between a chapter from one section and a chapter from another is not very clear. In truth, all the stories that follow, like my own, could have been placed in a different section.

CRITICAL SELF-REFLECTION

Because first-generation students represent a variety of backgrounds, experiences, and needs, it is not possible to predict with any accuracy what will be meaningful to you in your journey. Nor can I, or any of the contributors of this book, tell you what direction you should pursue in school. We can help illuminate the crucial elements to college success, but it will be up to you to decide precisely which path to follow. You will have many options available to you at college, which will require you to determine and discover what you need to get from your time in school and how to go about doing it. One important tool in helping you to determine what you need is self-reflection.

Self-reflection involves metacognitive (the act of thinking about thinking) "processes supporting self-exploration for the purpose of attaining self-knowledge, motivated by self-curiosity" (Barkai & Hauser, 2008, p. 115). It is a process of looking inward to critically explore and consider your thoughts and feelings, including what informs them, shapes them, and impacts them. Self-reflection "is related to human agency (the ability to exercise control over one's experience) and self-efficacy (the beliefs underlying this competence)" (Barkai & Hauser, 2008, p. 116). This form of introspection helps you to cultivate a deeper emotional awareness, which allows you to know yourself more fully. It is this type of self-knowledge that allows you to more effectively utilize the resources available to you, navigate relationships with others, feel strong and resolute in the face of hardships, and feel more mentally stable and fulfilled.

The stories in this book may offer you a sense of belonging and community, as well as practical tips, advice, and strategies. They also offer opportunities for self-reflection. Each section of this book ends with questions to reflect on, in a section titled Critical Self-Reflection. These questions can be read and considered on your own, in group discussion with peers, and/or in discussions led by faculty, staff, counselors, or others. The questions are designed to assist you in looking inward to explore your reactions to the content of the book so that you may better know yourself and, consequently, better know what you need to get from college.

THE STRENGTHS OF FIRST-GENERATION STUDENTS

First-generation college students bring many strengths to their campuses. They bring a special work ethic, interconnectedness, family bonds, and wisdom, and they offer an alternative perspective. First-generation students are eager to learn and highly motivated to succeed. They are impressively self-reliant and independent. They take pride in their ability to attend to their families' needs as well as their own. Some have already overcome adversity in their lives, and they bring the resulting confidence and resilience with them too. (Nunn, 2019, p. 4)

It can sometimes be difficult to appreciate those strengths because the system that these students enter into is not designed to promote them. Students do not fail in the system; rather the system fails them. How do we redress postsecondary education in ways that highlight the strengths and abilities of these students so that more people can be successful? There are a handful of books, programs, and organizations focused on the needs of first-generation students. They frequently take the approach of focusing on educating first-generation students on how to adjust to college's expectations. These services help students be more successful and happier while in college. The assumption, however, is usually that the student is the one who must adjust to the environment. Colleges and universities need to make significant efforts, however, to adjust who and what they are as well. We have a model of colleges that is outdated and designed for white, middle- and upper-class men. Newer generations of students entering college have different backgrounds and different talents and, therefore, different needs. Sometimes the conditions at college not only do not allow the strengths to emerge but also suppress and silence them.

Higher education institutions must critically examine the new landscape, better understand the needs of their students, and then examine themselves with an eye to determining how best to serve an increasingly diverse population of students. This no doubt will entail changing attitudes and customs. Although more studies on the experiences of first-generation students are emerging, there is still much to learn. One study, now over 20 years old, found that for the fall semester of 1989, 43.4% of all students were first-generation (Nunez & Cuccaro-Alamin, 1998). There is some indication that the number of first-generation students is rising, due to greater access to higher education and the belief that it "is essential in the United States for economic advancement and success, both individual and national" (Harris & Gonzalez, 2012, p. 1). It may be that over 50% of current students enrolled in 2- and 4-year colleges and universities meet first-generation status (Davis, 2010).[4] This means that first-generation college students are now the majority, even though colleges and universities do not treat them as such.

College largely remains another step in an academic pipeline that privileges white middle- and upper-class men, leaving others behind to struggle. We are living in a time when students are taking out massive amounts in school loans, tuition is rapidly increasing, state financial support of public colleges is decreasing, and the promise of

---

4. Due to differences in how first-generation college students are defined, as well as differences in which types of postsecondary schools are studied (2-year versus 4-year), there are different data about the number of first-generation college students. Cataldi, Bennett, and Chen (2018) found that the number of first-generation students overall is decreasing; however, this information was based on a definition of first-generation college students that excludes any student who has had a parent attend any college.

a stable middle-class existence seems like a myth to the younger generation. We must transform our institutions "to attend to the wider set of educational histories, adult responsibilities, and cultural sensibilities of our entire student body, rather than the narrower set of lived experiences that many of us imagine that a 'typical college student' has had" (Nunn, 2019, p. 5).

This book, therefore, has several purposes. First, and perhaps primarily, it aims to decrease the isolation and alienation that first-generation students feel. For marginalized groups, the importance of normalizing experience cannot be overstated. For first-generation students, these stories may help you to breathe a sigh of relief and realize that you are not alone and that the stresses you experience are not your fault. The mentorship and advice offered in the book help to bridge the gap between first-generation and continuing-generation students and offer first-generation students some of the benefits that continuing-generation students enjoy. Second, this book seeks to help faculty and administrators better understand the experiences of first-generation students and determine how they can implement changes that increase inclusivity. Third, this book holds a mirror to the institutional norms that keep first-generation students, low-income students, and students of color marginalized and create real barriers to their success. It is past time for colleges and universities to abandon ineffective, antiquated, and discriminatory pedagogies and methodologies maintained over generations.

You can approach this book in several ways. You can read it from cover to cover or use it as a reference, selecting chapters that capture your attention at a given time. Know that even if the author is in an unrelated field or appears to have experiences that differ a great deal from your own, you never know what may arise during your own experience in college, what may shift over time in your interests and pursuits, and how tidbits from a seemingly unrelated position could benefit you. Explore each essay with an open mind and highlight what resonates and stands out to you.

Onward . . .

SECTION I
STORIES FEATURING ACADEMIC EXPERIENCES

ADAM J. RODRÍGUEZ

The stories that first-generation college students tell often contain some experience of adjustment, big or small, to the new and different academic standards and expectations of college. The disadvantages that first-generation college students face, sadly, are rooted in social class and often begin in an academic pipeline that starts as early as birth. These disadvantages can include inadequate elementary schools, middle schools, or high schools that do not prepare students for the academic expectations of college. They may include an absence of extracurricular tutoring and direct parental involvement in academics and a lack of resources. Moreover, first-generation students may lack exposure to a college culture that rewards proactive and direct engagement to build collegial relationships with faculty and staff.

College is often considered to be further along a continuum of academic rigor. Although there is some truth to that conceptualization, it is also fair to say that college sets its own standards of academic performance. There are rules, standards, and norms that when followed contribute to college academic success. These include writing styles, testing formats, increased reading requirements, and ways of studying and preparing. Many first-generation and low-income students get their first exposure to these new academic systems when they begin college. They may feel unprepared and behind their peers, which may lead to a sense of inadequacy or a feeling of not belonging. The academic challenges are compounded when students must manage work and family responsibilities and lack the time or resources to receive additional tutoring or academic support.

Research tells us that when compared to their continuing-generation counterparts, first-generation students have lower SAT and ACT scores; lower high school GPAs; lower reading, math, and critical-thinking skills; and lower first-college-term GPAs (Davis, 2010). Perhaps most significantly, and naturally quite related, as a result of the inequities in the academic pipeline, many first-generation students "do not know *how* to study very well" (Davis, 2010, p. 39). What hides behind those statistics are the socioeconomic factors that contribute to first-generation student challenges. Culturally, we have a poor understanding of academic performance and often associate it primarily and directly with generalized intelligence (the type of intelligence measured by IQ tests). This attitude is often internalized by students. So when we face academic hardships, it is not uncommon for us to lose confidence and feel that we do not belong. Not only is this cultural belief about intelligence incorrect; it diverts attention away from the social injustices that lead to the differences that place us at a disadvantage in academic readiness. Academic performance is a product of several variables, which includes intelligence but perhaps even more importantly good study skills, access to quality instruction, freedom from significant social and psychological stressors, adequate rest and nutrition, and a familiarity with the standards and norms of academics at colleges and universities.

Assefa was a college sophomore enrolled in an abnormal psychology course I taught. His mother was born in Ethiopia and as a young adult moved to the United States, where she found regular custodial work. His father was a musician born and raised in the U.S. who struggled to earn a reliable income. Assefa grew up in Los Angeles, where he attended a series of barely adequate schools. He was bright and curious, so he did well throughout his time at his various schools, but it required very little effort for him to excel. When Assefa, as the first in his family, began college, he struggled greatly, initially earning mostly Cs and a few Ds. He was, however, able to establish a solid social life, making several close friends at school while being active in two campus organizations.

In his course with me, during his second year of college, two aspects became immediately apparent when I started to receive assignments from him. The first was that Assefa appeared to be grasping the concepts of the course exceptionally well. He had a sophisticated insight and understanding of complex psychological concepts. The second was that he had a very difficult time clearly communicating those ideas. His papers were unclear, unfocused, meandering, and poorly written overall. Beyond the poor writing were core ideas and thoughts that clearly demonstrated Assefa was a talented and intelligent young man who had simply not yet developed strong writing skills. I met with Assefa to discuss his papers and his struggles. During our conversation, he revealed that he was experiencing similar struggles in his other classes. He was confident in his abilities because he had always done well in school, but he did not fully appreciate that he was not well prepared for the expectations of college-level academics. Up to that point in his life, school had not been challenging, did not teach him writing skills, did not help him develop study skills, did not help him think critically about material, and did not encourage him to develop relationships with faculty and staff that would enhance his academic work and buffer him against academic setbacks.

Although Assefa's challenges were primarily academic, the interconnectedness of multiple forces quickly turned one problem into a complex, multidetermined set of problems. The stresses he experienced in his coursework were making it harder for him to participate in the campus organizations he was a member of and kept him from spending time with friends. They were also causing him to feel inadequate and had begun to erode his self-esteem. Fortunately, we were able to identify some of Assefa's struggles relatively early and help him get support.

Although the stories in this book are divided into academic, social, and psychological categories, these are interrelated forces that can exacerbate or strengthen one another. In this section, you will find narratives by students in which some part of the academic aspect of their experience in college was prominent—sometimes as a challenge and sometimes as a strength. You will likely notice very quickly, however, the interactive contribution of the social and psychological aspects to their overall experience as well. None of these domains exists in a vacuum. The good news is that colleges and universities can take steps to mitigate the differences in academic preparedness of first-generation students and help them "catch up" to their continuing-generation peers; even more importantly, these steps need not be drastic. We will learn more about these in the chapters that follow the essays.

CHAPTER 1

Anthony Vargas
Student Affairs, Campus Living University at Buffalo

My name is Anthony Vargas, and I am a Dominican who was born and raised in a neighborhood called Washington Heights in New York City. I am a first-generation U.S. marine, college graduate, and full-time student pursuing a master's degree in higher education and student affairs at the University at Buffalo (UB). I currently work as a professional staff member within the Campus Living Department at UB. I am in my first year as residence hall director for one of the first-year undergraduate residence halls and in my fourth year within Residence Life, which began with my role as a resident advisor. Among my many responsibilities, I help supervise 18 undergraduate paraprofessional staff members, assist with educational strategies for the residential curriculum, oversee the conduct processes within a residence hall, assist with large-scale programming, and serve on an "on-call" rotation for a residential area.

Growing up I would often hear my mother say, "My love, all I ask is that you earn a college degree and we can hang it up in our home. I will then know that it was all worth it." Besides the incentive she supplied, I knew from childhood that I was passionate about helping others, especially those who looked like me or came from a similar background. I wanted to give back to my community, which had given so much to me. I live by the saying "Each one teach one." When I became a resident advisor, I realized I wanted to pursue a career in student affairs. I found that through this role, I could show support and care for minoritized communities within the realm of higher education and help those that face hardships within their college experiences.

APPLYING TO AND PREPARING FOR COLLEGE

Raised in what is known as Little Dominican Republic, I attended high school at the Washington Heights Expeditionary Learning School (WHEELS) in Upper Manhattan. At WHEELS, we had a college access room where there were dedicated advisors who helped our helped our large enrollment of Hispanic/Latinx families with the college application journey. Although I knew I had enough support from WHEELS and my family to ensure I would be able to go to college, I had no idea how to get there. I recall receiving my first acceptance letter, from the State University of New York at Potsdam, and privately wondering whether I should be happy or scared. The thought of moving away from home, being on my own, with all the pressures of having to succeed in college—a place that was unimaginable in so many respects—was nothing short of terrifying. As my graduation date got closer, my decision of which school I was going to attend changed by the end of each week. My decision constantly fluctuated, sometimes because I was having doubts, but mostly because I was afraid. It scared me to think about how much my family members, friends, and school were investing in my future. Failing out of college was a possibility that I did not want to think about; however, it was very much a real worry.

My indecisiveness and worries led me to submit another application and apply to my final school, the UB, on June 22, 2015, just a few days short of graduation day. When I received my acceptance letter, I could not believe it. I thought that I was going to be rejected, especially because I did not believe I had the grades or potential to succeed at the UB. Another layer of panic arose when I needed to figure out with my family where I was going to live because my application was so late that Campus Living was at full capacity and had to add me to their waitlist. My family was fortunate that Campus Living was able to provide me a space on their south campus. Nevertheless, the fear of moving alone to an unknown place that was 400 miles away from home was still extant.

EXPERIENCES IN COLLEGE

When my family dropped me off at the UB South Campus, I remember sitting outside of Clement Hall and watching the vehicle drive away. This specific moment was filled with fear and, worst of all, as I have mentioned, the unknown. It was my first time being over 6 hours away from home with no family nearby, which caused me to feel somewhat isolated. The difference between me and my classmates quickly became evident when I found myself working more at my jobs than having fun, attending university events, hanging out with others, or living the "college life" like all my other floormates and classmates were doing. When most of my friends and floormates were going out to eat and to explore the new city we were all in, I found myself saying, "I can't. I have work." Reality hit me when people would ask me, "Why are you always working?" Not being able to live the "college life" made me feel like I was different—a feeling I would have most of the time that first semester. I was different from my friends and different from what a "typical" college student was. I did not see many students working a job, much less two, while attending school. However, I needed these two jobs. I did not know how to create a balance between work and school. I struggled. My two jobs kept me working on some nights until 2 or 3 a.m., and I still had thousands of dollars in student loans. After my first term, I failed two courses, had an overall GPA below 1.0, and received an academic warning from the university. I immediately felt like a failure. I felt like I had failed my family, who had immigrated to this country for a better life. I felt like I had failed my high school and community back home because I simply could not make it in the place they all believed that I could. Moreover, I did not feel like I belonged at this university.

My involvement with my Residence Hall Association allowed me to build connections with the building's staff members. After experiencing many challenges, I decided to share my struggles with the residence hall director assigned to the building. The hall director told me that college was typically a tough time. Nevertheless, I was set on returning home. I was determined to go back to New York City and attend a City University of New York school so that I could be closer to home. My hall director told me to reflect on my experiences and to try and look at some of the positives at the institution. "Sometimes," he told me, "we get so wrapped up in our own lives we forget the good that is happening in our own community." I was encouraged to reflect on my experience thus far, to give myself grace, and to try again at the institution. Defeated but committed to giving this another chance, I took an introductory philosophy course during the winter session. My thoughts were that I could increase my GPA through an introductory course and try to get back on track as soon as possible. Naive as to what to expect from that course, I struggled again. I struggled to the point of failing the course, earning my third F at the UB in my first 6 months at the institution. Every day I would think, "Is college for me?"

One thing that I felt was missing was a sense of community. Growing up in Washington Heights, the sense of being part of a community was never missing. One afternoon, as I was walking through our student union, I overheard some Latino music coming from a room. Of course, I followed the music. Once I arrived, I saw my community. *Mi comunidad.* I saw a bunch of people who looked like me, spoke just like me, and whose smiles resembled those of my cousins. As soon as I got there, members of the Latin American Student Association (LASA) ran to the door to welcome me into their space. This would be a community that I would grow to love, care about, and share amazing memories with. During my undergraduate studies at the UB, I served as a member of the dance team for 2 years with LASA and served as their president during the 2019–2020 academic year. I will always cherish the impact that LASA and its members had on my life and academic journey and hold those memories close to my heart. As we say, "LASA for life."

CONTRIBUTORS TO MY SUCCESS

Whereas the beginning of college was extremely difficult, in some ways due to the difficulty in connecting with others, I appreciated many aspects of my undergraduate career. My ability to become successful was heavily influenced by my family, my partner, my mentors, the LASA community, and those friendships that I developed within the institution.

My family's values of always giving back to others and fighting for one's community reminded me why it was so important to "stay in the fight" and continue school. My partner always believed in me and reminded me that I was needed in these spaces. We reminded each other that we both were going to make the change needed in our communities. My mentors provided me with great advice, opportunities, and support to keep me focused on the mission. Finding my home away from home within LASA at the UB was honestly a main reason why I was able to make it through the Buffalo experience while still missing home. The friendships I made taught me a great deal during my time as an undergrad, including how other people experience the world of higher education differently because their backgrounds and experiences play such a major role.

ROLE OF FAMILY

When I was working until 2 or 3 a.m. at one of my jobs, my mother would stay up some nights to make sure that I would not fall asleep while doing my homework, or she would call to make sure I made it home safe. Even 400 miles away, I felt as though my family was right there with me. Whenever I went more than a few hours without writing in our family group chat, my family would flood me with endless caring messages. My brother, cousins, aunts, and uncles would constantly remind me of how proud they were of me and how much they missed me. I would always feel loved, even on the other side of the state.

Through all the hardships I faced in college, I had to acknowledge that I could not tell many of my family members (except for my brother and some of my cousins) of the struggles I was facing because we all were first-generation students (something that was an unheard-of concept to me in undergrad). Not being able to share my college struggles with my family or feel they would be understood was very isolating at first. I had often looked to my family for answers, but this experience was different because they were unable to help me figure out some of these issues. This realization sank in, and I failed to understand why it was so difficult to simply be understood.

"It's okay *mi hijo* [my son]. We're going to make it through. I believe in you, Choni." This is a phrase that my mother would say to me many times throughout my college experience. The support of my family means the world to me, and whenever I thought about giving up, I remembered that it was not about me. Throughout my life, I have always kept in mind the long nights and hard work that my family put in to provide for us. I remember that it was my family that fought for me to have this very same opportunity. I would tell myself that the only way to make sure I paid my family back for it and showed my appreciation was by making sure that I worked as hard as I could to become successful.

TIPS AND ADVICE

As a first-generation college alumnus, I recognize that some of the issues I faced were due to being first-gen: the feeling of being alone (or not feeling welcomed in a space), often being confused, and sometimes being afraid of the unknown. Many of these feelings are common among first-generation students, and they might be the same ones that you are experiencing.

First-generation students, I want to tell you that I am proud of you. I am proud of how far you have come and where you plan on going. Remember to look at your identity as a first-generation student as another tool on your tool belt instead of as a deficit or a negative identity. As first-generation students, we must look for those resources that sometimes might not be as readily available to us as they are to some of our peers. Nonetheless, the journey to strive for greatness is what will make you all great.

I want to underscore the importance of mentoring. Mentors are of vital importance in helping people be successful. One of my mentors at the UB was my professor Dr. Stephen Santa-Ramirez, a Latinx and a first-generation student, who allowed me to be real with my struggles while also giving me hope and the wisdom I needed to become successful in spaces where first-generation students struggle, along with some spaces (like higher education institutions) where the presence of BIPOC individuals is not and/or was not welcomed. To see Dr. Santa-Ramirez produce necessary research, advocate for his communities, and serve others while holding similar identities to my own made me feel validated and hopeful that I, too, could one day make similar contributions to our world. His example gave me confidence that one day I could be a mentor to another first-generation student or Latinx student in the way that Dr. Santa-Ramirez was for me. So, I want to say thank you, Dr. Santa-Ramirez.

A final piece of advice I will give you is to remember you are not alone on this journey. There are many first-generation alumni, and there are many first-generation students who are navigating these same struggles and obstacles. We are here for you. First-generation students thrive and show the rest of our society why our voices matter and why we belong at the table for these conversations. Keep up the great work, and be proud of how far you have come.

CHAPTER 2 MAPPING OUT COLLEGE TO CAREER GOALS IN REAL TIME

Jeremy Edwards, PhD
Lecturer for the Program in Writing and Rhetoric at Stanford University

My name is Dr. Jeremy Edwards. I am an educator, researcher, critical scholar, author, son, brother, nephew, and a beacon of inspiration and hope for my family. Over the past few years, I have been working as both university instructor and education researcher; however, my experience teaching spans over 6 years, and my research, which addresses educational inequities and access to higher education for historically marginalized populations, spans over 10 years. My work involves assisting college-transitioning students, connecting them to career goals, and addressing student developmental models designed to support their academic and career pathways. In my research, I examine the structural components of education and provide recommendations for infrastructural changes that should be implemented for all students to succeed academically and professionally.

I am the product of two loving parents with family members across the western and southern regions of the United States. My family never obtained many college degrees, yet they considered education to be an essential foundation for opportunity, growth, and prosperity. In this way, the prospect of receiving formal education and a college degree was instilled in me.

My undergraduate education provided me with the necessary tools to successfully earn a PhD and attain my current position as a university professor. Being involved with departmental research and federally funded research-intensive programs gave me the opportunity to work with professors and graduate students on major research projects that would be presented at symposiums. Being a member of various professional organizations on campus gave me essential learning experiences, such as how to work with people and communicate ideas, what it takes to be a future graduate student, and the importance of research to address systemic issues in education. While my knowledge and skill set has evolved over the years, my involvement during my undergraduate college years provided a stable foundation from which to continue pursuing my professional goals.

APPLYING TO AND PREPARING FOR COLLEGE

In high school, I was involved with honors and advanced placement (AP) classes, which usually emphasized the importance of attending college. I also frequented the College Career Center, as the counselors sometimes had updates about colleges, programs, and other opportunities that high-performing students like myself qualified for. During each academic school year, staff representatives from college outreach and mentorship programs visited my high school's College Career Center. Toward the end of ninth grade, I commonly received summonses from these university-based programs to speak with their staff about applying. Programs like Early Academic Outreach, Upward Bound, and Posse visited the College Career Center regularly, which is how I became aware of the various precollege programs for prospective college-bound students. By 10th grade, I applied for and was accepted into a college preparatory program called Vice Provost Initiative for Pre-College Scholars (VIPS), headquartered at the University of California, Los Angeles (UCLA). My decision to apply to VIPS derived from the numerous one-on-one sessions with my former mentor, who made sure that as a high school student I enrolled in the proper courses, participated in leadership roles, and learned about different types of colleges. Completion of VIPS also qualified me for a $20,000 scholarship if I was accepted to UCLA, which influenced my decision to apply. This program was created in response to the direct student action demonstrated on the UCLA campus regarding the decline in Black enrollment numbers during the early 2000s (VIP Scholars, 2021). The program was birthed from student activism and advocacy for increased Black student representation on campus.

VIPS had a social justice orientation and became responsible for preparing some of the highest-performing Black students in the greater Los Angeles area. As a member of VIPS, seeing the representation of Black staff, faculty, and students who were involved in the program boosted my confidence as a young Black male scholar. It removed the barrier of feeling "less than" or being perceived as "inferior" despite my intellectual capabilities. VIPS provided the opportunity for 28 rising high school juniors and seniors across multiple school districts in the greater Los Angeles area to participate in an intensive summer program in which we lived in the UCLA residential dorms for several weeks, enrolled in college courses, and were immersed in the college atmosphere for two consecutive summers prior to senior year. This program became the backbone of my critical scholarship about the systemic issues prevalent in education, including, but not limited to, student tracking systems, AP course disparities, and deficit-based curriculums. My high school counselors, teachers, and VIPS mentors instilled a college-going culture, notifying us about course selection, dual enrollment, extracurricular activities, and, most importantly, college application requirements.

With the support of the career center and academic programs, I was fully prepared to apply to college. The mentorship I received from VIPS, especially, prepared me for the rigor expected of a college student in terms of writing college-level papers and helped me adjust to a faster-paced curriculum, learn about notetaking and preparing for exams, and build rapport through vocalizing my needs and concerns to instructors and administrators. The program provided workshops on financial aid and other funding sources, SAT/ACT test preparation, A-G requirements, community service, leadership work, and other college-preparation content that could assist our successful entry into college. I remember applying to 11 schools, getting accepted into 6, with UCLA being my final selection.

EXPERIENCES IN COLLEGE

My first year in college was drastically different from the subsequent 3 years—mainly because I was so new to the environment and the expectations of college. Even with the workshops and support from mentors and advisors telling me what to expect, actually experiencing it firsthand was a totally different reality. Academically, I found myself feeling behind in comparison to my peers. My college friends would brag about the latest A they received on a paper or exam, and I would remain silent, wishing I received those same marks.

I entered college as a pre-sociology major, but I never took any courses for it. I had planned from the beginning to switch majors, transferring into the College of Engineering to become a computer engineering or computer science major. The plan had derived from conversations I had with former mentors regarding the college application process. Depending on the school, applicants can choose two potential majors. My former mentors encouraged me to strongly consider my major selection because majors can be housed under different colleges (e.g., College of Letters and Science, College of Engineering), and there may be more demand for some majors than positions available, which influences the applicant's chances of getting accepted. To maximize my chances of acceptance, I chose two different types of majors within the College of Letters and Science: the first selection was computational math and the second selection was sociology. I was accepted as a pre-sociology major. Applying to be a sociology major had been a difficult decision, as I had applied to other universities with majors in either computer science or engineering. However, I understood that I could ultimately choose my own path and plan accordingly as I progressed along my milestones.

I would find out that regardless of major, each student must still take the prerequisite courses to officially get accepted into the major, which usually takes at least 1 year. First-year students often shop around for various majors, and they are commonly undeclared or switch majors several times within the first 2 years of college. Each department has an undergraduate advisor, with whom students are highly recommended to meet, especially those students who have an interest in a specific major. No one wants to waste time, money, and energy on courses that will not contribute to successfully completing college.

My career goals changed over time, but engineering was initially an industry I saw myself in. To obtain this goal, I knew enrolling in math and science courses was inevitable. The required STEM courses, including chemistry and calculus, were incredibly rigorous. I experienced many academic challenges early on, which ultimately affected my GPA and my confidence as a high-performing student. Despite my college preparation, I did not have a strong grasp on the content of math and science courses, given the difference in material and the intense memorization and practices needed to perform at a high level on a weekly basis. After my first year, I received several Cs and a majority of Bs, which dropped my GPA to 2.8, the lowest of all my years of schooling. To be clear, I had average to low performance in classes outside of STEM as well, which reduced my confidence even more. Although I was already serving in the office for the National Society of Black Engineers (NSBE) my first year, and I was confident in pursuing engineering as a major, the effort I had put forth thus far had not translated into high grades. This was one of the first times that I had to really contemplate my future as a student in formal education. I had no idea what to do, but I knew something had to change.

After my first year at UCLA, I continued to feel unsatisfied with my academics. While I was involved on and off campus professionally (e.g., taking on leadership roles in areas besides engineering) and socially (e.g., connecting with peers, being involved with community organizations, doing volunteer work for prospective students), my dissatisfaction with my academic progress after my first year did not allow me to feel a level of fulfillment that others may have felt. And then it happened—the day that would change my trajectory and allow me to find purpose on my academic path. At 19 years old, I attended a PhD dissertation defense for a well-known leader on campus who happened to be one of my mentors. Witnessing how my mentor responded to the questions being asked by the dissertation committee was so inspiring it gave me the certainty that this was something I wanted to do. I had already been conducting research during my freshman year, but I had never fully considered going on to pursue a PhD or anything similar. My main objective had been to pursue something that would make a difference for people and communities across the globe. At this point, I knew I had to get it together. I had to figure out how to not only increase my GPA but also find an academic path that fit me.

The summer before my sophomore year, I created a 13-week plan that involved reading books, writing letters to myself as a form of affirmation, searching for different majors and courses to take for the upcoming fall quarter, and finding new ways to actualize my goals. These 13 weeks prepared me for the task at hand. My goal for sophomore year was to find a major, take the prerequisites, successfully get into the major, and get more involved with research and other similar research-intensive programs. After speaking to a friend who had recently declared a psychology major, I thought, "Why not try Intro to Psychology to see how things go?" I ended up loving the content in the psychology program, and the rest is history. I took all the prerequisite courses during my sophomore year, achieving much better grades than the year prior. By the end of my second college year, my GPA had finally returned to a 3.0, which was a significant milestone for me considering my first year. I also became more involved with research as part of a research program through the Academic Advancement Program. I was well on my way, as deciding what type of courses to take began to get easier, and my goals became clearer and more focused as time progressed.

By my third year, I had been accepted into the Ronald E. McNair Post-Baccalaureate Achievement Program, a federally funded TRIO program designed to increase the number of historically minoritized professionals working in academia, especially as faculty members. Acceptance into this program was another indicator that I was following the path I had designed during those 13 weeks prior to my second year. After reflecting on my freshman year and applying myself differently, I began to see my hard work pay off in many ways. I was a McNair scholar for 2 years, leading to applying to graduate school. This program prepared me for the rigors of graduate school and allowed me to see how my potential could be actualized in real life.

So far, I have been speaking primarily about academics in describing my college experience because the academics affected other areas. Once I got my footing academically, the social and professional realm (e.g., networking with peers, taking leadership roles) took off. I was highly involved throughout my college years, whether it was research, service, work, leadership, event planning, or other experiences. My major challenge was believing in myself no matter what—that I had what it took to overcome any academic struggles I faced. My earlier struggles taught me the importance of having a plan. A plan can shed so much light on a situation, allowing one to envision a much clearer path forward. Sometimes, the more an individual gets involved, the more people may expect of that person, and it can become an overload. However, staying involved can also be the way out of systemic turmoil and is helpful to reconfiguring one's purpose. I finished college with a 3.4 GPA, earning a bachelor's degree in psychology and a minor in education studies. Despite my initial academic difficulties, creating a plan that challenged these initial obstacles helped develop my level of scholarship in ways I never imagined.

CONTRIBUTORS TO MY SUCCESS

The mentorship I received from distinguished faculty and staff; the support of family, friends, and colleagues; my research training opportunities; and the strength developed through facing challenges contributed to my overall success. Not only did I develop as a scholar; I also grew into my adulthood as a young Black man striving to effect change, make a difference, and contribute to correcting structural inequities in education and dismantling systems of unfreedom in societies across the United States. During commencement, out of 7,000 graduates, the chancellor announced my name while delivering his speech, acknowledging my acceptance into the education and psychology master's program at Harvard University. Hearing my name announced in front of thousands of graduates and proud families validated my journey toward success even more. Although I ultimately decided to attend University of California, Santa Barbara, to pursue my PhD in education, it felt satisfying for myself, my family, and my friends to hear my name over the loudspeaker, affirming my purpose and dedication to my future. From those difficult nights of feeling like an academic failure as a freshman to successfully getting into a PhD program, with multiple graduate program offers, I was ecstatic and motivated to continue my pursuits. These accomplishments confirmed the old saying "Whatever you put your mind to, you can accomplish."

ROLE OF FAMILY

At a young age, my family instilled in me the need to focus on school. This meant getting good grades, performing well in school, and going to college. Although my family did not have a history of attending 4-year universities, they knew that college would provide opportunities that I would not otherwise have. In this case, my family provided the foundation for me to achieve academic success and consistently strive for more. Upon reaching college, I relied extensively on my mentors and guidance counselors, who had the appropriate knowledge to help me prepare for and apply to college. In the end, my family did not have to worry about my college applications or whether I was able to fund college. My family provided moral support and was always there when I needed someone to talk to. They understood why education mattered so much, and they influenced me, especially in my viewing it as an opportunity for upward mobility. Hearing about my family's financial woes to the point of needing to find a new place to live added pressure for me to not only finish college but to ensure I could provide for them. They were not forcing this on me, but I felt obligated to relieve them from these burdens. I felt I had a responsibility to make sure they didn't experience long-term financial struggles, opening them to new possibilities within their own lives in terms of what they could achieve for themselves.

The growing pains of transitioning from adolescence to adulthood occurred during college as well. Sometimes I experienced pushback about my newfound ideas and perspectives on different subject matters that I developed from my experiences taking courses, conversing with peers and faculty, and being involved with social and political organizations. I believe that each college student represents their family in some way, but more importantly, each student grows into themself and builds the capacity to speak for themselves and be their own person. Thus, being stern in one's beliefs can sometimes create minor conflicts between one's newly developed identity and family members' traditional perspectives and customs. Despite any obstacles I encountered, the personal journey of developing into a scholar and young adult during my undergraduate college years was an amazing, profound process, especially with my new sense of independence and responsibility on campus.

TIPS AND ADVICE

The following advice is based on my personal experiences as described above.

1. Find a supportive network comprised of peers, mentors, advisors, instructors, and staff who are reliable and trustworthy.
2. Maintain a daily and weekly calendar or planner that includes tasks, assignments, goals, events, breaks, or any additional area of importance for tracking and time management purposes.
3. Pick at least 1 day out of the week just for yourself (i.e., no courses or scheduled tasks). If you cannot pick a full day, then schedule a half-day block for your own personal leisure as a form of self-care.
4. Select a major that will challenge your way of thinking and contribute to your personal growth and career pursuits.

5. Get involved with campus organizations, especially those involving leadership roles. Doing so will help you learn about campus structures, improve communication with peers, and gain valuable knowledge and skills that transfer to the workforce.
6. Do not just take courses and stay in your dorm. Use your time in college to learn about yourself, learn about others, and figure out what your personal and professional goals might be.
7. If you plan to work, take a job that will benefit you both financially and professionally.

CHAPTER 3 SUCCESS IS NOT A LINEAR PATH

Ivonne Martinez
Pursuing Master's in Data Science

Although my story feels very personal, I know that many parts of it are not unique and are similar to the context in which many Mexican American first-generation students live. I was born in a small border town in Mexico called Piedras Negras, Coahuila. My mother and father both worked as office assistants and made a decent living. Neither love nor food was ever missing from our home, but my mother dreamed of a better future for her children and knew that a border town like Piedras Negras could not offer that future. When my mother found out that my father was born in the United States, she begged him, until she was able to convince him, to have the family immigrate. About a month after my father left, we packed our belongings into big black trash bags before following him to San Antonio, Texas.

APPLYING TO AND PREPARING FOR COLLEGE

Adjusting to the United States was initially difficult for our family. We had to adapt to a new environment while living in constant fear of discrimination because we did not speak the language. My father was able to secure a position as a warehouse worker while my mother dedicated her days to cleaning strangers' homes. When my mother would work on the weekends, she would take my sister and me to help her. She would often tell us to study so that we would not have to end up working as a maid like herself. Every moment she could, our mother would remind us of the importance of education. Although I was only 6 years old at the time, I was able to understand that the reason my parents left everything behind and moved to the United States was so that my siblings and I could have a better education. My parents believed that education was the key to a better future—not only for us but for the generations to come.

My father and mother both come from very tough backgrounds. My father never talks about his personal life, but my mother would often tell us stories about him. Both of my father's parents died when he was 14, and although he had an older brother and sister, he and his younger brother grew up alone. My mother came from a very poor working family. My grandfather was taken out of sixth grade to raise goats on a farm, and my grandmother had to stop attending school after the third grade to help take care of the children at home. My mother was expected to help with the home responsibilities as soon as she could work. I know my parents would have loved the opportunity to obtain a higher education if they had been given the chance.

The importance of education, though predominately unspoken, was alive in my family. Although they did not know much about how the school system worked, my parents were as encouraging and involved in our studies as they could be. As immigrants, my family could only afford to live on the west side of San Antonio, where many impoverished neighborhoods were situated. Growing up in that neighborhood made me feel as if I had only two choices: work hard and go to college or get married and work retail. I knew that the first choice would let me escape this cycle and provide for my parents in their old age. I made sure that everything I did could be added to my résumé for when college applications came around. I knew that paying for college and following the right path depended almost entirely on what I did during my teenage years, so I focused on my grades and was involved in many different extracurriculars. I was in University Interscholastic League, debate, One-Act Theater, First Robotics, and TRIO. I also performed community service on weekends. As a result of my single-minded focus, I never really cared what the "cool kids" in high school were doing. Besides, I knew our goals were different.

I was determined to go to college. I dreamed of applying to Ivy League schools and to every scholarship that crossed my path, but when my SAT scores came back, I feared the scores were not good enough. Although I was the salutatorian of my class and had an extensive list of awards, my average SAT scores reminded me that I came from a broken school system. Back then, I thought I was one of the best in my class, but I was also aware that my high school was at the lowest national and state academic level. I knew I would not be able to compete with students who came from better neighborhoods and could afford SAT tutors. Due to my SAT scores, I ended up applying to only three universities, all of which were relatively close to home. I was aware that I would qualify for these schools due to Texas's "top 10% law," which guarantees students who graduate in the top 10% of their class admission to all state-funded schools. In the fall of 2017, I started my bachelor's in mathematics at the University of Texas at Austin.

EXPERIENCES IN COLLEGE

I was extremely excited to move to a new town, meet new people, and start college. I felt as though I was starting my life and that all my hard work had paid off. I was the youngest of three, and although both my sister and brother had warned me about how hard college might be, I did not understand what they meant until I attended my first lecture. Although I had taken college credit calculus in high school, I decided to enroll in Advanced Calculus at my university. I loved mathematics and thought the class was going to be fun, but on the first day of class, Professor Phillip Uri Treisman was talking about the fundamental theorem of arithmetic and how to prove that $1 = 0.9999$. I looked around the room to try and find another student who looked as lost as I was, but at that moment, I felt as though I was the only one who was not understanding the lecture. Nevertheless, I believed that everything would be fine and that I would eventually be able to catch up. I was determined to do well in the course and attended all the extra help sessions available, but my confidence rapidly decreased with every day that passed. Not only did I feel as though I did not belong in the class; I also felt as if I did not belong at the school. My classmates would talk about the summer trips they would often take with their family and the multiple language courses that their high schools offered; in contrast, my school was always struggling to find teachers willing to teach in the district. My comfort zone had disappeared remarkably fast.

My insecurities seemed to consume me, but I was not ready to give up on myself. I knew that the only way to overcome my self-doubts was to reach out for help. Erica Winterer was Professor Treisman's right hand and the teaching assistant for the course. She was at every lecture and always held extra help sessions for any student who wanted them. Both Professor Treisman and Erica believed in their students a great deal, providing them with all the emotional and educational support they could offer. I studied often and never missed any of the extra sessions, but when I failed the first major quiz with a 67%, I lost it. I was not sure what was working and what was not. I never had to study in high school. Everything had come so easy to me. I was worried that I was going to fail Advanced Calculus although I was only 1 month into it. I felt stressed, out of place, and ashamed to have failed what I felt was a simple quiz.

After that first quiz, I decided to attend a one-on-one meeting with Professor Treisman to see what I could do to succeed in his course. On the first Saturday morning after receiving my score, I met with Professor Treisman in his office. I entered the room and sat down quietly. I did not know exactly what to say and was afraid to open my mouth as I felt tears gathering. It was so hard for me to accept that I had failed and that I was struggling to understand the material. Professor Treisman did not provide me with any guidelines to succeed but instead consoled me regarding my doubts. He said that he had noticed all the hard work that I had put into his course and that I should not give up. He asked me to trust him and the teaching process that he had implemented for so many years. I was not sure what to say or who else to talk to about my fear of failing. I knew my family would be willing to listen and that they supported me no matter what happened, but talking to them about my struggles at the time would have made them feel 10 times heavier than they already felt. Telling my family what I was going through would have made my failure seem more real. Although I did not know what the outcome might be, I knew that the only choice I had was to believe Professor Treisman and Erica when they said they believed I would be able to succeed in the course.

I kept attending office hours and asking for help. Even after receiving a 59% on the first midterm, I was sure everything would eventually make sense because I already knew more than I had known before. Erica not only met with me often after class to talk about the material but also checked in on how I was feeling emotionally. Professor Treisman and Erica were there every step of the way to provide their support in any way they could. At some point in the semester, I felt my grasp on the concepts was slowly getting better, I could do some of the problems myself, and my spirits were improving. Then everything fell apart again.

At first I was sure I was going to pass the second midterm. I had studied for countless hours and attended all the extra sessions that were available. I was even able to solve some of the hard problems on my own, but the day before the exam, my mind went blank. I started to dread the idea of failing the exam again and kept doubting my ability to pass it because I had failed the other exams. My anxiety kicked in and I started to cry hysterically and let the tears drop on my notes. I was so scared of failing the second midterm that I could not focus and return to studying. Because I could not focus, I decided to try and sleep my feelings off. However, that night I was unable to get any rest and kept turning in my sleep. As time counted down to the midterm, my anxiety continued to increase. I remember getting ready that morning very absent-mindedly with my feelings showering over me. I got on the bus and started crying on my way to school. I knew I was going to fail that exam and would not be able to do anything about it. Before I entered the classroom building, I sat down in the courtyard, deciding to calm myself down, resolved to get it over with. Although I thought nobody would notice or care about the emotional wreck I had become, as soon as I entered the building and sat outside my classroom, Erica rushed over. I could feel the tears rolling down my face as she took me outside to talk to me. She helped me calm down. She had talked to Professor Treisman, and they both agreed to let me take the exam over the next 2 days. The extra 2 days did not help my anxiety, and I ended up with a 55% on the second midterm. I was steadily doing worse with every exam I took. I was so tired of having my efforts be wasted and even questioned whether I was good enough to be a mathematician.

Professor Treisman and Erica believed in me wholeheartedly and encouraged me to persevere. They knew that many students with similar backgrounds were struggling as much as I was, and they believed that everyone should have an opportunity to succeed. A month away from the final, they announced that if students' final exam score was higher than their class average, their final score would replace their class grade. I knew that this was my last chance to pass the course. I was sure I would be able to pass this time if I continued to study and was able to teach myself the main concepts. I started rereading and reviewing my notes. I looked over all the previous exams and homework assignments. Erica invited me to a small study group composed of three other women with similar backgrounds. We all seemed to feel very insecure about the course, but as time passed, we were able to work together to solve problems. It took some time, but soon we were all able to teach each other. In the study group that I had created early in the semester, I was finally able to explain some problems to my friends, unlike before when I would just listen to the conversation. Everything was finally making sense!

On the day of the final, I woke up and dressed for the exam. Unlike before, I felt at ease. I walked confidently to class and sat down to start my exam. It all seemed to make sense, and I was able to answer every question in the exam. It was the first time in the semester I had finished an exam and turned it in before the time was up. I was not sure if everything was right, but I had a feeling I had passed. Later that day, I received an email from Professor Treisman and Erica congratulating me for not only acing the exam but getting the third-highest grade in the course. After reading that email, relief and extreme happiness rushed over me. It was the first time in the semester I cried from joy and not anxiety. Although it might not sound meaningful to others, that was one of the greatest accomplishments of my life.

It is now inconceivable to me that 4 years ago I did not believe in my own abilities and considered dropping out of college. The system had made me believe that Latinx people in the United States were just not made for STEM. After a few semesters, I was able to believe in myself and understand that the road to success takes many unexpected turns; I was finally able to live up to my full potential. After finishing my undergraduate degree in mathematics at University of Texas at Austin, I decided to pursue a master's degree in data science. In the second round of applications, I was able to apply to all the Ivy League schools that I had not applied to the first time around.

CONTRIBUTORS TO MY SUCCESS

Although I have faced many other more challenging situations in my academic career since Advanced Calculus, I learned to never doubt my abilities and to believe in the process. College is hard, but it is much harder if people do not have a support system that believes in them or do not have enough courage to believe in themselves. I discovered how important it is to ask questions and find people who are willing to help me grow. The moment a person decides to give up on themselves might be the moment that matters the most. I have failed and I have dropped a course or two, but I was always able to recover.

There is an old saying: "It takes a village to raise a child." It was only after my graduate career that I was finally able to understand what that meant. Looking back at my life, it is hard to say who exactly contributed to my success because I strongly believe that all the people who have crossed my path have shaped who I am today and what I will become. From a young age, I had people in my life who influenced me to take the right path. My mother involved herself as much as she could in my early education, while my father playfully teased me to have better grades. I learned a lot by watching my siblings, Ileana and Leo, as they were the first in our family to strive toward obtaining a higher education. I also had a few wonderful educators, like Erica and Uri, who helped me realize my potential, as well as many friends and mentors who took the time to share their knowledge with me. My success is the product of all these people's positive impact on my life.

ROLE OF FAMILY

As a first-generation college student whose parents gave everything to provide me with better opportunities, I must say that at times it can feel burdensome to deviate from the ideal path that our family might have in mind for us. Whether this burden comes from failing college courses or deviating from a safe career choice, I remember that my family members have always been willing to listen to me and believe in me. Although it is sometimes difficult to talk to them about my struggles, they are a big part of who I am today and the reason why I continue working toward a better future.

TIPS AND ADVICE

Thanks to the journey and the people along the way who helped me grow, I am now a graduate student at Harvard University and will be graduating in 2023 to pursue a career in STEM. This is an achievement nobody in my family could have ever imagined. Although I am in graduate school and seem to have my life together, in some ways I am still the same girl as before who stresses and feels anxious about failing. Although my imposter syndrome has followed me, I no longer let it define me. I know that if I put my mind to it, I will be able to accomplish what I set out to do. The beautiful thing about being human is that you can adapt and learn at an extraordinary speed. Failing, learning, and getting back up is a part of life, and we must push our limits once in a while to reach our goals. With that in mind, I have a few tips for you:

Never give up. The moment you decide to give up and stop trying is the moment you decide to lose. Although sometimes it feels like our effort is not accomplishing anything, it is never wasted. As long as you do not give up, it all becomes a matter of time and not of wasted effort.

Have patience. Growing and learning take time. A lot of work and dedication is needed to accomplish everything that you might aim to accomplish, but do not beat yourself up for failing. Most success comes with some failure.

Always ask for help. Asking for help can be hard, but asking for help sooner rather than later is far and away better. It is also easier to ask someone for help than to struggle alone.

Do not lose sight of your goal. Although there were many times in my college career when my feelings consumed me, I never lost sight of my goal. That helped me focus on what was important, and it will help you too.

Surround yourself with the right type of people. The people you surround yourself with can encourage and inspire you to do better. It is important to find the right support network that will encourage you to not give up and to believe in yourself.

CHAPTER 4

Desireé Vega, PhD
Associate Professor, School Psychology

I am an associate professor in the American Psychological Association–accredited and National Association of School Psychologists–approved school psychology program at the University of Arizona. I took this position in 2016, having taught for the prior 3 years in the school psychology program at Texas State University. Before entering the academy, I worked as a school psychologist in the Omaha Public School district for 3 years. As a young Afro-Latina raised in Brooklyn and Queens, New York, I never imagined myself living anywhere other than New York. I also never envisioned obtaining a PhD and being a university professor, which speaks less about my belief in my capabilities, though imposter syndrome creeps up every now and again, and more about my being the first in my family to go to college. I simply never knew what my career possibilities were.

As a professor, I teach graduate-level courses to prepare future school psychologists. My research addresses three main areas: (1) identifying best practices in the training of bilingual school psychologists; (2) preparing culturally competent school psychologists; and (3) advancing the educational success of African American, Latinx, and emergent bilingual youth. Through my leadership and service activities, I am involved with various committees at the national level and I engage with first-generation students on the University of Arizona campus. I would say that my role as a faculty fellow at the Thrive Center at the University of Arizona has been most relevant to my interest in first-generation college student success. The Thrive Center is composed of multiple programs, including the First Cats program, which is designed to meet the needs of first-generation college students. Although my role was minimal compared to the amazing work the staff and student employees engaged in on a daily basis, I held office hours every week in which I met with students and discussed a variety of topics, including career options, graduate school, and research opportunities. I also engaged with students at events and programming for first-generation college students. This role was and remains particularly meaningful to me because as a psychology major in college, I learned that without a graduate-level degree, my career options would have been severely limited because a doctoral degree is required to become a psychologist. Being able to connect with undergraduate and graduate students and share what I have learned on my journey is impactful, especially because as an undergrad I often did not know who I could turn to for advice or even what questions to ask.

APPLYING TO AND PREPARING FOR COLLEGE

Applying to college can be a stressful process. Being a first-generation college student without adequate supports can compound these feelings. I cannot recall when I started thinking about college, but I remember receiving college brochures in the mail early in my high school career. I received information from univerisites across the nation, and I was both terrified and thrilled about my options. My high school sponsored a multiday college tour trip every year, but for some reason I was unable to attend. However, I did visit a few nearby universities on trips hosted by my high school. These visits were helpful in giving me a sense of what college was like, including what campuses looked like and what services were offered to students. At that point, I did not know what I was going to study in college, although I thought I wanted to study in a field related to business, such as accounting. Without having any real knowledge of what my career options and possibilities were, I felt unprepared to make this decision. I applied to several universities across New York State, without declaring a major of interest, which can make narrowing down the selection process difficult. All I knew was that I wanted to go away for college and live in a dorm; therefore, I did not apply to any local univerisities that would enable me to commute.

I had a conversation with my math teacher and track coach, Mr. Connor, about where I was applying, and he told me that I needed to talk to my parents. It was then that I realized I had been navigating the process independently without including my parents in my decision-making process. I spoke to them soon after, and they were agreeable; I am fairly sure they trusted my judgment, but they did not ask any questions. Nonetheless, although I had good judgment, reflecting back, I really did not know what I was doing or why I selected specific universities. Most were in the State University of New York (SUNY) system, which narrowed down the process for me, but others were private, and I did not understand the tremendous cost related to attending them.

After receiving acceptance letters and financial aid information, I was pretty set on attending SUNY-Binghamton University, mostly because I had heard it was the top school in the SUNY system. Other than that, I had very little knowlege about it and had not visited the campus. Visiting campuses was not an option due to the costs required for travel and accomodations. My family and I did make the trip to Binghamton for an event for students who were accepted for admission, and my parents then put down the deposit to secure my attendance. It was a great day; I felt that everything I had been working for had paid off.

EXPERIENCES IN COLLEGE

My undergraduate experience at SUNY-Binghamton University—four hours from Brooklyn and Queens, New York, where I grew up—was exciting and frightening in many ways. First, it was a major culture shock for me. New York is extremely diverse, and growing up my schools and neighborhood were predominantly Latinx, Caribbean, and African American; so for most of my life I had not experienced being the minority. I felt homesick and isolated at a university in the middle of nowhere, where I received questions from my white peers about my brown skin and curly hair. In addition, unbeknownst to me, the university was experiencing overcrowding in the dorms and was unable to accommodate everyone who wanted to live on campus. They had instituted a policy that freshmen would be given first priority for campus housing, and because space was limited they were placing three students into each double room. For that reason, in my first semester I was thrust into not only a new environment but also into small quarters with two roommates. I am an introvert and I like my space, so this arrangement was not ideal. Moreover, having two white roommates was a lonely experience, particularly because one grew up in a rural one-stoplight town and had had no prior interactions with people of color. My roommates bonded quickly, but I did not share many of their interests; I felt isolated and missed my friends and family back home. The first semester was rough too because I was enrolled in Microeconomics, and after miserably failing the first exam I dropped the class. I was also struggling in my Introduction to Psychology course, which had an enrollment of over 400 students. The large lecture hall environment was intimidating and did not accommodate my learning needs. Honestly, I was afraid of failing and letting myself and others down. The experience was eye-opening because I had been a top-performing student up until then. I was worried that I was not college material.

Nonetheless, it was all a blessing in disguise. I dropped Microeconomics, which allowed me more time to study for my other courses. I also grew to like Introduction to Psychology and subsequently decided to take another psychology course in my second semester, which led me to major in that area. In addition, the university gained some control over the student housing crisis, and I was able to move into a designated triple room next door to my original roommates. In this new living situation, one of my roommates was of Jamaican descent and grew up in Brooklyn and the other was from Puerto Rico. I had a greater connection with my new roommates, and that made me feel more comfortable joining student organizations, which were culturally based and allowed me to develop a sense of community as I got to know people from similar backgrounds with shared interests.

As is often the case for students from low-income backgrounds, financial challenges permeated my college experience. I remember buying textbooks for the first time and not having enough money to buy the books for all my courses because they were so expensive. I was terrified of the consequences of not having the books purchased for the first week of classes, and I worried about falling behind. Also, because scholarships did not cover my entire tuition, I had to take out student loans. The thought of accumulating debt was scary and not something I completely understood. I am still working to eliminate the financial burden of my schooling.

CONTRIBUTORS TO MY SUCCESS

Reflecting on what contributed to my success in college, I remember spending a great deal of time in the library in my undergraduate years. I studied in the library on a daily basis, and I did not take my college experience for granted. Part of me also feared failure, because I was the first in my family to go to college. So I worked really hard. I also felt unprepared and that I needed to work harder than my peers; this motivated me to study whenever I could.

A major source of mentoring I received as an undergraduate was through the McNair Scholars program. I learned that the program was designed to increase doctoral degree attainment among students from underrepresented backgrounds, including low-income, first-generation college students and students of color. I had decided to apply, and I remember being extremely nervous the day I submitted my application. I was worried I would not be accepted and thought perhaps I should not apply after all. However, I did apply and was accepted! The McNair program was instrumental to my becoming a faculty member. I learned about the process of applying for graduate school, received course preparation for the GRE, and was able to engage in research opportunities with faculty members and contribute to conference presentations. Through this experience, I realized my love for research, which sparked my interest in a career in academia.

The program coordinator for the McNair Scholars program, Karima Legette, was phenomenal and helped me gain confidence in feeling like I belonged and deserved the opportunity. The program also provided a supportive atmosphere and comradery with other students from similar backgrounds with similar academic goals. I also worked on campus at a child development center for children with disabilities. This opportunity helped me to gain leadership experience, as I supervised the student workers in my senior year. The work also helped shape my career pathway as a school psychologist. I knew I wanted to work with children, and working with children with developmental disabilities and learning disabilities helped me better understand the population I wanted to serve and the context in which I wanted to work.

ROLE OF FAMILY

My family provided encouragement, and they believed in me when I did not believe in myself. They saw my potential and knew I could be successful in college; therefore, they were supportive of my leaving home to attend college. I understand this is not the case for many students from collectivistic cultural backgrounds. Nonetheless, whereas I enjoyed being able to develop my own identity, the difficulty with being away from home was worrying about what was happening there. As the children of two working parents, my two brothers and I had many responsibilities at home, including cooking, cleaning, and caring for each other. This meant that I had to learn to balance my new role so it would not interfere with my studies. It was a challenge but necessary for my success.

TIPS AND ADVICE

At times, I felt alone and lost in navigating the college application process. Once in college, I wish I had known what questions to ask to get the support and guidance I needed. I remember my high school counselor provided information on scholarships, but I do not recall having concerted assistance in negotiating the ins and outs of the college application process. I firmly believe the responsibility falls on school personnel to disseminate information about the college preparation and application processes, particularly to students who lack experience with them. However, based on personal and anecdotal experience and extant research, I know this is often not the case for a variety of reasons. Therefore, it is important for future first-generation college students to advocate for themselves and seek out support and assistance. Thanks to the technological advances that have occurred since I applied to college in 2001, the internet is now a great resource for answering questions about college-going processes. An internet search will yield an abundance of websites with information on financial aid, scholarships, completing college applications, studying for tests, and preparing personal statements. After obtaining information, future first-generation college students may consider meeting with their school counselors to obtain more in-depth information and get answers to lingering questions.

My experiences with student organizations both as an undergraduate and as a graduate student were critical factors in my retention. I do not believe I would have thrived academically, emotionally, and socially without supportive friends and mentors. Therefore, I strongly advise current first-generation college students to get involved in an organization that is central to their interests and/or identities. Because being a first-generation college student can be stigmatizing and isolating, finding others who share these as well as other intersectional identities can help you build community, destigmatize this status, and foster a sense of belonging. Many universities now have centers and/or programs to support first-generation college students, including student organizations. I encourage students to take advantage of those opportunities.

CHAPTER 5

Yvonne M. Luna, PhD
Associate Vice Provost and Professor of Sociology

I never imagined myself as a professor. The possibility really did not enter my mind until I was studying for a PhD. I took my first academic position at Northern Arizona University (NAU) in the very cool mountain town of Flagstaff, Arizona, in 2004, where I remain today. As I was attempting to finish my PhD, I did not feel ready to be in the job market. My husband had recently passed away, and I was simply trying to get my life back in order. After his diagnosis, the toll of his illness forced me to put my academic career on hold. Two months after his death, I resumed my graduate studies and my graduate teaching position at Arizona State University (ASU). Looking back, I am thankful for the opportunity to do so, as it forced me to refocus.

The following year, in 2004, one of my professors handed me a printed job advertisement from NAU for an assistant professor of sociology position. Yes, back then we passed around hard copies! I applied, was one of four finalists, and ultimately was offered the position. Because I continued to work toward my PhD, NAU hired me as an instructor for the 2004–2005 academic year and gave me 1 year to finish my dissertation. No pressure! Breathe! I made the deadline, and my tenure as assistant professor started the following academic year. In 2011, I earned a promotion to associate professor and today occupy the rank of professor. I served as chair of the Department of Sociology at NAU from 2016 to 2021 and am now associate vice provost for curriculum and assessment.

As a professor, I feel passionate about teaching. One of the primary reasons is the impact professors can have on students. My experiences as a first-generation college student taught me that. My position as associate vice provost, and previously as department chair, allows me to have an impact on students in a broader way. The decisions I make impact all our 28,000 students in some way, about half of whom are first-generation. My own experience as a first-generation undergraduate student helped prepare me for this career.

APPLYING TO AND PREPARING FOR COLLEGE

In high school, I worked for a law firm as a receptionist. Back then my goal was to be a secretary (now we refer to this job as "administrative assistant"), and I took classes to prepare myself to be one. A high school teacher referred me to a potential employer—a woman looking for a kid to answer phones. I interviewed and was hired. While working as a receptionist/secretary at that law firm during high school, my career goal shifted to becoming a paralegal. Being a paralegal required an associate degree, which amounted to 2 years of postsecondary schooling.

I knew quite a few high school classmates who attended the local community college, Central Arizona College (CAC), and I thought it was a good option. After graduating from high school, I applied there. My sister had recently attended and was able to show me some of the ropes. I also asked questions of "grown-ups" who had college experience. Although my mom never went to college, she went with me to the CAC campus and stood with me in several lines as I negotiated the process of registering to take placement exams and classes.

My parents could not pay for my college education, but going to CAC was affordable and allowed me to continue working to pay for school bills. My mom offered me free room and board at home. The combination of work and a free place to live worked for me. I felt thankful for both. However, because I now worked full time at the law firm, I could only take a couple of classes at a time. I never planned to be a full-time student. Eventually I changed my mind about that too.

Later, when I decided to go to a university, I felt really scared. I did not know what to do, where to go, or how to go about doing any of it. I remember driving to the campus one day, parking my car, and walking around trying to figure things out. I had some semblance of knowledge because by that time I had experience with two community colleges, and I knew that the registrar's office was a good place to start.

EXPERIENCES IN COLLEGE

Being a community college student was not much different from my high school experience. The number of students in my classes was similar, the teachers were local residents who were familiar with the surrounding communities, and I knew many of my classmates. However, because I worked full time, I needed to prioritize my job and so I took night classes at CAC. Students in these classes were like me—they had other responsibilities during the day—only they were a bit older and many of them had children. In addition, instead of being on campus from 8 a.m. to 3 p.m. like in high school, I was now a full-fledged adult, or at least so I thought. I had to structure my time and practice a different kind of discipline in order to get my homework done, attend classes, and go to work. I found I did not have much time to stray from my responsibilities. Being busy kept me focused.

When the end of my studies at CAC was approaching, I applied to the paralegal program at Phoenix College (PC). I had been confident that my good grades at CAC and my law firm experience would gain me entry; however, all I needed was to meet the minimum GPA requirement and have an ability to pay (i.e., my job). Attending PC turned out to be a life-changing experience, allowing me to venture out of my small community on my own. Much larger than CAC, with fewer ethnically diverse students, PC was smack-dab in an urban center. I made the decision to continue to live in my hometown, earning wages at the law firm, rather than move, which was not only cost-effective but also allowed me to embark on a new experience while also feeling a sense of grounding. After my first semester at PC, my brother died in a car accident, and I moved back in with my mother, who was severely grieving the loss of her child. After a short stint out on my own, moving back helped her and made life easier both financially and emotionally for me, as I also grieved.

PC provided a good segue between community college and university life. I realized how much I enjoyed being in school, being a student, and how much I loved learning and the intellectual exchange that a college experience offered. After a year working as a paralegal, I resigned my position at the law firm to continue my schooling on a full-time basis. Going to the university closest to me, ASU, made the most sense. Student loans made it possible.

I remember feeling like a lost puppy when I first stepped foot on the ASU campus. The campus felt so large and spread out, with thousands of people. Fortunately, I had taken many of the general education classes at community colleges, so I did not have too many large classes. My classes ranged from 40 to 75 students with the exception of a geology class, which was a program requirement and had at least 300 students in the class. I connected with a couple of women who sat close to me, and although we did not develop long-lasting friendships, they made that class bearable. Another course stands out in my memory: a political science class with about 100 students. I received a B on an exam, which for me required a meeting with the professor. In those days, email did not exist as a way to communicate with our professors, so I went to Dr. Pomp's (a fake name) office hours. When I arrived, another student was meeting with him. I overheard Dr. Pomp tell her she was smart and she should set her sights on law school. As she walked out of Dr. Pomp's office, she glowed. I felt certain I would get the same cheerleader talk. I wanted to understand what I had done to earn a B; prior to his class, I had maintained straight As. I began to explain that I had studied really hard. Dr. Pomp responded that apparently I had not studied hard enough and sent me out of his office. I was devastated. I cried. I wanted to drop out of school right then and there. Instead, I gathered myself and went to his class just a few short minutes later. That day in class, our topic was affirmative action. He split us up into groups and tasked each group to come up with arguments in support of or against affirmative action. Oddly, at least to me, he gave kudos to all the groups who chose the anti–affirmative action perspective. He did not seem to care much for the pro–affirmative action viewpoint. I do not recall what side of the argument my group took; however, I came to a hard realization that day: As a Latina, I needed to work extra hard to prove my worthiness, and despite popular belief, race gave me no privileges. In fact, most of the people around me had no understanding of their own privilege. I had to demonstrate that I was as smart and deserving as the other students.

A frustrating aspect of university life was dealing with the university bureaucracy. Many times I could not find answers to my questions, which left me wanting to give up. Simple tasks like figuring out how to get financial assistance and get a parking pass proved very challenging. Once I figured something out on my own, though, I felt a sense of accomplishment—just as I did when I turned in a paper or earned a good grade. Despite the many challenges, I enjoyed meeting people, forming friendships, and learning about the lives others led outside of the small town in which I grew up. What I learned allowed me to make sense of my personal life, my own biography. As an undergraduate, I started to see the big picture. I realized that my life experiences were shaped not only by my own individual choices but also by larger social structures and history. I fell in love with sociology. The more I learned, the more I realized I had so much more to learn.

CONTRIBUTORS TO MY SUCCESS: I DIDN'T DO IT ALONE

My family contributed the most to my success. They modeled behaviors that served me well. Both of my parents read. I remember clearly our dad always reading a book, our mom reading to us almost every night, and our family reading aloud together. My parents prioritized reading so much that they ordered a complete set of encyclopedias and paid for them monthly, on a payment plan. Thanks to them, I learned to be a good reader. In fact, my grade school teachers often called on me to read, and I was proud of that. My parents were too!

Similarly, teachers throughout my life expressed confidence in me, from my first-grade teacher, who had me help her grade papers, to the high school teacher who sent me on the job interview at the law firm. She deserves special tribute here. I remember her profound influence, not only because she exhibited confidence in me but also because she was Mexican American/Chicana like me. I did not realize it then, but looking back, this aspect was significant. I knew I could relate to her. I remember a Chicana instructor at PC, both an attorney and a teacher, who similarly impressed me. These women are partially why I am so passionate about teaching. They served as positive role models, and I want to be of similar service to students.

Like many first-generation students, I worked so I could attend school. I needed employers to allow me the flexibility to take classes at various times. My first employer at the law firm supported me in this way, and I appreciated it. In addition to accommodating my school schedule, they allowed me to use the computers after hours to do my homework, and one of the attorneys even read my homework assignments and offered constructive feedback when I attended paralegal school. Later, I worked at the county juvenile probation office while attending ASU, and they too allowed some flexibility in my work schedule.

Although being both a full-time student and an employee kept me very busy, the bonds and friendships I formed as a student also contributed to my success. Study groups, lunches, and hanging out with classmates proved critical. I did not realize the importance of these bonds and relationships then. However, now that I am familiar with the scholarship on retention and persistence, I have a better sense of how my positive social interactions and attachments to an institution helped me stay in school. Those same connections and relationships are what will help students stay in school rather than drop out today.

ROLE OF *MI FAMILIA*

My sister and I are first-generation college graduates. She is a nurse practitioner, and I have a PhD. My mother, Isabel, who passed away about 11 years ago, worked at a factory, and my dad, Richard, was an underground copper miner. They worked hard all their lives, and although they never had a formal education, they are the smartest people I know. Why do I say that? Because they taught me values that serve my sister and me well every day of our lives both in and out of academia. They taught me lessons that helped me get along with others and be a leader. They taught me to work hard, to be kind to others, to treat people the way I want to be treated, to be humble, to share the credit, to read, and to try and improve myself so that I can improve others. In short, they taught me how to have a positive impact on people's lives. These are the life lessons that contributed to my success.

On a similar note, my mom allowed me to live with her when I could not afford my own housing, and through her employer I had health insurance until graduate school. These privileges allowed me to stay in school. Despite all of this, I definitely experienced some hardships too. I took on somewhat of a parental role with my mother after my parents divorced and my brother passed away. My mother struggled with depression. At times I helped her manage some of her responsibilities, like running the household and paying bills. There's no question that this added to my heavy load of responsibilities and stress, but I believed it was my duty to help her, and it allowed me, in a little way, to reciprocate for everything she sacrificed for me.

TIPS AND ADVICE

From my perspective as a teacher and scholar, as I reflect on my first-generation undergraduate experiences, I have some personal tips and advice to offer:

Desire and curiosity. You've got to want it. You must be curious. Reading fostered my curiosity. Pick up (or download) a book and take a trip or go on an adventure through the words on the pages that spark your imagination. Doing so will heighten your desire for learning.

Persistence and perseverance. Lean on people (e.g., family, friends, advisors, professors, mentors) when the challenges feel overwhelming. There are so many types of resources available to students today; take advantage of them. Go to mental health counseling. Go to tutoring. Seek academic assistance. Participate in clubs and campus events. The first few times may feel uncomfortable, but it gets easier and a lot more fun. Ask for help. These behaviors will help you persevere and persist.

Ask questions. As you might guess from reading the previous paragraph, there really is no such thing as a dumb question. Ask lots of questions. People are more than happy to answer them. Ask questions in class. Ask about campus resources. Ask your friends to hang out, in person! Ask your classmate to go to a campus event (or go alone)! Go to your professor's office and ask what you can do to get the most from their class. Ask about scholarship opportunities. Ask. Ask. Ask. Got it? If not, ask.

Be vulnerable. When you ask questions, you are letting people know a little bit about you and what you may not know. That's okay. Be brave—let people know you exist. More importantly, let them know you crave knowledge—that you do not claim to know it all, and you want to know more. In short, you are letting people know you want to be successful. Be visible. Participate in events and activities. Research clearly shows that all kinds of opportunities are linked to social networks. Most of us first-generation folks don't have our own social networks as undergraduates. I didn't. Start building yours today and it will reap rewards tomorrow and for years to come.

CHAPTER 6

Maria Dykema Erb, MEd
Director of the Newbury Center, Boston University

My name is Maria Dykema Erb, and I am a proud first-generation college graduate. Throughout my more than 3-decade career in higher education and student affairs, I have witnessed the definition and recognition of the first-generation college student identity and the evolution of student services that serve this population. I, myself, did not even realize that I was a first-generation college student until 2009, when one of my graduate student assistants shared with me the book by Alfred Lubrano, *Limbo: Blue-Collar Roots, White-Collar Dreams*. Learning that being a first-generation college student was a thing put into perspective all that I experienced as an undergraduate student. Today, I am the inaugural director of the Newbury Center at Boston University, which was established in 2021 to foster the holistic success of first-generation undergraduate, graduate, and professional students. Through professional and personal development workshops, social activities, and engagement with faculty, staff, and alumni, a close-knit first-generation community has been established and has created a strong sense of belonging among the students. My own personal experience has led me to the pinnacle of my career, in which I now serve as the person I needed in my life when I was in college.

APPLYING TO AND PREPARING FOR COLLEGE

Even though I was a straight-A student and was the salutatorian (ranked second academically in the senior class), and even though I was involved in numerous extracurricular activities and received many awards, I did not aspire to attend an Ivy League school. My highest aspiration was attending Champlain College in Burlington, Vermont, which was at the time a 2-year associate degree college largely focused on applied business majors, such as accounting, court reporting, and secretarial science.

When my friend Melanie, who was also a first-generation college student, started her college search, she was looking into a career in hospitality management. That intrigued me! I had stayed in a Marriott hotel once during high school and could picture myself as the general manager of a large chain hotel in Hawaii wearing an amazing business suit like they wore on *LA Law* (one of the top TV dramas back in the 1980s). I thought I was quite clever in choosing a major in which I was guaranteed a job when I graduated; hotels would always need managers.

EXPERIENCES IN COLLEGE

In August 1988, I started my college career at the University of New Hampshire (UNH). No one clued me in to the fact that I should have arrived much earlier than I did that day. I had been assigned to a "built-up" triple, which was a euphemism for three students in a room designed for two. My two roommates arrived earlier than me and claimed the two beds that were on the floor level and the only two desks in the room. I was left with the top bunk of the bunk beds, half of a wardrobe area for my belongings, and no desk. Needless to say, this was not the best way to start my college experience.

My parents did their best to help me, even though they were not familiar with the college environment. My mom made herself busy, cleaned as much as she could in my room, and executed that last ceremonial act performed by most parents when dropping their kids off for the first time. It was an act that symbolized my official separation from childhood and the start of a new life in college—she made my bed. Finally, with nothing left to do, it was time for them to drive back to Vermont. I walked my parents to their car in the parking lot, said goodbye, and gave them hugs; that day was one of the few times in my entire life that I have seen my mom cry.

My first semester of college was a disaster academically. I had a GPA of 2.83, and for a student who received straight As in high school without having to study, it was a crushing blow. When I returned to school after winter break, I had to meet with the chair of the Hotel Administration Department, who expressed deep disappointment that I had not done well my first semester. I would have to repeat Macroeconomics in the fall, and I was also at risk of losing my Sheraton Hotel Corporation scholarship if my GPA did not improve by the end of that semester. I was terrified; losing my scholarship would mean having to drop out of college.

I went into the Dean's Office of the business school to meet with my academic advisor to see how I could improve my GPA. Her suggestion was that I study harder and manage my time better, but I did not know how to do that or where to get the necessary academic support and tutoring assistance. I am sure there was an academic support services center, but I never thought of it because I believed what many other first-generation students believe—that I had to figure it out on my own. I had to focus more on my academics and spend less time socializing with my close friends, and I also needed to figure out new study strategies because obviously what I had been doing was not working. I also knew that I had to somehow get involved in campus activities. In high school I had been the queen of extracurricular activities, but I had thought it better to not get involved in them the first semester of my first year to allow for more study time. That turned out to be one of the biggest mistakes of my college career. I was not sure what club or organization I would join, but I knew I had to do something that would force me to better manage my time.

When I started college, my parents informed me that I had to pay for school myself because attending was my choice. My parents knew about free money via scholarships and figured I could earn plenty of money that way to pay for school. The entire financial aid application process was a mystery to me. I filled out as much of the application as I could figure out and then had my dad fill out the rest with his asset information. For my first year of college, I received a refund from my student account and did not have to pay anything because I had the Sheraton scholarship and various local high school scholarships. However, no one explained to me that I would have to eventually pay for college because most of the scholarships were only for 1 year. As each year progressed, I ended up having to take out more Stafford loans to cover my expenses. Moreover, I did not fully understand the impact of taking out loans and the implications of paying them back after I graduated. At that time, dealing with the financial aid office was always an anti–customer service experience. I dreaded meeting with their staff because they were not student-centered, and I had difficulty understanding all the financial aid lingo as a first-gen student.

Another way that I tried to pay for college was to become a resident assistant in an all-women residence hall. However, having come from a co-ed hall, the job was not what I had expected, and I ended up resigning after the first semester. The next year and a half off campus was difficult because my financial aid was decreasing, leaving me with minimal income during the school year. I was envious of my peers who did not have to work and who would talk about their fantastic spring break trips and summer travels. Meanwhile, my life consisted of going to class, volunteering as a campus tour guide, working as many hours as I could at my part-time on-campus job, and trying to find some spare hours to socialize with my friends in the least expensive way possible. Food became a coveted commodity, and the staples on my shopping list for my weekly trip to the grocery store consisted of ramen noodles, a loaf of bread, peanut butter and jelly, and a couple of frozen dinners. I was at my skinniest during those years because I was on a strict diet plan—not by choice but rather because I was starving.

I fulfilled my degree requirements, but my required courses were not engaging me in the way I had hoped, and moreover they did not seem purposeful. I discovered that I really enjoyed sociology courses and ended up with a minor in sociology, but changing my major at that point would have added another year to my stay at UNH. In addition, I had no idea what I could do with a sociology degree. Coming from a working-class farm family background, I didn't think sociology was a practical choice. By my junior year, I was ready to drop out of college and work full time. Making a weekly paycheck seemed much more productive than paying for my education and earning next to nothing with my part-time job on campus.

The only financial support that my parents provided me while I was in college was the old family car to use as my source of transportation and my car insurance, but that car was a crucial part of my life. Despite the mechanical headaches, I was able to get around easily and be independent, and I did not have to go home over winter or spring breaks.

CONTRIBUTORS TO MY SUCCESS

Despite the many challenges I encountered as a first-gen, I was able to find my way. My success in college was due to the important role models and peers who were able to provide me with what I needed. At the start of my first semester, my resident assistant Marcy's dedication to ensuring that all the new students got off to the right start made all the difference in my life. She helped me with the transition from high school to acclimating to a college environment, and she connected me with my fellow residents and introduced me to her friends across campus.

Sheila, a fellow hotel administration major, became another close "lifetime" college friend. She too was a first-generation college student and the daughter of two Irish immigrants. As a city girl from Boston who was the fourth of six siblings, she was fun and assertive, and I could hardly believe her chutzpah. I lived vicariously through her, and she became my voice. She helped me gain self-confidence in college so I could eventually speak for myself.

In my sophomore year, another friend introduced me to Toni Taylor, the associate director of UNH Institutional Research. Institutional Research was the office responsible for surveying students and alumni and providing data and reports to the university administration. Because I didn't qualify for the work-study program due to all of my financial need being met through the Pell grant and scholarships, I was fortunate to find a part-time job for hourly wages; I worked through winter and spring breaks to help pay for school. That job was important to me for many reasons: I was able to earn a paycheck to help with daily living expenses, I acquired a baseline education and understanding of higher education data, and I met one of my lifelong mentors. Toni helped me get through my 4 years at UNH; she was a strong role model and a second "mom" to me. Toni represented consistency and stability and was an excellent listener. Sometimes she did not say much to me at all, but when she did I could always count on her for her words of wisdom. All first-generation college students need a "Toni" in their lives.

The most influential people in my professional career were the staff in the Admissions Office, where I was an admissions tour guide for 3 years. My three mentors who encouraged me to pursue the field of admissions instead of the hospitality industry were Dave, Gary, and Eric. These professionals took the time to explain the world of admissions to me and helped me envision myself in higher education as a profession. I realized I felt more committed and passionate about being on a college campus than working in the hospitality industry. I had already worked for several summers at a summer resort, which was in my degree field, but found it less than fulfilling and more like a job. In the spring of 1992, the University of Vermont was hiring two assistant directors for their admissions staff. With the support of my mentors, I submitted my application; they were also able to network on my behalf with the associate directors at University of Vermont. After 4 years in Durham, New Hampshire, it was time to return to Vermont, my home, to begin my professional career.

ROLE OF FAMILY

I am a Korean adoptee who was raised culturally as a conservative Christian Dutch American on a dairy farm in Vermont, so the role of family and its relation to the intersections of my identity are significant to me. Statistically, I should not have even been accepted to college, let alone graduate with my bachelor's degree. I cannot remember when I decided to go to college, but I always knew I had to go. It was not because my family held higher education as a value and encouraged me to pursue that dream; my parents had only middle-school educations. I wanted to get off the dairy farm and do more with my life than marry a dairy farmer, which was the path my peers and I were supposed to follow. My parents did not think college was very practical; they believed I should simply get a job after high school like my older siblings had.

When I reflect on my high school years, it is clear my parents never said I could not go, but I now understand that they did not know what kind of support they could provide me. They could not even provide the financial piece, which I had to do on my own. This is a common frustration for first-gen students today—their parents simply do not know how to support them because they have no context for the college-going experience.

I do recall aspects of my personality that showed streaks of independence early on. I had questions that were at times inconvenient for those who were attending to my Christian education. As a child, I went to church twice every Sunday and attended a Christian school from Grade 1 to Grade 8. In eighth grade during Bible class at the Christian school, I daringly asked, "How do we know if Heaven really exists?" To my heartfelt and sincere question, I distinctly remember the teacher harshly responding, "If you were a real Christian, you wouldn't ask a question like this. You better read your Bible more." That day, when I was shamed in front of my classmates, was a turning point for me and my faith. In ninth grade, my questions only increased. The major conflict for me was that I was supposed to "love my neighbor" but not _____ (fill in the blank). I was in a community that held absolute truths, and anyone who did not believe in salvation directly through Jesus Christ and failed to follow the appropriate doctrine was wrong in their beliefs. That included Catholics, Jews, Muslims, LGBTQIA+ people, and the list goes on. There was an expectation that I would make a public profession of faith in front of the church community as a teenager, but I refused to go through with the ceremony merely to fulfill my parents' and the church community's expectations. Much to the dismay of my parents, I chose to never make a public profession of faith.

By the time my first year of college was over, I stopped going to church completely, except when I went home for breaks and was expected to attend on Sundays. I have met many first-gen students who have had similar experiences to mine when it comes to religion. We dismantled what was taught to us growing up, and some of us ended up completely walking away from religion, while others rebuilt our faith and religious expression on our own terms. It turned out that college afforded me the opportunity to further explore my religious and spiritual identity. During this time, questions about my faith reached a breaking point, and I took my "personal leap of faith." I still believed in God but questioned whether the way he was portrayed to me during my childhood was the God that I felt was in my heart. To me, God was compassionate and loving instead of merely angry and punishing. I went through the process of trying out two on-campus student ministry organizations and attending some local churches.

Religious parents who have first-gen college students can sometimes view college as a threat, and it may cause a lot of fear within the family. I believe that going to college further solidified my faith in God because I had the privilege of examining my beliefs. I finally returned to a church on a full-time basis when my first child, Alexa, was born.

Although I am a transracial adoptee, race was never discussed in my family, nor did my parents have the knowledge or capacity to even approach the subject. I was never considered Korean but rather as just one of the family who was loved the same as all my parents' other kids. Therefore, I had little awareness of, nor did I anticipate, what the campus would have to offer first-generation college students and students of color. UNH was a predominantly white campus, and I barely saw anyone who looked like me. I think there was an office of multicultural affairs, but I never felt like I belonged there. I did not think I was "Asian" enough due to not speaking Korean or knowing about my culture, and I was more familiar with the white experience, having been adopted into a Caucasian family. There was not an ounce of Korean culture in me other than my appearance.

In the entire Hotel Administration program, there was only one other student of color—an African American student named Shawn. One day both of us were informed by Ann, the program's administrative assistant, that we were going to the Minority Hoteliers Conference at Cornell. Neither one of us could understand why we were chosen to go because we were just "Shawn and Maria." My friends were shocked that I was considered a minority. Shawn and I hopped in my car and headed off on the long drive to Cornell.

At least Shawn had more familiarity with the African American culture than I did. I stayed with a group of young women in Ujamaa House, the residential learning program that celebrates the culture of the African diaspora. That was my first real encounter with groups of people of color. I felt like such a fraud because I could not identify with an Asian community. How could I identify with other people of color when I had never had the experience?

Could I recap what the Conference for Minority Hoteliers was all about? No. However, the experience of being part of a large group of people of color for the first time was a memory that stands out for me. It was a whole new world, and at the time I did not know how to deal with the situation. I was among peers who looked like me, but I still felt so different from them. Today, I can appreciate the richness of that experience and how it was part of my racial identity journey.

TIPS AND ADVICE

In retrospect, I know that I missed out on a lot during my college experience. I was not aware of what I missed until I learned more about the challenges that first-generation students face. I had classmates who talked about studying abroad and experiencing a different culture. All I knew was that it was very expensive to study abroad, or so

I thought, and that automatically eliminated the possibility for me. How could I go overseas when I could barely pay for college in Durham, New Hampshire? I did not know that financial aid or scholarships might also be possibilities for study abroad. Some of my classmates went to places as far away as Switzerland for unpaid hospitality internships in the summer—opportunities that seemed unattainable to me. I self-selected myself out of the process without even asking any questions, something that many other first-generation students do too.

Even now, many first-generation students believe they cannot study abroad or attain a paid internship. However, the good news is that now, because of the increase in research on the first-generation college experience, we know more about how first-generation students contribute positively and uniquely to a campus community and what resources need to be provided to reduce and eliminate the barriers to success. I am grateful that I am now in the position to help first-generation students at Boston University find the resources they need to thrive just like their continuing-student peers.

What advice do I have for you? Never suffer in silence. I promise you, there are many other first-generation and low-income students who feel the same way you do. Find and use your voice. Ask for help and look for resources like a first-generation student initiative or program on your campus. Find out what academic and career resources are available to you. Do not be afraid to ask how to receive additional financial aid or emergency funding if needed; food and housing insecurity is real. There are so many people on your campus who believe in you and want to cheerlead you all the way to the graduation stage. Seek out those mentors who will assist you while you are in college and beyond. Always be aware that the brief interactions with people who help you today may lead to lifelong mentor relationships and friendships. Manage those imposter syndrome voices that whisper, "You do not belong here"—quiet them as best you can. Know that you belong on your campus and your presence makes the campus community an even richer one. I offer all of this to you as someone who has been in the exact same shoes as you.

CHAPTER 7

David Winston, MD, PhD
Forensic Pathologist

I have been a forensic pathologist for over 25 years. I am currently employed at the Pima County Office of the Medical Examiner in Tucson, Arizona, and I have been at this office for 20 years. My main responsibilities are to determine the cause and manner of death for persons who die suddenly and/or unexpectedly. Other duties include discussing autopsy findings with family members; meeting with attorneys and law enforcement regarding criminal and civil proceedings associated with these deaths; testifying in court; and teaching undergraduate, graduate, and medical students, as well as pathology residents and forensic pathology fellows. My biology degree and my undergraduate work-study research experience provided the groundwork for my graduate and medical education, in which I completed both PhD and MD degrees.

APPLYING TO AND PREPARING FOR COLLEGE

I had no clue what I was doing when I was applying to college. I attended a Catholic high school that provided a core curriculum for those who planned on attending college. At this high school, I earned college credit in English and history. My high school had a career guidance office, and many college representatives made recruitment visits. However, when I met with my assigned counselor, I did not feel this counselor gave me any real guidance regarding my decision of which college to attend. Because I was the firstborn and no one among my parents, aunts, uncles, and grandparents had attended college, I did not have any family members to ask about their experiences. Eventually, I applied to several in-state and Catholic universities. As the acceptance letters arrived in the mail, I would look at the anticipated financial aid awards, knowing that the majority of the financial burden of college was on me. Ultimately, I selected Saint Louis University (SLU) because of the relatively small student population and financial aid package (SLU sponsored my high school college credit). I decided on biology as a major because I enjoyed my science and math classes in high school. My initial plan after college graduation was to seek employment as a field biologist for a state or national wildlife agency; I had no plans to attend graduate or medical school.

EXPERIENCES IN COLLEGE

Overall, my experience at SLU exceeded all my expectations. I met a core group of friends who were essential to my success. We still keep in touch via email and social media. Because all of us have professional degrees, we often travel for educational conferences and try to meet in person whenever we are in each other's vicinity.

Even though my childhood home was only a 30-minute commute to the SLU campus, I did not own a car, so I elected to stay in the dormitory. On check-in day, I was quite anxious during the 30-minute drive from the house I had lived in for the past 12 years. I had spent time away from home at various summer camps, but those lasted a week at most. At these camps, I never had to configure a schedule that would include class attendance, part-time employment, and laundry.

Several of my high school classmates also attended SLU; however, all were women, so I had to rely on the dormitory lottery for my roommate. I received my roommate assignment about a month prior to moving into the dormitory. This was 1981, so there was no social media or email to foster a relationship prior to the start of the semester. Our first communication was at check-in. He spent the entirety of the freshman orientation period in a hotel with his parents. Once classes started and he began living in the room, numerous incompatibilities surfaced. For example, he would unclip and hide the handset of the shared landline phone in various places around his side of the room, including under his pillow, in his desk, and in his chest of drawers. In the pre–answering machine and cellphone era, this meant that if I wanted to answer the phone and he was not there, I had to search his side of the room for the handset. Four weeks into the semester, another student on our floor had to take a medical leave of absence from college, so I petitioned for, and was granted, a change of room. I had this new roommate for the remainder of my years at SLU even though he was a Chicago Cubs fan, the rival of my hometown favorite St. Louis Cardinals. Fortunately, my friends and I were able to laugh about the situation while it was happening. I was lucky that the opportunity to switch rooms essentially fell into my lap and that I could stay on the same dormitory floor. If this opportunity had not presented itself, I believe that I would have consulted with my resident advisor or one of the dormitory directors to see what options were available.

I graduated with a BS in biology and a certificate in German. I enjoyed the majority of the courses I studied. My favorite class by far and away was Natural History of the Vertebrates, a class in which we would take monthly weekend field trips birdwatching and lifting logs and rocks searching for reptiles and amphibians. During spring break of that semester, two of our professors supervised a university-sponsored trek to the Everglades National Park. We spent the week camping and documenting our observations. I still have my field notebook from that class, and to this day I enjoy observing and photographing wildlife.

A part of my financial aid package was work-study funding. I had three jobs in college, including documenting dormitory visitors, dishwashing in the dorm cafeteria, and working in a research laboratory at SLU College of Medicine. This research job was instrumental in shaping my career, as I will describe. My least enjoyable time in college was the hours I spent washing dishes in the cafeteria. I was fortunate that I only had to do this for one semester. The only silver lining about the dishwashing job was that I used it as motivation to get me through the tougher times in college, especially preparing for calculus and organic chemistry exams and writing papers for my philosophy and theology courses. I would often motivate myself by muttering, "You need to get this degree or you may have to wash dishes for the rest of your life."

One of the biggest transitions to college life was the need to acquire time management skills to juggle lectures, studying, part-time employment, and a social life. The differences in the courses between high school and college required an adjustment on my part as well. Initially I found the college courses more difficult due to the expected knowledge base and the pace and profundity of the lectures, especially the science classes. My notetaking habits changed, and I had to learn how to write faster yet still maintain legibility. I discovered relatively quickly that cramming a night or two prior to an exam, which worked well in high school, was not going to be the road best traveled for college. I decided to pace myself by learning the material over time instead of relying on memorization. Eventually what worked best for me was to at least skim the relevant sections in the book or the syllabus prior to the lecture. Doing this preview prior to the lecture is the number-one tip I give my current students.

I quickly discovered that whereas I had no problem arriving on time for 8 a.m. classes in high school, this was not the case for me in college. The major reason was that I rarely made it to bed before midnight in college. I was able to schedule classes and work so that I finished both by 5 p.m. This allowed me to have time for a leisurely dinner before deciding how to divide up my evening between academics (studying, writing papers, or preparing lab reports), fitness (participating in intramural sports or working out at the rec center), and socializing. I did not have weekend work hours, so unless there was an exam in the upcoming week, I would only spend a few hours studying on the weekend, usually on Sunday night.

CONTRIBUTORS TO MY SUCCESS

I believe that having a core group of friends played a major role in my success. Two of these friends were also biology majors. It was helpful to be able to discuss the lectures, prepare for exams, and review laboratory assignments with these friends. It was even more helpful to have a peer group with whom to discuss the struggles of nonacademic life, such as worrying about financial aid, having to juggle a job with classwork, and relationship issues.

One of my friends who worked at a medical school research laboratory introduced me to Dr. Andrew Lechner, a research scientist who was looking for work-study employees. At first my duties were limited to washing glassware and retrieving journals from the library. As I gained experience, Dr. Lechner increased my responsibilities and decreased his direct supervision. By the end of my undergraduate career, I was performing unsupervised experiments, ranging from basic assays to thin layer chromatography and operating an electron microscope. These experiments led to my first scientific publication. I believe this experience was probably as important as my GPA with regard to being accepted to graduate school.

Having a source of stress relief was essential to my success as well. I would take time out nearly every evening to go to the campus recreation center. I was active in intramural sports throughout college and joined the SLU rugby team for 2 years. I think it is important to take time to exercise, and participating in sports was my way to accomplish this. I still keep active by riding my bike and hiking to alleviate job stress.

ROLE OF FAMILY

Initially my parents did not understand my desire to attend college. My parents were raised in a farming community in southeastern Missouri in the same small town where several previous generations had resided. My ancestors either worked the family farm or sought employment with the local industry or shops after high school graduation. My parents were unique in that they moved approximately 60 miles north of their hometown after they were married, but they did not attend college. My parents were concerned about the cost of college for me because they could not contribute very much toward paying for it. It was helpful that I earned a scholarship and was awarded a grant, but I still had to apply for a student loan and seek employment because I chose to attend a Jesuit university instead of a less expensive state university.

TIPS AND ADVICE

Take advantage of on-campus housing and a campus meal plan for at least the first year. For many, moving from the comforts of your parents' home to a sparsely furnished dorm room is a huge transition. You will have plenty that will occupy your time (e.g., classes and studying, social life, and laundry to name a few). A campus meal plan eliminates the extra burden of having to take time to shop and prepare meals. I think it is best to postpone meal preparation responsibilities until after you have adapted to the college experience. Living on campus is an invaluable way to make new friends, and you will soon learn that many, if not all, the other students are just as anxious about college as you are.

Take time to meet your professors, especially those who teach your favorite classes. I enjoy talking to my students, not only about the coursework at hand but also about their ambitions. In addition, you will likely need letters of recommendation for internships, graduate schools, or employment, and it is much easier to approach someone with whom you have established a relationship.

Find ways to travel. Many colleges have weekend trips, fall and spring break opportunities, or summer travel excursions. Be creative and see if you can travel to friends' homes for breaks or long weekends. On two separate Thanksgivings, I traveled to Chicago and Indianapolis to spend time with friends' families. In return, these same friends spent Easter weekends with my extended family. At the end of one summer, a group of us traveled to Boston to spend a week with a friend.

Take care of yourself. Find time to exercise, whether it be organized campus activities or community team sports or solo efforts like running, swimming, or yoga. Make efforts to eat healthy food. However, it is also okay to deviate and enjoy some good junk food, especially during late-night study sessions or after a stressful exam. Last but not least, have fun. These years will fly by and before you know it you will be employed with a plethora of financial and familial commitments.

CHAPTER 8

Mike Santaniello
Professor of Sociology

I am a college professor of sociology, an academic advisor, and a mentor; these are positions I have held since 1985. Previously, I was a full-time truck driver for 14 years and a teamster for 10. I also spent many years as a construction worker full time, part time, and as my father's helper. I have helped countless students choose a major, stay in college, graduate, find a satisfying career, get into graduate school, and pass it all on. Helping working students succeed against the odds has been my life's work.

APPLYING TO AND PREPARING FOR COLLEGE

My father, who grew up poor, loved building things and wanted to become an architect. His high school curriculum prepared him to study architecture in college. When he received a scholarship to attend college, he spoke to his father about it. His father (my grandfather) asked him, "What do you want to go to college for? College is for sissies." My father never attended college, deciding instead to become a New York City police officer like his father. My father always stressed the importance of education to me, and he undoubtedly wanted to support my dreams, not crush them. Even though our family had very little money, he sent me to an expensive and highly ranked Catholic high school: Chaminade in Mineola, New York. Every one of the 312 graduates of the Class of 1970 attended college. I was in some honors courses, and I had many great teachers who inspired me and/or pushed me to work hard and aspire to do "something" with my life.

I was also one of the few working-class kids there. I rubbed elbows with the sons of some of the local political and business elite. In my senior year, I took sociology as an elective, and I loved both the course and the teacher. I began to really understand what my family's "place" was in the pecking order of American society. I also learned about some of our society's major social problems, including poverty, inequality, racism, and sexism, and I became obsessed with trying to help "fix" all that was wrong and in need of fixing. I started dreaming of finding a way and a career through which I could help change the world.

My high school social studies teacher inspired me to become a high school social studies teacher, and that became my reason for going to college. Which college I would attend really was a simple decision, because as I saw it I had very few realistic choices. My parents had no money; therefore, I could attend either the local community college (which I saw as a glorified reform school) or State University of New York at Stony Brook, an hour's commute from home. Then, another option presented itself. My father told me that a relative could help me go to Cornell on a partial scholarship (football and track). However, my father had already chosen my high school for me, and I did not want him to choose my college as well. Therefore, I decided to commute to Stony Brook. Going away to school did not seem to be an option because I knew that I had to work and was needed at home. At that point I was the family chauffeur, driving my mother wherever she had to go, alleviating that duty from my father, who was always working. I also began to help financially at home, paying for my own car, insurance, and gas, and doing other chores. Unfortunately, my parents had no clue how to apply to colleges and for financial aid, and they knew it. My parents always emphasized that if I ever had a question in school, I should ask a teacher. So, I asked my high school guidance counselor and several of my teachers for assistance. They were happy to help; they showed me what to do, I followed through, and I was accepted.

EXPERIENCES IN COLLEGE

I began my freshman year as a social studies/secondary education major with hopes of becoming a high school social studies teacher. As a sophomore, I decided that I preferred teaching college rather than high school. I had been an edgy kid growing up, and I realized that dealing with the immaturity of adolescents in general, particularly edgy ones, was not what I wanted to do. Therefore, I changed majors. I had loved sociology since my first course as a high school senior, and I changed my major to sociology with the goal of becoming a sociology professor. This was a very easy decision. Being a sociology professor seemed like a great life to me, and all I had to do was learn the field of sociology and be myself.

Generally, I enjoyed my experiences at college. I was blessed to have had numerous excellent professors in college, and I had a few that first semester. Without a doubt my most positive experience in college was having so many professors who could serve as role models for me. As a future teacher, I watched professors closely, and I was constantly thinking about what they were doing and how they were teaching. Writing this now, it sounds a bit bizarre, but that is what I did. I looked for cues and clues: I examined what worked well and what did not. I asked myself, should I do this, or could I do that? Was the professor getting their point across in the best way? Sometimes I looked so closely at *how* they were teaching that I occasionally drifted away from and missed *what* they were teaching.

Many of my professors were passionate about their respective fields, which drove their teaching. My passion for sociology has always driven my teaching as well, even after 34 years. I also believe that no matter how difficult the challenge, one must approach it with a positive attitude. Reading Viktor Frankl's (1997) study of concentration camp survivors in *Man's Search for Meaning* taught me that each individual ultimately has control over their attitude and that having a big problem and a negative attitude amounts to having two big problems. To quote Captain James T. Kirk, "I don't believe in a no-win scenario." Most of my professors were down-to-earth (with PhDs), direct, and approachable. I was lucky to have professors with these qualities in both my undergraduate and graduate (Columbia University) studies. Professors Gerald Suttles, Herbert J. Gans, and Lewis A. Coser all were accessible and helpful, despite each having a substantial reputation in the field of sociology and on campus. With these examples, how could I ever be stuck up to *my* students? The one exception to those gifted teachers was an education professor in my second semester. After each of several class meetings, I would respectfully approach her desk, which was surrounded by her "Clickettes" (her little group of docile and devoted fans), to ask a question, but I always got an *attitude problem* from her. She often frowned, rolled her eyes, or otherwise looked disgusted or disinterested in my query. I suspect now that she did not like me because of my working-class appearance and demeanor, my edginess, and because I asked her challenging questions. To me, "question everything" is and was the key to academic discourse. It felt to me that the other students who gravitated to her desk were, like her, prisses, who both dressed and acted like they had never worked a hard day in their lives. I did not understand any of this fully then, and this professor really rattled my cage. Her attitude toward me was qualitatively different than that of most of the teachers I had ever had, and she temporarily shook my confidence in my ability to become a good teacher myself. The course grading was midterm 50%, final 50%. I earned a B on her midterm and felt that I did at least as well on the final (although it was not returned) but got a D in the course. I felt unjustly screwed. When that semester's grades came, I had a 2.25 cumulative GPA, including a C and a D. I thought to myself, "Stupid! You want to be a teacher. You must know something." If that professor had ever intended to inspire me, it likely would have been to drop out of college to keep what she may have felt was my proper station in life. Instead, I became inspired to become a better teacher and person than she ever would be. She also helped nudge me to a 3.8 GPA for my last nine semesters of full-time study. At that point, I knew that students like me needed understanding and approachable teachers.

After studying social class differences and their implications throughout most of my professional life, I always go back to Sennett and Cobb's (1993) *The Hidden Injuries of Class*. One key way that members of the privileged elite maintain their control and feeling of superiority over their "underlings" is to make them feel inadequate and inferior. That professor's technique worked on me then: a first-generation college student who had not yet even read Sennett at that point in my education. Today, whenever a fellow first-generation student tells me a similar story about how they were treated badly by a teacher, parent, or boss, I go crazy. One of my favorite mantras, which my students hear repeatedly, is that the only difference between us (professors and other professionals) and you is that we have been in school longer. In fact, I take it one step further. I tell them that anyone who disrespects another to prove their own superiority has instead proven their own inferiority.

Social class and economics also affected me personally as a college student. I worked full time while attending college full time, and I always knew that hard heavy labor jobs often paid more than minimum-wage service-sector jobs. For that reason, I drove a truck full time primarily in Brooklyn and the Bronx, delivering refrigerators and washing machines up countless flights of stairs. As an undergraduate, I usually attended classes Mondays, Wednesdays, and Fridays between 9 a.m. and 5 p.m., and between classes I ate lunch in my car, read, did research for term papers, and/or studied in the library. During the semesters, I worked 3 10- to 12-hour days per week on Tuesdays, Thursdays, and Saturdays. I spent Sundays doing schoolwork, after which I would watch football or baseball. During the summer "vacation," I never took classes because I worked 50 to 60 hours per week. Throughout much of my career, my boss, a teamster trucker, was incredibly supportive of my going to school, although he himself was not college educated. He and his brothers were working-class men who built a trucking business by loading trucks and making deliveries themselves, and this boss clearly was the heavy lifter of the family. His support of my going to college was like my father's support. Whenever I needed an extra day to write a term paper or study for an exam, I could take a day off. In return, I was dependable and hardworking and usually had heavy runs in difficult areas. I also must confess that once per semester, I would miss an entire day of classes, and I always spent that day "off" writing a term paper.

I also helped out at home, both financially and with errands. Although I dated, school and work were typically more important than girlfriends. I earned money because I had to pay for everything that I needed and to support my family. I never felt like I was missing anything important because helping my parents was the classic example of the expression "What goes around comes around." They helped me immeasurably: to do well in school, to aspire to attend college, and to succeed academically, and I am eternally grateful for that. In my dissertation research, an interview study of working-class college students, I found that many other first-generation college students had similar stories to tell. Most of them said they were "very organized" and had "hectic" or "crazy" schedules and lived lives similar to mine in college. Often their families also had major financial problems and stresses. My research showed that their parents were the reason most of them made it. There is no need to send sympathy cards, however. I really did not miss anything I felt was important, and my work ethic has been an incredible asset. In fact, when I finally got to graduate school, I did very well and earned fellowships in part by outworking most of my fellow students. I finally earned my PhD 15 years after I completed my first master's degree. Another mantra I toss at my students came from that experience: "College is mostly an endurance test, and you have to do some *work*!"

CONTRIBUTORS TO MY SUCCESS

Outside of family factors, three factors above all others contributed to my "success." The first was my work ethic, which was experience based and fueled by stubbornness and determination. I flat-out refused to give up and constantly fought to stay in school. The economics of doing so were difficult and relentless. Money was always a problem, but I understood that education was the only solution. I worked full time and attended college full time. I left school briefly twice, and my bachelor's degree took 5.5 years to earn. After my father was severely injured at work (three fingers cut nearly completely off by a power saw while working in construction), I paid the mortgage for 6 months, including during my last semester, then graduated. The second key was teachers. Whereas my grammar school teachers provided the foundation, my high school teachers pushed me to aspire and to question, and my college professors were my mentors and guides. I assessed every professor's personality and sought out and latched on to those who were down-to-earth, accessible, and obviously enjoyed helping students. They helped me immeasurably, especially with questions that my uneducated parents wanted to answer but could not. The third key was finally finding what I wanted to do with my education and my life. That made staying in school and doing well so much easier. I worked very hard to become the best, most accessible, and most down-to-earth professor I could be. My many gifted teachers were my living examples.

ROLE OF FAMILY

My parents were the reason I made it. They kept a roof over my head, fed me, kept me out of jail (I fought and was very good at it), and took care of me. My mother, who was a high school dropout, read to me when I was a baby and taught me the alphabet when I was 18 months old. She was my master teacher without a degree. My father, never a big talker, told me when I was 15, "Mike, you've got to go to college. It's really important. But I can't help you with it. We just don't have the money." The pain on his stern face screamed at me, "Go to college!" Without making me feel guilty, both of my parents educated me as a child about how hard it was for them financially. My parents created no hardships; they taught me economic realities and gave me a strong work ethic. Their struggles gave me my strength.

TIPS AND ADVICE

First, you must understand *why* you must get a 4-year degree. Without at least a bachelor's, most young Americans today will endure a lifetime of struggles, suffering, and financial stresses. With a bachelor's, you will make a lot more money—far more than most of your uneducated peers could ever dream of making. The income gap between high school grads and 4-year college grads is huge and has been growing for at least 40 years. That extra income will help you pay off your school loans and take care of your parents when they get older. Let's be honest: Most first-generation college students are in college because of their parents. With an education, your chances of having a career that you really enjoy is much greater. So, pick your major based on your interests and hopes and dreams. Many of you have heard your folks say, "We want you to do better than we did." What are they lacking? A college degree. How do you do better than they did? Get a bachelor's. Let the fear of financial struggles help drive and motivate you. Latch on to the good examples in your college life who want to help you: your best and most down-to-earth teachers. Let them help, guide, and inspire you. That is what we do! Finally, just keep peddling! Your hard work will pay off. Don't stop! Do your best, for you and for your work, your life, and your parents.

CHAPTER 9

Lynn Pepin, BSE
Completing PhD in Computer Science

I am a first-year PhD student who probably does not get enough sleep. I spend my days performing machine learning and cybersecurity research at the main campus of the University of Connecticut (UConn), located in Storrs, Connecticut. Storrs is a rural setting, surrounded by trees, farmland, parks, trails, and rolling hills. On an autumn day, with a crisp breeze and golden and crimson leaves overhead, the campus and its surrounding area is large and quite breathtaking—if not a bit overwhelming—for a new student. Even the smaller, regional UConn campus that I initially attended felt a bit large to me. Still, as a first-generation college student who was struggling to find my bearings, I saw the Storrs campus as a symbol of adventure, freedom, and knowledge—a place of growth, especially after I had been through the complicated process of applying, planning finances, passing final tests, and graduating from high school.

During my undergraduate years, I devoted my time to my studies, fascinated with the field I had embarked upon. I realized only months before graduating that I wanted to pursue a research position, and so I applied to a PhD program in the same school. Here I am now, spending my days reviewing academic articles, studying for my classes, writing code for experiments, and interacting with other scientists in my field. I am right where I want to be.

I was lucky to have guidance from counselors, advisors, and students who walked this path before me. So when I heard about this book, I was excited to have the opportunity to share my experiences and potentially help other first-generation college students. I hope that my experiences can help you as others have helped me.

APPLYING TO AND PREPARING FOR COLLEGE

For most of my life, I never thought about college. Nobody in my family went to college, and it seemed financially impossible for me to go. Nobody told me that I should go, what scholarships were, that I should apply for them, or even that my hard work would make me a good prospect for college. I thought college was only available to rich kids.

That was until I was 17, when I learned that I was on track to graduate at the top of my high school class as valedictorian, making me eligible to receive UConn's Presidential Scholarship, which amounted to roughly $40,000 of tuition paid over 4 years. Suddenly, college was a possibility for me.

Because I had only one school to consider, UConn, applying to college was easier for me than for some others. In retrospect, I wish I had known about other colleges, but UConn was the only university I knew anything about. At the time, I did not know that other universities offered substantial merit-based and need-based scholarships. I was even unaware of the existence of Harvard and its prestige until *my last year as an undergrad*. I had a great education at UConn, but I wish I had spent more time considering all my options and what I wanted out of my education.

Attending UConn required that I win the scholarship I mentioned earlier, which meant I had to keep my GPA in the first or second spot of my graduating class. If I recall correctly, I managed this by a few hundredths of a GPA point. Maintaining this GPA was a lot of work and increased the heavy workload I carried as a high school senior. For these reasons, I did not have the time to look into or consider those options. Most of what I did know about applying to college was spoon-fed to me by my wonderful counselors and advisors, by UConn's orientation, and by a friend of mine, Connor, who had gone through my exact same situation only a year before me. Having his advice was a massive help, and if you have a friend like that, I recommend seeking their advice. I do not know how I would have been able to do it without him.

After a great deal of help, I was finally accepted to UConn, having received the Presidential Scholarship. However, when I learned how much I would receive in federal loans, I realized I could not afford room and board at the main campus in Storrs. I attended the regional Avery Point campus instead, which was a bit like attending community college; in doing so, I was able to save thousands of dollars and experience a much easier transition into the college experience. After three semesters, I was financially ready to attend the Storrs campus, where I finished my degree.

EXPERIENCES IN COLLEGE

Thanks to orientation materials and advisors, my experiences in college were not as hectic as the application period. At Avery Point, I did not have to handle the overwhelming size of the Storrs campus while also learning the intricacies of college life. I had three semesters to become acclimated to classes, to studying, and to the many other facets of UConn student life before also learning how to live alone, in a dorm.

Nevertheless, there are many aspects of college I wish I had found out about earlier than I did: like what a credit is and its importance, how grades are calculated, how GPA works, the weird and intricate rules of UConn's general-education requirements, the various kinds of degrees, and the differences between undergraduate and graduate studies. I also wish I had known earlier about the dynamics of professor-student relationships, the value of visiting my professors in office hours, what a teaching assistant is and their role in classes, and how to get textbooks cheaper in my first semesters. This is not an exhaustive list. Most importantly, I wish I had known how to ask "stupid questions" earlier and who to ask. (Turns out, you ask your advisor.)

Combined with the work ethic I developed in high school and the serenity the UConn Avery Point library offered over my household, I was able to continue to be an effective student. When I moved to the main campus, with more distance from my family, I was more able to focus. Over those 4 years as an undergrad, I believe I was moderately successful, and not only in my academics but also socially and emotionally; I made a number of friends, formed new relationships, progressed a great deal in my identity as an LGBTQ+ individual, and turned into a coffee snob who could make good coffee. Hell, following my academic/professional successes, I am now literally a scientist, with scientist friends, and I am helping write a book! This is more successful than I ever imagined myself being when I was younger.

CONTRIBUTORS TO MY SUCCESS

Ever since I was young, I have kept myself organized. I kept my papers in order, I kept myself aware of important deadlines and dates, and I studied upcoming syllabus topics and finished homework before it was due. I also devoted time to studying and good sleep and avoided drugs and alcohol. For work, I took on tutoring, which helped me maintain my skills from previous subjects and made future classes easier. I even tutored other folks in classes of mine, refining my understanding of the material. Basically, I did everything I could to keep myself ahead in class. This was especially instrumental in my first three semesters attending Avery Point, as I suffered some setbacks due to familial issues, which I will describe presently. These setbacks were not as disastrous as they could have been due to my ability to stay "ahead."

Speaking specifically to students who want to pursue computer science, I also learned some extra skills that made all my programming assignments much easier. First, I developed personal programming projects in my free time and I took on internships. These types of real-world experiences are invaluable. Second, during these projects I learned to use the Linux terminal and Git, which boosted my productivity as a software engineer greatly. Plus, the internships also left me with the money I needed to actually finish my degree, making them an important contributor to success.

Finally, I avoided making excuses. As an example, I would hear other students frequently say, "The professor doesn't teach!" This can be true, and classes can be more difficult due to a bad professor, so in these classes, like most others, the textbook becomes an essential resource. You must take an initiative in your own learning and learn to explore and study a subject independently, without distractions. On the topic of distractions and excuses, I would like to expand on one large factor that contributed to my success in college: having distance from my family for the first time in 18 years.

ROLE OF FAMILY

I will be blunt: My family was physically, emotionally, and at times even sexually abusive to me and to one another. During my high school years, that house was a difficult, disruptive, and painful environment. I do not know how I managed to study and work in it. During my first three semesters of college, when I was commuting from home to Avery Point, I finally had a place removed from that house where I could study and work. Since I still lived at home, I suffered in that house for those three semesters. I do not want to get into the details of specific events, but know that these difficulties were persistent. It took effort to remain successful and healthy.

Once I moved to the main campus at Storrs, I had almost 24/7 distance from my family. I was able to sleep soundly in a safe environment. Noises outside my room were no longer a cause for my adrenaline to spike. I was able to form positive relationships with people. I could study without being interrupted by fights. Distance from my family was the single best thing for my mental health, personal growth, and development as a person. If you are a soon-to-be high school graduate in a similar situation, I hope you can find similar independence, freedom, and growth.

In an odd way, I am lucky in that my parents played almost no mentorship or emotional support role in my adult life. They had not gone to college themselves and had little advice or support to give me as a college student. If they had, I might have found myself relying on them for support, undermining the independence I was building. I also had very little financial dependence on them after my first paid internship in 2016. This financial independence is not common, and I see how friends who are financially dependent on abusive family members experience even more stress.

TIPS AND ADVICE

If you're reading this section, that means I get to ramble on, not once but *twice*, about what I consider important for success. I covered a lot previously, and I will not retread much of that ground here. However, there are a few key things to cover. First, recall my friend Connor, who went through the exact same situations as I did as an applicant, only 1 year prior. If you have such friends who are willing to share advice, get in contact with them! Take advantage of as much information and help as you can get during the application process, as it can be overwhelming. Second, *stay organized and keep on top of things*. This is important for pretty much every aspect of life. Be aware of dates and obligations. Keep a to-do list, a calendar, whatever works for you. Also, locate your classrooms early. When I first arrived on campus, it was large, and I knew only a few places. I took my schedule and sought out my classroom buildings so that I knew the paths I would take. Fourth and final piece of advice: *Take care of yourself*. Regular sleep and hydration are important. Make sure you know what health services (mental and physical) exist near your campus. As a student, I was unlucky in that I did not have any services within an hour's drive that took my insurance; I had to make sure I did not get sick or injured. Even when I was in the worst of moods, in the most depressed or self-injurious of mind-sets without a care for self-preservation, I was able to convince myself to sleep, to rest, to clean my wounds, to take a walk and clear my head, or to seek the help of a confidant. If you ever find yourself in such a place, I hope you can help yourself as well. A piece of advice that I was given once was that the mind needs a healthy body and vice versa. I know it's a privileged thing to say "just stay healthy," but it is important that you do so as much as you can.

Of course, everything I wrote above is a list of imperatives—what worked *for me*. Ask others what worked for them. Keep note of what works for you and use it. I wish you the best of success as a student and the best of luck in your near future!

CHAPTER 10   FROM NORTH PHILLY TO FACULTY: *TESTIMONIO* OF A FIRST-GENERATION LATINX COLLEGE STUDENT SURVIVING AND THRIVING AT A HISTORICALLY WHITE UNIVERSITY

Stephen Santa-Ramirez, PhD
Assistant Professor of Higher Education, Department of Educational Leadership and Policy, University at Buffalo

> "*¡Venceremos porque nacimos para triunfar!* We will overcome because we were born to triumph!"
>
> —Motto of Latino America Unida, Lambda Alpha Upsilon Fraternity

I am currently an assistant professor of higher education at the University at Buffalo, whose operations take place on the unceded ancestral territory of the Seneca Nation of the Haudenosaunee Six Nations Confederacy. My story, from North Philly to faculty member, is the *testimonio* of a first-generation Latinx college student surviving and thriving at a historically white university. My professional experiences in higher education and student affairs (HESA) include multicultural and LGBTQ+ affairs, residential life, and migrant student services. In addition to working and teaching at University at Buffalo, I have worked for the Philadelphia Freedom Schools, Michigan State University, the University of Texas at Arlington, and Arizona State University. As a first-generation college student navigating the complexities of higher education, my involvement in various organizations and finding people and campus spaces of belonging (described later) led to my interest in working professionally in HESA and eventually becoming a professor for a graduate program that supports the development of researchers and administrators in higher education settings.

My diverse personal and professional experiences in higher education, as well as my identity as a scholar-practitioner-activist, have played formative roles in my involvements and the development of my research agenda, which centers the lives and knowledge of historically marginalized and economically neglected collegians. By employing critical and asset-based frameworks, my scholarship investigates campus racial climate, first-generation students' sense of belonging, college student activism, and the various ways race, ethnicity, and im/migration inform the educational experiences of collegians who are Latinx and undocu/DACAmented. In my writing, I utilize *testimonio* and critical race theory, which allow Black, Indigenous, and people of color (BIPOC) to share salient life experiences, injustices, and human struggles, which are often erased by dominant discourses. They also allow me to enter this conversation by centering my knowledge, positionality, and lived experiences, which in turn, I hope, will create space for reflection and healing.

APPLYING TO AND PREPARING FOR COLLEGE

As a result of historical and contemporary racist policies and practices that have affected the lives of many with intersectional identities (e.g., BIPOC and low-income), we enter college from high financial need socioeconomic backgrounds, endure various levels of discrimination and microaggressions, and navigate challenges with white ideologies, especially at historically white institutions. Unfortunately, I experienced some of these challenges prior to entering college. Before sharing a pivotal moment, let me briefly provide some context of my arrival to high school and some of my involvements.

I attended the Franklin Learning Center High School in Philadelphia. At the time, this was one of the few public high schools in Philly that offered academic majors. With a passion for the arts, I was encouraged by my middle school guidance counselor to apply as a performing arts major. Although I was hesitant and quite honestly a bit nervous about the unknown, I decided to apply and audition. I was granted acceptance, and for the next 4 years I would take public transportation 1 hour away from home to engage in my passion for the arts. While at Franklin, I was class president from my sophomore year to graduation day. In addition to being a student leader, I worked diligently to maintain good grades to be competitive for college admissions committees. To be fully transparent, I do not remember anyone ever sharing the significance of getting involved in student organizations and activities of interest (e.g., sports and community service) to make myself more marketable in college application pools. I simply wanted to be part of a leadership team that did good work alongside and for my classmates while also advocating for our collective needs. However, I do recognize that this leadership position may have appeared favorable to college admissions committees. Therefore, if possible and able, I would encourage others to get involved in at least one organization of interest prior to applying to college.

As a first-generation college student from a high financial need Puerto Rican household, I did not have others in my family to turn to for college advice. However, I was fortunate to receive their support as I became involved with a nonprofit organization in Philadelphia, Congreso de Latinos Unidos, which assisted us teenage affiliates with college applications, answered our questions, and accompanied us on campus tours. The staff at Congreso were a blessing to me and many of my Black and Brown peers in Philly.

I was able to utilize the great team at Congreso to help me navigate necessary components of the process, such as the Free Application for Federal Student Aid and college applications; however, as many BIPOC high school students with college aspirations find out, some individuals attempt to stifle our goals and act as gatekeepers (Obama, 2018), and my designated high school guidance counselor proved to be one of them.

When I approached him (a white cisgender heterosexual man) to support me with preparing to submit my applications and potential fee waivers to 4-year institutions, he stated, "People like you don't go to college." I was shocked and confused at hearing that statement, which was quickly followed by, "I can help you with applying to CCP [Community College of Philadelphia]." As mentioned earlier, I had a decent academic record (top 10%) and was the class president. As soon as the guidance counselor uttered those words, I knew it was because I was a Brown person from North Philly—not because I lacked intellect or leadership abilities. I knew that in his world "people like you" meant people who were unworthy of attaining a higher education that was initially designed for and is "meant for white folk."

Reflecting on that moment, I realize now that I was privy to how systemic racism plays a significant role in shaping many BIPOC communities' life trajectories (e.g., mass incarceration and lack of opportunities for professional advancement and generational wealth). I also was aware that I was going to encounter some people in life who have racist ideologies and may try to belittle my accomplishments and stifle my success. At this pivotal moment, I made an active choice not to let him win. I knew my worth and talent, and he would not be the gatekeeper that kept me from achieving my goal of attending and graduating from college. Disappointed but not broken, I left his office and never returned. I then turned to the other school counselor, a white cisgender woman, Amy Miller, who validated and affirmed my aspiration to attend college. She took me under her wing and assisted me in the ways my designated school counselor was supposed to but chose not to. Every time I received a college acceptance letter in the mail (this was well before email notifications became the norm), I made a copy and slid it under his door—16 in total.

EXPERIENCES IN COLLEGE

After careful thought and consideration, I was excited to enroll at West Chester University of Pennsylvania (WCU). Having been born and raised in a high financial need family in a predominantly Latinx community in North Philadelphia, I experienced a bit of culture shock. WCU is a midsize historically white university. At the time of enrollment, my residence in West Chester, Pennsylvania, was approximately 1 hour from home. Among a sea of white folk, I quickly learned that to survive and thrive as an undergraduate student, I needed to find a community of *mi gente*—individuals who share similar cultural backgrounds, interests, and life experiences. Soon after, I became involved with a social and advocacy student organization that catered to Latinx students, the Latin American Student Organization (LASO). Through my involvement as a general member and on the executive board, I found a community and a sense of belonging via this counterspace where I could be my authentic self.

LASO planned on-campus social and educational events that centered on the history and experiences of Latinx people writ large. During my first year, after organizing and participating in a winning performance, consisting of the beautiful sounds of salsa and bachata music at WCU's homecoming parade, we collectively decided to start the first Latinx-based dance troupe on campus, Mas Flow Dance Team. As a cofounder and team captain, I led my peers in various routines centering Latinx music and dance styles. We performed at several events, including WCU's annual homecoming parade, a plethora of campus events (both at WCU and surrounding universities), and the annual Philadelphia Puerto Rican Day Parade. I remember being especially proud when we placed among the top three performances as first-time participants. During the latter half of my second year, due to the absence of Latino-based fraternal organizations on campus, my line brothers and I became founding chapter members of Latino America Unida, Lambda Alpha Upsilon Fraternity (LAU). As an active member and chapter president, I built close bonds with *mis hermanos* while celebrating our different cultures and continuing to host programs and events that catered to the needs of Black and Brown students. Between LASO and LAU, the experiences and time spent together allowed many of us to build a strong rapport and become each other's family away from home.

Shifting from my social experiences to academics, although I could have done without some of the mandatory electives and prerequisites, I took courses based on my interests in college. However, I was caught off guard by the amount of reading required of college students. I remember spending ample time in the university library, reading and completing various class assignments. At the time, I was not a proficient reader, which means that I was never properly trained to actively read lengthy texts while simultaneously retaining what I was reading. I often found myself rereading the same page because once I reached the end, I did not remember most of what I had just read. Thus, I trained myself in the library to read various books and articles efficiently while memorizing key points and taking notes on the side of the page(s) in order to retain the significance of the literature.

One of my earliest college memories is walking into my first course, COM 101 (public speaking), taught by an African American man and fellow first-generation college student, Dr. Timothy Brown. He was one of the very few Black professors on campus, and that representation meant the world to me. Once I declared my major as communication studies, I was fortunate to have Dr. Brown assigned as my academic advisor. College was also where I could be truly independent, living on my own and connecting with people beyond the geographical boundaries of Philadelphia. Furthermore, in college I began to find my "voice" as an advocate, recognizing the lack of Black and Brown people on campus and getting involved in spaces from which I could speak on behalf of a larger student body. Thus, besides becoming an executive board member of LASO, and the Latino recruiter intern for the Admissions Office, I was a WCUR campus radio host, where my catalog and conversations centered Latinx music (i.e., reggaeton and salsa) and issues, and I was invited to join committees and to visit the university president's home, where I was able to provide insight on the needs and wants of Latinx collegians and students of color writ large.

During my time in college, I recognized my full potential and the agency that I did not always know I had. I found some of my lifelong friends and *hermanos* (fraternity brothers), many of whom have continued to be an indispensable part of my life journey over the years. I am happy to say that most of my undergraduate college memories consist of joyous moments in community with peers and faculty/staff. I am incredibly proud of a few of my decisions in life. Attending and graduating from college is at the top of the list.

CONTRIBUTORS TO MY SUCCESS

Without a doubt, a salient factor to my success has been my intrinsic motivation to obtain a college degree and advance socioeconomically. The connections I made on campus via various student organizations (i.e., LASO, Mas Flow Dance Team, and LAU) played a significant role in my development and holistic student success. Through these organizations, I built a community with others who shared similar backgrounds and experiences. We supported each other personally (e.g., celebrated birthdays and accolades) and academically (e.g., creating study groups and sharing internship/scholarship opportunities). For example, I recommended a Latina peer of mine to an internship opportunity. A couple of years later, she encouraged me to apply for a summer internship at an insurance company in their Public Affairs Department. As it turns out, this internship was what jump-started my full-time professional career.

In addition to my amazing peers, I formed positive fem/mentoring relationships among professional staff in student affairs, including a Black woman in admissions, Dr. Angela Howard (my internship supervisor); a Black man in the Office of Multicultural Affairs, Dr. Kendrick Mickens (my work-study student worker supervisor); a mixed-race woman in Residential Life, Marion McKinney (a senior leader in the department I worked in as a resident assistant); and two white folks, the vice president and assistant vice president for student affairs, Dr. Matthew Bricketto and Diane DeVestern. These individuals collectively looked out for me and met with me whenever I needed to talk through a work, personal, or academic issue. For example, to discuss a matter related to one of my supervisors on campus, I went to Dr. Howard's office, and she provided me with the encouraging words and guidance I needed to work through the issue. Moreover, Dr. Mickens would sit and speak with me about various opportunities to consider. He would also text me when there were campus events where food was available. My friends and I did not have a lot of money, so free food was always something we looked forward to. When I was preparing to graduate, I was honored to have Dr. Mickens ask me to be the student keynote speaker for the multicultural Kente graduation ceremony.

When I decided to depart from my first postcollege career in the corporate sector, Dr. Mickens played a significant role in guiding my decision to pursue a master's degree and career in HESA. He helped me to realize the opportunities and my potential for doing social justice work as a HESA professional. Diane DeVestern helped me develop a "winning résumé" and walked me through the pros and cons of applying to various graduate programs. Finally, Marion McKinney, Dr. Brown, and Dr. Bricketto graciously agreed to write recommendations for my application. Between my organizational involvement, my peers, and my professional fem/mentors, I successfully navigated and persisted through college to graduation and received guidance to advance professionally postgraduation.

ROLE OF FAMILY

Although my family did not fully grasp what I was going through in college, they always supported me and were rooting for me. My success in and after college was and continues to be a family win. Fortunately, I never felt pressure from my family to stay home and not pursue college. Although separated, my parents were both incredibly supportive. When I was accepted to WCU, my father drove me to the school for a "Check Us Out Day" (where I first met Dr. Howard, who oversaw this program hosted by the Office of Admissions). On day one of my collegiate journey, my father helped me shop for necessities and dropped me off at my residence hall. Moreover, my mother would visit me every few months, a couple of times sleeping over in my residence hall and later campus apartment. She brought groceries and cooked delicious Puerto Rican dishes for my friends and me. This was one of my mother's ways of showing her support for my academic journey. I could not go to my family members for direct guidance, but they constantly affirmed and validated my being in college—always reminding me that they were proud.

Ten years after my undergraduate graduation from WCU, I was honored with the Legacy of Leadership Award. My mother accompanied me as my date, and all of my fem/mentors mentioned throughout this chapter were in attendance to celebrate this accomplishment. During my speech, I publicly thanked them all, including my beautiful mother, for believing in me and instilling in me the knowledge and skills needed to continue doing good and important work for other students, especially those who are first-gen and underrepresented in college.

TIPS AND ADVICE

Having now graduated as a first-generation student with my bachelor's, master's, and PhD, in addition to working professionally in HESA, I have gained loads of insight over the years. My involvement in organizations and finding people and campus spaces of belonging were critical components of my journey: together they led to my interest in working professionally in HESA and eventually becoming a professor for a graduate program that supports the development of researchers and administrators in higher education settings. Everyone's college journey is different, with various factors to consider. Some people have access to federal- and state-level financial aid, and others do not (e.g., individuals who are undocu/DACAmented im/migrants). Further, some people consider attending college directly after graduating from high school or receiving an alternative diploma. In contrast, others decide to enroll in higher and postsecondary education as older adults with spouses, children, and full-time employment. The great thing about college is that there are various types of institutions to consider, based on individual wants and needs (e.g., community college, online/distance learning, trade school, public and private universities, and Native/Hispanic/Black-affirming institutions). To anyone considering higher and postsecondary education, I would suggest thinking through your desires, aspirations, wants, and needs (e.g., going away for school versus staying close to family).

If possible, I would highly recommend reaching out via phone and/or email to admissions office staff and coordinators of academic major(s) of interest to ask any questions you may have about enrollment, fee waivers, scholarships, campus life, and so forth. These individuals are hired to assist and are waiting for you to reach out. Finally, when applying, do not feel pressured to share your trauma in your statement of purpose. You may read some "tips and tricks for applying to college" that wrongly perpetuate a view of first-generation and racially minoritized students from a deficit lens and encourage applicants to solely share struggles and generational trauma (see for example Stern, 2021). Do not feel obligated to do so. We are more than obstacles derived from whiteness and racism; thus, it is perfectly acceptable to highlight joyful moments as well as the assets and skills you possess.

For currently enrolled first-generation students, know that you are worthy and that your being and your skills are needed in these collegiate settings. First-generation students have various assets to contribute to their campus community and academic programs, including various aspects of cultural capital (i.e., aspirational, familial, navigational, resistance, and social). Hone in on what you contribute to your respective colleges inside and outside of the classroom. Always remember that you are the talent, and they are fortunate to have you. Another piece of advice is, if possible, reach out to HESA staff and faculty who you relate to for potential fem/mentoring relationships. Having multiple fem/mentors to assist in various aspects of your personal and professional development can be affirming and beneficial to your holistic success. If you need a starting point, there are formal peer and professional staff fem/mentoring programs you can partake in through various HESA campus departments (e.g., Office of Multicultural Affairs).

Moreover, try to remain true to yourself and what makes you happy. If possible, major in what brings you joy, surround yourself with people who have similar interests, and do not be afraid to step outside of your comfort zone and befriend others whom you may not normally engage with. You never know what kind of lifelong relationships can emerge. Furthermore, if others have helped pave the way for you, I recommend paying it forward to other first-generation students. We do not have to navigate these institutions alone.

I began this chapter with a motto from my fraternal organization, LAU: "*¡Venceremos porque nacimos para triunfar!* We will overcome because we were born to triumph!" I was introduced to this powerful motto back in 2006 as an undergraduate student, and it continues to motivate me as I persist in this journey called life. Always remember, you are the author of your story, so make it one you are proud of.

Critical Self-Reflection 1

Adam J. Rodríguez

After reading through the first 10 stories, what stood out to you? Some of these experiences may have felt very similar to your own, and some may have seemed quite different. You also likely read tips and advice that you are familiar with and some that you had not considered previously. As you read through the stories, no doubt some parts stood out. It may have been Anthony's worries about failing out of school, Jeremy's concerns that he may be perceived as "inferior," Ivonne's anxiety about her performance in a class, or Maria's early academic struggles. Personal stories are powerful and can impact us emotionally, sometimes at great depth. The critical self-reflection sections of the book are designed to explore these dynamics and more.

Each section begins with two standard questions, followed by a series of discussion questions that are unique to the particular section they cover. All questions may be explored independently or with others. Try to create intentional time and opportunities to reflect, more than once, on these questions on your own—through journaling or during private moments. Return to them over time as your thoughts and feelings may evolve and shift. Also look for opportunities to explore them with others. You may explore them with your therapist, with a close and trusted friend, in a group of peers, in a group led by a high school guidance counselor, or in a group led by a college academic advisor, mentor, professor, or other university staff member.

TWO PRIMARY QUESTIONS

1. As you read through these stories, what came up for you?
2. Having read this group of stories, what advice would past, present, and future you give to yourself?

The first question, What came up for you?, appears to be relatively simple but is actually quite challenging. It asks you to take note of anything that you read, in any part of the book, that caused you to experience some significant *feeling* while you were reading it.

It does not matter what the feeling was. It may have been excitement, joy, enthusiasm, confusion, worry, dread, sadness, or any number of other emotions. You may only be aware that you felt something but be unable to identify the specific emotion. There is no "correct" form that this will take. The feeling is the important part. It is a signal that something you read has special meaning for you. The first step is to simply note the fact that you experienced some significant emotional response; just be aware of it.

The next step is to reflect on that emotional response. This step involves asking yourself to increase your awareness of *what* you felt, in an effort to understand it better and to explore the many dimensions of it. It may still be inchoate. Ask yourself, What does it feel like? Where does it appear in your body? What thoughts come to mind? Does it elicit any memories? As you reflect on and explore those emotions, your mind might take you to an unexpected place—one that may even seem irrelevant, nonsensical, or confusing. I consider this metacognitive process to be "play." Play in this context involves allowing your thoughts to be directionless, without specific goals; it is to let your mind take you wherever it wants to and appreciating that you are exploring. Here you are simply observing, being curious, and discovering, not attempting to find solutions or answers.

By paying attention to the emotional experience, and the accompanying thoughts and sensations, through this form of play, you are discovering something about yourself. Whatever evoked this response while reading will occur again in the future in some form. When you do have that feeling again, you will be familiar with the experience and will find more to be curious about and to consider. It is in these moments of emotional impact that we ultimately discover meaning. It may be that in the process of play we recognize something valuable to us that we want to remain attuned to and pay attention to. We may also be responding to a warning of something painful, which we want to be protective about.

The second question empowers you to act as an agent of information and advice, while connecting with your own thoughts and feelings through time. Having read and digested these stories, what advice do you have for yourself? Consider not only the advice you currently want to give yourself but also what the younger version of yourself or even your future self might want to say. How might the advice look different in each of those scenarios? What factors contribute to the change in the advice? The idea here is that you stretch your own experience beyond what is presently in your mind. Sometimes, especially in novel or pressured times, we can become fixated on a way of thinking that is narrow and relevant only to the current moment. A wider lens can help us consider ideas outside of that perspective. It can challenge us to project ourselves backward and forward in time to consider the values and ideas that were previously important to us or that someday may be important to us. Play with the idea of giving yourself advice, not just as your current self but also as an older and younger version of yourself.

FURTHER DISCUSSION QUESTIONS

What follows are larger questions that have emerged for each of our authors and are worthwhile answering for yourself. They are not specific questions that warrant a specific answer, but rather each item below represents a general domain that contains multiple questions that may stimulate thoughts, ideas, values, or feelings that you can begin to elaborate on. You will have in your mind the stories you have read, and they will inform how you think about these questions. What is important here is to approach these items with a sense of curiosity and exploration.

1. How might you know if you need academic support or help? What are the signs or indications that help would be beneficial or is needed? What might interfere with your ability to ask for and receive help?
2. What feelings arise when you think about asking for help? Does contemplating it feel uncomfortable in any way? Does it feel shameful or embarrassing? What may contribute to those feelings? What types of help do you feel more comfortable asking for than others? Are there any types of help that feel unimaginable to ask for?
3. Reflecting on past academic experiences, think about the times you were successful in school and the times you were not. Consider what contributed to that success and what stood in the way. What types of academic experiences do you aspire to? What do you want to accomplish in the future? What are those things specifically? What do they look like? What form do they have? What influences them?
4. Can you identify an academic role model? This could be someone who possesses qualities that you aspire to. It may be a professor, a high school teacher, a graduate student, or a peer. What are those qualities? How did they obtain them? What do they do that you respect or admire? In what ways would you like to be like them in the future? In what ways would you like to be different?

SECTION II
STORIES FEATURING SOCIAL EXPERIENCES

....

ADAM J. RODRÍGUEZ

Although Western culture emphasizes individuality, humans are, by nature, social creatures. We rely on and need relationships with others for support, for emotional connection, and for our overall mental well-being. Many first-generation students come from communities in which relationships are heavily emphasized, within and outside of their families of origin. The hyper-individualism that college culture promotes can feel like a culture shock. Adjusting to college is a challenge for nearly all students, but first-generation students often feel different from our peers—alone, uncomfortable and unsure of our place, and unclear of how we fit in or if we ever will. Many of us enter college feeling like we do not belong.

College is not just about grades, although we often think of it that way. It is about networking with professionals and building relationships with faculty and staff. It is also about forming friendships (some of which may last a lifetime), a sense of community, and a feeling of belonging. It is about developing collegial relationships with peers and learning from and teaching one another. College is about study groups and also parties, clubs, organizations, and sports. College is a social endeavor as much as, if not more than, it is an academic one in which "feeling like you are part of the college community is a crucial component of undergraduate life" (Jack, 2019, p. 27). College is a time of individuation and maturing into adulthood. In order to build relationships, one must feel that the culture and environment of the school promotes inclusion and helps create opportunities for social engagement, or at the very least does not explicitly or implicitly create obstacles for students. Jack (2019) notes that

> students who do not feel welcome at a college do not avail themselves of the many opportunities and resources that are available. Campus life is often more stressful for these students than for their peers, hampering their ability

to focus on various tasks. They tend to underperform and to give up more easily. Students who delay integrating into the larger college community also have less access to social support from their peers and from the college as a whole—support that proves crucial to success both in college and in the labor market upon graduation. (p. 28)

Colleges and universities can actively create opportunities for their diverse student populations to meet and socialize with others, from campus organizations to residence halls to experiences within the classroom. They can also knowingly or unknowingly ignore the needs of marginalized groups, like first-generation students, which exacerbates these feelings of isolation.

Bianca was a first-year student at a prestigious university who was referred to me for psychotherapy by the college. Like many students, she initially reached out to college counseling services due to very general feelings of anxiety, sadness, and a lack of motivation. Early in our sessions, she talked to me about feeling that she was "not right for college" and that she did not "belong there." At first, Bianca thought her feelings were due to not being "smart enough" to succeed in college, but as we talked she began to realize that her discomfort at school had far less to do with her academic ability and much more with feeling different, alone, and misunderstood. Bianca grew up in a somewhat small town, the child of a Black mother and Guatemalteco father. Neither of her parents had gone to college and both worked long hours, leaving Bianca to spend a lot of time on her own.

Bianca was attending a prestigious, predominantly white institution that professed inclusion and support of people of color yet had very little diversity on campus; this meant that many of its students, faculty, and staff had had limited exposure to communities of color or individuals from lower-income backgrounds. Bianca struggled with forming new relationships in general but found this to be even more difficult at a predominantly white institution where most people could not understand her. Very few people on campus looked like her, shared her customs or traditions, listened to the types of music she listened to, or ate the types of food she ate. Bianca regularly faced microaggressions from students, faculty, and staff. She dealt with repeated attempts from others to touch her hair, was asked about "where she was *really* from," and was told "how articulate" she was. Bianca found herself withdrawing further and further from others. Attending class felt intimidating and unwelcoming. She felt that faculty and staff were judgmental and unapproachable. Already tired from work, she began to miss more classes and quickly got behind in her coursework. She started to isolate herself in her dorm room, feeling depressed and anxious and without anyone to lean on. These forces increased her isolation and loneliness, which created a vicious cycle. Naturally, her academic work suffered.

Social belonging and acceptance in school goes beyond having friends. Without connections we cannot function let alone thrive. Difficulties in feeling like we belong and feeling like we can form meaningful relationships affect our mental health, well-being, and performance in class. The stories from this section prominently feature some aspect of the social experience of college. For some students, feelings of isolation and lack of community became a major factor in how they felt about college. For other contributors, it was the ability to find community, either soon after beginning school or after an adjustment period, that became central to their experience at college and contributed to their success. As always, please keep in mind that these stories may have prominent aspects of the social, but they also contain elements of the academic and psychological.

CHAPTER 11 THE LITTLE GIRL FROM GAY, GEORGIA

Patricia Harris, MA
Senior Director of Education, Operations, and Initiatives, University of North Carolina at Chapel Hill

A nurse (let us call her Brenda) at Warm Springs Medical Center named me Patricia, which means "noble," but no one calls me that but my mother, Cynthia (aka Simp, aka Teen Mom—don't judge me). My family calls me Polly, which has several "Virgin Mary" associations, but of course I defaulted to the word *rebelliousness*. Most people know me as Trish, which according to the trusty Urban Dictionary (2010) means I am "a sexy, strong, sensitive woman who is straightforward and honest. A person who makes a great friend. Loyal almost to a fault, funny, thoughtful and loving. . . . Someone you want on your side" (para. 1). According to the same source, I am also a person who "will always stand up for herself and what she believes" (para. 1). This must've been written by Brenda, because my God, the accuracy of it. I am a self-proclaimed troublemaker, an agitator if you will, and a proud disruptor who speaks truth to power. All of these characteristics are well suited to my newly appointed role as the senior director for education, operations, and initiatives in the Office for Diversity and Inclusion at the University of North Carolina at Chapel Hill. That was a mouthful; I am ridiculous and seem "too much," so the title seems befitting. I have been working in higher education for almost 20 years, focusing on college access, admission, and recruitment, with a commitment to educational equity and improving outcomes for historically marginalized students. I have held positions at Dutchess Community College, Marist College, Bard College, University of Georgia, Clayton State University, and Duke University. Most of my career has been centered on cultivating strategic partnerships to creative innovative solutions and structural change. As stated on my LinkedIn profile (insert sarcastic undertone), I am a connector (aka The Plug), a collaborator, a conduit for change, and unapologetically Trish.

As I type these words, I clearly recognize the impact that my education at Savannah State University (SSU) has had on my life and why I have been consistent in my efforts to stay intentionally connected to the institution and community that helped to shape my life's path. As an alumna of SSU, the oldest public historically Black college and university (HBCU) in Georgia, I am a staunch advocate for HBCUs and have a vested interest and commitment to their purpose, promise, and beliefs; these are not only grounded in a rich tradition but also represent the natural evolution of the institution's mission. SSU's guiding foundational credo is "You can get anywhere from here," which is woven into the fabric of the institutional culture. This credo guides the high morale and commitment that faculty and staff demonstrate in their service to students and the community. SSU provides a culture of caring—one that prepares students to contribute to their communities by building their confidence and instilling them with the audacity to be leaders and the hope to realize their dreams. It is a culture that helps bridge the academic achievement gap and plays a vital role in delivering better futures for the Trishes of the world: you know, Black, female, country, first-generation, poor, unpoised, unpolished, and nappy around the edges. It is a culture that cultivated my Blackness in a way that I had never before explored; it was that environment that taught me to be proud of and honor my colloquialisms (that Southern twang just touches the ears a little differently); it was the place that lifted me up, dusted me off, and guided me when I was lost. It was also the place that granted me the opportunity to have experiences that most people read about in books or watch on the History Channel.

I distinctly recall an experiential learning assignment for my African American Studies course. Our professor decided to hold class at the First African Baptist Church, the oldest Black church in the country. I remember walking into the church for the first time and being in absolute awe. Most people might view the beauty and artistry as mere elements of another beautiful church. However, during the lesson, I was able to feel, touch, and smell a part of history that connected me to my ancestors. Hidden in the stained-glass windows, the church pews, the ceiling, and the floorboards were designs and messages that signified that the church was a stop along the Underground Railroad. I will never forget the eeriness and immense sadness that I felt when I placed my fingers through the breathing holes in the floor. An experience like this affected me in ways that I cannot adequately describe; the only word that comes to mind is *transformative*. Needless to say, SSU set the foundation for my transformation and charted a path that has allowed me to dwell in my purpose and live a life above the floorboards (breathing freely) with my face turned to the sun.

APPLYING TO AND PREPARING FOR COLLEGE

Someone once told me that "demography does not have to be your destiny when there is intervention involved." Education was my intervention—my saving grace and my way out of Gay, Georgia (population 110, according to the 2020 U.S. census). Let's take it back to 1999–2000, my senior year at Greenville High School. After securing (aka, begging for) two SAT/ACT vouchers and three application fee waivers from the guidance counselor, I decided to apply to college. I did not know waivers were a thing until my friend Keisha asked me if I had received my vouchers. The teachers and staff loved Keisha, so they shared resources with her, and like a true friend, she shared them with me. I was the troublemaker, the girl with the bad attitude and potty mouth who argued with her bipolar mother in the hallways; I was the one who wore a secondhand minidress to the prom, drank stolen wine in coolers after school, and was deemed unworthy of free college application waivers. I was troubled indeed, but I had a praying grandmother and a beautiful mind; therefore, I still managed to earn a spot in the top 10% (number 8 to be exact) of my graduating class. (There were only 97 of us, but I'm still a genius or whatever.) Anyway, I obtained my vouchers, filled out those confusing SAT forms, forged my parents' signatures (it was for a good cause), walked to the end of the dirt road (you know, like our grandparents who walked 5 miles to school), and placed the packet in the mail. However, in true Simp and Trish fashion, the night before my SAT exam, my mother and I had another one of our frivolous arguments, which meant she would no longer drive me to the exam the following morning. The test was scheduled for 8 a.m.; I woke at 6:30 a.m., got dressed, and did what any other troublemaker would do—stole my mom's minivan and drove 30 minutes to the testing site. I had to get out of Gay by any means necessary. I knew my mother would forgive me once the acceptance letters started rolling in because she would then have her bragging rights among her church friends.

Clueless and misguided, I followed the only examples I had—my aunt, now in her early 90s, attended SSU but transferred to the University of West Georgia to be closer to home. Accordingly, I applied to both schools. I also met a cute boy at the Georgia Youth Assembly who was going to Clark Atlanta University, so I applied there as well. I received a random letter from the University of Georgia congratulating me on my academic accomplishment; so guess what? I applied there too. Clearly, there was no strategy, and I had no idea what I was doing, but I did it anyway. I received acceptance letters from all four institutions. Thanks to former governor Zell Miller (God bless his soul), the Georgia Lottery (and all the good Christians in the lottery lines), which funds the HOPE Scholarship, and my above-average GPA, I was awarded the HOPE Scholarship, which covers the tuition cost for Georgia high school students pursuing higher education at public and private institutions in the state of Georgia. I shared all my offers with the guidance counselor, because she needed to know that I was stepping outside of that box that she had tried to put me in. That brought my petty little heart so much joy, but she retaliated by not entering my HOPE Scholarship information into the statewide system. That's a story for another time, because I have to move on. Ultimately, I decided to attend SSU because it was the farthest away from Gay and it felt like home when I went there to take the entrance exam. At the time, I had no idea of the significance of HBCUs nor how my life would be forever changed by attending one.

EXPERIENCES IN COLLEGE: I LOVE MY SSU

On the day I left for college, I woke my father to say goodbye. He responded with, "Where are you going?" I replied, "To Savannah for college." He asked, "Do you need money for that?" He reached into his wallet and gave me $100. My mother and I packed the car; she drove me to college, helped me set up my room, gave me a keychain and a kiss on the forehead, and drove off. I did not really hear from either of my parents during my time in college—not because they did not care but simply because they did not know how to support me on this journey. However, I could always depend on my granny to give me $20 in towels and my aunts to keep me stocked up on personal care items and fuzzy socks. No one really knew my major or "what I was doing down there." If you ask my mother, she would say I was studying to be a child psychologist. My father thought I was studying law, and the rest of my family thought I was working with troubled youth like myself. In reality, I majored in sociology with a minor in psychology, so they were all kind of close. My family would comment on how much I had changed and grown in such a short time. I attributed that growth to the professors who nourished both my stomach and my mind and offered unsolicited advice and support ("Harris, don't marry that Jackson boy; he ain't no good." I didn't listen).

Handing out free school supplies at Thunderbolt Elementary, planning activities for the elderly at Tara Nursing Home, and providing resources for teenage parents were my normal Saturday-morning activities. These were the spaces that allowed me to lean into my purpose as a servant leader. I became more self-confident, gained autonomy, and developed a greater appreciation for other people's perspectives and stories. SSU is also where I was introduced to my college roommates (my toots) and friends who became family. They are the ones who are there during the highs and lows, bad weaves, poor decisions (just know that good times were had—thank God we all had praying grandmothers), marriages, divorces, baby showers, birthdays, fancy promotions, and the slowing of metabolisms. My SSU family are the ones I chose (except for Yalonda—she kinda jumped out of some bushes and made us be her friend. Now I'm the godmother to her only son). They were there for me when I could not rely on Simp and Michael (that's my daddy). These connections were an invaluable part of my collegiate experience. I learned that you do not have to share genes in order to be family. If I had to do it all over again, I would choose SSU every time.

CONTRIBUTORS TO MY SUCCESS: TELL THEM WE ARE RISING

One of the first contributors to my success was SSU. SSU's campus was a place where culture was curated and where young Black scholars were free to express themselves through dress, art, music, dance, and Black research and scholarship. There was an expansive catalog of courses centered on what it meant to be Black: like Psychology of the African American Experiences, where we engaged in a deep exploration of the African retentions; Urban Sociology (we basically examined critical race theory and talked about how dope Black people are in spite of racism and being considered chattel at one point); and the Sociology of Religion (y'all know we had to talk about Black Jesus). It was all Black everything. I mean the entire diaspora. From Paine Hall to "the circle" and the grassy plains and palms abound, it was a place where I belonged; it was mine and I loved every second of it. From the long registration and financial aid lines to the freshman-year experience course where I constructed my first résumé and learned about the school's rich history.

My experiences outside of the classroom were also key to my development as a leader and my purpose. I participated in Dress for Success Wednesdays (it was all about professionalism—you know, the white patriarchal norms that try to keep us in a box), campus community service days (if you were not volunteering you felt left out; I clocked over 300 community service hours my first year), experiential learning opportunities, classes that focused on the double consciousness of being Black (yeah, we had the whole light-skinned versus dark-skinned debate), cookouts on the yard (everyone loved the Que chicken), those hazing-ass peer counselors (this was my first experience with a peer mentor), the step shows (I fell in love with Alpha Kappa Alpha), homecoming (my first HC was lit), hanging in the café, the Gullah Geechee cultural influence ("say deh"), the fresh seafood from Bobo's, $2 chicken boxes (I'm not sure that was chicken), and parties in the "old old gym," the "new old gym," and the "new new gym."

"Tell them we are rising," the powerful statement given by SSU's founder Richard Wright, was pivotal in setting the bar, the pace, and the necessary mind-set for the institution and its stakeholders to create an ecosystem of resilience and achievement. This conviction was instilled in me during my first week on SSU's campus and has echoed throughout my academic and professional careers. I remain passionately driven by the unlimited potential given to me by my alma mater and will work with all stakeholders to ensure that these standards are not compromised and that SSU provides a blueprint for students to rise and achieve the greatest level of success. This credo gave me the self-assurance to trust my own power and to have the gall to simply be me. It is where I truly began to know and believe in my inherent worth and belonging in the world. It was faculty members like Dr. Ja Jahannes, Dr. Turray, and Dr. Gardner (God rest their souls) who nourished my potential with their unconventional mentorship, signed me up for advanced courses when they thought I was being complacent (aka, lazy), urged (aka, forced) me to tag along when they gave guest lectures, and invited me into their homes for Sunday dinners. I can never repay them for what they did for me, so I simply pay it forward by modeling the mentorship and guidance they gave me.

ROLE OF FAMILY

My family simply did not know how to show up for me, so they didn't. The sentiments of my mother's forehead kiss faded, and the $100 my father gave me were long gone. There were no visits to campus (my dad would ride down with my aunt to visit a cousin who followed me to SSU, but he never came to visit me, and that hurt), no celebration of milestones, no check-ins. At first I hitched rides homes for the holidays and breaks, but eventually I just stopped going home. I had to grow up quickly and figure things out on my own. I would be the one who left Gay and never looked back. With that came a lot of pride from my family and the local community, but for a very long time, I resented them for having such great pride in my "success," because I had been "the girl with the bad attitude," the one who was not gonna make it, the disrespectful one (because I defied their rules), the one who became a surrogate daughter and sister to my roommates' family when mine was absent, the one who was forced to be a "real adult" before I was ready. I barely knew how to spell *resilient*, but they should definitely add my picture next to the words *resilient af* in the Urban Dictionary. Anyway, I'm no longer resentful. I am cool now, but it took a lot of tears, bad decisions, and therapy to get here. If you do not have a therapist, I advise you to get one.

TIPS AND ADVICE

As Shannon Sharpe said, "I learned to embrace my frailties, so that no one else could make me feel inferior about them. Savannah State gave me that and much more." So, this is what I say to you. The world will tell you that you are not enough, or that you are too much. Do not believe them. You are enough. Being underestimated is one of the biggest competitive advantages you can have. Embrace it. Find or create spaces that are big enough to hold you. They (I have no clue who *they* are) will try to censure and silence your voice; that is when you will need to discover the sovereignty of your hum and the strength of just waving your hand. And when they try to restrict your movement, that is when you will bend and learn a new dance (not like the ones on TikTok—those are fads and you are greater than that). Don't you dare stop speaking your truth, whetting your hum, or doing your dance. Finally, never let anyone narrate your story; remember you hold the pen, which means you have the power to tell it your way. Own that power.

CHAPTER 12   IN MY OWN WAY

David Hernández
Associate Professor, Latina/o Studies
Faculty Director of Community Engagement,
Mount Holyoke College

I am a professor at a liberal arts college in New England, where I have worked since 2012. My first position was at a large public university in Southern California, which I assumed after completing my doctorate in 2005. Initially, being a first-generation student of color was a hurdle to overcome. As an undergrad, I was isolated and different from the majority of students, and I occasionally wanted to quit—once quite seriously. Professors, peers, and some of the parents I met noticed all this, yet they seemed to be a bit indifferent to my plight; as a result, my sense of belonging never gelled. Nevertheless, I pushed through, made friends, earned good grades, and had a good time. I knew I was experiencing something that would come and go only once. So, I stayed.

It is interesting, especially as a Latino professor, to witness some of these same issues decades later. First-generation students come in all shapes and sizes, but I still see a version of myself all the time—uneasy, deeply out of place, without support from home. I gravitate toward these students because they can easily fall through the cracks, as the common narrative for student success often excludes them. My personal first-generation experiences set me apart from my colleagues, and as a professional, I think they help me do my job better.

APPLYING TO AND PREPARING FOR COLLEGE

Applying to college was a challenging and eye-opening experience. I did not know anyone who applied to college—well, sort of. My older brother had applied and was accepted to a local state university, but he never registered for courses or attended. As teenagers who were only 2 years apart, our relationship was competitive, volatile, and seething with anger, so we did not speak about the process with one another. I never saw his essay or any of his materials. My brother would have been the first in our family to attend college, and as I look back, our dysfunctional familial relationship with education burdened him as much as it did me. The only difference is that I applied, was accepted, and opted to attend a university. Admittedly, this was done less out of a sense of ambition and more to escape the tensions of home life.

The application process was an isolating experience. I paid for the entrance exam—the SAT—myself, with money from part-time jobs I held since I was 15. If there were preparation courses, such as there are today, I was not aware of them—nor would I have had the ability to pay for them. My mother, a housekeeper who worked for cash under the table, might have helped, but I never asked. This speaks to the tension and skepticism surrounding higher education at home. The central message I received from my family about education was that it was a waste of time and paled in comparison to getting a job at the local lumber store, the UPS, or other places where my brother and my many cousins worked. Even worse was the presumption that I would screw it up. "You'll be back," family members said, even on the day I left for college. Nothing in my academic profile suggested that I would, only my family's distrust and low-grade contempt—perhaps jealously—of me.

I should say that applying for financial aid was an impactful experience. I completed the FAFSA form myself and asked my mother to sign it in the appropriate places. Nonetheless, I had to determine our family income and ask my mother the requisite questions. I was stunned when I learned my mother's annual income from Aid to Families with Dependent Children (AFDC, or "welfare") was somewhere between $4,000 and $5,000 annually. This was not a brief adjustment period in our lives; it was sustained downward mobility. As a result, I came to understand my mother in new ways. She raised three sons on her own with this paltry income. Like virtually all other people on "welfare," she worked side jobs for cash to make things work. We never went on a vacation or owned luggage, and we lacked a lot of things, but I was never hungry, my clothes were clean, and our home was tidy. My mother did this. It was a tremendous lesson as I set off for college.

EXPERIENCES IN COLLEGE

I have experienced being "first" at all levels of my education and career. Strung together, these firsts constituted a series of peaks and valleys, always beginning at the bottom of a steep learning curve. During these transitions, I experienced repeated patterns of anxiety, adjustment, and eventual excellence only to begin again many times over. I faced an information vacuum throughout college. Other students seemed to know about education abroad, campus interviews, and internships. It seemed as though the university was full of secret opportunities that I simply did not have access to. I did not even know where the gym or computer lab were, and I was afraid to ask for fear of attracting unwanted attention.

In particular, during my undergraduate years, I felt invisible. My racial and class differences from the majority of white upper-middle-class students did not expose me to direct discrimination necessarily, but something more insidious—neglect and invisibility. My peers did not see me. They looked past or through me. They bumped into me. I felt like a piece of furniture. To counter this invisibility, and because I felt out of place and ignored by my mainstream peers, I made the mistake of making the learning process adversarial. I focused on besting the persons who I thought were looking down on me. I was the Mexican guy who sat in the back, who was different, and who did not seem like he belonged. In those days, grades might be posted on a professor's door for all to see. I remember once rushing to see my Economics grade, only to run into another student there. He was the sort of student that I presumed judged me negatively. My name and grade were first on the list—the top score. The other student expressed disbelief: "I can't believe that's you," or something like that. That was the only thing he ever said to me. Mission accomplished.

I often succeeded at, and even innovated, this adversarial approach. For example, in my courses, I noticed that students would sort of claim space in the form of certain seats in the classroom. I could never muster that sort of entitlement. I did not like drawing attention to myself—in fact, I never entered tardily to a classroom because I loathed the moment when a sea of heads turned to see who had just arrived—so I gravitated to the back of the room. I would remain seated there the entire term, with one exception. For in-class final exams, I would arrive earlier than normal and claim the seat, often in the front, of one of the students who I perceived to be a bully, or a snob, or a know-it-all. No one ever told me, "Hey, that's my seat," and I would have likely offered it to anyone who asked for it back. Maybe it unnerved my adversary and maybe it did not, but it was my way of pushing back.

I did not have an arsenal of such maneuvers—just the one, and although it was a form of motivation, I now believe that besting others was a short-term solution that actually lowered the bar of what was possible at the university. It still ensured that those I disliked (or who disliked me) held all the cards. They were in the center of my world, where they had always been. My performance was based on theirs. I believe I paid a price for this perspective because I never reached my potential in my undergraduate years. I accomplished a lot. I overcame adversity and succeeded in an uncomfortable environment—one that probably reached the level of hostility for others who had more challenges or were more damaged than me. However, in hindsight, I believe I could have done better.

CONTRIBUTORS TO MY SUCCESS

I am not so sure that I experienced academic success so much as social success in college. I earned good grades and graduated with high honors, but I did not engage deeply with the material or take advantage of the more scholarly opportunities. I did not write a thesis or study abroad. I cut corners by sacrificing sleep in order to pull all-nighters. Little did I know that years later I would not recall anything from those study sessions. For me, the social challenges were tougher than the academic ones, and I focused on this area of my experience. I worked 20 hours per week while in school and plenty more during the summers. Working hard was part of my identity.

I also never returned home, staying in my college town until graduation. I immersed myself in the college-living experience but to a lesser degree the scholarly one. I made lifelong friends. I fell in love. I felt independent and alive—feelings that I valued and that made it all worthwhile.

ROLE OF FAMILY

My family's initial reaction was of distrust, indifference, and some back-biting. Yet over time, as I remained in school, I think they saw that I was growing up and having interesting experiences. They were interested in and impressed with the social aspects of school. They saw that I had very close friends. My brothers visited a couple of times in order to party and hang out in the social scene that I had cultivated. A cousin did the same.

My parents, who divorced when I was 9 years old, never visited me on campus except on graduation day, although home was a mere 90 miles away. Where I teach in New England, I see this a lot also—families may be poor, cannot travel because of their immigration status, or as in my parents' case, they are unsupportive or do not know how to provide support. Every year, during "family and friends" weekend, I joke with working-class, first-generation students, asking if their folks are taking them and their friends out to an expensive restaurant. We all laugh at the absurdity that we collectively understand. As far as financial support, I did not receive any. In my financial aid letter, the line for "family contribution" was always zero. My parents struggled financially in their individual lives. Their impoverishment was not due to lack of effort; they hustled. I admired them for that and never expected or asked for a dime.

TIPS AND ADVICE

It is difficult to tell people to persevere, as if it is that simple. However, I am convinced that feeling out of place is not that unusual. For persons of color, queer people, the working class, and many others whose experiences are different from the majority, this feeling is common and expected. It may be difficult at first, but as I learned from an early age, transitions are hard, they feel uncomfortable, and it is natural to want them to stop. However, they are not only doable and occasionally enjoyable; they also bring unimaginable rewards—independence, ingenuity, and scrappiness. This is the difference between first-generation students and those with histories of higher education: We cannot imagine the depth and length of educational transitions on our own, because we are on our own. The rewards of higher education are there for us too. So, I say, *Be brave, persevere, make friends, ask for help, and help others who are struggling more than you.*

For success, I urge students to play the long game. Set your own standards, and learn from everyone around you. Be yourself. Think. Ask questions. Share your perspective. Remember, the skills and hard knocks that first-generation students bring to the table are unique and constitute major contributions to the classroom.

Finally, I advise first-generation students not to compare themselves to everyone around them, especially those for whom higher education is a given intergenerational experience that draws family members together. For first-generation students, it is often the opposite. Higher education pulls us away, almost permanently, from our families. Our incompatibility with the university also becomes transposed to home and family. As such, comparisons will only steer students to the pedigree that they do not possess. You can succeed in higher education. You can and you will, but you will have to do it in your own way.

CHAPTER 13

Jenny Lieurance
First-Generation Specialist

My name is Jenny Lieurance and I currently work within higher education at Washburn University in the Center for Student Success and Retention as the first-generation recruitment and retention specialist. Even though I have only been in this profession since July 2020, my long-term goal has been to help students like me gain access to, succeed at, and graduate with a college education. In my current position, I work toward first-generation initiatives, including teaching first-year seminar courses and advising the first-generation student organization and the living learning community. It is an honor to work in this role and to be a part of other first-generation college students' journey. My college experience was pivotal in leading me to where I am now: Not only did it provide me with the qualifications for my role, but it also exposed me to the possibility of working at a university in the first place. At Washburn, I found mentors who provided crucial advice that helped me be successful. They encouraged me toward experiences that allowed me to excel and graduate on time. Due to the significant role these relationships played in my experience, along with their support and direction, I can now provide similar advice and guidance to my students.

APPLYING TO AND PREPARING FOR COLLEGE

I grew up in a small town in Kansas, where only a few people talked about getting a college education, usually referring to one of the state colleges in town. Although my teachers, family, and friends wanted me to have a college education, it always felt way out of reach to me. Nevertheless, the idea stayed in the back of my mind. I knew education could be a new door to open or an exit path out of the struggles my family had, but I honestly did not know how to get to college. Fortunately, I was a part of Advancement Via Individual Determination (AVID), TRIO, and Gaining Early Awareness and Readiness for Undergraduate Programs (GearUp) programs, and so I had many people who encouraged me to consider college and who were willing to walk me through the steps to get there. AVID is a program centered around strategies to advance students from elementary school to the college level through building their organizational, critical thinking, and writing and reading skills. TRIO, a federally funded grant program that has many branches across the country, is designed to help students from disadvantaged backgrounds apply to, succeed in, and graduate from college; its programs extend to children in middle school and help individuals all the way through college. GearUp is also a federally funded program for low-income students in middle and high school. For each of these programs, from my early middle school years throughout high school, I had a teacher encouraging me to apply. Despite this encouragement, I remained unsure whether college was for me.

Throughout high school, I visited colleges with those various programs. By the time I was in my second semester of junior year, I started to feel like it was crunch time. I took the ACT and began looking at colleges, with mainly one in mind. By my senior year, I applied to five universities (mainly because we were required to apply to at least three in my AVID class) as well as to numerous scholarships. I can still recall getting praise from classmates, teachers, friends, and family; yet, I still felt I would never get into college, let alone succeed if I were to be accepted. I always felt this tension of doubt within myself—mainly because I was not sure that college equaled success no matter how much I was told that it did. Then again, I had a great deal of support from people who knew I could make it. I struggled with these two tensions, which I now know was a manifestation of imposter syndrome. As much as people said, "Jenny, you belong" or "You can do this; you are so smart," I was unsure of my own capacities or if I could believe what they told me.

The summer prior to college, I mainly worked a ton as a camp counselor and did not focus on, nor prepare myself for, college. I learned in late June that my family was moving, which encouraged me to switch my decision regarding schools—from the school I had hoped to attend prior to learning this news to Washburn University, because it would be closer to family. I knew then if I was going to college, I could not be far away from my family. However, I had already declined an offer from Washburn University. I still remember calling the Admissions Office at Washburn, feeling that there was little chance they would let me reverse my decision. To my surprise they did, but I confess that at that moment I was still uncertain whether the college experience was for me. I felt this way not only due to the cost of college but also because the idea of college remained so out of reach; only a few in my family had ever even tried it. To me, college was for elite students who had the money or who were legacies—not students who were breaking off and creating a new path for their family.

EXPERIENCES IN COLLEGE

As with most first-generation students, my college experience started off as challenging. I was trying to fit in, trying to succeed, and trying to pass. Everyone around me seemed to be joining clubs, making friends, and feeling at ease with their new surroundings. However, I was struggling with a variety of stressors, from getting barely passing grades to feeling like I did not belong and feeling that I had no one to turn to who could understand. My college experience only turned around when high school mentors and friends encouraged me to jump in. Once I moved on campus the second semester of my first year and started to get involved in campus activities, I finally began to feel like a college student. I began to feel like I was worth all the effort that those around me had put into me.

Within my first 2 years, I took courses in leadership, communication, poverty studies, and women's studies. I learned about topics I never knew existed before. Through my coursework and involvement, I took my first-ever flight—to Washington, D.C., for a leadership conference—and then quickly turned around and flew to Nicaragua for a group study trip abroad. As a group in Nicaragua, we completed service work and then reflected on how the experience affected us. In the last reflection, I talked about the pressures of being a first-generation college student. On my return, I began to discover that helping students like myself was a career I could aspire to. I began working in our First Experience Office, helping other first-year students transition into the college environment.

By my junior year, I knew that college was exactly where I belonged. I was enjoying helping students transition and succeed in the college environment. I was able to help them through all the little bumps and red tape that had tripped me up at first. I assisted with the new summer bridge program, and I created a first-generation student organization. I wanted to build the community I felt was nonexistent my first year. I was also building a community I felt I could always come back to.

As my senior year came and went, I was brought to tears knowing I was leaving the environment that had built my values, confidence, and a life that I never had before. Walking across the stage was the ultimate moment that finally reassured me that all those high school teachers, friends, and family who somehow knew it was possible for me were right. It was. That day, with each step, I was reminded of the people, memories, and life-changing moments that helped me grow within a short 4 years.

CONTRIBUTORS TO MY SUCCESS

I believe that what contributed to my success was the people around me: the faculty and staff who encouraged me to lean in to the college experience and try new things. They gave me opportunity after opportunity to learn, and they challenged me to grow when I thought I had grown already. Without those opportunities and development, I am not sure I would have ended up in the career that I am in now.

There was also my high school AVID teacher and friends who encouraged me to give college another shot. Without them I would have dropped out and never graduated in the first place. In my freshman year, my roommate gave me hope that people like us belonged in college—that a first-generation college student could be someone with a college degree. I attribute my success also to the many papers-to-projects that made me think and really learn what my thoughts and ideas were and what I could hope for. Sometimes these projects felt like too much to handle, but they taught me how to manage my time wisely. Finally, my friends and family always reminded me of why I was doing all this in the first place. They gave me courage when I felt I had none.

ROLE OF FAMILY

My family played a large role in this entire process. Family is my everything and why I work as hard as I do. I have seen them all work tirelessly to meet success, which is one of the many reasons I entered college in the first place. From a young age, I was taught that people can work their body or their brain, and it is each individual's choice which. I wanted to work my brain. Throughout college, I felt as though I would show people whether college was possible, and if I failed, then no one else would ever try. Some of my family members were encouraging throughout, and some thought I was wasting my time. My dad in particular was one of my largest supporters and someone I would always call, whether it was to cry during times when it felt like college was not for me or to celebrate my successes. However, as much as he was one of my best supporters, he would always say, "Jenny, I am not sure what to tell you, because I have never been in your shoes before." My family's support ranged from phone calls to sending some money to showing up for family weekends or banquets. They were always there cheering me on, even if they had their own doubts.

Some of the hardships I encountered included discovering some of those doubts and being told I was not there for my family. I had already felt a great deal of pressure to not waste money, time, or energy. Therefore, hearing about birthdays, holidays, or other big and small moments that I missed out on because I was in school was very hard. I hated feeling like I was failing them, when the whole reason I was doing this was to show them it was possible, that our last name could mean something beyond our small town.

TIPS AND ADVICE

Know that you belong. Until I met my freshman-year roommate, there were numerous times when I felt like I was one of few, if not the only, first-generation college student at Washburn University. Once I discovered that she and I both came from a similar background and were both first-generation college students, I no longer felt alone. Seeing her succeed gave me the strength to realize that I could too, even if it would be one of the most challenging times in my life. Know that whether you meet someone like yourself on your campus or not, you belong. You are in college for a reason, and students like you are carving paths that will change our world for generations to come.

Find your support system at college, whether it be friends, professors, staff, or mentors. Whether I was having the best time or the worst in college, my support system helped get me through it. My support system believed in me when I did not believe in myself. They helped me get to where I am today.

Professors teach in lecture/classrooms and have separate office spaces. The night before my first day, I prepared myself. I wanted to make sure I was not that lost freshman. Being a first-generation college student, I knew I needed to at least *seem* like I fit in. However, the next morning I discovered that my preparation fell short because I wrote down all my professors' office numbers and not their classroom numbers. After being directed to my first class, I quickly figured out that the location of the professors' offices was different from where we had class. No one had told me this, and as much as I knew this environment was vastly different from high school, I genuinely thought that like high school the teacher taught where their desk was.

Lean in to the college experience. Live on campus, get involved, and take opportunities that challenge you to grow. During my first semester, I was not involved, had no friends, and wanted to drop out. I ended that semester with a 3.0 GPA and a D in College Algebra. I moved on campus after listening to the advice from some high school friends and my AVID teacher. There, I met my freshman-year roommate, who introduced me to anyone and everyone. By the end of that semester, I had gotten involved, began establishing my support system, and completed the term with a 4.0 GPA. Because I chose to lean in to the college experience, my college experience was worthwhile, and I am in the career I am now in. I chose to grow into a person who wanted to help educate others.

It is okay to not know everything—ask for help! I constantly hear my colleagues at orientation telling students to ask for help and see the students brush off that advice. I even recall doing the same as a student. Yet please, please know that those faculty and staff are there for a reason—to help. That help can take many forms—from educating you in a classroom to guiding you through the admissions process or even helping you find a building. You do not have to act like you know everything to fit in. If you knew everything, you would not be in college. Besides, if I have learned anything over the years, it is this: Whether or not you are a first-generation student, asking for help when you do not know the answer or where to find the answer is the best thing to do. Asking for help when you need it will likely always save you time and who knows what else.

As my dad would say, "I am proud of you, young lady." This chapter is dedicated to my dad, or Old Man, as I would say. His inspiration and love allowed me to believe in myself and to have a first-generation story to share.

CHAPTER 14

Glynis Boyd Hughes
Grant Writer and Storyteller

I am not only a first-generation college graduate; I am also a post-traditional student who began intentionally planning a career at 49, for the first time, when I returned to Virginia Commonwealth University (VCU) to complete my undergraduate studies in 2017. I started my higher education journey at 18—a high school dropout from an impoverished background with a 3-year-old daughter, big dreams, and no real plan for how to get there. I succeeded on this journey despite these and other obstacles that could have stopped me in my tracks at any point. In March 2021, I arrived at the end of my graduate studies only to find that the dream of a full-time, satisfying career remained elusive for me. I was hired as a REV coach with Reynolds Community College in Richmond. REV is an acronym for Re-Employing Virginians, a 2020 Virginia grant initiative to provide educational support for citizens who have lost their job or had their hours cut as a result of the COVID-19 pandemic. There are a few simple eligibility requirements, and when they are met, Virginians can receive a semester of college classes in a high-need area the state has identified (such as health care) at no cost. The position was grant funded and temporary—slated to end December 2021—and I was somewhat hopeful it would turn into a full-time position. Also, Reynolds has a special place in my heart, having given me my start. I never forgot that, and I gave 100% to my position. After 6 months, when the full-time job had yet to materialize, I acquired an as-needed position as a grant writer, which I love but which is also not full time.

Admittedly, my early background of poverty sometimes makes it challenging to simply love what I am doing when I know within weeks I will lose my "steady" income source. I struggle with this, as I work my part-time jobs with one eye on my bank account and the other on job ads—so much so that *balance* is only a word for me, not a reality. As a 54-year-old woman pursuing a dream that so many take for granted—having a career of one's choosing, not merely a job—at times it is difficult to not question the validity of my choices, especially when all the while that little voice, emerging from the deficits of childhood, says, "Who are *you* to be happy?" Add to that my being the first person in my family to not only acquire but even want any kind of formal education, and you have the makings of a reality series if anyone ever wanted to throw money my way. In spite of all this, I can say that I use my education daily, especially my higher education takeaways (thank you, Paulo Freire)!

APPLYING TO AND PREPARING FOR COLLEGE

I excelled in school as a child, as I took to what was required as easily as if I had "lifelong learner" written into my DNA. Yet I also remember a mother who never acknowledged my accomplishments, events in which the only people cheering for me were teachers, and the nagging feeling that somehow if I continued on this path, this dissonance with my family would not improve. I was right.

I dropped out of high school in the fall of 1984, having returned from giving birth to my daughter in January of that year. I was in a 10th-grade homeroom and was taking two ninth-grade classes I had failed the year before. I had been on maternity leave the latter part of my ninth-grade year, and home-based learning did not exist then. When I returned to school post baby, a boy in one of my classes asked me what I was doing there, and I answered, "I'm doing my work." He said I should not be there because I had a baby. With my nonexistent self-esteem and sense of belonging, that was all that was needed for me to walk out and never go back. I began working at a job a classmate helped me get—at a Kentucky Fried Chicken that had recently opened in our neighborhood. I knew that a $3.35 an hour job, which was what could be expected for a high school dropout, would not provide the basic necessities, much less the tools for life my daughter deserved and I wanted, and I knew that education was my way to get there. I had no network or social capital as we call it now; it was going to be a true test of girl versus world. The question was, *Could I do it?* Would the words of that boy from class keep me from the dream I so desperately wanted: to attend college?

I cannot recall how I latched on to the idea of college. I was a bright student who wanted to be involved in everything school had to offer, yet there was little in my home life to encourage educational aspirations. As a child, I was often ostracized because I did not wear the "right" clothes, was dismissed by my peers as "weird," and knew that even if I had friends, I could not have them over to my house for a visit because of the everyday chaos that was my home life. Yet two teachers, the late Delores Brunson, my second-grade teacher at Fairfield Elementary School, and Diane Carter, my English teacher during my time at Mosby Middle School, turned out to be pivotal for me. Both teachers, and especially Diane in later years, recognized my natural inclination for learning and nurtured it through the simple yet powerful combination of positive regard, active listening, and never letting me forget I had so much more to do in the world. With all that was difficult in my life, to have an adult whom I admired and respected listen to me was the beginning of my having a dream that should have seemed out of reach: *Perhaps I could go to college.* To be listened to is a radical act, especially from the perspective of a child, because it affirms that the person being listened to *has something to say that's worth listening to.*

By my 18th birthday, I finally had enough courage to apply to Reynolds Community College. At the time Reynolds had an "ability to benefit" policy, which meant that students could apply and get in without a high school credential but could not graduate without one. At 19 I took the GED test, passing it on the first attempt. At the time I did not think very much of this—but now I recognize it for the accomplishment it was and its importance in ensuring that my educational journey would continue.

EXPERIENCES IN COLLEGE

I remember semesters at Reynolds in which I alternated between excelling and failing, depending on what was going on during my two-to-three-job work life. I had a toddler and a $250 a month apartment, and I could barely make enough to live on. Sometimes wanting to be a great student was not my motivation—my financial aid refund was, because it meant I could buy my daughter a warm coat or actually fill my fridge for a change. In the midst of this, I found ways to engage in school: I had a work-study job in the student center, working with students who had difficulty in writing classes, I served as treasurer in the Student Government Association, and I helped plan many a student activity, which unfortunately I could not often attend because I was always working weekends at KFC. I remember managing to get off on Halloween one year. I rented a princess costume and spent the evening at the annual costume bash we always had at Reynolds's downtown campus. It was the most fun I'd had in years: nonstop laughter, guys asking me to dance. I looked beautiful, without a care in the world, and much like Cinderella, I never wanted the night to end.

I transferred to VCU in 1996, fully intending to finish an undergraduate degree in psychology. However, I had imposter syndrome, and as an indication of how deep it went, I wanted to pursue psychology so I could become a "doctor" (psychologist) and go back to my old neighborhood and impress the folx there. When I had my daughter at 16, people in my neighborhood were betting on how many kids I would have by 18. I had put no real thought into what it meant to get a degree in psychology and there was no one to talk to about it. Advisors were as helpful as they could be—but most of the time they were only graduate students trying to get their hours in. I remember one advisor I had at VCU, Raymond, who told me that college was a marathon, not a race. All that mattered was finishing. His words would go on to frame my life, because I left VCU in 1997 to accept an unbelievable job—as a social worker for the Richmond Department of Social Services. It meant my yearly salary as a shelter worker would triple to $30,000—more money than I had ever made—with benefits. I planned to return to VCU within the year, after completing my probation, learning my job, and getting settled. I was a single mother with a growing daughter who had never made more than $9,800 a year in her life. There was no way I could turn down that job.

It would take me 31 years to arrive back on VCU's Monroe Park campus to finish the studies I began at 18. Ironically, the catalyst that brought me back to campus was the same that induced me to leave in the first place. My social work job no longer felt good; I was losing connection with my work. My job had evolved into more of a "paper pusher" role, and that brought me no joy. Although I had left VCU originally for a "real" job, earning a salary with benefits, returning to finish was always my plan. It is important to share that while I knew accepting a job that literally tripled my income was the right decision, I struggled with feeling like a failure for leaving college.

CONTRIBUTORS TO MY SUCCESS

No first-gen story would be complete without giving kudos to educators, the tireless superbeings who invest in students day after day. Delores Brunson, circa 1975, was my second-grade teacher and the first adult to negotiate time with me; she would give me 5 minutes to read at the beginning of class and I would pay attention for the rest. In addition, I often thought of Diane Carter—my dear English teacher for sixth to eighth grades, to whom I remain close to this very day—as I faced challenges in those early college years, remembering how deeply she had invested in me. Jack J. Green, the late publisher of the *Voice* newspaper, who hired me as a staff writer even though I had no prior experience, taught me to show up 100% authentically, as well as the importance of checking facts and the right spelling of folx' names. Dr. Christine Cynn and R. Dale Smith at VCU were especially impactful, along with Dr. Bryant Mangum and Andrew Spencer. These amazing people, each in their own way, invested in me deeply, which is no small thing.

The truth is we have so many people who affect us, some by telling us we will do well, and some because they do not believe we will—and while I am not choosing to name those folx, I thank them too; they annoyed me, and I had to prove them wrong. Yet if I had to name that one person who has been the wind beneath my wings, it would be my partner and best friend, Gary C. Hughes Sr., whom I have known 20 years and been married to for 10. He has supported me, encouraged me, listened to me, and done anything he could to help me be successful in college. One of the greatest was giving me his full blessing so I could leave my social work job to resume and focus primarily on my studies, working whenever, as well as when I went to graduate school. My degrees have my name on them—but I share them with Gary because this was no solo journey.

ROLE OF FAMILY

I learned what it meant to be a first-generation college student within the last 6 years, upon my return to VCU. I connected this identity with pioneers of the past, explorers of new lands, trailblazers, and my ancestors because this is what it means to be the first to achieve college graduate status in your family. The irony of being a first-gen, with all its drawbacks, is that the mind-set keeps me focused and determined to succeed, as it has my entire life. Of course, not all of us come to our higher education journey with the same support and challenges. Some first-generation students represent families who express only love and joy at their accomplishment, with everyone seeing it as a win for the clan. Then there are those like me, who come from families in which these types of endeavors are ignored, ridiculed, or simply used as a way to make the student pursuing education feel as though they have committed the greatest crime of all: wanting a better life because the one they have is not good enough—the implication being that the lives of other family members must not be good enough either.

In the circles I now occupy, I definitely get more respect—but those relationships have not weathered the test of time. In other words, the people who think the most of what I am doing and who I am have literally just met me. They think well of me because they value what I am doing, more so than who I am, because they cannot possibly know me well yet. This does not detract from these relationships, and I am sure many will be sustained through time, yet it does give me pause on occasion.

Reflecting on my education as a first-gen, I am reminded of something that I only observed after the fact, not so much while I was living it—the sense of being in two worlds and trying to find acceptance in both. To people who are from where I come from, I am considered an anomaly; people "like me" do not exist. Many of the students I went to high school with are dead, ended up on drugs, or simply checked out on life although they are still physically alive. Within my birth family, my academic and other accomplishments hold little merit because "book learning" has no value where I come from.

I would be remiss not to add that now, years later, even without the support of family, my efforts have yielded other fruit: I have a grandson who began college in the fall of 2021, after insisting he was not interested, and he aced his first semester. Now he's all in. My daughter, his mother, who also never wanted college, has signed up to begin the practical nursing program at Reynolds next year. Even my husband went back to college and has a year of undergraduate studies left. Sometimes what we do is not simply for us—we are creating a foundation for the future, for those we know and those we do not.

TIPS AND ADVICE

When all is said and done, and I mean this with my whole heart, I believe being a first-gen is a unique phenomenon. There is so much about this journey I have mucked up because there was no one there to guide or help me—but I never gave up. When I talk to other first-gens, they share similar stories. Just imagine if everyone had that kind of energy, that type of attitude that "no matter what, I'm getting what I came for" wherever they went in life. I know it may sound funny, but I feel a bit sorry for the students who will never know what it is like to have to trust themselves to see a goal through—*no matter what*. I feel this way because I realize that if nothing else, we first-gens know what we are made of and that we can most definitely get it done. We may not always be clear, or we may fall off at times, and even lose our way trying to find our way—but we cannot be counted out.

I am a strong advocate for teachable moments and takeaways. If I could offer my handy travel kit for first-gen success, it is this:

1. *Ask questions.* The question you do not ask is the one everyone needs to know the answer to. Be bold and confident that no question is dumb or stupid. Think about it—no one can know everything. I really think this is why Google searches are so popular.

2. *Communicate.* I cannot emphasize enough how important it is to connect with and stay in touch with your professors. For example, my husband, a first-gen, was struggling because he was having work issues. I advised him to talk to his professors, even if he did not go into the issue in great detail; the point was to let them know that he cared about the class but was under a lot of stress that was affecting his classwork. Both professors thanked him and helped him to work out a plan for the missing work, and he finished with two Bs. Do not underestimate the importance of communicating and believing that professors really do want you to succeed.
3. *Be proactive and learn the lay of the land.* Check out the scholarship site months ahead of time to see what they will want from you. Do research on the careers you are interested in, including scheduling informational interviews. Connect with at least one person in your class so you have a "check-in pal." Remember that the skills you are using for your studies have real-world applications.
4. *Learn to accept rejection, failure, and error with grace.* You are wonderful all on your own—but so is everyone else. No one can be excellent at everything. It is not possible, although social media will try to make you think otherwise. A larger perspective may be important to consider when you do not get what you want, something does not work out, or you get passed over for something that you think is for you. The seeming failure or rejection could be the best thing that ever happened to you. What is for you is for you—own that.
5. *Be open to the possibility of you.* Maybe you came to college to be an engineer but keep finding yourself coaching middle schoolers. Maybe you have a knack for organizing but are determined to be a teacher. The juxtapositions are endless—they really are. Sometimes we find ways to meld our various talents together, or we do something totally different. The cool part is you can get a lot out of life if you do it right—and your first-gen cred can get you there. Trust yourself.

Sometimes it is still hard for me to believe I finally finished college, all the way to getting a master's degree and postgraduate credentials, after age 50. And earning a PhD is not off the table. My first-gen student identity is one I cherish because the core of it is resiliency, creativity, and this maddening, intractable belief that my dreams can come true. So can yours.
#FirstGenForTheWin

CHAPTER 15

....

T. Mark Montoya, PhD
Associate Professor of Ethnic Studies

"I am a recovering political scientist who teaches ethnic studies, studies the U.S.-Mexico borderlands, and publishes about teaching and learning. I do not belong anywhere." This is how I used to jokingly introduce myself in academic settings. I now know I belong, and so do you! Negotiating academic borderlands is what we do. While my actual "academic" biography—the one on my departmental website—speaks to my educational credentials, it makes no mention of the academic borderlands I have confronted, challenged, and crossed. It also makes no mention of the 9 years it took to receive my PhD. Instead, it highlights my research and teaching foci, my contributions to "the field," and my recent scholarly publications. In the third person, my biography also speaks to my involvement on campus and beyond. Finally, my bio ends with revealing that I (Dr. Montoya, by this point) have won numerous teaching awards.

It is strange to see these things in print. It is weird because it feels self-aggrandizing, and it is bizarre because I have read others' biographies and felt in comparison like an impostor—someone who has not really done anything. My academic and work background are not the whole of my existence; however, my experiences as a first-generation college student guide me. As such, I hope to help other university faculty understand the myriad issues first-gens experience. Many are not aware of the needs of contemporary first-generation students, even if they were themselves first-gen. The reason is simple—many first-gen folks understand their past frustrations as a "normal" feature of college life. College is supposed to be difficult and confusing, right?

APPLYING TO AND PREPARING FOR COLLEGE

I do not think there was ever a doubt I would go to college, but there was a lot of hesitation on my end while I was there. There still is. Notwithstanding, one might say I was destined for college. While I am a first-generation college student, I am not the first in my immediate family to obtain a college degree. My brother did that. At 10 years older—a brother plus co-parent—he provided me with specific guidance and knowledge, having worked for his university's financial aid office. Like our parents, he knew I would succeed in college. He even bought me a huge book that listed each university in the United States, including an extensive summary and a succinct informational sidebar documenting student population, popular majors, campus size, and so on. This was a *huge book*, printed on what I would describe as phonebook paper. I would literally flip through the book for hours—marking states, cities, and universities where I would like to live and campuses I would like to visit. It was more daydreams than anything.

Due to my family's financial limitations, I was never actually going to go on multiple campus visits; so instead, I imagined, and I dreamed. I marked some schools because they were huge. I highlighted others because I loved college hoops. I circled various art schools, and yes, placed question marks next to various seminaries. I also marked my very own state schools as the most realistic options. I also rather enjoyed crossing off cities and states where I absolutely did not want to live. In the end, I only applied to two schools—my state university and Loyola-Chicago. What I recall of the application process is all the forms. Paperwork! Without my applying there, my hometown's university admitted me and offered a scholarship. Even long-shot Loyola welcomed me and sweetened the deal with some $8,000 "Hispanic" scholarship and an offer of work-study. I believed it to be some sort of mistake.

When it came to what I could realistically do, I chose to attend New Mexico State University. Compared to what I knew, and as clichéd as it sounds, everything there was bigger and better. I was now a college student. I do not recall preparing, because I did not know what to prepare for, but I had made it. I even had a typewriter! Unlike other first-generation students, I did not choose a major "for the money" or "for the job." Instead I chose my major—history—for the chance to eventually become a college professor. I was destined to have college be my life, one might say. Wow, history was such a hard major.

EXPERIENCES IN COLLEGE

I sweated—a lot. Not because I was hot but because I was nervous, anxious, *and* excited! All the time. I would sometimes wear an extra layer of clothing to hide it, but then I got hot, and the process continued. During my first semester, I was to meet with my major advisor—a graying history professor. On the morning of my advisement, I repeatedly went to the professor's office, knocking on the door about six different times. Without taking into account the teaching, research, and service they did—and certainly not really knowing what office hours meant—I assumed professors worked a typical 8-to-5 job. Frustrated, I went to the department office and asked where the learned professor was. A very kind and patient woman explained to me about office hours. Figuring I was eager to get my paperwork signed, she said to me, "You can talk to the chair." Confused, I replied, "But I'd like to talk to a person."

Other than this incident, my college experiences were not ones of any real distress. In other words, I would not say my experience as a first-generation college student was traumatic, hurtful, or painful, but it *was* difficult, confusing, and with more hindsight, tough to navigate. Do not get me wrong; I had my share of tears, hardships, and awkward moments, but no real suffering. What helped is that I found my people, which was a great thing. They were mostly ethnically and demographically similar: Latino first-generation college hoops fanatics who loved Mexican food. One was my roommate and fortunately my best friend from high school. The others lived in the same residence hall. We quickly formed a community while walking to the first basketball practice of the season. Not the first game but rather the first practice, because you have to go somewhere to find your people. Go somewhere! The five of us, all from disparate majors, formed a social group, and we held each other accountable. We really did contribute to each other's success. Without each other, one or all of us may have quit. Upon reflection, I was seeing myself in other people. I am painfully shy, so intentionally setting out to find my people was challenging. Fortunately, my people found me too.

I did not seek official student support, help, or services, because I did not know I needed them; nor did I know support systems existed. This was the early 1990s, and to my knowledge, any student supports that existed were for folks with low grades or deficiencies. I luckily remained a pi scholar: 3.14 GPA. There were tutors and labs, which I purposely did not visit, because I categorically believed that I was in my academic situation alone. Who knows? I may have been a "whole pie" scholar had I asked for help. The one time I did go to an office for career advice, the poor soul at the front desk immediately called over a counselor to speak with me—I mean an actual psychologist, not an employment or guidance counselor. Shared office space, I assume. It must have been all the sweat. Did I look nervous? Did I not ask the right questions? What were the right questions?

CONTRIBUTORS TO MY SUCCESS

It is amazing how much fear can play into one's successes or failures. Because of my anxieties, I decided to pay attention to what others were doing and to follow their lead. When I finally did get brave, I purposely talked to my Latino professors, many of whom, now that I think about it, were Latinas and Chicana feminists. Upon further reflection, I began to see myself in these influential people. I followed their lead. One of them said, "You should go to this lecture tonight." "Where is it?" I asked. I followed and I mimicked. They would wave at friends. I would wave at acquaintances. They sat in the third row; I sat in the fourth. They would nod and take notes. I would nod and doodle, and then, before I knew it, I too was taking notes.

I am so extremely fortunate to have gone through my undergraduate education having learned with and from Chicana feminists. They were certainly doing the "invisible labor" many other professors could not or would not do. I later asked one of them, "Um, excuse me, I'm so very sorry to bother you, but I don't know what to do with the rest of my life. Do you think you can help me?" My questions were often so convoluted that I would not doubt I actually asked that question in this way. I asked for a letter of recommendation. I asked for help. I found my next support system. Too often, students drop out or are pushed out when they lose contact with their support systems. Colleges and universities need to provide first-generation students with a continued sense of community and connectedness, and they need to hire faculty who are reflections of their students.

ROLE OF FAMILY

My immediate family—my mom, dad, brother, and I—were quite functional, particularly in terms of being practical. "What can we do, given our income, to get this boy an education?" Student loans! Oh, all the student loans. I just paid them off. If I was "doing good," there did not seem to be any issues with supporting my education. My parents would put some money in my bank account when I needed it, and my brother would send mail with words of encouragement or a funny cartoon he found in a magazine. He was essentially sending memes via mail—real mail, like from the post office. My family did their best. They did what they could, but the studying was all on me. Functioning was all on me. Not functioning was also on me. Any hardships that came from my family were less on them and more internalized. I could not "do bad." I could not quit. I could not disappoint them. Remember, it was a setup. I was the "college boy."

TIPS AND ADVICE

There is no one blueprint for success. There are several. These are strategies. Strategies are plans or approaches. Your approach might not take you to your assumed endpoint, but do know that as you navigate academic borderlands, you have many possible approaches. For 8 years I spoke at Northern Arizona University's new student summer orientations. My talk was called "Strategies for Success." I did not come up with that title, and I do not know if I was actually offering up strategies for success, but I developed an acronym to help guide the talk: SUCCESS.

S is for (brace yourselves) success. Know what success is for you. Success is subjective.

U is for uncomfortable. You will have uncomfortable moments. Be prepared to do the hard stuff because growth and education are all about discomfort. Learning is uncomfortable.

C is for chaos. Doing what you need to do will take time and effort and may require some room for chaos. Knowledge is about process, not outcome.

C is for commitment. Commit! Do not do tomorrow what can be done today. Confront, challenge, and cross academic borderlands today.

E is for experience. Learn from your experiences. Learn from your mistakes—sometimes you may be your own best teacher.

S is for self. Be yourself.

S is for shifting. Shift! There is no one way. There are multiple ways. There will always be borders on your path to success. Negotiate academic borderlands. Ask questions. Even if you do not know the right questions. Ask for help. You are not in this alone. It is intimidating, but I know you can do it. Please, do not give up!

Whereas college is indeed complicated and sometimes mystifying, we first-generation college students often start in a predicament that continuing-generation students do not experience: We are without the benefit of handed-down advice about resources, timelines, unwritten rules, and the like. We have started the "race" on an unequal and increasingly crowded field, where the lack of social and cultural capital adds additional hurdles. Research has shown folks like me must proactively address the specific needs of first-generation students to cultivate ALL students' successes. It is not enough to get you to college without equipping you with the tools first-gen students need to graduate—the tools ALL students need to graduate.

CHAPTER 16

Joyce Stewart
Senior Academic Lecturer, English Department

I have been a college instructor since 1998 and am currently a senior academic lecturer in the English Department at the University of Wyoming (UW), where I teach a variety of writing classes, including first-year composition. I served as the director of the first-year composition program for 5 years. I primarily teach first-year students in Bridge, a support program for students who have been admitted to the university with conditions. Students must enroll in the Bridge program at UW if they do not meet the GPA and/or ACT/SAT requirements set by admissions. In other words, a condition of admission to UW is enrollment in our program, which includes taking first-year composition for first-year seminar students in Bridge. These courses run on a cohort community model, in which students attend these courses with the same group of students. Students in Bridge also work with professional advisors from the program and with faculty who are trained to work with this population of college students and are invested in supporting students who are deemed "at risk" when it comes to completing college/university.

My students call me Joyce or Ms. Stewart, whatever they feel comfortable with. Working with first-year students in Bridge is what is most important to me because I want to advocate for marginalized students who may have trouble navigating the transition from high school to college. My experiences in college as an undergraduate student do not directly link to my current teaching position, except that I had wonderful, patient teachers; they were great role models for me in terms of showing me how important it is to connect with and build students' confidence.

APPLYING TO AND PREPARING FOR COLLEGE

My advisor's office seemed to be a room that would only randomly appear a few times in my high school experience—a faraway place that could be found using a magical map that could only be deciphered by the "smart" girls at my school. These girls, I imagined, had taken some kind of prerequisites that allowed them to find and read that map: one that I did not own nor understand.

In reality, of course, my advisor's office was not hidden, but for me, at age 17, it might as well have been. My advisor was a nun, which made some sense because I went to an all-girls' Catholic high school. However, this was during a time when few sisters still worked for these kinds of Catholic institutions, and because very few nuns actually taught us, my advisor's being a nun only added to the mysterious nature of advising and future college plans.

To this day, I do not know how my father paid for me to go to Catholic school; he made only about $100 a week in his job as a superintendent (we got to live in an apartment in the building for free). In the last year of high school, tuition was $4,500 a year, which was a lot of money in 1990. My high school was considered a "college preparatory school," but the only time I remember having a discussion about "preparing" for college was when my advisor told me I would not get into any "real" colleges. In a school in which so many girls got straight As, my ranking was too low and my SAT scores rendered me "not college material." She said that the best I could do was apply to the community college across the street from my high school. Students in my class would sarcastically call it "the Harvard on the Hill," but I was so clueless I did not even get the joke.

My father, though a great believer in education, never once discussed college with me, nor did my mother. Neither of them had gone to college, and my father's highest level of education was the sixth grade. The only people I remember asking me about college were my friend Merlin's parents. They were immigrants from India. They knew I had struggled in our high school but still asked me if I had applied to colleges and encouraged me to do so.

I did not want to go to the community college across the street from my high school because it felt like an extension of high school. I found out about a small Catholic 4-year college in a nearby town. My "application process" included talking to a man in admissions a few weeks before the semester began. Because my father's salary was so low as a superintendent, I qualified for Pell grants, which covered most of the tuition.

At my college, nuns worked in admissions (I could not seem to get away from nuns); they literally filled out the financial aid forms for me, which was tremendously helpful as neither I nor my parents knew how to do so. I am not sure why I was admitted to this school. I believe they wanted to grow their enrollment (there were only 1,200 students attending). At the time, I remember thinking that they may not have looked at my transcripts carefully or there had been some oversight. Whatever the case, I soon found myself enrolled in college.

EXPERIENCES IN COLLEGE: THE ENJOYABLE AND ANNOYING

Transportation to college was one of the first challenges I faced. I did not have a car or even a license. My father needed his station wagon for work, and my mother never learned to drive; she took buses every day to her jobs as a home health care worker. When I got into college, my father had told me that he would drive me in the mornings and I would have to take two buses to get home. I knew that commuting home would be time-consuming, expensive, and sometimes scary (at night), but doable. Soon, I found a friend who was kind enough to drive me home; we synched our classes so our schedules, for the most part, matched.

I soon discovered that I liked school and that with some effort I could be good at it—something I had never felt in high school. The classes were small, and unlike in high school, I could take courses that I was interested in. The professors were kind and invested. After being encouraged by several of my English professors to do so, I became an English major early on. I was always a fairly decent writer, and I loved reading stories and poetry, but I had never thought beyond the moment or class I was in. I never thought about what kinds of jobs English majors could get or what kind of career paths were possible. The best part of majoring in English was there were not that many of us, and as a result, we formed a little community. There were not that many professors in English either, so I often had the same professor for several classes, which helped the professors really get to know me and I them.

However, these feelings of "sneaking into college" or not really being "college material" followed me throughout college, especially in my first semester. I remember getting a 59% on my first psychology exam and thinking to myself, "See, you don't belong here." As time went on, however, I became more confident and started to get good grades (even having straight As a few semesters). Nevertheless, my lack of belief in myself was still there, in different ways. For example, I never applied for scholarships because I did not think I would get them. In addition, in applying for graduate school, I would not have anyone review my application materials (a huge mistake for anyone applying for anything!) because I was afraid my professors or other staff would think that my applications were not strong enough—and might reveal that I did not really deserve the success I had had in college.

My college was a commuter college, which really worked for me because I was living at home and working in the evenings in retail (Sears lingerie, to be precise—sounds like an oxymoron, but it was a real department). My classmates, for the most part, were similar to me in terms of socioeconomic status and/or were first-generation students and/or had immigrant parents. We did not have college parties or big campus events. Folks went to class, then they went home or to their jobs.

I loved my school, but I did miss out on some opportunities. I always dreamed of studying abroad, but by the time I learned that this was a possibility, it was too late. I had to finish college in 4 years if I wanted my financial aid to continue. I also remember being hungry at college and not having enough money for lunch some days. My embarrassment over this was actually more painful than the hunger I felt. Luckily, I had a small appetite and most days a kind friend or acquaintance would spot me and buy me a burger. I also had a part-time job that allowed me to pay for these kinds of expenses. However, I had to be careful to not take on too many hours at my job, especially during midterm and final exams, or I would fall behind in my studies.

Finding the money for other expenses was more difficult. For instance, I dreaded having to buy school books, which were not covered under my grants, and often only bought the books at the last minute, right before a reading was assigned in class so I would not make the mistake of buying a book that the professor ended up not using. I sometimes did fall behind in my coursework if I did not have the money for a book, but I started to learn little tricks to make sure I did not fall too far behind. I would copy pages from my friends' textbook or borrow an upperclassman's copy. If I really trusted the teacher, I would tell them I did not have the money to buy the textbook. This often resulted in their lending me an extra copy they already owned. Because I was an English major, many of my books for class were not textbooks but classic literature, such as novels or books of poetry, and I was able to borrow those from the library. What I remember clearly was the anxiety I felt when it came to buying books and how time-consuming it was to find ways to solve this problem.

Despite these financial challenges, I never felt like giving up while I was in college. I attribute this resilience to the fact that I was doing well in college—much better than I had ever done in high school. The smaller college environment allowed me to have a great relationship with my professors and other college staff. I also knew that compared to many of my peers, I had it easy. I did not have to work full time. I did not have children or a family member to care for, and I had a family who, although they did not understand how college worked, supported me in my academics. I was also accustomed to having no money. Because my family had struggled financially for years, there was nothing new about not having enough money for things like lunch or books. As each college semester went by, I became better at knowing how to take advantage of the resources I had personally and the resources that were offered to me by my small school.

CONTRIBUTORS TO MY SUCCESS: WHAT WORKED FOR ME

I believe the most salient factors that contributed to my success were that tuition was almost fully covered through grants and that the classes were small. Not having to worry about paying for school played a major role in being able to continue and graduate. The small class size allowed me to always be engaged. Every professor I had knew my name and encouraged me in their feedback on my work.

I did not have any school-related jobs or internships; advising was fairly easy to navigate in such a small school (and do not forget I had those financial aid wizard nuns). I remember once being asked to work in the college writing center in an unpaid position, but I did not take the job because I needed to work after school and could not give up my part-time job for an unpaid position.

In terms of fortitude, I still did not have a lot of confidence in myself, but I finally did feel like I could do well in the vast majority of my classes. I had mostly gotten Cs and even some Ds and Fs in high school, but in college I was getting Bs and As in almost all my classes. The best part of college was starting over fresh, where none of the professors knew I was a "bad" student. So, in a way, I reinvented myself and became a "good" student.

Most students at my college were busy after school with their jobs, and some of them, who were older than me, were also raising families. However, as luck would have it, days before college began, I convinced a friend of mine from high school (her parents would not allow her to go away to college, so she had planned on going to "Harvard on the Hill") to come to this small liberal arts college with me. We helped each other persevere in college, but the truth was that she helped me more than I helped her. She gave me rides home (and sometimes to) school, spotted me for lunch when I had no money, and shared her notes if I was out sick. We are still best friends today.

ROLE OF FAMILY

To understand the family support I received, I will need to relate a little about my parents. My father had a ritual when it came to leaving notes for tenants. He would write out the note on a piece of paper, something along the lines of, "Please use only quarters for the dryer; other coins do not work." Then he would ask me to rewrite the note. He hated his own handwriting and did not want the tenants to see it. I thought it was silly at the time that he should be that self-conscious; however, I imagine that if I had only made it to the sixth grade, I would be self-conscious about my handwriting (and a lot of other things) too. This handwriting ritual indicated that he thought that when it came to education, I was already above him. I could never ask him for help on an assignment (in high school or college), but I always knew that he supported me in any way he could. After all, he paid for me to go to a private high school (he could have sent me to the local public school), and if I owed some money after my Pell grants, he would give whenever he could. He would never let me skip school (high school or college), and every now and again he would say, "Learn all you can." He never said it, but I knew he was proud of me. He still is.

However, in some ways, my family held me back as well. They lacked ambition and belief in themselves. My mother, who was well-read and intelligent, had a serious problem with self-esteem. She had gone to nursing school when she was young but contracted tuberculosis and had to quit. Although she had many subsequent opportunities to go back to school after healing, she never took them. She seemed resigned to working as a deli-counter clerk and/or as a home help aid, as though it were the best she could do. Now, as an adult, I realize she could have been anything and would have excelled in university. Believing in myself was not instilled in me in high school or college, and it has taken me a long time to build my self-confidence; some days I still struggle.

TIPS AND ADVICE

Find an advocate in at least one person. If it were not for one single professor (thanks, Dr. Weibe) who joined the faculty in my last year as an undergraduate, I would not have applied to or gotten in to graduate school (low GRE scores). Dr. Weibe encouraged me to apply to a program where he had a connection. Going to a good graduate program changed my entire life as a scholar and as a person.

Use the resources available to you and advocate for yourself. While it is important to find someone to advocate for you, this might not be easy or happen organically; therefore, you must use the resources that are available to you. As mentioned previously, when I was applying to graduate programs, I did not have anyone look at my application materials. This was foolish, as there were professors and other staff I could have reached out to, but I was scared to ask for help. These folks exist in all kinds of institutions and they love to help, so reach out to them! Do not be afraid.

Surround yourself with students who are serious about their studies (i.e., find "your people"). By the end of high school, I had discovered a group of students who read a lot, went to museums, and were interested in the world around them. They had fun in high school but also cared about getting good grades. I found this group a little late in my high school career but knew I wanted a similar kind of community in college. I noticed that serious students scheduled time for studying and completing homework in between their home or work schedules. They were smart, and most of them enjoyed the same kinds of activities as I did. Find those students who are serious about their schooling—sit beside them in class and say hello to them in the halls. Find people you have something in common with. These are "your people."

Reach out to first-generation professors, staff, and alumni. Whatever higher ed institution you are in (or are thinking of applying to), there are first-generation instructors, professors, and staff working there. Sometimes you can identify these individuals because they are involved in some sort of support program for first-gen students; if they are not, ask your advisor for this information. First-generation faculty and staff will know what you are going through as a first-generation student and know how to get you the help you need. They are glad you are in college and at their institution.

Do not let standardized test scores discourage you. I was 44 years old before I did well on a standardized test. I had to take the GRE as part of my application for a PhD program, and finally, after struggling with standardized tests my whole life, I received a respectable score on the verbal section and a perfect score on the analytical writing part of the exam (I did not do well on the math section, but I did not need to for my field of study). I thought about all the times I had dreaded these tests. The acronyms haunted me: the SAT in high school and the GRE for my master's. I always had weak scores, and even on my retakes I had mediocre scores at best. At the age of 44, I had finally "cracked the code" and learned how to answer the questions quickly and got a feel for the rhythm of the tests. In the grand scheme of things, if you want to get into college, do not let a weaker score on a standardized test stop you. There are lots of colleges that do not require standardized tests, and for some colleges the tests are only a formality. I know many students who were successful in college (or graduate school) despite their poor standardized test scores. I am one of them.

CHAPTER 17

Kevin L. Wright, EdD
Senior Equity Facilitator/Consultant at the Center for Equity and Inclusion

My name is Kevin Wright (he/him), and I am from Las Vegas, Nevada. Currently, I serve as a senior equity facilitator/consultant for the Center for Equity and Inclusion, based out of Portland, Oregon. My role involves raising consciousness, building skills, and developing strategies to socialize and operationalize equity efforts throughout organizations. My commitment to racial justice, equity, and inclusion are rooted in my approach to shifting cultures and processes one system at a time to advocate for historically marginalized individuals. I speak the language of the unheard, collaborate with company and community partners, and provide support to other key stakeholders with an intersectional and equitable lens. Coupled with my 8 years of working in student affairs and higher education, my labor and service is currently focused on racial justice and equity. My experiences as an undergraduate student led me to this work. If it were not for the support my advisors and mentors gave me, I would not have graduated, and I would not have discovered the heart work I am doing today.

APPLYING TO AND PREPARING FOR COLLEGE

Originally, I did not want to attend college because I did not think that college was meant for me. My goal was to enlist in the military after high school in order to serve my country. My grandfather fought in World War II and served in the navy. However, my plan of enlisting was quickly taken away from me. Due to health reasons, being the only man in my immediate family, and being the last person in my bloodline, I was deemed ineligible to serve—a decision that came from every branch of the military. When I realized the military was no longer an option, I sought out resources to apply to college. As a high school student, I attended a college preparatory academy and studied engineering. This decision led me to explore the field of engineering and obtain a degree to work as an electrical engineer. I went to every college fair, attended every financial aid workshop, and disciplined myself to apply for at least four scholarships a week.

Searching for these online and seeking assistance from my teacher in the Advancement Via Individual Determination (AVID) program helped me learn about multiple opportunities I could take advantage of. AVID is an initiative designed to assist potential first-generation college students to successfully graduate from high school and seek college admission. I applied to 16 colleges and was accepted to 15, all of which provided various levels of financial aid packages. When it was time to decide on which college to attend, I simply followed the money. Northern Arizona University (NAU) offered me the most financial aid, an affordable meal plan, and discounted housing. Also, NAU offered an electrical engineering program. Another attractive aspect was its location in Flagstaff, Arizona, which experiences all four seasons and is only 3.5 hours away from Las Vegas. Regardless of which college I chose to attend, I wanted it to be out of state, to make sure I would be challenged and would experience something new.

Institutions typically hold orientation sessions over the summer. These sessions are designed to inform incoming students about campus resources that will help them throughout their undergraduate career. Incoming students often arrive to orientation with their families, but that was far from my experience. No one in my family ever had the privilege of taking time off from work, especially in the middle of the week. No one in my family felt comfortable driving to Flagstaff, Arizona, either. My journey to college consisted of sitting on a Greyhound bus for 5 hours, with three luggage bags and $300 to my name. Within 10 minutes of stepping off the bus, gathering my luggage, and walking a mile to campus, I found myself gasping for air every few minutes; I was not aware of how much the altitude change would affect me. When I finally arrived at my residence hall, I was checked into the wrong room and my meal plan had not been activated yet. I bought only a few snacks because the price of food was significantly higher in Flagstaff than in Las Vegas. I did not have much contact with my family because my phone did not have good reception thanks to my service provider. To say the least, my first few impressions of navigating college indicated that I was off to a rough start, and classes had not even started yet.

EXPERIENCES IN COLLEGE

The Classroom

For as long as I can remember, I never felt empowered as a student in the classroom. Going to college reaffirmed that mind-set and triggered imposter syndrome. Imposter syndrome is that little whisper in your ear that asks you, "Are you supposed to be here?" "Do you deserve this?" and "Are you good enough?" I did not understand the process of choosing the type of classes I needed to take, which is why I chose random courses based on their titles. None of them was enjoyable. I shared this frustration with my academic advisor, and she told me I was feeling this way because I was a first-generation college student. That was the moment I was first introduced to my identity as a first-gen. My academic advisor told me that my first-gen status came with many benefits and just as many obstacles. After our conversation, I went back to my residence hall and reflected on my reason for being in college. My academic advisor was one of the few college resources I actually trusted. I only met with her because my residence hall director, a Latinx man of color, had made the suggestion to ensure I felt supported in other areas of campus. She listened to me, gave me advice that was specific to my individual circumstances, and was never difficult to access. At first I had been skeptical of meeting with an academic advisor, but my first impression of her debunked every assumption I'd had. I was struggling with the idea that maybe I had gone to college because others expected it of me and not because it was my own decision. Each day, I would go to class and not feel connected to the classroom space, the curriculum, or the instructor; I was just another warm body taking up space and giving money to an institution. By the time midterms came, I knew I wanted to continue being a college student, but I was not sure if I wanted to continue attending NAU.

Reslife

Dorm was the word I always heard when people referred to where they lived during college. NAU introduced me to the term *residence hall,* which were buildings where students lived. They provided a lounge, games and movies, an exercise room, and a computer lab. All these resources were provided by the Office of Residence Life, which had the nickname "reslife." I was offered rent at a discounted price if I decided to live in a space with two other people in a room that was initially designed to accommodate only two people. As a broke college student, I was always thinking about money, and anytime I saw an opportunity to save money, I took advantage of it. My residence hall truly was a tight-knit community, even tighter among the students of color. Our residence hall director was visibly present, the resident assistants facilitated awesome programs, and the other students in the community always found a way to have a good time. While I mainly hung out with the other people of color within the residence hall, I was fortunate to not have negative experiences when interacting with white students. Many of the white students I met were welcoming, progressive-minded, and did not feed into negative aspects of their whiteness. Even 12 years later, I have managed to stay in contact with many of those I met there. Living on campus was an enjoyable experience; I met a new best friend, my future best man, and current colleagues that also work in higher education. When times were rough in college, I always knew I could go back to my residence hall, hang out with my friends who were also first-gen, and renew my sense of hope that everything was going to be okay.

Campus Involvement

To put it simply, I was the overinvolved student. I held at least one position in every organization I was a part of, and I explicitly contributed to the 80-20 student leadership narrative, which is an informal perception of who holds leadership positions on campus; it means roughly 80% of the student leadership positions available are held by 20% of the overall student population. With this narrative, the same select few students attend every club or organization meeting and every leadership conference and work at the same places. Some argue the narrative is beneficial because there is consistent leadership, with someone to depend on for any given task. However, others argue this narrative contributes to burnout and low retention. The latter argument is that students invest more time in their extracurricular activities and less into their academics, treating their leadership activities as their major while their academics serve as their minor. Yet, this problematic notion sometimes remains unchecked by the very institution that promotes and encourages students to get involved in the first place. For me, getting involved in different activities was not about building my résumé, showing off my leadership skills, or seeking recognition. Getting involved was about developing a connection to the institution, making new friends, and learning more about myself. As a student in the K-12 school system, I was living under everyone else's expectations. As a college student, I wanted to learn about the expectations I set for myself.

CONTRIBUTORS TO MY SUCCESS

Student Support Services (SSS) was a major contributing factor to my success. All the other entities I was involved with either came from or were somehow connected to the SSS TRIO program. I met my first few mentors through this program, joined a business fraternity, and founded a chapter for another fraternity and sorority. And through SSS I obtained my first job in student affairs, where I served as an orientation leader. Needless to say, I never got involved with something on campus without running it by my advisor in the SSS program first because I trusted their judgment in evaluating what was best for me. Because of SSS, I continually stretched beyond my comfort zone in many aspects of my identity. As a Christian, I challenged myself to attend services at the Catholic Newman Center to learn about other communities within the Christian faith. As a cisgender, heterosexual man, I became an intern at the LGBTQIA Services and Support Office to learn how I could further advocate for queer and trans folx. I confronted my fear of speaking in front of large audiences by presenting a workshop at a national conference with 5,000+ attendees. None of those things would have happened if it were not for the SSS program.

ROLE OF FAMILY

My academic advisor warned me that my first-gen status was going to have its obstacles, but I did not think those obstacles would involve family. After my first semester of college, I went home for winter break. When I first arrived home and was greeted by my mother, I immediately felt something was different. When I had a family dinner with my mother and sister, it did not feel like family members having dinner together. Instead, it felt like a mother and daughter were having dinner with a guest they were meeting for the first time. Coming back home for the holidays was not a family reunion for me. Instead, it was my mother and sister mourning the loss of the son and brother they knew before he went off to college. My friends from high school felt this way too; the conversations we used to have were no longer the same, and they felt it was because

I went to college and some of them did not. The feeling of loss was mutual; I could not talk to my family or friends back home about my current struggles. After a few of these brief encounters with familiar faces, I started to feel guilty about going to college. The people who had pushed me to go to college and supported my decision to go out of state were the same ones who later shamed me for that decision. This is known as first-gen guilt—something I still struggle with as a full-time professional and three-time first-gen graduate. This obstacle taught me the difficult skill of letting go, which is what I had to do with many of my friends back home. As for my family, we are still trying to develop a new relationship with each other.

TIPS AND ADVICE

To all first-gen students, both current and incoming, I advise you to not hesitate to ask for help. When I got to college, I thought asking for help was a sign of weakness. However, had I not asked my mentors for assistance, I would not have graduated. Without the help I received from the caring individuals at NAU, I would not have attended graduate school to pursue a master's degree, and I would not have later pursued a doctoral degree. Also, I advise you all to make sure you do not waste time. Do not waste anyone else's time, and definitely do not waste your own time. For each person who has willingly helped me get to where I am today, I am doing all that I can to provide assurance that their investment in me was not wasted. Keep your circles tight, and make sure you are always in good company with people who continuously lift you up—not bring you down. Admittedly, I got too caught up in having a lot of acquaintances and lost sight of who was actually a friend. Finally, do not let your degree define you—you were enough before you got it. While that piece of paper holds weight, there is more to who you are than what is printed on that degree. Stay humble and keep moving forward!

CHAPTER 18

Sonja Ardoin, PhD
Associate Professor and Program Director,
Student Affairs Administration

I grew up in the small, rural community of Vidrine, Louisiana. Most would not consider it a "real" town because it lacks a zip code and there is not a stoplight to be found. One can only note its existence by the school and volunteer fire department that boast its name, both of which are within a 10th of a mile of each other. It is one of those "if you blink, you'll miss it" places. No matter how many other places I have lived (at least eight) or will live, I am proud to call Vidrine home.

I come from a family of farmers, and I lived on the land where my maternal grandparents tended rice and soybean crops most of the year and crawfish lakes during the season. Our homestead was precisely 1 mile from Vidrine High School, which was the K-12 school I attended for my entire primary and secondary education. My MawMaw taught me to utilize the library in the next town over for the joy, learning, and escape books afforded. My parents worked blue-collar jobs at various local businesses and instilled in me the habit of hard work and engaging in one's community. I played every sport offered in our area and learned how to drive in my PawPaw's farm truck in the middle of a field.

Teaching was the future my family envisioned for me because it was a "good" steady job in our area, and I leaned in to it from an early age, "teaching" my stuffed animals and dolls. Also, the mantra of "get an education so you can have a 'better life'" was impressed upon me as a child. No one ever defined what "better" meant, but I understood it was different from what we had. College was seen as the key to this, but I would have to figure out how to get there (literally and figuratively) and how to pay for it.

As fate would have it, teaching did end up being my future. I went on to earn three degrees in education and become a first-generation college student turned faculty member. It was not a direct route though. My career began in 2006 as a student affairs educator, and I spent 10 years as a full-time practitioner at five different universities while also holding several concurrent roles as instructor or part-time faculty member. I loved being part of the learning process—whether inside or outside of the classroom. However, it was not until 2015 that I was able to overcome the concern that "people like me" could be faculty members and conceded to my desire (and fate's push) to have the classroom be my primary "office." Now, I spend my days preparing future student affairs practitioners and advancing scholarship and practice on how colleges and universities can better serve first-generation college students, students from rural areas, and students with poor and working-class backgrounds. I could not be a faculty member without my three degrees, yet everything I do in my role is influenced by my identities—including my first-generation college graduate status—and my drive to have the voices of historically excluded and underserved students heard and their experiences understood.

APPLYING TO AND PREPARING FOR COLLEGE: LSU WAS MY HARVARD

I distinctly remember the first time I visited Louisiana State University's (LSU) main campus in Baton Rouge. My older brother had been invited to attend a prospective student program, which included a campus tour and a football game. My family made the 1.5-hour drive to Baton Rouge, and as a seventh grader, I went along for the ride. I recall walking with my parents near Lockett Hall and telling them, "I am going to go to school here one day." They seemed less assured than I was and mentioned that the two local community colleges were also great options and much closer (within 20 minutes) to home. But, from that day forward, my mind was made up: It was LSU or bust.

I knew I had to put in the work to realize my goal. LSU was only in reach if I could qualify for enough scholarship money to pay for it. This translated into a need for an almost perfect, if not actually perfect, 4.0 grade point average, a quality ACT score, and applications to every scholarship I could possibly qualify for. In essence, I saw it as a numbers game—the higher my scores and the more scholarships I applied for, the greater my chances of receiving funding. So, I focused on my classwork, met with teachers and the guidance counselor to ask questions and gather recommendation letters, and took the ACT test four times—in less than 2 years—to earn what I believed was a high enough score to be competitive. I applied for every scholarship possible, including ones from the local fire station and nearby Walmart. Thankfully, the state also provided a tuition assistance program, which had similar academic qualifications. My diligence and the support of my family, teachers, and guidance counselor resulted in a numbers game win for me: I graduated from high school with a 4.0 GPA and a 30 ACT score and was positioned as a recipient of the state's tuition assistance program and a competitive applicant for several local and university scholarships.

In the late 1990s, most higher education institutions recruited students "the old-fashioned way"—through direct mail. So, after I received my final (and highest) ACT exam score, I began receiving mail from various colleges and universities throughout Louisiana that were trying to recruit me. I was always excited to review the glossy brochures of colleges I had never seen in places I had never visited (yes, in my own state), but I remained steadfast: LSU was it for me. I was aware that I needed to hedge my bets though, and I ended up applying to three state institutions—LSU (of course), Louisiana Tech, and the University of New Orleans. I had never visited the latter two, but they were both a bit farther away from Vidrine, which appealed to me as I wanted a new experience. I also wanted to compare scholarship packages because money—whether or not I wanted to admit it—was a factor in my decision.

Being the mail-checker in our house, I grabbed the mail one day and drove into the carport, where I filtered through the items. One was a regular-sized envelope from LSU. I vividly remember holding the letter in my hands and thinking, "This is it. This letter determines my future." I opened it, alone, in the second-hand 1995 Chevy Blazer I drove. When I saw the word "congratulations" I cried. LSU was, in fact, it for me, and I had gotten my shot at that "better life" that everyone kept referring to. The next task was to figure out what all of that would mean.

EXPERIENCES IN COLLEGE: FINDING MY TIGER STRIPES

I began my college experience in a way higher education scholar-practitioners would not recommend: I moved into an off-campus apartment with my best friend from high school. We did not know that living on campus was typical or that we might do better academically and socially in that environment. Nevertheless, we ended up living together for 4 years in that same apartment and both graduated within 4.5 years of our fall 2000 starting semester.

Transitioning to college was in part a move from being a "big fish in a small pond" to a "small fish in a big pond." I was used to being at a school and in a place where everyone knew me and my family, where people were similar in culture and language, and where I knew how everything worked. LSU was the opposite. Almost no one knew me or my family, people made fun of my Cajun accent and asked a lot of questions about my hometown and culture (yes, even in the same state), and there were many systems, policies, and ways of being that I did not understand or know how to navigate.

Academically, I did pretty well, although I did struggle during my first semester with writing in the way my English 1003 professor preferred, and I was confused by why my Survey of the Arts teacher hated us (really, he did—he told us that!). I made efforts to visit my faculty members during their office hours to ask about assignments and have them further explain some concepts. I particularly enjoyed my history professor, Dr. Gaines Foster, and reveled in his office library. He was gracious enough to indulge my interest in his subject area, so I enrolled in every course he taught and he became my favorite undergraduate professor.

Within the cocurricular, I had some setbacks. I applied to many student organizations during my first year and was only accepted into one—a first-year student committee for student government. This was a shift for me, because in my small, rural high school, I had been fortunate to always make the team or win the election. My first fall semester at LSU taught me that my "insider" status did not accompany me to college and that I would have to figure out how to navigate this large campus as a new and unknown member. Unlike some of my peers, I was not coming to campus with a large group of friends from high school, connections through my parents' careers or alumni status, or prior involvement in state-level leadership programs (such as HOBY or Girls State), which were not available in my community. I figured I had a choice: Give up or keep trying. As my rural community and working-class family had taught me, the former was not an option, so I reframed my mind-set to be grateful for the opportunities I was afforded and keep trying. I applied for activities that captured my interest until they either worked out or I decided they were not meant to be. It was a powerful lesson about change, humility, resilience, and connections.

Fortunately for me, that first-year student government committee turned out to be a breeding ground for networking, and many of the students I met through that committee would hold significant student leader positions on campus in our later years, serving as editors of the student newspaper, student government cabinet members, fraternity and sorority chapter officers, business school standouts, orientation leaders, and other high-profile roles. They helped me transition to the "big pond" of LSU, shared their connections and resources, and helped me grow into a "bigger fish" on campus than I ever imagined I could be. In subsequent years, I found my core engagement in the orientation and extended orientation leader groups, student government, and honor societies. Through these opportunities, I met advisors and university administrators who become mentors for me and inspired me to explore a new career option—higher education administration and student affairs, which I would not have considered (or known existed) without my campus involvement. These organizations and their members not only made LSU my second home but also directed me to a fulfilling career path. Today, they continue to influence their career fields and communities, and I still call many of them (both peers and advisors) friends; they serve as "social capital" and direction givers in my life, and they make me feel at home.

CONTRIBUTORS TO MY SERENDIPITOUS SUCCESS

My success as a first-generation college student was due to a combination of strategy and circumstance, which some might also call luck. Admittedly, even some of the strategy was propelled by necessity. For example, visiting faculty was key to my academic success, but I did not do it for retention or networking because I was unaware that it would be helpful in that regard. Rather, I went to see my faculty members because I knew I needed good grades to keep my scholarships and thus stay at LSU, to better understand the course material, or to write in ways that were more "academically appropriate" so I could get those good grades. I also was not aware that cocurricular engagement assisted with retention and sense of belonging. I merely wanted to meet people and contribute to the community.

It also helped that some of the other students I met, and became close with, were other first-generation college students from small, rural areas in Louisiana. Compared to people I met from Baton Rouge, New Orleans, or Shreveport, who were less familiar with my Cajun culture and often from different (e.g., more affluent) social classes, these folks understood my background. We could discuss our families, our challenges, and our blessings. They grasped why I sometimes felt simultaneously like an imposter at LSU and a traitor to my home community. I was not afraid to go to their hometowns or invite them to mine. They "got me." So, my success was a triad of sorts: (a) get to know faculty and let them know me, (b) get involved on campus in some way, and (c) find community with those who shared one or more of my identities.

ROLE OF FAMILY: IT'S NOT MY DEGREE, IT'S OURS

While my family—both my parents and grandparents—could not assist me much financially or help me navigate the myriad new processes and expectations that higher education presented, they were my "cheerleaders" throughout my undergraduate experience. They consistently asked me how school was going, attended events with me on campus so that they could be involved, and celebrated moments of success with me. My mom would make the 1.5-hour drive to Baton Rouge sometimes just to take me to dinner or wash my clothes; it was her way of "doing something for me." My grandfather would always give me $10 when I came home on weekends as his way of buying me lunch one day that following week.

Did they always understand what was happening, why I had to study so much, or why I decided not to come home for some family event? No. However, they supported me in the way they knew how and made an effort to be there for me. Moreover, when I became the first person in my family to graduate from college, they were, in fact, all there: my parents, my brother, both sets of my grandparents, my aunt and uncle, and two first cousins. That day is burned into my memory, particularly the moment when my maternal grandfather—my PawPaw—held my diploma and remarked that he never thought he would be able to hold one of those in his hands in his lifetime. Thinking about that moment still makes me want to cry. That moment solidified the awareness that the degree was not only mine—it was ours. I recognized that while I was the one who was afforded the opportunity to pursue higher education, it was the history, sacrifices, and support of my family that allowed me to persist.

TIPS AND ADVICE: "MY TWO CENTS" OFFERING

I am hesitant to give advice to anyone, particularly other first-generation college students, because each of our experiences is unique based on our combination of social identities (e.g., race, ethnicity, gender, sexuality, social class, age, ability), the dynamics of our families, the geographical place we call home, the type of institution at which we are enrolled (public, private, 2-year, 4-year, large, small), what we are studying, and other life circumstances. First-generation college students are not a homogenous group. Yet, there are similarities in our experiences and we can learn from and encourage one another. Therefore, I will offer my "two cents" with three suggestions for others who also identify as first-generation college students:

Ask all the questions. As a first-generation college student, the language, processes, and ways of being in higher education were often new and frequently confusing to me. So, I asked a lot of questions—of my faculty members, advisors, and fellow students. My questions included everything from where buildings were to what a "blue book" (blank exam booklet) was and where I could buy one. Sometimes the only way to learn and acclimate to college is to ask questions. I promise, you are not the only one wondering.

Give some grace—to yourself and to your family. As with any new experience or transition, you will need time to learn how to function in the space and to figure out how it may influence you or you may influence it. You will fail or come up short sometimes. That is no reason to quit though; we learn from those setbacks. So, give yourself some grace. And share that grace with your family too—they are also experiencing higher education for the first time. Although their well-meaning advice or support may seem misplaced or frustrating at times, or they may not fully endorse your pursuits, remember they are also in new territory.

Be proud! Earning any higher education degree (associate's, bachelor's, or graduate degree) is a big deal. Although it may seem like "everyone has a college degree now," that is not factually true. The reality is that fewer than half of the people in the United States have earned a higher education degree. So, be proud of your status as a first-generation college student and seize the opportunity! I am proud of you.

CHAPTER 19

Kamina P. Richardson
Assistant Program Director and Pre-Law Advisor for Legal Studies Program at Temple University's Fox School of Business

My name is Kamina P. Richardson, and I am the assistant program director and pre-law advisor for the legal studies program at Temple University's Fox School of Business. I have been in this role for 9 years and I love it. My responsibilities entail working with students who major in legal studies and business students who are interested in becoming lawyers or judges in their future. I mentor students from different socioeconomic backgrounds and am the faculty advisor for a first-generation student organization that provides programming and services for students navigating college life. Education saved my life!

I'm a first-generation graduate with a bachelor of science degree in business administration and a master of science in organizational leadership. Through these degrees, I developed the acumen to understand how businesses work in this ever-evolving world and how to navigate relationships and office politics within an organization. Due to both of my degrees, I have been successful in securing a higher education position and longevity in this role.

APPLYING TO AND PREPARING FOR COLLEGE

My experience navigating the college admission and application process was not a traditional one. In high school, we were told to apply to colleges before we graduated. I completed those steps per our guidance counselor and was accepted into eight schools. However, we were never told what to do once we received letters of acceptance. I grew up in a household in which no one was experienced in college enrollment or financial aid, and no one could offer guidance in preparing to be a college student. Because of this, my dreams of having a degree were delayed. Those acceptance letters fell through because I did not know how to undergo the process of paying for college. I felt my only option was to work. For 5 years after high school, I held several temporary jobs in various locations outside of Philadelphia. Then, one of those jobs offered a degree program through a cohort program that partnered with two other companies. I decided to enroll and begin my college experience at age 25.

EXPERIENCES IN COLLEGE

I was considered a nontraditional student because our classes met at an off-campus facility instead of on the college campus. Students were given an advisor who helped us navigate the financial aid process, course selection, and additional services the college provided to its student body. Because our classes were held off campus, I made sure to go on campus every chance I got on my days off. I wanted to experience college life and be around students who looked like me. I was the youngest person in my cohort, and many of my "peers" had worked for the company for 20 years or more. I had nothing in common with them because I was just beginning to understand who I was and what I wanted to do with my life.

My experience working on my bachelor's degree was unique. My classes offered an understanding of the business world, which tended to focus on revenue, producing more products, and servicing customers without building relationships. Those courses taught me how to navigate roles in operations, marketing, accounting, and human resources. I had a hunger to learn more, which led me to visit the campus, where I built relationships with administrators and met students who were also struggling to complete their degree while working. At the same time, I had to realize that those customers were me. As a student, I was also a customer and I did not want to be just another body in their statistics. Therefore, I learned how to navigate my learnings with my work experience and drive change in my personal and professional life.

The most challenging part of my undergraduate college experience was not feeling a connection to the college because we were provided services outside of it. I was part of their student body, but only from a distance. I was in an accelerated degree program in a classroom that was created in a business location. I was away from my peers as a young adult but surrounded by seasoned professionals with 20+ years of work experience. I was forced to advocate on my own behalf because staff waited for students to enter their office. The advisors focused on course selection, financial aid, and tuition reminders. At the time, no services existed for students like me working 40 hours a week, living from paycheck to paycheck with a small family. I suffered from food insecurity, lack of transportation, and lack of a support system to guide or mentor me. To shorten the distance between myself and the campus, I started to build a path to Peirce College that allowed me to talk to the administrators, build relationships, and network to understand the process of human engagement when pursuing a career in education. Initiative and my love for learning helped me graduate in 2003.

My daily routine at college involved working on homework, building my résumé, and creating search requests for business acumen books in the school's computer lab. Along with the classroom experience, I began to learn the ins and outs of academia. I became aware of the obstacles that come with some programs, like my own, and how students feel when they are first-generation and lack a mentor. My coursework allowed me to pursue companies and my work in them with fervor. Being a nontraditional student who needed to work to survive, I excelled because I knew a little of everything needed to maintain a business. My social circle began to expand because I was coming out of my introverted shell. In my temp and seasonal positions, I began to build relationships with other individuals who were pursuing their education in a similar manner.

In 2006, with my degree and my tenacity, I became a program coordinator for Drexel University's Lebow College of Business. In this capacity I was helping directors and managers provide graduate school services and degree options for working professionals and undergraduates. This was my dream job, as education and learning were becoming my passion. Also in this position, along with finding myself, I was helping students to discover or to move closer to achieving their career goals. It was a perfect fit. My degree paid off in many ways, and the mentorship I was missing was included in my personal and professional goals.

After 2 years at Drexel, I was promoted to program manager in charge of providing students with experiential learning initiatives; these included outside-the-classroom programming that enhanced their educational pursuits and internships, externships, business plans, and case competitions. In 2011, the program's grant ended and so did my career at Drexel. Finding another job in higher education was difficult because all the schools required a graduate degree for student advisors. Therefore, my next feat would be pursuing a master's degree. I started my master's program in 2012 and graduated in 2014 with a job at Temple University, where I have been since.

Although my undergraduate studies gave me a good grasp on business operations and efficiency, I lacked a comprehensive understanding of human relationships. My graduate program began to fill in what I had missed in my education. While pursuing my graduate degree, I learned about myself, how and why people do things, and what that means in the business world. My graduate education helped to supplement an area of learning that I desperately needed if I planned to continue working in higher education—how to build relationships before taking on tasks. I began to understand the importance of building solid relationships with colleagues and customers. I was also aware that my fears, obstacles, and mistakes in life were connected to my family and environmental factors: I was too bossy, arrogant at times, and willing to forgo professional relationships to rise in the company. These traits made me expendable because my relationships with colleagues suffered. My graduate coursework unpacked the psychology of people, company culture, and how politics play out in business. I had missed all that as an undergraduate student with no mentor. I found it during my graduate program, and it allowed me to become a better mentor, coworker, and supervisor in my current role.

CONTRIBUTORS TO MY SUCCESS

The knowledge I received from the start of my college experience as a working professional to the completion of my master's program taught me to trust the process of unlearning what I had been taught and relearning what makes sense for my own life. I realized that my mistakes and experiences could serve as a cautionary tale and a thought-provoking story as a mentor inside and outside of academia. If I knew then what I know now, I would have asked my high school guidance counselor more questions and I would have reached out to the schools that accepted me instead of assuming I could not pay for college. I did not know that reaching out to the college's financial aid department is encouraged. I was hoping for a full scholarship so that I did not need to worry about the details, but a partial or a predetermined amount of merit scholarships covered only so much. I also could have advocated for more money based on my academic standing, but I did not know it at the time. My high school guidance counselor did not know and neither did my mother or her friends. So, my educational pursuits stalled for several years.

ROLE OF FAMILY

Education saved my life! There are many things I have completed in my life that are firsts. As I reflect on my life as a 40-year-old African American woman from Philadelphia, the experience I truly missed was having a mentor—having guidance from someone who looked like me. The advisors that I reached out to at Peirce College and the Philadelphia College of Osteopathic Medicine were my biggest fans because I admitted to them that "I didn't know" many things and I was unafraid to say, "I need help." They encouraged me to look within, look at my family systems, and forgive myself and others in order to move forward.

Once that happened, I was able to form better relationships with my mother and brother and lean in to my family for support. Sometimes looking at the past and seeing the harm that comes from being silent and not questioning our parents and family leads us to be silent to our own facilitated trauma. We tend to encourage others to do us harm because we become voiceless. As a first-generation student and now graduate looking back on my life, I realize I should have spoken up more, asked more questions, and continued to be seen. Once I found my voice through education, I was able to utilize that voice in the face of disparities, inequities, and student goals, and in balancing my work and social life.

TIPS AND ADVICE

My advice for first-generation students starts with high school goal-setting. While in high school, find a mentor in the business world who is on a career path that is in alignment with your goals. Look to someone who has a similar socioeconomic background so you can hear crucial advice that will help you when applying for college. In addition, work with your guidance counselor and ask questions about the college application process. Find out what scholarships are available for first-generation students and what college expenses total not only for the first year but for all 4 years. This is information that must be shared with your immediate family because their financial information may need to be included during your college years.

As a first-generation incoming college student, make connections with your primary advisor, financial aid, and career services during your first semester. Know their names, the services they provide for students, and what you will need outside of the classroom. Also, when taking courses, get to know your professor through their office hours and *always* read the syllabus. At the end of the semester, provide verbal feedback on the course if you enjoyed it and stay connected to the professor through their office hours or social media platforms. Once you reach your senior year, those connections with professors will enable you to request letters of recommendation for grad school or reference letters for your career.

As an advisor and mentor, I tell students to invest in business cards during their time in school. Students do not carry their résumé around, and when networking with business professionals, school administrators, and the community it is always good to have a card on hand as you exchange information. On their card, students tend to include their school's name, a QR code to their LinkedIn page, their major and/or minor, contact number, and email address. Business professionals will be impressed that you are prepared to network and "seal the deal."

Finally, be mindful of what you post on social media platforms. Read a lot of books that go against your views to learn the art of debate and having crucial conversations. Be prepared to argue both sides of a topic. Read books on history, marketing, philosophy, constitutional law, economics, and finance among other fields. Post the interesting concepts you found through the art of reading and build your own professional social circle. This latter advice is important since first-generation students tend to think we are a small population. We are out there, so taking the initiative to engage in public and on social media will widen your access to people who can open the door to opportunities, such as internships, jobs, and associations that enhance what is being taught in the classroom. Access and being accessible to business and academic spaces will increase your confidence, networking skills, and resilience in the face of rejection. You will get tested by people, and reading, writing, and critical skills will prove to be your armor.

Always remember that change is constant. As a first-generation student, you will be changed by confronting obstacles and experiences that will seem trying and difficult. Those challenges are part of the process of unlearning and relearning how what you experience fits into your life. Be gentle with yourself, and remember that your college experience will prepare you to be an active part of a world that involves you. Your path begins with you becoming more self-aware and will continue to encourage your self-actualization as you navigate failures and create successes.

CHAPTER 20

Emilee Claire Inez
Admissions Representative, University of Wyoming

My name is Emilee Claire Inez, and I am currently an admissions representative for the University of Wyoming (UW). During my undergraduate time at UW, I discovered a passion for working in and around the college admission process. The feeling I had when I was able to help students find comfort on a college campus was nothing short of a high. For example, as a student ambassador, I was giving a young African American girl and her father a tour of campus, and she asked me a myriad of questions, but the one that stuck with me was, "Are there other people like us here?" Being of mixed race myself, I was able to reassure her; she looked at her father and said, "Okay, you know I'm coming here, right?" After graduation, I briefly worked for first-generation students who were admitted with support programming, but I quickly realized that I was once again yearning for that high. I have been in my current role for about 5 months. During that time, I realized that one of my biggest motivators is to help students find a bit of clarity in the haze that is the college search process.

APPLYING TO AND PREPARING FOR COLLEGE: BEFORE THE BACHELOR'S

While growing up in Southern California, I was fortunate to attend a private high school that was focused on college readiness. Each time a college representative would come to campus, our counselor would send around a signup sheet, and if the tiny meeting room for college presentations filled, then the students with the lowest GPA would be cut from the attendance list. Unfortunately, that was always me. In my 2 years of signing up for every list that came my way, I was allowed to go on zero college visits. I had been told for so long that GPA and test scores were only a portion of the college application process and that a student's extracurriculars were a huge factor. I am sure my family can still recall the meltdown that ensued when not a single college that I applied for even asked about the clubs I belonged to. For years, I had participated in clubs, going above and beyond, all for the sake of putting it onto my college application. The realization that all that work was in vain was absolutely devastating to my 17-year-old self.

My high school counselor had voiced some doubts regarding my readiness for college, even going so far as to suggest I take a bit of time off before starting. I still remember the anger that seethed in me when those words fell from her mouth. In retrospect, I think I was frustrated by her distrust in my abilities, but over time I came to the realization that I had been having the same doubts. She did not know that I had not gotten into any school I had applied to, but an immense feeling of failure haunted me. I later learned that I needed to send in my transcript and test scores independently from my application. I had used the common application, which was explained to me as an application that was one and done. Therefore, I assumed that I was done as soon as the application was sent.

Regardless of my failure to be accepted or the inevitable doom I felt by being waitlisted, I wanted nothing more than to go away to school and get what I thought was the only true college experience. My back was against the wall, and I was grasping at straws to find a way out. I applied to the UW on a whim in late April of my senior year, completely unaware of the doors I was opening for my naive, spite-fueled self. Soon, my parents and I were flying thousands of miles from home to visit a school in a little town none of us had ever seen, which I would later learn would be the perfect place for me to flourish.

EXPERIENCES IN COLLEGE: GROWTH IN UNDERGRAD

Throughout my time as an undergraduate, my first-generation student identity took many forms: first, as an excuse for misunderstanding, then becoming a chip on my shoulder through the frustration of not understanding, to eventually maturing into a badge of honor. I wore that badge proudly, quite literally in the form of a button on my backpack, and figuratively, because I had finally come to understand that I had fought for every bit of that understanding.

College was the most invigorating experience imaginable. Media had only taught me the polarities of college student life. In my mind, a student either never left the library or never left the bar. That perception could not have been more wrong. My childhood friends asked me about my life in the far-off land of Wyoming in excruciating detail. Having had experiences that no one I knew had, both at home in California and in my new home in Wyoming, was interesting. I always tell students that the transition from home to hometown is something that happens slowly but also all at once.

I spent the majority of my first semester of college holed up in my dorm room, terrified of the world that existed beyond the threshold. I felt like I had missed the boat to make friends because I was still in shock that I had moved across the country alone. Eventually I settled in and accepted my niche as the overinvolved yet under-the-radar girl, or so I thought. As time went on, I discovered that I was far less inconspicuous than I had imagined. Every time I encountered someone who knew about me or the work that I did for UW through clubs or admissions, I felt justified in taking up space in college. I could occupy that space with pride and feel justified that I had made the right decision to do the scariest thing I had ever done.

One of the more difficult parts of my undergraduate experience was not knowing when to celebrate accomplishments or what accomplishments were worth celebrating. Growing up, I had always been a person who easily fell into leadership roles. The luster of those achievements tarnished as I aged, and so did my need to feel celebrated. This became a bit of a problem when I was in college because it was hard to convey to my family and friends the difference in grandeur of an accomplishment in a collegiate setting. When I was a senior in college, I was elected to be the chairman of the College of Agriculture and Natural Resources, the highest student-elected position in the college. My parents were, of course, ecstatic, but I could hear the slightest tinge of hollowness in their excitement, which I can only assume came from not knowing the full breadth of the honor. The trouble of not knowing what to celebrate is still a problem for me and far from resolved; however, I have come to realize that it is not from a lack of caring, at least when I think of my parents' perspectives, but rather from a lack of understanding.

CONTRIBUTORS TO MY SUCCESS

Admitting to myself the strength in asking for help was one of the most challenging things I have done to date, but it maximally contributed to my success as a college student. I felt like I was exposing myself in a way that was deeper perhaps than even being naked or any other form of vulnerability I had previously known. I remember asking a lot of questions of my friends, usually under the false pretense of clarification, as if I had any idea what was happening around me. I felt so alone in my misunderstandings that I thought I should keep them all to myself. I struggled with the worst imposter syndrome. I could not understand how I had skated for so long when I felt like I understood so little. I do not really remember when I first reached out for help, but I am pretty sure I was screaming for it unconsciously for a long time before I finally did. I could not feel how heavy the weight I was carrying was until I took a step back and asked for help bearing the load. Telling my friends that I wondered how anyone had any confidence in me and having them reassure me that everyone feels that way was nothing short of liberating. I would go in to have these chats with my supervisor and mentor, and she would just let me talk and talk and chime in when she saw fit. I did not see it as asking for help but rather as sharing my concerns, half hoping they would fall on deaf ears. However, they did not. Makayla wound up being one of my biggest sources of help in my college career, and I can truly say I would not be nearly as successful or the person I am today without her guidance and willingness to always listen. For almost my entire experience in college, I had wondered whether I was genuinely this confident or whether I had built up such a strong facade of confidence that I was about to teeter off the top, destined to fall. In asking for help, I found not only the strength to see it was not a facade but also the strength to persevere.

ROLE OF FAMILY

My parents have always been the most supportive people in my life, and I cannot imagine that I would be where I am today without their unconditional support. I know that my parents and brother tried very hard to be supportive, despite not having experienced what I have. I know this because when I told my mom that I was one of the few students at freshman orientation without a parent there, she was devastated. I held on to that for a long time, first in anger but then in fear that the incident would make her feel she is unable to give me the necessary support.

I wish I could say the same about my extended family, but unfortunately I cannot. I think my grandmother wanted badly to be supportive, and do not get me wrong, she was, but her traditional Hispanic values are too deeply rooted. When I was about to leave for my freshman year, she looked at me and asked if I was sure I did not want to stay and start a family; and at my graduation party she asked when I was going to move back home. I cannot tell you which incident broke my heart more. I know that she did not understand why I would move so far from her, being that I am the only one of her grandchildren to not live within an hour's radius. I know that she only wanted all her babies near to her. I understand her sentiments come not from a place of anger but from love so immense it is beyond understanding.

As my time in college went on, I realized how little I actually had in common with some of my cousins. At first, when I went home for holidays and breaks, I could not wait to share with them what I was learning and experiencing. In this, however, I was met with very minimal interest. By sophomore year, I had become a captivating fun fact book for my youngest cousins, but they lacked the ability to have in-depth conversations that I so deeply craved. I made sure to still always share with them my experiences, so they could see that college was not all that the media makes it out to be. While I cannot speak for them, it always seemed like my extended family was watching a sporting event in a different language, looking around and cheering when everyone else did but never quite sure exactly what had just happened.

TIPS AND ADVICE

I have a couple pieces of advice for first-generation students. The first is that there is no correlation between knowing what you want to study and success. The idea that in order to be successful you have to know what you want from the beginning is an absurd expectation that we place on the youth in our society. I changed my major four times. With each change, I felt like I was a failure until I realized that not studying what brought me the most joy would be failing myself. Moreover, at 19 I would have told you that studying a major in theater, art, or any humanity was a waste of time. After much time, I began to see that we would have a miserable experience as humans if it were not for the beautiful things people create—the same people who study the humanities. So study what brings you joy. I used to argue that you should not spend money on something that will not return the investment, and I am glad that I can finally see beyond that feeble-minded argument. Beyond merely studying what brings you joy, do whatever brings you joy in college. Seeing the juxtaposition in the student carrying a briefcase and wearing a full suit and the student wearing pajamas and riding a scooter makes me happy because I know they are happy in their choices. It goes so much deeper than just physical appearances. College is a space for students to explore so many aspects of their lives, including interests, hobbies, careers, sexual orientations, and styles of dress. Basically, college is a place for you to find out who you are and to live freely as whoever that may be.

Critical Self-Reflection 2

Adam J. Rodríguez

Having read the stories in this section, you will once again notice that certain parts of stories stood out. It may have been T. Mark sweating with anxiety, Joyce's embarrassment at her hunger, Jenny finding her place and sense of self at college, or Kevin finding that returning home was not the family reunion he may have hoped for. Personal stories carry enormous emotional impact, which means that it is likely that you are going to automatically think about where you have similarities to and differences from our authors. When engaging in self-reflection, we assume that those similarities and differences will emerge; therefore, we aim to explore our reactions with even greater depth. To that end, we return to our two primary questions for exploration.

TWO PRIMARY QUESTIONS

1. As you read through these stories, what came up for you?
2. Having read this group of stories, what advice would past, present, and future you give to yourself?

Recall from the first critical self-reflection the idea of play. There are many situations in college in which you will need to come up with concrete, clear solutions to problems. This is a form of work. You are working to resolve an issue. Self-reflection is not nearly as linear or goal directed. It is not about finding an answer to a problem. It is about non-linear thoughts and feelings, introspection, curiosity, and discovery. This is play. In play, we let our mind wander and take us in directions that we may not have anticipated. There are parts of our mind, outside of our conscious awareness, that have knowledge and understanding that we do not have access to. Play can help us access that knowledge. As you read through these stories and discussion questions on your own or in a group, remember the notion of play, being curious and open and discovering what new places our mind unwittingly takes us.

FURTHER DISCUSSION QUESTIONS

What follows are groups of questions. I am not presenting a specific question that warrants a specific answer. Rather, each item below is a more general domain that contains multiple questions that may stimulate thoughts, ideas, values, or feelings, which you can begin to elaborate on. You will have in your mind the stories you have read, and they will help inform how you think about these questions. What is important here is curiosity and exploration. Note that the use of the term "relationship" here refers to any type of relationship—platonic, romantic, familial, professional, or otherwise.

1. What types of relationships do you envision yourself having in college, and how do you imagine they may be helpful to you? Which traits and qualities do you value in relationships, which energize and revitalize you, and which provide strength and power? Which relationship qualities deplete and drain you? When you reflect on the most meaningful relationships you have had, what stands out to you as the most fundamental qualities of those relationships? Who are you in those relationships? What roles do you play?
2. What are the types of social environments in which you find yourself thriving the most? Think of the environments in which you have felt the most content, satisfied, comfortable, understood, and supported. What did that environment look like? Who were the people around you, and what were they like? In what ways did they support you? What can you do in college to try and create some version of that environment? What is necessary in a social setting for you to feel safe and vulnerable?
3. What does your family mean to you? How will or how has college impacted your relationship to family? What has changed in your family, for better or worse, since you started college or started preparing for college? What sorts of impacts have those changes had on you?
4. Consider the groups and environments that you have been around in the past, and consider how, during and after college, you will be exposed to different groups and environments. What do you imagine will be the benefits and drawbacks of being in these new environments? How will your old relationships change? What may you have to give up from your old groups? What will you benefit from in the new groups you enter into? What might it mean for you to straddle both groups or cultures? How are you different with each group? How do you hold on to the things you value while recognizing that your environment has changed? How can you be thoughtful about navigating both environments, appreciating that both groups provide different values to you?

SECTION III
STORIES FEATURING PSYCHOLOGICAL EXPERIENCES

ADAM J. RODRÍGUEZ

> When you're socially isolated *and* worried about money and struggling in all your classes, it doesn't feel like three distinct problems. It feels like one big problem.
>
> —Paul Tough, *The Inequality Machine: How College Divides Us*

Isaiah, a student I worked with as a psychologist, faced consistent problems in college, which made the campus feel unwelcoming and dangerous, left him frequently wanting to quit school, and eventually led to a severe mental health crisis. Isaiah had grown up in a tumultuous household in which he endured regular psychological and physical abuse from his mother and stepfather. Among a host of other issues, his parents' abuse and neglect resulted in Isaiah missing a year of middle school and a year of high school before being kicked out of his home and spending the last years of high school homeless. Despite missing 2 years of school, suffering abuse, and being homeless, Isaiah applied and was accepted to a prestigious college in the Bay Area, where he arrived with dreams of becoming a physician. He was talented, driven, and incredibly intelligent.

Upon arriving on campus, however, Isaiah instantly felt like he did not belong. His peers could not relate to him, which caused him to struggle to build friendships. Although, like nearly all campuses, the institution stated that it embraced diversity and advertised itself as a progressive and open place, Isaiah repeatedly encountered professors, administrators, and other students whose behavior was sometimes confrontational and dismissive and whose interactions revealed they did not understand him. When Isaiah went to the financial aid office early in his first term to ask questions about how his loans and scholarships worked, a staff member was condescending and disrespectful. He perceived the staff member's behavior as reflecting an attitude that he was an ignorant and negligent fool who should already have the information he was seeking. Another early experience, this time a meeting with his department's dean, went no better.

He was once again rejected, this time being met with a series of microaggressions by the dean, who at one point called him "irresponsible" when he confessed to not knowing which prerequisites he needed for a course. Isaiah had multiple problems in the classroom with professors, several of whom were brash and uncaring. One referred to him as a "bad influence" on other students, several others called him lazy, and some cast accusations against him. One baselessly accused him of being a drug addict. The feedback he received on his papers did not address his writing skills but rather ridiculed his thoughts and experiences as ridiculous or naive. Isaiah felt like every day was a fight. He was losing confidence in himself every step of the way.

The competitive, neoliberal ideals of the university directly conflicted with Isaiah's values. His ideas, attitudes, and perspectives about college were unconventional, but they were substantive. The school faculty and administrators, as well as his peers, were overwhelmingly white and from an affluent background, and with their unconscious biases they had no doubt formed stereotypical assumptions about Isaiah's character. Students and faculty rejected his ideas because they did not fit in with their traditional experiences, and rather than embrace his alternative views, they disregarded and shunned him. Consequently, he often felt isolated and bad, which activated feelings of worthlessness and hopelessness and heightened his defensive and protective impulses. He told me that his regular experience was that he "very, very rarely could be [himself]." Here was a young man who had overcame immense challenges and had brought numerous strengths to campus, but his rejection by faculty, administrators, and peers—because he was "different" from others—silenced his strengths and pathologized him.

Toward the end of his second year of college, the culmination of ostracization, rejection, and disregard led Isaiah to a significant mental health crisis. Frustrated, desperate, feeling completely alone, and in intense despair, Isaiah, in the middle of the school term, booked a one-way ticket to another country with the intention of ending his life. Isaiah courageously reached out to me via phone while he was away, and we were able to get through the crisis and find a way for him to return to the United States. Upon arriving he found that his professors had dropped him from his classes and placed him on academic probation.

Despite Isaiah's attempts to talk with his advisors about his struggles, the institution made no serious effort to understand what led a promising student with intelligence and fortitude—the type of "diverse" student that the university's website displayed as merrily walking around campus and studying—to abruptly stop attending courses. His absence in class was viewed solely as an administrative matter. There was no outreach or even curiosity. As his psychologist, I spent hours conducting phone calls, writing letters on his behalf, and completing forms to try and get someone on campus to understand that this young man had experienced a critical mental health crisis and needed support—not punishment or ostracization. Isaiah spent even longer periods of time meeting with staff to explain his situation.

After two appeals and three letters written by me on his behalf, Isaiah was finally readmitted, but on academic probation, which only added to his stress and difficulties.

A bright and driven young man with a history of trauma arrived on campus eager to learn. Rather than embrace and support him, many seemingly well-intentioned people, locked into their own ideas of who a college student should be, provided an unwelcoming and judgmental environment.

We all arrive at college with our own psychological history, which shapes our experiences while in school. Some students enter college having had relatively few difficult experiences in their lives. Other students have had difficult relationships with family; experienced trauma, homelessness, or food scarcity; endured significant poverty; or suffered through depression or anxiety and must attempt to be good students while managing myriad thoughts and emotions associated with those experiences. Other times, a student may experience a traumatic event while in college. Many common elements of college culture, like too little sleep, increased stress, separation from family, and alcohol and other drug experimentation, can trigger or exacerbate mental health challenges. In addition to their histories, first-generation students come to campus and must then deal with academic overwhelm, feelings of not belonging, insecurity about their ability to be successful, and confusion, isolation, and loneliness. Moreover, they often meet with discrimination, microaggressions, or outright hostility while struggling with feeling responsible for the family they left back home, intense anxiety about money, and angst regarding the costs of upward mobility.

In this section, we see stories in which some aspect of the author's psychological life played a significant role in their college experience. The writers here bravely discuss their internal experience. Our psychic life is an incredibly important part of being a student, but unfortunately many stigmas about mental health remain. As you read these stories, note not only the psychological aspects of the story but also the manner in which external circumstances in the authors' lives influence those aspects. You will also notice the impact emotional experience can have on academic and social life, with all these forces acting on and influencing one another. Even if we are fortunate to not experience trauma in our lives, many first-generation students live with feelings of isolation, imposter syndrome, loneliness, self-doubt, and other insecurities. We will also, sometimes, need support for those difficult experiences we had prior to school. It is my sincere hope that we can work to destigmatize mental health and support one another.

CHAPTER 21   TO THE GARDEN THAT BLOSSOMED SEEDS OF DREAMS

Ulises Morales
Executive Assistant

I am the child of immigrant parents who envisioned a life in a place that surpassed their horizons and who sacrificed everything to give me and my siblings the life they could have only wished for. I am the child of parents who wake up every day and do everything in their power to make my siblings and me feel connected to this foreign land beneath our feet and who allowed me to dream on this land. I am no longer a child, but I am the result of the sacrifices they made. I am a first-generation college graduate from California State University at Monterey Bay. I wish my journey was straightforward, but like many first-gen students' experiences, it was far from it. If as a student you ever felt different, alone, confused, or unheard, or were petrified of speaking up in class, then I can resonate with you. My name is Ulises Morales, and I too felt those things during my experience as a college student.

Before I dive deeper into my experiences, I want to acknowledge that being first-gen is not necessarily a story of overcoming obstacles; it is not always a story of hardships. Yet, it is always a story that deserves to be celebrated, for you and your loved ones, because you managed to blossom in a space and in soil that was not designed for you to do so. Your story is unique to you and you only, so own it. Claim all your accomplishments no matter how small and continue being yourself throughout your journey.

APPLYING TO AND PREPARING FOR COLLEGE

Reflecting on my journey feels like a full-circle moment for me. In the beginning of my college journey, I feared sharing my thoughts. I have always been a quiet student, so sharing my story means a lot. My drive and desire to go to college stemmed from my family's sacrifices, from knowing how hard they worked to put me in the position that I am in today. Before college, I spent many of my high school summers working on job sites with my dad. He paints homes, often big homes, and the work he had me doing was no joke. Although my dad never let me do much of the painting, I taped, applied caulking and mud, and did lots of sanding during those summers. Those walls needed to be smooth. He picked up on the smallest of details, so I needed to make sure I did my part accordingly. I learned so much during these times, but what I remember the most is how tiring every single day was. Yet, I would never show how tired I was or how much I wanted to stop. In my eyes, my dad was, and continues to be, the greatest. He never complained about anything.

Organically, I gravitated toward wanting to be just like him. In my view, I was preparing myself, learning under him, to one day be an amazingly hard worker just like him. I shared this aspiration with him one night when we were making *elotes asados* (grilled corn on the cob) in the backyard. I told him, "I want to be just like you—work hard just like you, Dad." My mind was made up. I knew working under those circumstances was hard, and there were days I did not want to go, but I wanted to be like my hero. We were chatting about that for a while, until he looked at me and said, "That's funny because when I was your age, I wanted to be just like you." I was confused. *He's telling me that he wants to be like me. What does that even mean?* I was just a shy and scrawny teenage kid. Why would he want to be like me? Although that confusion rattled me, I soon understood what he was telling me. He opened up about how he had always dreamed of being able to go to school. Back in Tarimoro, Michoacan, where he is from, he did not have much. He did not even have enough money to pay the bus fee to go to school. He always dreamed of going to school, but he needed to work merely to pay for the bus fee, let alone the school fee. I then had an insight that shaped my academic trajectory forever. He gifted me the opportunity to do something that he could only dream of doing. From that moment forward, I knew that I would embark on this journey. It was something bigger than myself, and now through the sacrifices of my family, my dreams were mine to manifest and obtain. It is scary being the first, but I was blessed to have the choice to pursue this dream, and so I did. I am now in a position to tell my dad, "We reached our dream. We did it. For our entire family. This is ours."

EXPERIENCES IN COLLEGE

Although I did graduate, college was not the least bit straightforward for me. I was an average student in high school, but I was blessed to be accepted into a handful of universities that believed in me. I began my college journey in the fall of 2017 at California State University at Monterey Bay. This new journey had many obstacles. It was my first time away from home. I did not know anyone. I was immensely shy. To be completely honest, I did not feel at home until my fourth semester of college. I had no one to eat lunch with for the longest time. I would try to eat as fast as possible so I could go back to my small dorm room that housed three individuals. Many nights I would hide under my blankets and cry over how out of place I felt. I would get anxious about going to class because I did not know anyone. I did not feel smart enough, and I was petrified of being called on in class because I did not know any of the answers and my vocabulary was different from my peers'. What kept me going was the strong will that my father instilled in me to keep trying, and I did keep trying. Even if that meant having to dedicate at least 1 day per week to going over class material at the tutoring center for an entire semester, I did it. I spent more time with tutors than anyone else I knew during the first half of my college journey. I was trying hard to not fall behind as a student. Still, deep down I knew that I was much more than just a student, and as an individual, I could not help but feel alone. I wanted to do good for myself, but I was completely isolated. Or so I thought.

CONTRIBUTORS TO MY SUCCESS

I dealt with imposter syndrome. Mentally I was terrified of this new transition, but physically I was present enough to get by; so I never slipped too far in any of my classes. Deep down inside I felt lost, and many times I questioned why I even pursued this journey if I did not fit in to the puzzle of it. However, I found an organization on campus that made me feel I belonged—like my voice and experiences were valid. That group is TRIO Student Support Services—an on-campus organization that I consider family and for whom I am forever grateful.

Before the start of my third year, I was given the opportunity to be a peer mentor for students in this program. I jumped at this opportunity because I knew that if anyone else was going through hardships, I wanted to help them. I am still amazed at how I was given the opportunity to apply for this position; still, I am forever grateful that I did. The experience changed how I approached the remainder of my journey in college because I was regularly connecting with students who were like myself. As I guided them and helped them find ways to nurture their visions and passions, I gained skills in communicating with others. That instilled confidence in my ability to open up in more areas. I was given the opportunity to have an impact in other people's lives, no matter how small, and that is something that I will cherish forever. That same confidence that my father instilled in me, I now had the opportunity to instill in others. No matter how difficult the journey may be, I learned that throughout it, there are people who allow us to see realities beyond what we can imagine for ourselves. There are people who create spaces where people like us are welcome. There are people who create a space for our voices and our difficulties to be heard and acknowledged. For me, those people were found in TRIO.

As a peer mentor, I was always encouraged to be myself. I love music, and so I was encouraged to implement that into my position as a mentor. I began sharing my interests and passions with others. I saw that my thoughts held value in my community. I no longer feared sharing what I was thinking. These personal growth achievements extended into the classroom for me as well. I began my personal growth journey.

It took me a long time to find my community on campus, but I am grateful that I stuck around long enough to find it. It completely shaped the individual I am today. Opportunities were opened up for me to the point where I am now actively working in the industry that I love most: the music industry. This entire experience took my way of thinking to another level. The anxiety I had carried due to my introverted personality began to deteriorate. My mind-set blossomed, and I always used that as a metaphor to help people who may have been having similar experiences. My home on campus became TRIO. Their support, combined with the support of my family back home, was everything that I needed to visualize the completion of this journey.

ROLE OF FAMILY

Although my family did not fully understand every step in my college experience, they were a huge support system for me. My mother would try her best to check up with me—to make sure I was eating. She would text me randomly, and we would even speak on the phone at times. I loved speaking to my parents on the phone because my "why" was further solidified with each call. However, they always felt guilty about calling me because they did not want to interrupt my studying, so we did not speak as much as I wished we had. I would also use the excuse of being busy at times. The truth is that before reaching out and finding my community on campus, I was having a hard time, and on a subconscious level, I did not call because I did not want them to worry about me. Regardless, I knew that they supported me.

The talks I had with my father before leaving for college never left my mind, and every time I returned to school from breaks, the look in my mother's eyes always told me how much she would miss me and how proud she was of me. No words at all sometimes told me the most. Those small moments were instrumental to my commitment to continue this pursuit of higher education. Remembering how fearless and relentless my parents were in their own lives also pushed me forward, especially on difficult days. I had to be fearless too, so I never stopped pushing forward, regardless of how difficult the going got. My family helped me to step through doors I did not know were there. I stepped through them while masking my fears and insecurities. I had to fake it until I became it, but without my family's sacrifices pushing me through those doors, I probably would not have accomplished what I did in college. Graduation was a victory for all of us.

TIPS AND ADVICE

The hardest experiences in life always teach us the most. For some, the most challenging part is actually believing you can do what you set out to do. At the start of my college journey, I was not quite sure where it would take me. For me, it meant transcending the norms of my family and community. I understood that all the answers would not be written out for me. I was okay with that, but that understanding did not make the experience any easier. My college journey took me somewhere difficult in the beginning, but when I look back, I also see that it was necessary. The experience shaped me, and I grew through those moments in ways I could not have anticipated. One of the most pivotal moments for me was the leap of faith I took by applying to be a mentor despite having anxiety in social environments. As people, all we can truly aspire to do is take that leap to grow and never stop learning about our surroundings and most importantly ourselves.

Being a first-generation college student is something that I take pride in. As a freshman, I had an idea of what that could mean, but it meant so much more when I finally completed this chapter in my life—not only for myself but for my loved ones as well. If any educator, coach, or other leader is reading this, keep in mind that the quiet kid in the room has a lot to say. It may simply be hard for them to open up at first. That does not mean those quiet students are not thinking. Honestly, the quiet folks always tend to be the best listeners, picking up on details that most people gloss over. Then when they do open up, sometimes just a few words can have the most profound impact. For me, those few words were the ones my father shared with me before the start of my college journey. We dreamed together and blossomed in a place where the soil was not designed for us to grow in. We did grow, along with the abundance of other beautiful flowers I met along the way.

CHAPTER 22

Mayra González Menjívar
Communications Associate

When I think about my higher education journey as a first-generation college student, I realize it began long before I ever stepped foot on a college campus or even knew what the common application was. Early in the summer of 2012, I had just finished my sophomore year of high school, and President Barack Obama had just passed the Deferred Action for Childhood Arrivals (DACA; U.S. Citizenship and Immigration Services, n.d.) through an executive order. To qualify for DACA, individuals had to have arrived to the U.S. before the age of 16, be under the age of 31 on June 15, 2012, and be physically present, having attained lawful status by the same date: be a student, have a high school diploma or GED, or be a veteran, without having been convicted of a felony.

I would be eligible for DACA that very summer I turned 16. My parents and I found an immigration lawyer who was taking DACA cases, and we diligently prepared my initial application to prove that I met the basic requirements and to demonstrate that I was the order's ideal version of a model immigrant. Kindergarten report cards, the certificate from my second-grade science fair, a tiny piece of paper that noted my entrance to the United States, and even a letter from the church I attended growing up were all copied and placed into a large manila envelope that my dad labeled "Mayrita DACA." We made the long early-morning trip to the Salvadoran consulate on Long Island, located about an hour from where we lived. We brought the envelope to our lawyer, finished filling out the application, handed over a money order for $495 to cover the fee, and submitted the application.

A few months after submitting my application, I received a letter from United States Citizenship and Immigration Services informing me that I was to go to one of their offices to provide biometrics for my work permit. A few weeks after that, my social security card and my work permit arrived in the mail. I was now able to obtain a driver's license and find a job to help me become more financially independent. Most importantly, because of my new status, I could now apply to colleges without fear.

APPLYING TO AND PREPARING FOR COLLEGE

In the fall of 2013, I began my senior year of high school. I was fortunate to attend a school that emphasized the importance of attending college. College recruiters regularly visited throughout the first few months of the school year to provide basic information about their colleges. In this environment, with my academic track record and my parents' encouragement, I saw college as an inevitability, one that I would relish experiencing. However, despite this, I found the application process to be nebulous and overwhelming. My parents attended school and had some college experience in our home country, El Salvador, but were unfamiliar with what was needed to apply to colleges in the United States, let alone how to support a child who was just beginning this journey for herself. They encouraged me as much as they could, but at times I felt as though they did not understand the stress and pressure I was under. The college application process is stressful by nature, but knowing my parents did not know how to help me made the process all the more daunting.

I was fortunate to have a fantastic English teacher who taught my advanced placement English class my junior year. She quickly became one of my favorite teachers, and I found myself confiding in her that I did not even know how to approach my college applications. She responded by inviting me into her classroom every day after school that fall so we could work on my personal statement for my applications, as well as any other essays I needed to write for specific schools. Many years later, I still credit her with helping me get into college.

My position in my family as a first-generation student made college applications difficult, but my immigration status made filling our financial aid forms not only difficult but nearly impossible. At the time I was applying to college and filling out the Free Application for Federal Student Aid, DACA was barely a year old. I remember sitting down with my dad for about an hour a day for a whole week, trying to figure out how to fill out the student aid application, the CSS Profile, and any other financial aid forms we needed to fill out. The real kicker was, I would not discover that I could not qualify for federal or New York State financial aid until I received my financial aid package in the spring of the following year. Then again, how would I know that when all the information I received about applying to college catered to a white, middle-class audience who did not have to worry about immigration status? I was an exceptional case for my school, and because I was undocumented, I felt like I did not have an adult I could trust in the building to answer my numerous and ultra-specific questions. Despite the questions and challenges that came with applying to college, I was able to submit all my applications and forms on time.

In the spring of my senior year, I was accepted to New York University's (NYU) class of 2018. NYU had been my dream school for as long as I could remember, and I greatly anticipated attending. In the months leading up to move-in day, I quickly learned about the kind of financial aid that had not been available to me because of my status. I had joined a Facebook group for students who were accepted to the university's class of 2018, and by the end of the school year, everyone had access to our financial aid packages through the university's portal. Many of my future classmates were asking about aspects of their packages that I had no idea about, such as Perkins loans,

Pell grants, and work study. This was the first time I was hearing about any of these, and I still had no idea what they were. I checked my own financial aid information on the portal, and the only thing that appeared was my scholarship. After a quick Google search, I learned that what my classmates were talking about were forms of federal student aid. After another quick Google search, I learned that I did not qualify for federal student aid. I felt like I had somehow been fooled. To me, DACA had been marketed as some sort of Hail Mary that would allow previously excluded undocumented immigrants to access higher education. However, access to higher education means nothing if affordability is not also addressed.

EXPERIENCES IN COLLEGE

The day I finally arrived on campus as an NYU student with my student ID in hand, I felt like I had finished a marathon, having successfully overcome countless hurdles that had been interspersed throughout. However, I had made it; I was on campus, my stuff was moved into my dorm room, and I was ready to take on college life. Or so I thought. During senior year in high school, our teachers had been very diligent about informing us that college life and college-level courses were much different than what our advanced or honors courses could prepare us for. I was now in charge of managing my own time. All 24 hours of every day. And while good grades came easy for me in high school and I rarely had to study, I had to teach myself discipline and learn what study methods were most effective for me in college. I had shared a room with my younger sister since the age of 10, and during the first week, I had to adjust to sharing a room and living space with two strangers I had never met before. Although I had only moved to Manhattan, just 2 hours from my family home on Long Island, I had to adjust to living without my family for the very first time.

My first year of college was also the year I realized I was suffering from what was termed at the time "undiagnosed depression." During my first semester, I often failed to do the assigned readings for my classes, and as a result, my class participation grades were lackluster. Although I was able to maintain a solid GPA that semester by adjusting my study habits, during my second semester, my depression became a bit more difficult to manage. My precalculus class grade suffered the most. I had been a great math student throughout middle and high school, and precalculus was supposed to be one of the easier math courses students could take if they were on a liberal arts track, which I was. Yet, the concepts did not land as firmly and as easily as they once had, and when the professor tried elaborating on the concepts he was teaching, it almost sounded like a foreign language to me. Although I knew many people were struggling in the class, my inability to understand the subject matter the first time around disappointed me and caused me to lose all motivation for doing my classwork. I would often miss lectures or recitations—a required review class, which had fewer students and weekly quizzes—because the mere thought of getting out of bed and going to class felt more like a burden than potentially failing the class did. I often neglected to do my homework because I failed to see the point of doing the work if I could not understand the material. For the first time in my life, I felt as though I was truly in danger of receiving a failing grade. I knew I needed to maintain my scholarship if I wanted to continue at NYU, and I knew a failing grade would put my scholarship in danger, yet I felt paralyzed at the thought of going to office hours to seek the help I needed.

I have a distinct memory of going to see my math professor one day during office hours, only to overhear that a few other students were already with him. Although I knew they were asking about the same exact problem from the homework that I had trouble with, I turned the corner and walked right out of the building, went back to my dorm, crawled into bed, and pulled the covers over myself in frustration. I felt embarrassed. The thought of asking for help in front of other people terrified me.

Come spring, my depression improved enough to enable me to finally ask my professor for help and for extensions on any assignments I had missed. I still felt embarrassed confiding in my professor. I remember my face getting hot and red with embarrassment, especially when he expressed his disappointment and asked why I had missed so many assignments. At the time, I still did not realize that I was depressed, and I was unable to offer him a valid reason for my falling behind besides saying, "I don't know." Thankfully, he gave me the extension and I was able to turn in many of my missed assignments. Although I eventually passed the class and was able to maintain my scholarship without going into academic probation, this experience made me feel like a failure. I could not comprehend why math, something I excelled at throughout elementary, junior high, and high school, suddenly became so difficult and demoralizing for me. That experience alone made me question whether I was cut out for higher education.

However, as the years went on, academics got easier and easier. During my sophomore year, I found a job babysitting for two different families in the city; thus, I had a source of income throughout the school year in addition to the money I saved from my summer job working at my hometown's ice cream parlor. At the end of that year, I declared my major in media culture and communications with a minor in Latino studies. I was in my wheelhouse, and I felt that I had really hit my stride. Long gone were the days of missed math assignments. I also learned that natural light, something I had little access to in my dark freshman dorm, hugely contributed to minimizing my depression. However, the following year Donald Trump was elected president of the United States, and as someone who had been paying attention to immigration policy since at least the age of 10, I knew this did not bode well for me or my family. Luckily, this time I was able to recognize when I was falling into a depression again, and although I was still undiagnosed at the time, I knew how to handle my symptoms and was able to greatly minimize their impact on my life, especially in comparison to the first time.

By the time I began my fourth and final year at NYU, I had already renewed my DACA once and would renew again immediately after my upcoming graduation. I arrived on campus that year excited about the classes I would be taking and ready to begin planning the next few steps after graduation. I had a great dorm with a fantastic view, wonderful roommates, and great friends, and one of my cousins had just moved to the city for his first year of college at a neighboring school uptown. Everything seemed to be coming up Mayra—that is, until I had my first class. That morning, President Trump announced that he would be ending the DACA program. I felt as though the universe was playing some sort of sick joke on me. While my peers were focused on ensuring that they met all their graduation requirements and the semester's deadlines, I also had to worry about whether or not I would even be in the country after graduation. My first week back was suddenly filled with phone calls with my dad about what a potential end to DACA meant for me, as well as calls with local reporters from back home who wanted to know how I felt about the news and how it would impact me and my family. With the publication of a few articles naming me as a DACA recipient, I had done the one thing I never thought I would do: I had come out to my hometown community as an undocumented immigrant.

Although everything turned out all right in the long run—a judge ordered the DACA program be reinstated with a continuation of renewals, and I was able to graduate in 4 years with an excellent GPA and an internship lined up—I know I missed out on many crucial college experiences due to my status. My dreams of studying abroad, which many of my peers at NYU had done, quickly dissipated before I could even send in an application. I found myself at a loss when it came to even trying to find an on-campus job until my final semester because I could not access work study. There were also more times than I could count when I found myself waiting for the rug to be pulled out from under me, causing everything I worked so hard for since kindergarten to slip right through my fingers. Being a first-generation college student is difficult enough, especially as I was unable to turn to my parents for specific advice or knowledge about how to navigate the higher education space. However, being an undocumented first-generation student from a low-income background felt like trying to play pickup soccer with Lionel Messi. Yet, despite the challenges and the disappointments, I know I would not be where I am today without my college education. I only wish it had been a little easier for me.

CONTRIBUTORS TO MY SUCCESS

There were many major and minor contributors to my success throughout college. My AP English teacher is one of the first people who comes to mind. Without her, I would not have been able to refine my numerous college essays well enough to make a good application. She was even able to clarify the application process for me as we worked together after school in her classroom.

Also, although I did not have a super strong relationship with my guidance counselor, her encouragement during our scheduled check-ins to talk about college helped me realize that I was definitely capable of being accepted by a top-tier school. NYU had been my dream school for as long as I could remember, but through most of high school, it had felt like a reach school to me. However, I experienced two key moments with my guidance counselor: First, when we created a list of schools that I would apply to. These schools included reach schools, safety schools, and match schools. I told her I was interested in NYU, and she responded by putting it in the match category, signaling to me that she thought I was more than capable of getting into a school that I thought I would have trouble getting into.

The second moment came at the end of my senior year, about a month out from May 1, which is otherwise known as college decision day. I had been accepted to two schools—NYU and SUNY Stony Brook, a state school only a 40-minute drive from my hometown. With the scholarships I had received from both schools, the cost of attendance would be about equal. I had a meeting with my guidance counselor to talk through my options and how to go about making such a monumental decision. She assured me that while Stony Brook was a fantastic school and that it was wonderful that I had gotten in, she felt I could truly blossom at NYU; that was exactly the push I needed to choose NYU.

In college, many of my professors contributed to my success. They were instrumental in their passion for the subjects they taught or in the way they structured their lectures and classes to make them engaging and interesting. One professor in particular taught two of my Latino studies courses. For one of her classes, we had to work on a final research project about a specific topic and its impact on Latinos in the U.S. The class size was small, only about 10 people. She was able to create a space in which we felt safe to ask questions, voice our opinions, and even talk about how the 2016 election affected us and our families. I decided to write my final research project on DACA: both its positive impact on recipients and how it falls short of truly comprehensive immigration policy. Not only did my professor help me feel confident enough to write about the subject as someone with lived experience, but she also created a safe space for me to come out to my class as a DACA recipient.

There are countless other people who played a role in my success. My partner supported me, especially when I had a tough time during my freshman year. My best friend provided much-needed respites from studying and would insist we walk through the East Village in search of treats. I also credit my junior year study group for my success in my two intro classes to media culture and communications. Other contributors to my success include the two families I babysat for, who continued to encourage me throughout the years, especially one of the mothers, who was Puerto Rican and understood some of the challenges I had faced on the road to college and the difficulties I was facing during college. I especially attribute my success to my parents, who always challenged me while also supporting me throughout school. However, if I were to write a list of every single person who contributed to my success, I would end up writing an entire book of names. When people say it takes a village, they are not lying.

ROLE OF FAMILY

My family provided as much support as they were able to, given that the college application process was completely foreign to them. Not only was I the oldest of my parents' two children, but my parents and I were all first-generation immigrants. Although they both had some level of college education from El Salvador, they had absolutely no experience with college in the United States. I do not even think I ever explained to them the difference between a public and a private university.

When it came time to apply, it really was just me, a computer keyboard, and my English teacher hashing out essay after essay. I involved my parents in the process when it came time to fill in our financial aid information, requiring our tax documents, which occurred about halfway through the process once all my essays were finished. They did not present many, if any, hardships during the process, and I suspect part of that is because they did not really know much about what the process entailed. Overall, I felt that they trusted me to make this big decision without needing much of their input. They had seen the work I had put into my education, practically from the day I started kindergarten. In addition, they knew that I was capable of making an informed decision about what was next for me after high school. My parents and my sister provided as much emotional support as possible, from the moment I began looking at college all the way through to graduation and move-out day. I know I would not be where I am today without their support.

TIPS AND ADVICE

There are three big pieces of advice to offer based on my experience. First, understand and know what you like outside of school and see how you can apply that interest to your academics. The beauty of higher education is that the scope of knowledge expands beyond English, science, math, and social studies. I applied to college thinking I would study something in the science field because I particularly enjoyed chemistry class in high school. However, I found out that math became very difficult for me, and I knew I would not enjoy going through those challenges for the next 4 years. I then looked at a list of majors and saw one that was media culture and communications. I looked at the classes related to the major and saw that a lot of them related to television, film, and internet culture, which happened to be three things that I had been really interested in throughout my life. Yes, the world needs scientists and mathematicians, but it also needs writers, artists, and communicators. Therefore, do not base your decision regarding your major solely on what classes you liked in high school, but take stock of the activities you enjoy outside of the academic setting.

The second piece of advice is to drop the class. If you are not feeling the class, the professor, or the courseload within the first week of classes, drop the class and swap it for a different one. Schools always have a "shopping period" during the first few weeks, in a process I liken to shopping for clothes. You get to pick and choose which courses and professors you would like to take, bring them with you into the changing room, and try them on to see if they are a fit. Although every major has its own requirements for graduation, with a few core classes that must be taken, chances are there are multiple professors teaching that precalculus class. If the teaching style of one professor does not seem like a fit to you, try out a different professor. When you try on clothes, you want to end up buying clothes that will fit and will last a long time in your wardrobe. The same could be said for the classes you take in college. You are ultimately paying for them, so you want to make sure you get as much as you can from each of them. There were multiple times throughout college when I dropped a course because it did not fit into my schedule, the workload was too much when added to that of my other classes, or the professor was not a fit for me and my academic needs. The "shopping period" exists for a reason, and you should feel free to take advantage of it so you can make your college experience the best it can be for you.

My final piece of advice is to know that you do not have to do everything alone. It truly does take a village, and that is exactly what I and many of my friends who were first-generation students or students from low-income backgrounds reflect on every time we look back on our educational journeys and career paths. Although I could not use my parents and family as a resource for information when applying to college or for help with choosing classes or a major, they provided the support and love that I needed to get me through the challenges that I faced throughout college. I cannot even begin to count the number of times a warm meal was waiting for me when I came home for the weekend or a break from school nor describe how much comfort that food provided. When I needed practical help, I knew I had others in my corner who I could turn to: my English teacher, my guidance counselor, one of my Latino studies professors, my study group friends, my partner. They all contributed not only to my success but also to my ability to thrive. Being a first-generation student can feel isolating from start to finish, but it does not have to be. I can guarantee you that the rich, white, legacy students at Harvard, Yale, and all the other predominantly white institutions do not get into those schools on their own. So, find your village and make sure you take care of one another.

CHAPTER 23

Kallie Clark, MSW, PhD
Educator and Researcher

My undergraduate experience was neither quick nor smooth, and for years I considered my rocky road through college as a deficit. I saw every stumble and struggle as a reflection of my inability to succeed in college. It was not until years later, when I became a college counselor—and had to reflect on my own experiences as a college student—that I realized my struggles in college were not a reflection of my ability to do well but of the challenging circumstances I experienced as a young person. This shift in perspective changed everything and filled me with a confidence that I had lacked for far too long. I realized that being a first-generation college graduate from a lower-income family could be an asset. My early challenges provided me with valuable insights into some of the obstacles my students face on their road to college success. After teaching and counseling for many years, I decided I wanted to use my experiences to improve the education outcomes of students beyond the walls of my own classroom.

Currently, I am a researcher at the Institute for Health Policy Studies at the University of California, San Francisco. I received my PhD in social service administration from the University of Chicago, where I was an Institute of Education Sciences Predoctoral Fellow. After graduate school I joined the Hope Center for College, Community, and Justice at Temple University, where I studied food and housing insecurity and access to mental health services among college students. Before graduate school, I wore many different hats, some more glamorous than others. I cleaned houses, changed diapers, served coffee, and sold flowers on the side of the road. My first full-time job, after completing a master of fine arts from the School of The Art Institute of Chicago, was teaching art courses at a charter high school. For 5 years I taught multiple subjects, including studio arts, digital arts, AP psychology, and summer school math and humanities courses. I then applied for a position as the school's founding college counselor and was hired. I have since published a college guide, taught graduate-level statistics courses at the University of Chicago, and produced my own podcast. Each of my experiences taught me something about myself or the world around me.

APPLYING TO AND PREPARING FOR COLLEGE

While my more affluent friends were taking SAT prep classes, I was trying my best to ignore the life of poverty that I thought was waiting for me on the other side of high school. Although I had little expectation of attending college, I enjoyed my high school courses and would have made a good candidate for college admissions. I graduated high school with a 3.54 cumulative GPA, took multiple honors and advanced placement courses, was deeply involved in music and the performing arts, and served as president of multiple clubs, and yet no one ever talked to me about applying to college. Needless to say, I had zero guidance when the time came.

My mother had been raised to think that college was only for rich people's children. She would tell me that "college is for doctors' and lawyers' kids." When I once asked her about applying to college, her eyes became teary and she snapped out a reply: "Don't you think I would love to send you to college? If I could, I would." The devastation I felt at watching my mother express her sense of powerlessness at her inability to offer me what more privileged parents could offer their children kept me from ever asking about college again. I did attend a handful of information sessions hosted by college representatives, but I could not imagine how I could ever come up with the cost of attendance, which could be $30,000, $40,000, or even $50,000. So I did the only thing I could do: I ignored it. I wanted to go to college, but no one had ever told me I *could* go to college.

Eventually, near the end of my senior year, a friend's mother convinced me to walk into the admissions office at the only 4-year university in the city of Sacramento—Sacramento State University—and apply for admission. As I sat in the admissions office waiting for my name to be called, I was convinced I would not be accepted. I imagined the first question out of the admissions officer's mouth would be about whether or not I could afford tuition. I, of course, would have to say no. His face would then sour with annoyance—exasperated that I had wasted his time—and he would ask me to leave. Those fears could not have been further from the reality. Transcripts in hand, I was admitted on the spot. The admissions officer was dumbfounded that no one had talked to me about applying to college. Given my high school GPA and financial situation, I received enough aid in state and federal grants to fully pay my tuition. I was completely confused. Did this mean I *could* go to college? I felt a great sense of gratitude for the opportunity to attend Sacramento State (Sac State), and at the same time, somewhere in the back of my mind, I also felt cheated out of what might have been.

EXPERIENCES IN COLLEGE

I attended Sac State for my first 3 years of college and then transferred to California State University (CSU) Fullerton to complete my degree. I fell in love with experimental psychology and received some of the best research methods training to date from the faculty in the Psychology Department at Sac State. Two of the most impactful courses I took were Logic and Reasoning, and Advanced Research Methods. Logic and Reasoning proved to be essential in training me to form sound arguments and avoid many of the errors in reasoning so many of us, especially college students, regularly encounter. Advanced Research Methods and Statistics required me to learn to code in Unix and interpret and summarize results for academic journals. While this was as difficult as it sounds, the course prepared me for the level of work I would encounter in graduate school.

One of the more unexpected challenges I faced early in college was coming to terms with how devastatingly underprepared I was in the mechanics of writing. I was a talented storyteller and poet, but those gifts did not help me attain the level of academic writing I needed to succeed in college. During my first semester, every paper I wrote came back laden with red marks. I was mortified. I knew I needed help. I now know that college campuses have academic support services specifically for students struggling with writing, but as a freshman in college, I had no expectations that a college would offer such support. My high school did not have a writing center, so why would I expect my college to have one?

Although students are often informed about academic services during orientation, I do not remember attending or even being informed about orientation at either of the CSU campuses I attended. Because I still carried a fear that I did not belong on campus, and that any mistake could mean being found out as a fraud and thrown out of school, I ultimately went to a place where I could seek help without having to disclose to strangers that I was struggling academically: the library. I checked out guides on grammar and APA formatting and applied myself to learning common college-level vocabulary. This self-learning approach was difficult and nauseating at times, but the payoff in skill development was enormous. Improving my writing allowed my papers to be critiqued based on the merit of their content rather than their mechanical problems.

Whereas I struggled with the formal aspects of essay writing in my small classes, I excelled in my large lecture classes, where many of my exams were in multiple-choice format. I was an incredibly disciplined student who attended lectures regularly, completed all required readings, and made study guides for myself. In these classes, I only needed to recall the information covered in the lecture or reading without also having to overcome the added barrier of language mechanics and spelling.

I did well academically in my freshman and sophomore years, but I was socially isolated. I worked nearly full time, which left little time for building friendships on campus. During my 3 years at Sac State, I never attended a single on-campus activity. Peers are a great source of knowledge of campus resources, and living and working off campus really put me at a disadvantage in that respect. I eventually did meet a small group of students when I began working at a café closer to campus, but our interactions were exclusively outside of school. I needed support more than ever when I was struck a devastating blow.

CONTRIBUTORS TO MY SUCCESS

When I was in my last year of undergraduate studies at Sac State, I failed out of school. Working 30 hours a week and going to school full time left me exhausted. I was barely holding things together when I was sexually assaulted by an acquaintance. I became anxious and found myself in a deep depression. I sought counseling and tried medication. I did everything I could to keep working toward my goal of earning my degree, but in the end my efforts felt as futile as trying to spin straw into gold. I was overwhelmed with the idea that I was failing at an opportunity that meant so much to me and my family. After all the time and effort I had put into my education, the thought of getting so close to the reality of graduation and then failing was devastating.

I knew I needed to start a life in which I could focus on school and school alone. I transferred to CSU Fullerton, yet I carried with me the fear that I would fail again. I poured myself into school. I had hopes of going to graduate school, but I was terrified that someone would find out that I had failed my last year at Sac State—that they would see *me* as a failure and that everything I had worked toward would fall apart yet again.

Although I did end up finishing my bachelor's degree, my education would have stopped there if not for my biological psychology instructor, Professor Meg White. She exposed me to the secrets of the mind and encouraged me to pursue my PhD. She was also the first person who told me I would make a good researcher. She once told me I was a "bright rat"—the best compliment I had ever received. She spurred my confidence. Although it took me a long while to make it to my doctoral studies, I credit her with fostering in me a belief that I could be successful.

ROLE OF FAMILY

My success in college did not happen due to my efforts alone. I may not have been born into a family that could provide me with a lot of guidance or financial support, but I always knew they were fully confident in my ability to succeed. My mother, in particular, was incredibly proud of my attending a 4-year college. That pride pushed me to keep going even when failure seemed inevitable. The greatest gift my mother ever gave me was my commitment to thinking outside of the box.

When I found myself unable to complete school at Sac State, I found a new way to succeed. I transferred to Cal State Fullerton, where I had a strong network of friends whom I had met through the theater world in Sacramento. We lived in the same apartment complex, and in many ways these friends functioned like an extended family. I could not have made it through college without the support and love of this beautiful group of people. They connected me to resources, normalized my struggles, and provided a type of stability I had missed out on in my early college years.

Circumstances in my family life also made it difficult for me to succeed in college. At the time, my sister was homeless and my brother was fighting multiple felony charges. I was watching my siblings' lives being torn apart and my mother's expectations for their future burned to ashes. Additional challenges that came with being a first-generation college student made my success even more difficult. I heeded my mother's (misguided) warnings against acquiring student loans and debt. Little did she know that not taking student loans would mean having to work full time—thus adding years to my college journey.

However, when I needed my family, they came through in a way I never could have imagined. When I moved to Chicago to pursue my master's degree, I found myself with an $18,000 bill. I was desperate. I did anything and everything I legally could to get that money, including being an egg donor, but I was still $10,000 short. My mother had been injured in an automobile accident and was unable to work. My stepfather was a grocery store clerk. They did not have much money. My prospects seemed incredibly bleak when I received a phone call from my mother. My parents had refinanced their house so they could get me the money I needed. This is not something that every parent can do or would do even if they could. Yet, they made it happen. That money made graduate school a reality for me. They came through when I needed them most.

TIPS AND ADVICE

There are so many obstacles that can present themselves along the way to earning your college degree. Lord knows there were more than I ever could have foreseen. I cannot boil my experience down into a few nuggets of advice, but I will share some recommendations I have given to my own students. First, whether you are used to getting straight As in your high school writing assignments or whether you are worried your writing will not be up to par, please visit the writing center before you turn in your first paper. You may find you do not need any help at all, or you may receive the help you need to keep from failing your first semester. Either way, you have nothing to be embarrassed about in seeking help. It is not anyone else's job to gauge the extent to which you deserve to be on campus. An admissions officer already did that, and they admitted you. Now it is your job to use every resource available to help you be successful.

Go to office hours at least once for every course you take. If you need help, please go as often as needed until you are back on track. As a college instructor, I can tell you that attending office hours sends a strong message that you take the class seriously and are willing to put in the effort needed to succeed. College grading is ridiculously subjective, and if you are on the cusp between an F and a D or an A and a B, attending office hours could tip the scales in your favor. Also, one day you may need to ask for a letter of recommendation for graduate school, internship, or employment. Building relationships with your professors is key to securing good quality letters. I can say without any doubt that I would not have been admitted to my PhD program if it were not for the tenacious advocacy of a faculty mentor of mine.

Finally, it is okay to be embarrassed. It is okay to be scared. As a first-generation college student, there may be many times you find yourself embarrassed or scared. You need to be bigger than your embarrassment; you need to be stronger than your fears. Allow yourself to feel embarrassed or feel afraid, then put on your boss hat and do what you need to do. Seek out the help or advice you need. Most likely people will be understanding and helpful. If they are not, that's on them, not you.

I remember one moment in an undergraduate course when the professor made an ill-spirited joke that if we did not do well in her class we would end up bagging groceries for the rest of our lives. The class laughed, but I did not. My stepfather was a grocery store clerk. I had a choice: I could let the words and the laughter of this professor make me feel less than deserving to sit in her classroom, or I could be bigger than my embarrassment and stronger than my fear. I raised my hand and explained to the professor that my stepfather had worked 30+ years as a grocery clerk to take care of his family and that I was proud of his hard work. I explained that he did not have the same opportunity as I did to attend a 4-year college. The professor's face went red. Obviously she had never expected the child of a grocery store clerk to be sitting in her class. By confronting her assumptions, and by giving voice to my experiences, I turned a moment that could have done great harm to my academic identity into a moment of empowerment: a lesson that has served me well ever since.

CHAPTER 24

Dawna Jones, MEd, MSW
Director, Mary Lou Williams Center for Black Culture at Duke University

As the director of the Mary Lou Williams Center for Black Culture at Duke University, I provide leadership and strategic visioning to the Mary Lou team to carry out the center's mission to foster a safe and affirming community that supports the diverse needs of Black-identified people at Duke University. Under the "student engagement" umbrella of student affairs at Duke University, I partner with student affairs departments, faculty members, campus and community members, alumni, and current students to offer programming, training, and community connections. I see my job as an opportunity to create a safe and welcoming space that allows members of our Black community to be fully authentic and enthusiastically supported.

For the past 12 years, I have been working in various capacities in student affairs in higher education. I chose student affairs as a profession because I never wanted to leave college. For me, college was a place of self-discovery, of finding my people, and of feeling confident and challenged, and, most importantly, it was where I felt like the best version of myself. I felt like this even in the midst of some of the hardest times of my life and despite all my shortcomings. College is where I learned how to ask for help and where I found the people who made me feel grounded and understood. It was a transformative experience for me, and I never wanted it to end. Therefore, I chose the profession that would help me stay as close to that experience as possible for as long as I could make it last.

In my first position out of graduate school, I found myself in a role that required more crisis management than I felt equipped to appropriately handle. This experience motivated me to take a few classes in the School of Social Work at the university I was working for during that time. In one of those classes, I found an additional passion and a professional home in social work. Social work felt, and still feels, like a calling for me. The social work code of ethics is so closely aligned to my personal values that I often wonder how I did not find my way to the profession sooner and more intentionally.

APPLYING TO AND PREPARING FOR COLLEGE

College was not optional for me. The question surrounding college was never a matter of whether I would go, only a matter of where I would be accepted. My mother never completed college herself, and maybe because of that she had high expectations of me. There was never a point when I thought I could decide not to go to college. There was also never a point when I did not want to go to college; college was just part of the plan. I was always excited by the idea of college, starting with my obsession with the television show *A Different World*.

Despite college having always been in my sights, I knew very little about the collegiate experience and the process of applying to schools. All I really knew was that I did not want to attend one in my home state. I wanted very much to get away from my hometown and branch out as far as I could. I had seen so many people from my neighborhood remain in the same place for their entire lives. I wanted to take every opportunity to get away and not look back. I stayed true to that mentality; I never moved back home after college, even though it would have been the financially expedient thing to do. As I reflect on the amount of student debt I accumulated, and knowing what I know now, I would probably make a different decision. Regardless, I wanted badly to do something that had not been done before. More than that, I wanted the chance to reinvent myself, to be in a place where no one knew who I was "supposed" to be. I wanted to shed the identities and assumptions that were thrust upon me of being a bully's easy target, or a spoiled Catholic schoolgirl, "Miss Think She's Smart," or so-and-so's little cousin/sister/best friend. I constantly felt misunderstood and misperceived, and I could not name it at the time but I was absolutely ready for the opportunity to decide who I wanted to be with nothing more than "Jersey girl" as a general point of reference for strangers.

In addition to the general lack of information that most first-generation students have when preparing for college, I also had the issue of being an incredibly stubborn person in my late teens, which meant that even if I had people I could ask for help, I seldom drew on them as resources. I had no idea what was important or what to take into consideration when I started to apply for schools. I certainly did not understand enough about the process to consider what types of colleges or universities would be the right fit for my needs. I really did not understand that "fit" was something I should be thinking about, nor had I assessed what my academic, social, or financial needs were in relation to the collegiate process. No one told me to consider whether I was the "large college" or "small college" type. I did not know to think about urban versus rural campuses nor public versus private. I did not consider the impact of choosing a predominantly white university over a historically Black college. "Fit" was not a term I could have defined then, but of course I now know that it encompasses all of these considerations and more.

As a result of my lack of knowledge, I applied to a completely random mix of institutions within a 3–6-hour driving distance from my hometown. I had not considered the differences between large or small schools, public or private, who might offer funding for low-income or first-gen students, or any of the important characteristics I advise students whom I support to think about. Looking back, what I remember most about the process is that I did not really know what to look for in a school. I chose most of the schools I applied to based on their name or their location. I applied to many of what I deemed at the time "name brand" schools. Those schools included the Pennsylvania State University and Howard University. I visited a few campuses—not as intentional college tours but more as opportunities to visit the few friends I had in college at the time. Although I did not apply to any of them, visiting them helped me to realize that I was indeed ready to leave for school. Ultimately, I ended up attending a university that I had not visited, which was approximately 3 hours from my hometown: Pennsylvania State University (PSU) in University Park. I wish I could say why I ended up choosing PSU, but I am unsure even as I reflect on it today. I did not know anyone who was planning to attend when I applied. It was a random choice—maybe a gut feeling. I knew the places I had seen were not where I wanted to be; those short visits may have been fun, but they did not make me want to stay. Although I do not know why I ended up at PSU, I am glad I went there. It turned out to be the right decision in every way except financially. The debt is my only regret.

EXPERIENCES IN COLLEGE

College was a mix of good, bad, and very challenging experiences for me. I had a great group of friends, mostly from the tristate area, whom I connected with early on through a friend I had known before I left New Jersey. I count myself lucky to have made that connection before I got to Pennsylvania in the spring semester, because by that point many people in my classes and residence hall had already developed their friend groups. The friends I made during that year are people I have remained connected to over the past 20 years. Many of us were first-generation students and/or from low-income households, and we pooled our knowledge to help fill in the gaps of navigating the college experience. This group of friends is what I remember most about college and was the most positive part of my time there. They would also play an important role in some of my worst times there.

My financial challenges persisted from my first year to my last, creating an angst that often distracted me from classes and extracurricular experiences, but the more consequential and least pleasant part of college for me was the depression I experienced. I managed depressive symptoms late into my sophomore year until my senior year, when I lived off campus. I recall many days when I was supposed to be in class or at work and instead remained in my dorm room in tears for no apparent reason. Fortunately, and unfortunately, a few of my close friends were having a similar experience and symptoms. There were days we did not leave our living spaces, but we kept each other safe through physical proximity because we knew we would not harm ourselves if we were together. Some days we coped with music, sharing playlists with one another and comparing our taste in music. Other times we coped by talking about what we were feeling, usually nodding in agreement about the difficulty of getting out of bed, remembering to eat, and rarely having the energy to shower or go outside for fresh air. Most times, it was just a group of three or four of us just sitting on the floor trying to make it through the day. Those days on the floor truly saved my life. That group of friends is one I still speak to frequently in my adulthood, and none of us have forgotten how we got each other through those dark times.

I was so depressed in my senior year that I slept through most of my days and hardly left my bedroom. I rarely attended my classes and performed poorly when I was present. The rubber met the road when I slept through a final exam and failed a required anthropology course. I do not recall contacting the professor to tell them what happened. I assume that my professor thought that I was unfocused or experiencing "senioritis," but I do not recall my professor ever asking what was causing my spotty attendance. I accepted my F and later retook the class, but if I knew then what I know now, I would have made my way to a case manager or academic dean for an intervention. However, at the time I could barely muster the energy to shower or eat, let alone advocate for myself to a complete stranger. I cannot be sure that it would have made a difference at that late juncture, but at the time I did not know such resources existed. I knew of the counseling center, which I did attend from time to time and did not find particularly helpful. My roommates knew what I was going through, but I do not think they knew any more than I did that resources were available that I could have turned to before failing that class.

CONTRIBUTORS TO MY SUCCESS

As a low-income student, I had many financial challenges that affected my ability to fully focus on my studies. These financial issues were most prevalent in my first year, and I acknowledge that before leaving for school I had not fully understood the depth of the financial constraints that my mother was under. Not long into my first semester, I received a notice from housing letting me know that I was in danger of losing my housing assignment if my past due bill was not covered within a few days. A friend who lived in my hall connected me with the staff at the Student Support Services Program (SSSP), a federal TRIO program. I credit that team for so much but especially for keeping me in school by helping me complete the right forms to get additional aid and cover my past due bill. After I received the financial assistance, I spent a lot of time with the SSSP team and went to them for everything from financial aid advice to academic support to support navigating the predominantly white institution whose bureaucracy I had, at times, not known how to manage. The director of that program, Dr. Audrey Kharem, became a counselor to both me and my mother. Dr. Kharem would often talk with my mom about how to support me when she had no idea how to be supportive through specific woes I was managing.

Academically, I had great professors throughout my time at PSU. Two faculty members in particular were pivotal in my success for different reasons. My first sociology class was taught by a vibrant and gregarious older professor whom I credit for being the reason I later chose sociology as my major. He drew me in with interesting concepts and encouraged me to ask questions, a behavior I had often been admonished for in high school. In encouraging me to ask questions and listening to my answers, this professor validated my ideas and inquiries and allowed me to embrace my interests in human nature and behavior in a way I had never felt comfortable doing before. He later invited me to be a teaching assistant for his course—my first foray into working in higher education.

A professor who taught a research course for seniors was also a contributor to my success. What I remember most about the course was his feedback on a paper that I was struggling with. I was frustrated that I could not seem to grasp the quantitative methods that we were supposed to apply in the course. I went to his office hours, and he told me that my "dogged pursuit to do better" was admirable and would take me places. That feedback stuck with me, even in defeat (I barely passed his class). In the same way as when elementary school teachers would tell me I was "gifted," it was the language those faculty members used that helped build my confidence even when I was not excelling. Telling me I could, encouraging me to do what came natural to me, and acknowledging my strengths in the pursuit of my dreams made me want to keep going on the days I thought I should give up. Those words made all the difference at times, because those really smart people believed I could do it and some days that was enough to convince me to keep going.

ROLE OF FAMILY

I talked to my mother a lot, probably every couple of days or so, during college. She sent care packages of snacks and socks and loving notes to remind me of her. The girls on my floors loved those care packages and looked forward to them as much as, if not more than, I did. My mother and I were close and I knew I could tell her anything without fear of judgment, but I did not always share what I was going through because I did not want her to worry. I knew that she would be proud of me no matter what, but I felt like sharing my insecurities and academic setbacks would be another burden on her in addition to the financial burden I already felt guilty about. I always felt supported by her; however, I still felt lonely because of all that I was not sharing. The rest of my family, although well-meaning, contributed mostly by adding emotional weight. I was constantly reminded of how proud I was making my mother, how smart I was, and how much my success meant to our family. These compliments were meant to be encouraging, but at times when I was not excelling academically they created additional pressure. Everyone believed that I could do this, that I was so smart, and there I was failing Econ. The fear of failure compounded all the other pressures I was experiencing. I think what I needed more than anything was someone to acknowledge that what I was doing was difficult and that it was okay if I was not "killing it" the whole time.

When I started working in higher education, I supported events like family weekend and parents' weekend. Only when I was working these types of events did I realize that I had only very rarely had visits from family members before graduation day, if I had had any at all. I recall my first family weekend as a student affairs professional and thinking to myself that I never participated in anything like that and had not recalled any of my friends doing so either. Maybe it is a memory lapse, but I do not recall even acknowledging that such a time existed, although I am sure it must have. It would have been a financial burden for my mom and other family members to come from New Jersey to University Park for a long weekend. For one, the hotel prices alone were astronomical. There were additional costs for gas, meals, activities, and time off work. It is something I could not have imagined asking them to do, nor do I think I would have seen any value in having them do so. I felt guilty enough for the financial burden I had created; I could not see myself expecting more.

TIPS AND ADVICE

Now that I work in higher education, I see many aspects of the higher educational experience that I was oblivious to as a first-generation student. I did not realize how many resources were available to help me with the challenges I struggled with most. While I knew that I had the support of trusted mentors and friends, I suffered in silence so many times when asking for help would have saved me from much turmoil. Admitting that I was too depressed to go to class at times could have helped me from failing or having to retake required courses. Explaining my financial circumstances could have possibly meant not working multiple jobs to cover my gaps. Listening to more of the advice I was given could have saved me some trouble as well, but pride can be a terrible hindrance.

The most important advice I can give you is to ask for help often and without embarrassment. Not every person or resource will be helpful, but there are a multitude of resources that exist solely to help students succeed. There is absolutely no shame in asking for help and letting people know what you need. In fact, finding out later that you suffered unnecessarily can create guilt and remorse. What I can tell you now and wish I had heard was, "You absolutely can fight this fight on your own, but you do not have to. There are people here who get paid to help you and there are others who simply do it because they care and they can. Later you will do it for others, so your debt will be repaid. Tell someone you need help, and save yourself the tears and heartache."

On a similar note, find your people. One of the best parts of the college experience, in my opinion, is that you get to build a community. College is where I met some of my best friends and had some of my most memorable experiences. Because of those friends, I made it through some of my hardest times. They were the ones who helped me see that I was not the only one struggling. They taught me lessons I could not have learned in a classroom. To this day, I am in touch with many of those same friends. We godparent each other's children, celebrate our wins, lament our losses, and reminisce about the old days as much as we can. Being a first-gen student made me feel different, and so did being Black and low-income. When I found my people, I realized that everyone has aspects about themselves or their background that make them feel different and a little insecure. Together, we got through it. I will not say that I could not have made it without them—I was dogged and would have found a way—but I am so glad that I did not have to do it alone.

CHAPTER 25   THE PATHS WE PAVE

Mytien Nguyen
MD-PhD Student

I *wasn't the first in my family to decide to go to medical school. I was the first with the opportunity.* My name is Mytien Nguyen, and I am a MD-PhD student at Yale School of Medicine. As an MD-PhD student, I am pursuing my passion in both medicine, to take care of underserved communities like mine, and science, to generate new knowledge to bring innovation to health care. The MD-PhD program is an 8- to 9-year program that is split into three phases: 2 years of medical school, 4–5 years of PhD in any discipline, and 2 more years of medical school. At the end of this training, I plan to pursue residency and postdoctoral training to become a surgeon-scientist, a position in which I will perform surgery and run my own research lab. Together, my education will total almost 20 years of medical and scientific training. In this short essay, I hope to share with you my journey, its challenges and rewards, and why it is important for more first-generation students to have the opportunity to pursue medicine.

Before we embark on this journey, I will share some personal information about myself that will help to put my story in context. I was born in Vietnam into a mixed-race family. My mom is Vietnamese and my dad is Black Vietnamese (an offspring of the Vietnam War). Neither of my parents were given the opportunity to finish high school. My mom had to quit school at grade 10 because her family could no longer afford her education. My father quit school at grade 11 due to the cumulative toll of the racism and exclusion he experienced as a Black man. College was never an option, as it was generally known that college acceptance was not possible for Blacks in Vietnam. For that reason, when a stranger approached my dad about the American Homecoming Act, an opportunity for children of Vietnam War veterans to immigrate to the United States, my parents did not hesitate to apply so they could provide an opportunity to me and my younger brother to pursue education. We uprooted our lives when I was 8 years old and resettled in Burlington, Vermont.

APPLYING TO AND PREPARING FOR COLLEGE

My experience of preparing for college began in the fifth grade. My English as a Second Language (ESL) teacher encouraged me to take and pass the state ESL test so that I could opt out of the ESL classes in middle school, which were scheduled at the same time as some honors-track classes. If I had not tested out of ESL in fifth grade, I would have, by systemic exclusion, not been on the honors track. As in most schools, students on the honors track were likely to be college-bound. My participation in the honors track exposed me to a group of peers who were focused on college preparation, including SATs, ACTs, and college visits. Thanks to these relationships with peers on the honors track, which I was only able to participate in because of the advocacy of my ESL teacher, I acquired necessary knowledge to prepare for college.

I first learned what being a first-generation student is like in freshman year of high school when we took the pre-SAT. Having been told a test was coming up that we should prepare for, I took the PSAT. When I received my score, I saw that I scored below average in all categories, whereas my peers scored in the 90th percentile. I was devastated and felt like an imposter among the other honors track students. My excitement for college was diminished and my future educational prospects seemed poor—that is, until I learned that my peers had taken Kaplan prep for the SAT. This experience taught me that despite being in the same high school classes and receiving similar grades, there would always be a gap between my classmates and me. My family could not afford Kaplan prep or any other college preparation activities. I knew then that I had to be creative, and that was when I started to pursue my own path, following my curiosity and passion for knowledge. I wanted to learn another language and came across a scholarship application to take a language class at the University of Vermont during my sophomore year. I found that I enjoyed the college class setting and applied again—this time to take Calculus I and II. I enjoyed the challenge.

With my college courses came expenses, so I worked part time as a waitress, where I also developed critical interpersonal skills I would need later on. Working part time also meant I could pay for the SAT, ACT, and SAT subject tests and apply to a greater number of colleges. When I began to apply for colleges and sat down with my advisor with my list of schools, he saw Dartmouth and Cornell and immediately told me that I should not waste my money applying to these schools. I was not the only student who was considering applying to these schools, but I was the only non-white low-income student who received this advice. Whether it was because my advisor did not think I would succeed or because I did not fit into the profile of a typical student who applied to these schools, I do not know. When I walked out of that meeting, I was devastated and doubted my aspirations more than ever. Moments later, I happened to run into one of my teachers, who asked me which schools I was applying to. I recited the list, expecting a similar dismissive attitude. However, my teacher told me that Dartmouth and Cornell had good English programs and that I should seriously consider majoring in English. That encouragement was the glimmer of hope that led me to submit applications to every school on my list.

Although high school counselors are generally knowledgeable, not every counselor will have the background and experience to work with first-generation students, and they will not always give appropriate advice. It is important to trust your gut and to pursue that dream school. It is more important to find mentors who believe in you and your dreams. Months later my first acceptance letter, from the University of Vermont, brought smiles to my parents' lips and my own. I was going to college, which is a testament to my parents' sacrifice and support. I received many rejections—including from Dartmouth. On the day of Cornell's decision release date, I logged into the application system with trembling hands, expecting a rejection. "Congratulations," I read; I read that first sentence more times than I can count. I ran into my parents' room, and before I could even say the words, I started crying. "I got into Cornell!" I managed to gasp out before I ran back to the computer to check again for the thousandth time. I was going to Cornell—me. More importantly, *we* were going to Cornell. An immigrant family, with parents who work two jobs each and were not able to graduate from high school, was enrolling in an Ivy League university.

EXPERIENCES IN COLLEGE

If undergraduate education is difficult for first-generation students, undergraduate premedical education is terrifying. The comfort that I found in the Calculus classroom at the University of Vermont did not prepare me for the challenges of premedical education at Cornell. The first courses I took as a biology major were called "weed-out" courses—courses that were extra difficult to deter students from pursuing medicine. I remember receiving my first biology exam grade—C, the class average—and crying in the lecture hall bathroom for half an hour. One month prior to this, my family had dropped me off at school. They felt so proud that their dream was finally realized in me being the first to attend college—and not just any college but an Ivy League school! But here I was, one month in and already failing. Once again, I was taken back to that feeling from high school of the gap between me and my peers. Like many other marginalized students, my success in this "equal" education opportunity was impaired by decades of resource deprivation. I quickly learned that the education structure was created with the privileged in mind and that to thrive in this structure a student must have the necessary resources, network, and financial means. Through an email, I learned about Cornell's Biology Scholars Program, which aims to create a community for marginalized students, and applied to the program in search of a community that mirrored my own. There I was able to find validation with others who had similar experiences. I also saw many of my peers transfer out of premed. These courses were truly weed-out courses, but they were disproportionately weeding out first-generation, low-income, and students of color.

For the next 2 years, I continued to struggle in pursuit of my dream of being a physician. As those struggles persisted, the impact on my mental well-being grew. Each holiday season when I would visit family, I found it hard to tell them the truth—that I was struggling mentally and that I was uncertain whether I would be able to get into medical school or even whether I would be able to graduate at all. The most devasting setback was when I received rejections from all the summer programs for premedical students that I had applied to. I had thought, *If I could not get into these programs, how could I get into medical school?* Even though I was passing my classes, I felt like a failure. During the summer, I decided to stay local and volunteered at the Somali Bantu Community Association of Vermont. Going back to the community I grew up in and revisiting my family's immigration experiences through the lenses of others helped ground me and gave me purpose. It reminded me that success is not a number—it is not one's GPA or number of leadership positions—it is doing what I love. That fall, I came back to Cornell, but not as a premedical student.

Like I had done in high school, that fall in college I stopped doing the things I thought I *should do* and started doing the things I *wanted to do*, like taking courses that were interesting to me. These courses included sociology and engineering. I fell in love with both. My sociology studies led me to be a public service scholar, where I delved into understanding community-institution relationships. My engineering studies led me to understand a whole new approach to education—one that is based on teamwork and collaboration rather than on the individual brand building of premedical education. It also brought me to research and to the excitement of creating knowledge and being on the edge of innovation.

CONTRIBUTORS TO MY SUCCESS

It takes a village, and every person needs a village of peers and faculty mentors who can facilitate one's development as a person and as a professional. For me, my mentors were pivotal in expanding my network and increasing my awareness of my own potential. It was through one of my mentors that I learned about the physician-scientist career—where I can pursue volunteerism, health equity, and research, which was a perfect fit for me. Throughout my journey, I have built up a team of mentors whom I have sought out again and again for support and advice. Mentoring fit will vary throughout the course of one's career, and the more perspective you are equipped with, the more informed your decision will be. Each time I have encountered a career decision or challenge, I have sought out the advice of more than one mentor. As a graduate student, I would seek out senior graduate students, postdoctoral fellows, and faculty for advice. It is much, much easier for me to approach my mentors now than it was for me as a college student. As a first-generation student who had "figured things out" by herself, asking for help and advice did not come naturally. However, this journey is challenging, and I would not have survived without the help and support of my many mentors.

Another important key to my journey is my almost-stubborn pursuit of my "why." My personal experiences of systemic discrimination and exclusion built a fire in me to advocate for marginalized populations. Therefore, every activity, every class, and every opportunity that I participated in was a step toward that goal; with each step, I was able to develop my "why" further. This solid foundation allows me to maintain my motivation and optimism when I encounter challenges.

I have lost count of the number of times I have failed, been rejected, or been disappointed in myself and my performance. As a first-generation college student, failure to me was akin to taking five steps back, whereas success felt like taking only one step forward. The most difficult lesson I have learned in this journey is to accept failure and fold it into my experiences—that is, to fail forward. As I began to accept failures and develop my personal approach to tame my instinctive negative responses to failures, I began to see that I grow more from my failures than from my successes. When I first started working in the lab, I failed at everything. My incompetency in the lab was horrific, so much so that I saw my graduate student mentor gradually losing respect for me. When I was back in the lab for my summer internship, I took a moment to reflect on my first lab experience and why I felt incompetent; it was due mainly to a lack of confidence in the new, unfamiliar environment I was in. To become comfortable in the lab space, I started by going into the lab at night when no one was around. Being in the space by myself allowed me to gradually make the space my own, and with that came a confidence that eventually led to my independence in the lab.

ROLE OF FAMILY

When I called my parents to share my failures, the first thing they would say is that if it was too difficult I could come home. It broke my heart every time I would hear this. My family is a big part of my why. This journey is not my journey but our journey. The only reason I am here is because my parents made that sacrifice to leave everything they knew to come to a foreign land and culture. My motivation to go into medicine was due to the health injustices that my family had to navigate. I see my family in every community I work with and in every patient I treat.

I am aware that as parents, my mother and father hated to see their children struggle in new, unfamiliar environments. My family is my support network, a sanctuary that will always provide shelter no matter where I am, regardless of my success or failure. Although I feel like I can share anything with them, there were many times that I held back because I did not want them to worry. I have realized that the instinct to not share with my family is the same instinct that prevented me from seeking mentors—a hesitation to burden others. Over the years, as my parents become more knowledgeable, partly through watching me and my brother vent with each other about some of the challenges we have experienced, I have come to share more and more with my parents, which has strengthened my support network.

TIPS AND ADVICE

My story is one of many that you will read, and I would like to impart some general thoughts that I wish someone had told me earlier in my training:

Be kind to yourself. You have worked hard to get to where you are, and you will undoubtedly continue to work hard, even if you do not necessarily perceive it as hard work. There will be mistakes, missteps, and failures, and it is so easy to internalize them. Often, these failures are external, created by a system that you have no control over and that was created to keep the poor poor. Every success you have is a step toward dismantling that system, and each one should be celebrated.

Keep an open line of communication with your support network. It really takes a village. As a first-generation student navigating earlier paths by myself, I developed an independence that served me well at times but that also presented a challenge when I needed to ask for help. It was not until medical school that I began opening up to my parents about my experiences, and the resulting support was wonderful. This goes for your peer mentors, faculty mentors, and friends as well. It is okay to talk about your challenges, to be vulnerable to those you trust, and to let them support you as you would have undoubtedly done for them.

Pursue your *path, not the path you think you* should *pursue.* Like so many other career paths, the premedical education path was created by non-first-generation individuals for non-first-generation students. As a first-generation student, this path may not be the best one for you. If you are like me and have failed trying to follow such a path, your failure is reflective of the program itself and not your competence as a future physician. Craft your own path. It may be completely novel, or it may be based on the paths of other first-generation college students in medicine.

CHAPTER 26

Sean Richardson
Pursuing Master's in Higher Education Administration

I am a current graduate student at Boston College studying higher education administration. I never thought I would be the one to say that, but here I am. I have been working in higher education since my first year as an undergraduate, when I worked as an office assistant in residential life before quickly becoming a resident assistant (RA), where I became more involved in my campus community. My experiences as a first-generation undergraduate student directly inform my work in higher education and have produced in me a strong desire to improve the system for other first-generation college students.

APPLYING TO AND PREPARING FOR COLLEGE

In high school, I found myself existing in a kind of limbo in terms of how I saw myself intellectually. I was the type of student that my teachers saw potential in, but I would simply not "deliver" every time. I would get nervous in the classroom. I was often too nervous to participate in class or too anxious to read aloud. I was afraid that I would not know a word or how to pronounce it in the sentence. I existed with that anxiety for all 4 years of high school. I always felt as though I did not belong in the honors classes, but my family pushed and fought so that I would be placed in them.

I was in a college prep program: Upward Bound at Rhode Island College. I saw my friends involved in a similar program and thought I should be on par with them; however, I had no idea of the commitment it would take. Although I successfully made it through the application and interview process, in my first semester in the program I adjusted poorly. I had to take the bus from my little home in Pawtucket on Saturday mornings before the sun was up in order to make it on time. I hated waking up early on the weekends, so I would show up late. I hated having extra homework for the Saturday academic classes, so I "half-assed" it on Friday nights. My behavior caught up with me, and I was called into a meeting to address it. I was asked if I really wanted to be a part of the program and whether I had what it took to be an Upward Bound scholar. Fifteen-year-old me had an attitude, but as the conversation went on, I was reminded of the other students who were not accepted into the program and did not have the opportunities I was receiving. This admonishment stuck with me. I felt like it was destiny and that I belonged there for multiple reasons—one of them being my commitment to my own educational goals. I internalized that feeling of being empowered to control my own destiny, and it changed my focus. I eventually went on to get a scholarship from Upward Bound, which helped me tremendously in the first year of my college career.

In the summer before my senior year, I found myself with a Google doc in front of me titled "College Essay, draft 7." I had written seven drafts of my college essay. By this time, I was 17 and had internalized the idea of always being excellent in my academics. Each essay draft was about something different: One was about losing my mother at 9 years old, another was about having an absent father, another one was about having an unconventional family dynamic, and yet another was about just existing as a Black student. My peers thought I was being ridiculous, but whenever I felt a spurt of creativity, I went to my computer and began writing another college essay. It felt wrong to sell my trauma, but "that's how people like us get into college," one of my peers mentioned. I was sold; I had figured out the game. I picked the essay that talked about the most traumatic thing that had ever happened to me, and with that, submitted my college application to 13 schools.

As I continued my search and received acceptances and denials, different factors popped up. Lack of funding was a major factor that deterred me from pursuing admission to certain colleges. Soon enough, I realized that location was a second factor. I chose Providence College based on proximity and funding. There was a notion that you had made it once you left Rhode Island, but stepping onto that campus felt like leaving behind everything I knew did not matter.

EXPERIENCES IN COLLEGE

I took my first steps onto the campus at Providence College as a full-fledged college student in July 2016. I was there as a Friar Foundations Student. I owe this program my life. Friar Foundations is a 6-week summer bridge program designed to help "at-risk" students. I was invited to the program in my admissions letter and found it similar to the summer academy for Upward Bound. I was once again going to miss out on summer with my friends. There were 25 of us there that summer living in a residence hall, taking classes, participating in programming, and ultimately, just living the college life—or what we thought it would be. My mentor was also an English major, but he was a senior. He worked with me to help prepare me socially and academically for college. The program was incredibly racially diverse. I felt seen and heard. I was taking three courses and, frankly, taking full advantage of this free opportunity. By the time the school year started, I had solidified my relationships with my friends and the campus community. And then everyone else came.

The first anxiety attack I ever had was in my campus dining hall during fall orientation in late August, after the summer program ended. I had walked through the dining hall, and my rose-colored glasses were shattered. I did not see a single person who looked like me. This would serve as a precursor to my experience in college.

Classes felt like a whirlwind. I was an English major, but in most of my classes I felt behind somehow. I had trouble understanding why I felt behind until I realized that it was just the nature of the game for someone like me. I was a first-generation college student, and I began to understand that feeling behind was as natural as breathing. I was not the only one; my friends from similar communities who were also first-generation felt the same way.

I made it to the second semester, thankfully, and continued with my English major until I had this one professor. The class was a writing and film class, and I was super excited about it until I got feedback on my first paper. I was told, "I do not understand a word you're saying." A lot of my identity up to that point was being a talented writer, as I was often told I was. I had gone to his office hours, read the text more closely, and still he said he could not grade any of my papers because, he said, "I can't understand what you're saying." I visited his office hours one last time to try to understand what was going wrong. He asked me my major, and when I told him it was English he made a face that convinced me to switch it. I left his office for the last time, disappointed and frustrated—not with myself but with him. On my way out of the English Department, I ran into another professor who suggested I keep the minor and take classes exclusively within it. I still loved writing and reading, so I kept the minor.

A lot of my challenges were social ones. I did not understand people being wealthy while also being in the same space as me. My first time recognizing this tension was when I was a second-semester freshman. Someone asked me and my best friend of 15 years, who grew up in the same community, where we vacationed. We simply looked at each other and laughed, but this kind of occurrence would continue to be an issue in my experience. He and I did not have the money to vacation anywhere but Pawtucket. We explained to this person that we went home. This experience helped me to see how traditional whiteness carried weight in a way I would simply never understand, no matter how smart I got.

I spread myself too thin in my first year of college. I had a club meeting every night. I was applying to be an RA. I was the vice president of my class. I was a very busy freshman. I wanted to find community with other Black students, but I also wanted to let everyone know I was actively looking to make a contribution to campus. As I spread myself thinner and thinner, I needed to stay up later and later to do homework. I found myself struggling to finish meals without thinking about my next move. I found it difficult to live in the moment.

As I moved through the higher education system, I began to realize that not only were there issues with diversity, equity, and inclusion, but that the system itself was not meant for someone like me—a Black, first-generation student. However, if there was not a space, I was determined to make one.

CONTRIBUTORS TO MY SUCCESS

What contributed to my success was the sheer motivation of being the first one. In the back of my mind there always existed this idea that I would be stronger on the other side. I believed that everything I went through would ultimately be worth it in the end. Along with my motivation for coming out on the other side with a degree, I think the community around me played a major role in my success. At a school like Providence, all the students of color stuck together as a means of survival. In the face of oppression, we stood our ground in our numbers. When it came to my academics, I attribute much of my success to the high school programs that prepared me for college. I was challenged in those programs to do well.

The work did not come easy to me. I had to work hard. I understood the rigors of college very early and was able to reach into my educational toolbox, which I had developed through Upward Bound and Friar Foundations. These were resources my peers did not have but that I was able to share with them. I would fit my classwork in wherever I could. I found friends in my classes I could study with. I talked through essay prompts with my professors who wanted to get to know me and help me with the coursework. I used different resources to hand in my best work because, ultimately, I was representing something larger than myself; I was representing a legacy. My degree was attained through my determination, my networks, and the work I put in during both high school and my transition into college.

ROLE OF FAMILY

I had an unconventional family situation. My older sister became my primary caretaker after my mother died when I was 9. I experienced a lot of anxiety surrounding the FAFSA and other documents because I did not know my official title. Was I adopted? Was I a ward of the state? My status was unclear, which was uncomfortable and confusing. My college counselors had limited experience with someone in my situation, so a lot of the time we were guessing about what to do. Thankfully, I was able to fill everything out correctly.

When it came to expected family contribution, my counselor glanced at me, and back at my sister, and we looked at each other. "Zero dollars?" I said. My counselor nodded. He understood a lot of the students he worked with. The family income for low-income students in Upward Bound was expected to be zero.

While I was in my freshman year, I once called my sister crying about how expensive college was. She told me to "shut up" and that "if you weren't meant to be there, you wouldn't be." She was correct. That quickly became my mantra. *If I weren't meant to be there, I wouldn't be.* I knew sometimes that my sister felt guilty that she could not be a larger part of my experience. She wanted to contribute to my education and advocate for me when it came to money and scholarships, but I knew my sister had herself to worry about. Most of the time, I felt alone in my experience, but I knew it was a rite of passage for the first person.

I was incredibly involved on campus. On top of my academic work, I was part of four different organizations, each of which constantly demanded different things from me. My family did not understand that part of my college experience. I found myself being bombarded with messages about how I did not talk to anyone anymore and that

I had forgotten about my family. As much as this frustrated me, I had to explain that I was not going straight from class to work to homework. There was so much in between that I tried to explain, but sometimes they did not understand.

TIPS AND ADVICE

Be yourself. As cheesy as this may sound, it holds true. In my experience I found that I wanted to make myself different. I experienced a lot of mental tension between wanting to reinvent myself and wanting to be my most authentic self. As an outsider, it is easy to feel as if you must put on a show or reinvent yourself to fit in, when really college is filled with so many people that you can always find someone to relate to and someone to develop a relationship with.

Find your resources. This can be difficult, but pay attention during orientation and identify academic resources and locate administrators you believe you can trust. Finding allies is super important. Developing relationships with these people helped keep me sane during my college years.

Get involved. I believe the college experience is much more than just doing your classwork and homework and then going to the dining hall. It is also social learning. You can definitely get that from being involved. I found some of my closest friends through being on Student Congress, being an RA, and being a mentor.

Finally, *do not let anyone dictate who you are to you.* You got there on your own accord, and you will graduate on your own accord.

CHAPTER 27 NAVIGATING UNCHARTED WATERS

Adj Marshall
Families Program and Policy Administrator
Massachusetts Institute of Technology

In my professional path, I have had a number of different roles and titles, but my work has had a singular mission: working in collaboration with others to create transformative educational and artistic experiences, which lead to positive change. My career path has been circuitous, which I have two ways of explaining: On good days, I am an explorer—a renaissance woman—passionately pursuing my dreams in far-flung places. On other days, I see myself as traveling a wandering, winding, often underpaid path, which I attribute to social class discrimination with its inherent social capital disadvantages and, moreover, a general lack of knowledge that has persisted from my first-generation college student experience into my first-generation professional career. Both of these frames hold some truth. My work has taken me from small college nonprofits in the U.S., to international peacebuilding nongovernmental organizations abroad with famous mural artists known for crafting some of the largest murals in the country, to elite educational institutions. I was even a self-employed contractor in welding—a particularly working-class field—which in its facilitation was a particularly upper-middle-class field. The through line of my career has been my investment in work focused on educational equity and socioeconomic inclusiveness, with an artistic lens.

While the link between the skills I gained in college and the positions I have held may not be readily apparent, because the latter vary so widely, I credit my institution's liberal arts education model for allowing me the flexibility to pivot my studies and explore a variety of fields without extending my time in college beyond the standard 4 years. Moreover, every institution I have worked for has appreciated my computational thinking and data management skills, strategic problem-solving mind-set, and ability to identify with the communities we support. Some of these skills I developed in college (as a computer science minor, which at times I wish had been a major), others came from my lived experience, and still others I learned from mentors on my career journey.

APPLYING TO AND PREPARING FOR COLLEGE

I began college with a commitment to be nothing like my parents. I had borne the hardship of their choices, and by 13 years old I had devised a blueprint of my own path. I would not become a teen mom, I would not drink alcohol, and I would do this thing I had never seen my parents do—work. The problem was I did not know what a job was or how anyone got one. I had heard of college and knew that it led to work, so I decided I would focus on getting there. My choice to go to college was pretty naive and completely uninformed, but it gave me a goal to work toward—and more importantly, a way out of the strained life I lived.

The need to fight for access and resources would become a recurring theme from high school through college. By the time I entered high school, which for me was 10th grade, I had amassed a small set of pamphlets and ripped-out magazine pages that offered ways to get to college. From these I had determined the course load and grades I would need to be eligible to apply. Among the signature items deemed necessary for entry to a "good" college were advanced placement (AP) classes. The problem for me was that AP classes at my high school were by invitation only, and I had not been invited. Upon petitioning for entry, I learned that invitations were extended to students based on their PSAT scores, and I had missed the cut-off by a single point. Gaining entry to two AP classes was a highlight of my senior year, but it would also bring challenges. My high school refused my petition to be excused from the required AP exam but did agree to pay my exam fees. In the end, the process felt somewhat futile, as I would earn over a 95 in each AP course but would not secure a test score sufficient for earning college credit.

In my determination to access college, I became involved with a few programs for low-income students; however, their models focused on access to information about colleges themselves, with almost no coaching on how to determine the schools that would be the best fit or how to navigate what seemed to me the most important part: the application process. My most pressing application questions were, How do I tell the colleges I am applying to that my family is homeless, without an address, or that my absent father is unable to provide income verification due to his late-stage alcoholism? Left to my own devices and with minimal guidance, I applied to a handful of local schools, none more than an hour's drive from my town, with no real strategy or sense of what made each school unique. The college I eventually chose to attend I had applied to on a last-minute whim, because it was one of a handful of schools on the common application. Whereas I had prepared myself well enough to gain acceptance to college, I had failed to find a school that actually fit my personal and academic interests.

EXPERIENCES IN COLLEGE: ASSETS AND DRAWBACKS

Upon my entry to college, I threw myself into my studies, partly because it was a welcome distraction from my family life, partly because I love learning, and partly because I had a lot to catch up on, having not been offered the same educational preparation as my private-school-educated college peers. My undergrad experience provided me with a plethora of words and concepts I had never been exposed to before—a new vocabulary with which to speak and write. I loved learning, debating, and critiquing these new ideas, but it did not come easy. It was a hard-fought journey. Expressing oneself in the written form is crucial to most liberal arts education models, and when I arrived at college, my writing skills were deemed inadequate. Having failed three opportunities to prove my writing sufficiency, I was placed in what might be described as a remedial writing course.

The only memory I have of this course is that it was the only one at the institution taught by an instructor without the title "professor." It was disheartening to be so aware of the fact that I had been deemed "in need," which one would think might warrant the best support possible, maybe the most lauded English professor at the institution; instead, I was provided with a contracted instructor pursuing their PhD from a nearby college. The instructor had no accountability to the institution or to our success beyond the single remedial English class. I cannot say that I did not learn anything from that instructor—I honestly cannot remember—but the part that has stuck with me more than any skills I gained was the institution's choice to offer those left behind less than the best support possible.

On a very basic level, college provided me with a roof over my head, a stable food supply, and a work-study job with pay; these aspects of the experience offered me the luxury of safety and security and thus the time to focus inward on my own self-development. For me, having these basic needs met was as important a benefit of college as the educational opportunities offered. However, even these were hard-fought. Throughout my time in college, I continually ran up against the silos of the institution, which forced me to tell my harrowing story again, and again, and again in order to receive the support and services that allowed me to be a student at the most basic level. Sometimes my reality was challenged as being unfathomable by the institutional services, and other times it was treated with appropriate care. In every encounter, no matter the outcome, I always walked in with a tightness in my chest at the prospect of telling strangers the innermost trauma of my life in order to be offered support.

As a freshman, I found myself navigating the long hallways of college almost furtively, quietly darting between the large archways of the turn-of-the-century building, afraid to cause a stir lest I be told that my acceptance to this institution had all been a mistake and could at any point be revoked. I carried with me a constant fear of being found out, believing that revealing my secret would result in the loss of my newfound status as part of the privileged elite—someone considered worthy of higher education. This imposter syndrome left me flailing. I cried many a night about my own inadequacy as a computer science student while struggling with my woefully underrepresented position as a woman in the field. I had made no close friends and joined no activities or clubs, and my roommates all chose to transfer to other colleges or move back home or off campus after our first year.

There was, however, a glimmer of hope through all this. I had encountered the academic fields of sociology and the pedagogical approach of service-learning, and these spaces recognized the lived reality of my prior life and actively fought to create change for a better future. I believed this area of study, and those who pursued it, would allow the two realities I experienced to live together side by side.

CONTRIBUTIONS TO MY SUCCESS

In my sophomore year, my journey took a 180-degree turn. I got more involved on campus to embed myself fully in the college experience. I became a resident assistant, earning extra funds and building my conflict management skills. I participated in athletic pursuits and activist initiatives. I changed my major, added a second major, and began to dream about studying abroad. Most importantly, I found my people: the "radicals" within my politically and religiously conservative institution. They were people like me—outsiders at the institution who had decided to embrace their experience by immersing themselves fully to create change from within through activism. In my junior and senior year, I relied on that support network of student peers and professors I had built during my sophomore year. They guided me through the journey of studying abroad, first in Ecuador and later in Western Australia, from which I traveled to the recently war-torn country of East Timor. They helped me to focus my research on topics that were relevant to my lived reality, including socioeconomic policies related to welfare reform and homelessness, and to build campaigns that challenged policies at the institution around domestic violence and sexual abuse. They funded my travels to Washington, D.C., to protest the war in Afghanistan, and pushed me to stand up for my values by funneling my energy and knowledge into initiatives to create change.

Ultimately, I learned to navigate college successfully. I found ways to get individuals within the institution to support my interests, even if they were not always aligned with the institution's interests. I got outside the four walls of the campus as much as possible through studying abroad and volunteering with local community-driven change initiatives. I took an active interest in working to change the institution and draw attention to its faults, which helped me not to feel like a victim of the system. I met with my professors in informal settings, not to talk about my academic success but to learn about who they were as people, which also meant that when I was facing academic challenges, I felt comfortable approaching them. Forming relationships with my professors had the added benefit of bringing me to the top of their mind when they sought out contributors to their writing projects or received opportunities they could pass on to students. Although my writing skills initially were deemed insufficient, they grew steadily. I still do not know how to effectively use commas, but I have come to be okay with that. There are some skills we can build and others that will always elude us. The important part is to recognize that our deficits are not fatal flaws but just a part of who we are. It is important to remember that it is okay to ask for support. My dear friends, a copy editor and a professor, collectively added over 70 commas to this piece upon reviewing it.

ROLE OF FAMILY

Whereas I eventually thrived academically as an undergrad, I very much struggled emotionally. I was managing the survivor's guilt of leaving my homeless family behind and the culture shock of entering a majority upper-middle-class college community, which was a far cry from my own poverty-class upbringing. Despite the fact that my family "resided" less than 5 miles from my campus, they never set foot upon its grassy lawns until the day I graduated. However, although my family was never present, they were also ever present.

One particular moment from my junior spring comes to mind. I sat behind my university-provided desk, which was too small for the task ahead. I had spread out as best I could four sets of taxes, a list of social security numbers, a set of FAFSA pins, a CSS Profile, a death certificate, and my computer. My eyes were bleary from hours of looking at the tiny print of paper tax documents and computer-screen FAFSA and CSS Profile questions. I had been tasked with completing not only my own taxes but those of the entire family, in addition to three FAFSAs and one CSS Profile, to ensure that my twin brothers and I would receive our Pell grants and other funds available to us as low-income college students. The death certificate stared back at me: a reminder of my father's passing after years of alcohol abuse. At the same time that it brought melancholy, it also brought relief—that I would no longer have to quantify and qualify my father's lack of involvement, lack of financial resources, or whereabouts to the government and to the institutions my siblings and I attended. I could now offer a simple single response: deceased, with no further explanation necessary.

My "family life" was extremely complicated, painful, and full of landmines that could create emotional upset for me and for those I shared my life with. When engaging with my family story, I chose two opposite paths. One path kept everyone safe—silence. The other blew everything up—weaponizing. On the silent path, I would hold back my family story, ensuring I would not be hurt by others' reactions while sparing those around me the difficult details and need to respond. On the weaponizing path, I drew out my family story like a sword, ferociously slashing others down for their lack of awareness and unbridled classism; my family story was used as a weapon to inspire guilt and shame in others. I was fearful and angry, and my emotions about my family manifested themselves in a variety of ways, including how I chose to convey who my family was and where we came from.

My family's never-presence exacerbated their ever-presence. The support I received from them was the recognition that we had survived worse than my college experience, and the hardship they brought was the fact that their existence was so far outside the lived reality of my peers that I was forced to choose between acknowledging their existence or concealing it.

TIPS AND ADVICE

Reflecting on my college experience, I see two glaring spaces in which the institution failed me. In the first instance, the college failed to recognize my lived reality as a student with nowhere to call home as not only a thought experiment in which I could focus my academic interests but also as a reality in which I had to live. In the second instance, the college failed to demonstrate to me how to draw connections among that lived reality, my academic passions, and a career from which I could earn a living that would allow me to pay back the loans I took out to attend college in the first place. Getting through college as a first-gen student is a difficult journey but one that is manageable once you learn the parameters. Figuring out what you will do after college is by far the harder part. For first-gen students, college is more than a safe space to lay your head or an education with a credential; it is and always will be the fulfillment of a dream that allows for one's future reality to be different from their past experience. It is a step toward meaningful work that is financially viable and a recognition that you have been deemed valuable within society. It is the framing—how you tell your story—that brings that dream to reality. As first-gen students we often have complicated histories that continually impact our life choices and the paths we take in our career.

If we look at our lives as a ship's journey, we are on a course that starts with our personal histories, which are familiar to us but complicated to others. Through our college experiences, we are set out into unchartered waters where we can feel adrift like a ship lost at sea; when we find our bearings, the course we set for ourselves and the aspirations we have for our career can seem unfathomable or misguided to the people and places from which we came. Our new sea legs can feel shaky as we interact with newfound shipmates and the environment within which we have landed. Our complicated history sometimes trips us up and at the same time propels us forward like wind in our sails. This journey, which is arduous, can also be exciting and exhilarating, exposing us to new experiences, people, and places literally and figuratively. At the same time the journey can be heartbreaking because it often takes us further and further from that familiar home and history.

Through our college journey we learn a form of code-switching I call framing. I encourage you to frame and reframe your history, your present reality, and your future, drawing through lines that tie the disparate parts of your reality together. That framing can change depending on who you share it with and in what context you present it. You can learn to highlight certain elements and steer clear of others as you become an inhabitant of two realms serving as a ship guide that charts the course between the two worlds. I wish you light and a compass on your first-gen journey from high school to college to first-gen professional.

CHAPTER 28

Clifton E. Shambry Jr.
Assistant Director of Life Design for Diversity and Inclusion

As an educator over the past 10 years who advocates for all students to accomplish their goals, I am grateful for the opportunities I have been afforded and am honored to provide my story on thriving as a first-generation college student and graduate. In sharing my story, I feel it is critical to first recognize the work done by others, which helped me get to a place where I could even think about furthering myself. Therefore, I honor all those who have laid the foundation and fought so that I can have the freedom to write, speak, and thrive, even while the world we live in wants to change the freedoms I have been afforded.

I am an assistant director for life design, a position also known as a life design educator. In that capacity, my goal is to help students plan a future in which they can live well and be joyful. We help students reflect on what they are curious about and provide a space for them to explore their potential interests and try new experiences so they may create opportunities to flourish. I have the privilege of assisting students through a journey related to all aspects of their lives, including their upbringing, to explore their identities and values in the process of discovering what they are passionate about.

THE BEGINNING: WHY COLLEGE

As a first-generation college alum, I am grateful to the people in my life who helped me achieve such a significant goal. My past has had an impact on my future in so many ways, from being homeless to now ensuring that my housing bill is the first one paid, and from moving 26 times in my life (18 times before age 18 and 8 times in 12 years) to creating my own home wherever I am. In this chapter, I hope to share a little about my journey to becoming a first-generation college alum.

A major part of my motivation came from losing my mother when I was only 10 years old, which left me, my younger brother at 9, and my baby sister at 5 to find a new home. The one thing I loved in myself—which I knew connected me to my mother—was the value I placed on being "smart," and along with it a love for education. This love is what sparked my desire to succeed in school, and it was reinforced at age 22 when I moved in with my oldest maternal brother and his spouse in 1999. To this day, a part of me still lives for my mother—to make her proud of me and the person I have become and am becoming.

In preparing for college, I struggled to understand what it meant for me to excel academically. Whereas the community at home viewed me as someone who was a high achiever, I started to question my intellect, especially when I reached Spanish 4 in my senior year of high school and saw junior students in the class doing much better than I was; it made me realize that I was missing something. I wondered whether I was behind or simply not excelling—living up to my potential. After thinking through this dilemma, I was oddly empowered to continue pushing onward—to "fake it until I made it." What I was making it to, I had no idea—good grades, a scholarship, or into a college. Either way, I was going to work hard, and luckily, I had a guidance counselor who helped lead the way to my considering attending college.

APPLYING TO AND PREPARING FOR COLLEGE

As the first in my family to undergo the process of going to college, I had a lack of knowledge of what it would take. I had no idea what financial aid was, why I should go to college, the type of college to attend, how to select the right college for me, how I would pay, and what programs there were to help me. I did not even know until I began college that I could be a part of a program specifically for first-generation college students. I discovered how crucial guidance counseling is to selecting a college and applying to it. I had a wonderful counselor who took the time to work with me to find the right colleges and apply to them, and even took me and friends to visit one college to ensure aid was in order. I found that although it appeared from the package I would be fully funded, it included $28,000 in loans every year for 4 years. I had not known when I received the funding that I would have to pay it back. That would have put me into debt by about $112,000, which is almost a whole house, or 200+ new game systems, or over 750 pairs of Jordan's sneakers. Needless to say, I did not go to that college. I decided to attend a community college for free, which was the best and at that time the only option for me, and then transfer to a 4-year institution on a scholarship. I did not know what was in store for me on my college journey—the good, the bad, and the growth.

EXPERIENCES IN COLLEGE

I became very involved as an athlete and then worked in various offices at my community college, all of which led me to learn more about myself. It was not until I was in college that I learned there was a term or phrase to express part of who I was and how I might approach college: I learned I was a first-generation college student. Having moved so many times before college, I was not always confident in my ability to excel academically despite being in the top 30 of more than 400 students in my high school graduating class. During college, I became more deeply aware of the challenges that were part of my life's journey, among which was not fully grasping the concepts that would be necessary to thrive in college. I received my first C- on a paper in my college-level writing class. I was a little distraught, as I thought I had been doing so well in college, yet I also realized grammar was not my strongest area. However, doubts in myself increased, and I began to feel as though I could not achieve the goal of furthering my education, which I knew would make my mother proud. Reflecting on all this, I wish I had had an opportunity to have a consistent experience, to not have challenges with writing, to have an opportunity to fall in love with the sciences, or to not struggle with grammar. Yet I believe these types of challenges truly happen for a reason. Speaking to others who had more knowledge of what I was going through helped. I spoke with many staff, including my cross-country/track and field coach and my scholarship advisors, who helped me by giving me encouragement and resources to stay on the path.

I also tried to think of new ways to connect with others and build new skills. In college, I was a student organization leader, a member of student government, and an athlete. I got involved in these organizations because I valued connecting with others, being engaged mentally, and learning new things. Engaging with others to help them thrive was helpful for my own journey as well.

CONTRIBUTORS TO MY SUCCESS

Many factors contributed to my success, including being part of a program that helped me acclimate to a college environment, having good academic advisors, and having experiences that helped increase my self-awareness, self-assurance, and motivation. In a New Jersey college, I was part of the Educational Opportunity Fund (EOF) program, which supported first-generation students, limited-income students, and those from educationally disadvantaged backgrounds who tested into at least one basic skills course. This program set me up for success more than I would have imagined. Thanks to this program, I received resources without feeling judged for benefiting from them, and I had peers and advisors who understood my experience without me having to explain myself. They advocated for me, helped me see beyond my faults and struggles, and helped me overcome the feeling that I was failing. I remember a time when I spoke to an advisor who helped me to realize that I was having a cyclical experience—something that happened consistently around the same time of year. This was a huge eye-opener for me, as I was able to then think about the experience and figure out a plan to prevent and/or work through that experience when it happened again.

Also, talking with folks like advisors in academic programs led me to travel and to have experiences I never thought I would have, including traveling to Beijing and Shanghai to study. I learned of this opportunity through hearing about other students' experiences in the EOF program, as well as from the lead faculty person of the learn abroad experience, whose class I took. Hearing about how these types of experiences changed students' perspective on life made me want to try it out, as I had been accustomed to traveling but not to another country. If my advisor had not believed in me, she might not have shared my interest with the program leaders, who helped find some funding so I could have that experience—an experience that ultimately helped me gain a new perspective on what it means to thrive through difference, difficulty, and barriers.

All the advice I received from EOF, my college involvement, and scholarship programs helped me to work through challenges—or take advantage of opportunities for growth—that I had not been aware I would encounter in college. Because of this program, I had many resources to succeed as a first-generation college student. I found a new community and a sense of belonging academically. Having many folks to reinforce the excellence within helped me to continue my journey.

ROLE OF THE FAMILY

I understood that I was the first to go to college and later learned in my collegiate journey that some of my siblings had attended college but had not graduated. Being the first meant that I could not ask my family for all the help that I may have needed, as they were looking to me to do as well as I had done in the past. While I was in college, my sister was doing everything she could as a single parent to raise five children—three of her siblings and two of her own children—all while working a full-time job taking care of more children. Living at home was not what I wanted either; I wanted to get away from being the oldest child (although not the oldest sibling) and from having to help with things around the house—yet as family members do, we help. Being away at school and then going home enabled me to see how I was growing into a new version of myself. Engaging in both worlds seemed to make those worlds become more distinct. Sometimes I appreciated the privilege of being in both spaces, but sometimes the code-switching became more challenging in both spaces and often felt performative.

I continued my journey to graduate school and am the first of 11 siblings to earn associate, bachelor, and master's degrees. I look forward to my nieces, nephews, grandnieces, and grandnephews having a higher educational experience without the challenges that I had. I am sure I will be able to help them by sharing my experiences, and I hope that better higher education support services will be implemented in the future to ensure that all students—regardless of background—are able to excel.

TIPS AND ADVICE

As I continue to grow and work in higher education, I hope to support other students' journeys by providing intentional and appreciative advisement, resource sharing, and motivation. Although I have benefited from what some might call intrusive advising, which perhaps should continue in some facets, it seems important for advisors to keep in mind how many first-generation students, including myself, have benefited from intentional and/or appreciative advising.

I hope that more institutions find ways to help students see themselves and their experiences as assets in their life journey rather than deficits. I hope more institutions find ways to ensure students develop a sense of belonging through immersive experiences, such as cohort programs, asset-based approaches, and connecting students so they can talk through their experiences and get involved in new opportunities. Advisors and faculty can better understand and recognize students' experiences—especially those from underrepresented backgrounds like first-generation college students—by consistently connecting with smaller groups of students so they can help these students thrive.

I'll leave you with these questions to work through. As agents of change, how will institutions and programs see success through their students' eyes? How will institutions, programs, and governments provide more funding to ensure scholars are able to ground their passions in studies that are aligned with their own interests to make our world a better place to live, work, and grow? To students, how will you take your life into your own hands and journey forward? How will you live your life joyfully and big? How will you thrive as a first-generation college student turned alum? What is your legacy?

CHAPTER 29

Raquel Gutierrez Cortez, MSCP
Associate Marriage and Family Therapist,
Associate Professional Clinical Counselor

My most recent position was as a service coordinator at a regional center in Northern California. Regional centers provide assessments, determine eligibility for services, and offer case management services for a wide variety of people in the community. In my role, I coordinated services and managed a caseload of 100 clients between the ages of 5 and 22. Services included in-home and out-of-home respite care, referrals for government services like independent living services, in-home support care, day care, day programs, camps, and residential group home placement. Among other activities, I helped with housing placement, assisted in the creation of individual education plans, and participated in transition meetings as I advocated for my clients. Each client had unique needs, including developmentally diverse students who wished to complete high school and attend college. I willingly provided such support.

My experiences in college confirmed that I wanted a career helping people. They also have given me the ability to further my career and work toward my dreams. A bachelor's degree in psychology or a related field was mandatory for many of the positions that interested me. My late grandfather always reminded me that something worth having never comes easy. It definitely has not been easy.

APPLYING TO AND PREPARING FOR COLLEGE

Although I am a first-generation college graduate, education has always been very important to my family. My parents did not have the confidence to go to college themselves, and neither knew the first steps of how to achieve a college education. Soon after graduating from high school, in the early 1980s, my parents found well-paying jobs and decided to get married, buy their home, and start their family. My father's career provided enough financial support over the course of 10 years to enable my mother to stay home and care for me and my brother. My parents sacrificed a great deal both financially and emotionally to provide my brother and I with private education starting in preschool. Neither of us ever received public education. They thought that private education would enhance my scholarly performance and increase my morale. My parents always encouraged me to do well in school, and I was rewarded for good grades.

My parents always told me that they did not want me to struggle financially in the future. They firmly believed that being a college graduate would provide success and an easier life. Many of their friends and family members who went to college were better off financially, and my parents attributed much of that success to their education. Going to college was not something that was optional; they were sending me to college by any means necessary.

I take pride in being a first-generation college student. I am proud of my parents for providing me with the best education they could afford and am forever grateful to them. Being a first-generation college student was a challenge though. I wish I had been better prepared before I applied. I had some college counseling in high school, but it was not enough. The application process was stressful, as were the SATs and applying for scholarships and financial aid. I had to make many phone calls to student loan companies. I was constantly confused about which loans to apply for. Learning all the terminology, such as the difference between subsidized and unsubsidized loans, deferment, forbearance, and interest rates, was overwhelming. However, in the long run, learning about the differences in the loans did not matter much. These student loans still resulted in significant debt. Each of my parents took out a Parent Plus loan for me in addition to my own student loan that was under my name. These three loans were in deferment during the 4 years I was in school. We figured that if we had enough money to cover school, everything would be okay. It was "out of sight, out of mind," until 6 months after graduation, when I had to start repaying these loans. A disadvantage of not knowing enough about college funding is that I now realize I should have tried to fund college independently as opposed to involving my parents financially. I most likely would have received more financial assistance. It has been 9 years since graduation, and not only do I still have student loan debt but my parents do too.

Because my parents and I did not know about applying to college, the admission process, financial aid, scholarships, or how to navigate the resources that were offered, I sought support from my guidance counselors and admission counselors. I relied on them to help me negotiate the college application process successfully. I suffer from anxiety, so I only wanted to apply for colleges within California and close to home but far enough away from my parents to live on my own. I had only attended smaller private schools in the past, so the thought of attending a larger state school or a public university was intimidating to me. My options were limited. Not only did I have to try my best to be accepted to one of my preferred universities, but the finances and tuition were a major factor. Once I was accepted to the universities, there were many more considerations to explore, and I had a lot to learn. I chose my university based on the monetary grants they offered me, location of the school, class sizes, and how comfortable I felt when I toured the campus. It turns out that I selected the perfect school for me.

EXPERIENCES IN COLLEGE

My experience in college was fulfilling. I had my areas of strengths and definitely areas of development. With the help of my academic counselor, I was able to identify my weaknesses and learn how to work through them productively. As a first-generation student, I sometimes felt I was at a disadvantage because I believed I needed to constantly work harder than my colleagues who had parents and grandparents who had attended college. Academically, these colleagues seemed smarter and much more comfortable than I was. I learned to overcome my fear of requesting help when I needed it, and I was not ashamed to utilize the school's resources to my advantage. In my freshman and junior years, I had visits with the on-campus therapist once a month. These visits served as a check-in to keep me focused and emotionally strong. In the first semester of freshman year, I had already learned a lot about myself and did some soul searching. Between participating in the college scene and having freedom away from home, I quickly learned how easy it was to fall off track and lose focus. I had too much time on my hands. I also knew that I had already come too far to make dumb mistakes. By the second semester of freshman year, I decided to get a full-time job. I began working 40 hours a week, including weekends, while carrying a full-time course load, leaving no time to party. My parents were hesitant to encourage my working because they wanted me to concentrate on studying. However, they were supportive once I demonstrated that working allowed me to do better in school while earning money. I paid for my own books and school supplies, and I had some spending money. I did not have to help my parents financially; however, I now wish I would have paid down my student loans while in school to eliminate some of my current debt.

Although I earned my bachelor's degree in 4 years, some classes were challenging, and I had to retake them in order to earn a better grade. I struggled most with statistics. I took it twice with the same professor and earned a D- both times. I put in a great deal of effort and used the professor's office hours to request support, computed practice problems, sought help at the tutoring center, and even hired a private tutor, only to still end up with a D- the second time around. Although I was able to graduate with this grade, eventually I would need to take the class again and earn a passing grade as a prerequisite for graduate school.

If I had the chance to do it again, I would have financed my own college education to free my parents of my student loan debt that we are still paying. Having a structured schedule and routine taught me how to allocate my time, become organized, and maintain a healthy lifestyle on every level: physically, mentally, socially, and spiritually. I had plenty of friends, I was in a long-term relationship, and I made time for fun after my schoolwork was completed.

CONTRIBUTORS TO MY SUCCESS

The academics of college can be extremely stressful. Additional factors, big or small, such as working, dealing with anxiety, or being in a relationship, can easily add more stress. Those were all factors that added to my stress level. There are psychotherapy services on nearly every college campus. I took advantage of seeing the college therapist on a regular basis. I felt safe, our discussions were confidential, and the best part is that the cost was included in tuition. I did not have to worry about finding and paying for a therapist. Through my therapy, I was able to manage my anxiety and develop the skills needed to sustain my job and relationships the entire 4 years of college.

I also sought help from my academic advisor, Dr. Don Stannard-Friel. He was amazing. He kept me on track and advised me of the classes I would need to take to reach my goal of graduating in 4 years. He also suggested that I further my education and earn a graduate degree because he saw my growing passion for my field.

As a Latina and a first-generation college student, I was a minority on college campuses across two parts of my identity. I felt as though I had to prove myself not only to my family but also to my colleagues and race. I wanted to be a positive role model to my younger cousins and future children. I knew I had to be successful and give back to my community and let them know that if I could get a college degree, they could too. Growing up, I participated in a variety of community service opportunities. I assisted individuals with severe mental disabilities at a psychiatric and medical care facility. I worked with the geriatric population. I tutored at-risk children from low socioeconomic backgrounds and worked as a life skills coach for incarcerated youth. I place tremendous importance on helping minority and underprivileged populations get ahead in life. Helping people succeed and overcome personal tribulations has always been incredibly rewarding to me. Every single one of these experiences contributed to my decision to major in psychology. I owe my success to my own hard work, to the assistance of my counselors and academic advisors, and, most importantly, to my family's consistent motivation and support.

ROLE OF FAMILY

My parents grew up with different family systems and ideas about college. Although they had different upbringings, they individually had the support of their family. They each could have attended college; however, they chose to work full-time jobs instead. My dad is a retired heavy equipment operator and started his career when he was very young. Upon graduating from high school, my mom worked at a hospital and has worked in the medical field ever since. My parents are two very bright, practical, ethical, and hardworking individuals. The fact that they did not attend college was very difficult for them. They put all that focus on ensuring that their children attended college. I could not have graduated from college and graduate school without the loving support of my entire family. When I wanted to give up or take a break from school, I could always call on my family for a quick reminder and a bit of encouragement to "finish strong."

TIPS AND ADVICE

Applying to college is not an easy task. There is much to consider, including taking a tour; deciding which colleges are best suited to meet your goals; funding college through student loans, scholarships, grants, and financial aid; deciding who will be responsible for paying for college; choosing a college; and declaring a major and possible minors. Be wise and studious about funding college. Use as many resources as possible.

Apply for scholarships and try to make college as affordable as possible for yourself. Being a first-generation college student, I did not know how to find additional resources to fund college. My mom heard about scholarship workshops and seminars, and she took me to each one that was held in the area. These events were helpful but overwhelming, and they were not free. They taught where to find scholarships and how to apply for them. I applied for approximately 20 scholarships and received 3. I qualified for the scholarships that required a written essay, a certain amount of volunteer work contributing to the community, and at least a 3.0 or 3.5 GPA in high school. If your GPA is high, I recommend applying for grants through the government and/or school because they can sometimes offer more compensation. My scholarship awards were decent and worth the amount of work and time, especially because I did not have to pay back the money. However, most scholarships are very competitive. Some of them were only for students of alumni parents, which was discouraging because I, like any other first-generation student, did not qualify.

It is important to pay attention to scholarship deadlines as well. Many valuable scholarship opportunities are lost because students do not apply in time. On the other hand, a student might be awarded a scholarship because they are the only applicant. I am proud of myself for applying for the scholarships, but the process was laborious, and I did not apply for as many in the following years. I regret not applying for more scholarships. I am certain I could have received more money to use toward school. Making student loan payments is challenging, and it sometimes feels as though I will never pay them off.

My advice to you as a first-generation student is to be cognizant about how you invest in your education. Study for a profession that will help you afford to pay your student loan debt. People choose to go to college in hopes of landing their dream job and getting paid well enough to live a comfortable life. My student loan debt has weighed heavily on my ability to purchase a home. No one advised me on what would happen after college in terms of debt and how it would hold me back financially. I most certainly do not regret going to college or graduate school, and I feel strongly that my hard work and education will continue to pay off in the future. However, even though I have a job that pays me a decent salary, my student loan payment is barely manageable. I work for a public service agency and am in the Public Loan Forgiveness Program, which means my student loans will be forgiven after I make consistent payments for 9 years.

Also, apply for financial aid without involving your parents if possible. Do everything you can to minimize student loan debt while still in school. Ask plenty of questions and inquire about resources. Utilize services available at your school. If you take out loans for graduate school like I did, consolidate them with your undergrad loans to make one payment.

My past and present career opportunities have allowed me to work with individuals with special needs, students, incarcerated youth, and a variety of persons from diverse cultural backgrounds. My goal is to continue to empower individuals and help them stay accountable for their success. Life is meant for learning, and learning can be done inside or outside of a classroom. I realize there is much more for me to learn and explore. I did not choose my career for the money; I am simply passionate about helping others become the best version of themselves.

CHAPTER 30

Karen Hill, BA
Completing Master of Science in Counseling

My name is Karen. My pronouns are she and her. I am a cisgender Black woman from the Los Angeles, California, area. I am in my late 40s and the single mother of two young adults in their 20s. I work full time at a public 4-year university as an academic advisor. I am currently in my last year of graduate school, earning a master of science in counseling. I started college in August 1992 as a wide-eyed 18-year-old who was ready to conquer the world. Twenty-four years later, I returned to a 4-year university as a last-ditch effort to earn a baccalaureate degree with little hope of accomplishing that elusive goal. Two years later, in May 2018, at the age of 44, I received my bachelor of arts degree in psychology; it was the same year my youngest child graduated from high school.

Right after graduation, I secured a full-time position at a public 4-year university, but the position was not in academic advising. Seven months later, I received a full-time job offer as an academic advising assistant at my alma mater in the same office in which I had previously worked as a peer coach. The summer before my senior year, I had decided to apply to graduate school to earn my master's in counseling because it would give me the most options. For the second time in my life, I applied to colleges without any idea of what I was getting myself into. That process was significantly different from the undergraduate one, and I learned many new lessons.

APPLYING TO AND PREPARING FOR COLLEGE

Why did I choose to attend college? I cannot pinpoint a reason. I knew that it was expected of me because I was the "smart" sibling. While my siblings were good at sports, fashion, and communication, I was the shy, quiet youngest child who read a lot of books and did really well in school without much effort. I loved school, reading, and the gratification of getting good grades and academic awards. My parents grew up in Alabama and Mississippi during the Jim Crow era of segregation. They did not have many opportunities beyond working. They both had blue-collar jobs, which I could not imagine myself doing, and they always told me that a good education was the way to make a good living. In my mind there were three options after high school graduation:

I could work in retail like my mother, I could work at a meat-packing company like my father, or I could go to college and have a career that I chose. I had worked retail for 3 months in high school, and it had not been a good experience. My father had to wake up at 2 a.m. to go to work in a freezer all day, which also was not appealing. Going to college was a no-brainer.

I found applying to college stressful. No one in my family had ever been to a university. One of my siblings had completed a certificate program at a trade college in another state and another had taken some classes at a local community college, but no one had applied to 4-year universities or for scholarships or completed the FAFSA. Because I am an entire decade younger than my siblings, it may not have been much help even if they had. In the early '90s, personal computers were relatively new and the internet was in its infancy. My college applications were all handwritten or typed on a typewriter. With no family guidance, I knew I would need a lot of help with applications, so I got a job as a teacher's assistant in the college counseling office my senior year of high school. I had frequent contact with the college counselors who came to deliver application workshops. They were a huge help in answering all my questions. My sister worked at a computer company and purchased a used desktop computer and printer from her company for me. I was able to use that to type my scholarship essays.

I applied for nearly every scholarship that came through the college counseling office at my high school. My boss was the college counselor, and she would proofread my submissions for me. When my college acceptances began coming in, I was reassured that I had done something right. However, the financial aid offers were another story. My father, who had not finished elementary school, and my mother, who had no collegial aspirations, simply handed over their tax returns and left me to figure out the mystery of FAFSA. I was 18 with no frame of reference for the information I was being asked to supply. The offers were even more confusing: Where did the cost of attendance come from? Were they charging me for travel expenses even though I only applied to local schools?

I went on every campus tour that my school hosted, even if I was not interested in the college, because I wanted a sense of what college was like. However, an overnight trip to a university that was 8 hours north of my home was truly frightening. Where were the adults who were supposed to ensure my safety and oversee my decisions? I chose to attend the University of Southern California (USC) because their scholarship and financial aid packet were by far the best, reducing any student loans I would have to pay back. In addition, no one else in my graduating class would be going there. At the time, I wanted to stand out and be different from the masses. USC was also considered one of the top schools in the country. Finally, it was the dream college of my boyfriend at the time, and his excitement convinced me that I loved USC too. I even borrowed his dream major of architecture.

EXPERIENCES IN COLLEGE

I moved into the dorms, even though the university was only a 20-minute drive from my house. I wanted to be independent and get away from my strict parents. Shopping for and moving into my dorm was the best feeling. The majority of people on my floor were also freshmen. My roommate, also from Southern California, was nice. She had a car, so from my perspective she was rich, although we never discussed money other than to split the telephone bill and mini-fridge/microwave rental. I was not prepared for life at a predominantly white institution with an affluent student body. My high school had been full of students from various minoritized populations—mostly students of color. I had expected greater diversity, and I was unprepared to be the minority both ethnically and financially. Sitting in my freshman English class hearing about summer trips to Europe or that sailing was an extracurricular activity at my classmates' high school made me feel unprepared, out of place, and alone.

My new friends were my saving grace. Living in the dorms was the best decision I made, as I met five amazing friends who lived in my hall. Although we had the best adventures together, they were also a source of distress. I did not feel like I fit in with them either. Everyone seemed to know what they wanted to study and where they wanted their future to lead, and they were doing well in classes. I, on the other hand, earned 10 out of 32 attempted units and was on academic probation by the end of my freshman year.

I was depressed. I felt I did not fully belong either at college or at home. I was academically disqualified after my fifth semester. Thus, I began my 2-decade relationship with the California community college system. I gave up on getting a degree. I had surmised that I simply was not as smart as I had been led to believe by my K-12 experience. Yet I loved learning, so I took any classes that sounded interesting. Sometimes I did well and other times I did not. I was still dealing with the depression and shame of having been kicked out of the university. Watching my friends go on to graduate while I had my first child widened the gap I felt between us.

I eventually got serious about earning my degree when my job in a local K-12 school district was constantly threatened due to budget cuts. I earned an associate degree in respiratory care in 2012, 20 years after graduating from high school. Through that experience, I learned that I thrived in a small-cohort setting. Our class consisted of 17 students, and we took all our classes together. It was an instant support group. We were all nontraditional students from different walks of life, but we banded together to get through the very strenuous program. Three years later I realized that respiratory care was not for me and that I needed to give my baccalaureate degree one last shot. I applied to one public university. I chose it because it was the closest to my house and I did not want a long commute.

At new student orientation, I attended a campus resource fair, where I learned about TRIO Student Support Services (SSS). Despite my fear of rejection, I asked the person at the table if there was an age limit for applicants. He looked stunned and replied no. I applied and was accepted into the program. Between classes, I spent time in the TRIO office studying and connecting with other TRIO students. I met two other single moms who were majoring in psychology. We became study buddies and supported one another through classes and life in general. Something internal had changed. My academic performance significantly improved and I was on the dean's list each semester.

During those final 2 years of a 26-year educational journey, I discovered a passion for working with other college students to help them overcome barriers to earning a degree. The first year was a year of self-discovery. I learned a lot about myself and what I wanted from a career beyond a paycheck. I was also a TRIO SSS participant. TRIO SSS helped me realize that I wanted to work with students like me: low-income, first-generation, parenting, returning, transfers—in other words, nontraditional students from minoritized backgrounds. I applied for and got a position as a peer coach in one of the general education advising offices on campus at the end of my junior year. The second year was a year of action. In addition to my job as a peer coach for new transfer students, I joined several professional organizations and secured a fellowship with a mentor/ sponsor to help me network and learn more about the various higher education careers. I also conducted informational interviews with several administrators on campus, most of whom were women of color.

My work as a peer coach provided me with direct access to a dozen advisors. I shadowed them, interviewed them, and learned from them. The academic advisors I worked with had bachelor's and master's degrees in various disciplines, and they had all entered the field in different ways. The only thing they had in common was that none of them began college with the goal of becoming an advisor. I learned that a master's in counseling is required to become a counselor in the California community college system and decided to pursue this path.

CONTRIBUTORS TO MY SUCCESS

I credit two sources with laying the groundwork for my success: a psychology course I took the first semester after returning to college, and TRIO. They helped me discover what was important to me and what I enjoyed. They started me on the path toward my career in higher education. In my psychology class, I did informational interviews and extensive research on my top three career aspirations. I also learned about networking and began connecting with administrators on campus to find a mentor. I wound up having several that were instrumental in guiding the last year of my undergraduate degree and the graduate school application process.

TRIO SSS played a major role in my ultimate success of earning my baccalaureate degree after several failed attempts. I had originally signed up for TRIO SSS with the hope of getting help locating resources or attending helpful workshops. What I received was so much more. The week before my first semester at California State University, Dominguez Hills (CSUDH), TRIO SSS had an orientation for their new participants. My TRIO advisor, Liz (a Latina woman), and the TRIO coordinator, Josh (a Black man), shared their stories. This was the first time I had seen people who looked like me and who came from similar urban areas share their educational struggles. I could relate to them. It was the first I had heard anyone speak of struggling in college and overcoming their challenges to complete their degree. I got goosebumps while they were talking, and something in my mind-set shifted. *I was determined to seek help this time.* In fact, for the entire first semester I would email Liz and Josh weekly updates. They were extremely busy, so I would send the update to Liz one week and Josh the next, alternating so that I would not feel I took up too much time or was a nuisance. In those weekly emails, I would describe my triumphs and struggles.

During my first advising session, Liz urged me to begin thinking about graduate school. I smiled and thought to myself, *I am not even going to finish this degree.* I was attempting my degree one last time out of necessity. I had two teenage children to support, and I needed to find a career outside the medical field. I did not truly believe I would be successful, but I had to give it my best shot. I wanted to be realistic with myself. Realism at that time in my life meant pessimism. It was no use. Her optimism and keen insight beat my pessimistic realism each time we met. She spoke positivity into me and helped me see my victories instead of focusing on my failures. Liz was in a master's program at the time, having overcome major barriers in her own life. Now here she was helping me and 159 other students earn their degrees. I began to think that a master's might be possible for me too. By the end of that first semester, I knew I wanted to go to graduate school. In an amazing twist of fate, Josh and I were 2 of the 25 students accepted into our graduate school cohort out of over 250 applicants. We became classmates, and I was able to repay some of the support he had shown me during my 2 years at CSUDH.

ROLE OF FAMILY

My family has always been my driving force. My father read the newspaper daily and watched channels like CNN every evening. He often told me to turn off the TV and read a book. He encouraged me to acquire knowledge for myself and not to simply take someone else's version of the truth as my own. My father's health took a turn for the worse a few years ago, and he died 18 months after I earned my BA. I wish he could see me earn my MS in a few months. My mother has always been available to provide emotional support, meals, assistance with my children, and whatever else I have needed. She gets things done and makes things happen. I could not have succeeded at any of this without her. Yet, she still does not understand college. She does not know the difference between my degrees, what my grad school major is, or what I do for a living. Nonetheless, my beautifully framed BA hangs above her bed, and she is incredibly proud of me. My children were my biggest cheerleaders, encouraging me, celebrating me, and driving me to succeed. My oldest child is a ray of sunshine and had similar struggles to mine during her 2.5 years in college. Her college journey ended as mine was restarting. My youngest child (they/them) is a super brain. They were the top-ranked student at their high school nearly every semester. I told myself that if they could put in all that work, then I could work harder. When I was receiving my graduate school acceptances, they were being flown to the East Coast to visit Ivy League colleges. They eventually chose Stanford University and remained on the West Coast. We will once again graduate together in spring 2022, when they earn their bachelor's degree and I earn my master's degree.

TIPS AND ADVICE

Through this journey I learned that one of my biggest obstacles was my mind-set. I tended to beat myself up mentally. I never asked for help at USC because I did not think I had earned it. I always thought I could have worked harder or started an assignment earlier. My parents had taught me to be independent, and I took it to heart. I told myself that I was not able to ask for help until I had given 100% from start to finish. However, I now know, given all the barriers I was trying to overcome outside of my academics, what I was asking of myself was not realistic. Moreover, giving 100% looks very different from one day to the next. It is not static.

It was not until I was in my respiratory care program that I began asking for help. I asked my classmates. I asked the professors. I asked the counselors. I learned that as a first-generation student there were many things I did not know, which meant that I was often unaware of what questions to ask. Sometimes I would simply tell someone the problem and ask if they had any ideas about how to solve it. By asking for help, I was able to secure a temporary job with the program director and receive a scholarship to help pay for expenses in the last year of my respiratory classes. It was a big deal at that time because I was on public assistance and literally had to choose between paying for gas to get to campus or paying for necessities for my children. Of course, I always put my children's needs first, but I was worried that I would not be able to stay on track and finish my program.

When I got to CSUDH, the negative mind-set returned. I was fearful of asking my professors for help. Eventually, I worked up the nerve to begin attending their office hours. I soon learned that they were not as intimidating during office hours. I had professors who seemed mean during lectures but were welcoming and understanding in office hours. After attending office hours a few times, I saw them differently in class—not as mean—because I better understood their expectations or I no longer took their classroom demeanor personally. I now knew a different version of them. Initially, I was really nervous about attending office hours. I developed a strategy to help me feel more comfortable. I did not want to look dumb or ask a question that I thought would upset them. Keep in mind that I only knew their classroom personas at this point. My strategy was to begin by asking a couple of questions that I already knew the answer to or asking for clarification on a theory that I felt I had a good grasp on. For example, I would ask, "Can you please provide some examples of Erikson's third stage of psychosocial development theory?" I asked questions like this simply as a way to begin a conversation with them. Once we talked about a topic for a few minutes, I felt more at ease in asking my real questions. Another strategy was to begin by asking about answers I had gotten incorrect on an assignment or exam. A third strategy was to ask how they arrived at this career or whether they knew they wanted to do this when they started college. Usually after the second time I attended office hours with a professor, I no longer needed to use these strategies. Most professors really do enjoy talking to their students during office hours.

My final piece of advice is to get involved. It does not matter if you are 25, 35, 45, or older. This is *your* college experience. The more involved you are, the more memories you create. Join a club, run for student government, pledge a Greek organization, or volunteer on campus. It will make a difference. College is not something we should do alone. It is a time to make connections, give support, and receive support, and, hopefully, it will be a time to look back on with fond memories.

CHAPTER 31

Henry Rosas Ibarra, Political Consultant

As the son of Mexican immigrants who grew up under Senate Bill 1070, Arizona's "show me your papers" law, I felt an innate duty to prevent another generation from experiencing the daily terror and fear that overshadowed my childhood. I walked my first political canvass in triple-digit heat when I was 14 years old and have been involved in electoral work ever since. Today, following the completion of my bachelor's degree, I am working as an associate for a local political consulting firm in Phoenix, Arizona, where I was born and raised. In my role, I assist in managing projects and clients in a wide array of industries—from political campaigns to nonprofits serving communities of color here in Arizona and around the country.

The desire to make the political process in Arizona more inclusive, accessible, and progressive is foundational to my core values; this desire persisted even while I was attending a university thousands of miles away. Up until March of my senior year, I believed I would work in a big city like New York or Washington, D.C., joining a national political organization or campaign. However, when I began writing my senior thesis in my hometown, I felt a fire in my gut—similar to the sense of duty I had when I was 14 years old. Only a couple of weeks after graduation, I was fortunate to receive an offer from a firm whose leadership similarly arose out of a post-1070 era. More importantly, I was grateful for my major and my thesis advisor, who afforded me the opportunity to reconnect with my 14-year-old self, ultimately pointing me toward my dream job and the opportunity to be in community with like-minded change makers.

APPLYING TO AND PREPARING FOR COLLEGE

My mother, who is a housecleaner, for years allowed me to accompany her into the homes of middle-class and elite Phoenicians. I did homework on other people's dining tables and on the staircases of multistory homes, but I never really thought about going to college. My state was consistently ranked near the bottom for quality of education. As I was entering high school, I knew that the education system was overworked and drastically underfunded. As I got older, I realized the systemic underfunding was a deliberate effort to keep students like me from succeeding. My mom knew that if I were to attend college, I would need external help. Luckily, one of her clients pointed me toward a local nonprofit that guides low-income Latinos through the college application process. At that point, I really began thinking of the future.

Starting in my freshman year, once a month on Saturday, I learned about various aspects of the college application process, including financial aid, essay writing, and how to tell my personal story. Over the years, I steadily acquired foundational knowledge of what this exclusive process was like. Halfway through, I was pulled into an incubator organization called the Arizona Ivy League Project. It had an intensive, purposeful curriculum focused on the application process and networking with admissions officers at Ivy League institutions. The organization eventually took us on a trip to the East Coast to tour these schools. My first time ever boarding a plane, I was amazed at what could be and thrilled at the prospect of living in Hogwarts-style homes and learning from an elite faculty. In another first, I was afforded the opportunity to imagine my life at an elite institution and what it would be like to occupy a space that for so long excluded people like me.

In conjunction with this learning, I spent my time outside the classroom pursuing my passion for public service and progressive politics. I received my first internship at a political consulting firm at 15 years of age through my volunteer work on prior campaigns. In addition to appreciating my tenacity, every individual I met was very invested in seeing me attend a good school. They offered coffee chats with alumni, essay revisions, anything they could do to make my wildest dreams come true. These people, whom I consider close friends now, believed that I could achieve something greater. It was this love and community that sustained me throughout my undergraduate career—even during the darkest hours. I am forever grateful and indebted to these teams. Building a strong community, particularly if one's high school is unsupportive or understaffed, is essential, not only to facilitate a successful application but also to provide the emotional support needed during and after the process. One of my vivid memories will forever be on "Ivy Day" when all the staff at the congressional office circled around a single computer and watched me open every admissions decision. When I was accepted to Yale, Princeton, and Georgetown, this supportive group of people helped me narrow down my eventual choice to Yale.

I chose Yale because of its well-roundedness in academics and the people I had met during admitted students' day—one of whom I am still close with to this day. After I chose Yale, I did not really consider what it would mean to prepare for this huge transition. In the summer before freshman year, I was bouncing between three jobs, hanging out with friends, and saying goodbyes to my closest mentors. I declined the opportunity to participate in a program for first-generation students that would have meant spending the summer before classes preparing both socially and academically; it is a decision I regret to this day. That program awarded students two academic credits and gave people an amazing cohort of fellow first-generation/low-income (FGLI) students to rely on. Academically, I was always behind on credits, and participating in this program would have given me much more parity with the rest of my classmates.

EXPERIENCES IN COLLEGE

The FGLI identity can, and unfortunately most likely will, induce feelings of loneliness and helplessness. On my first day at Yale, I moved in and unpacked by myself. Whereas my suitemates laughed with their parents and headed to fancy dinners, I was forced to be content with saying a quick goodbye to my family at the airport. The same was true during parents' weekends, alumni weekends, and other events in which my peers could feel the warmth and familiarity of having their parents with them in an institution that made it hard to feel any semblance of community. In time, I even became resentful of my FGLI friends with families nearby because they could visit easily on holiday breaks. They did not have to make the 3,000-mile, $450 round-trip trek that I had to make (and yet I did so frequently my first year because I was *that* homesick).

However, going home was not always as comforting as I hoped. When I came home from university and detailed my experiences to my friends and family, people listened but did not understand. In the closing months of my freshman year, I began to realize that I was an outsider not only at Yale but very quickly at home as well. In my experience, this tension continues to be unresolved but can be lessened when students find a group of friends with similarly strong attachments to home. During my summers, I also made intentional efforts to reconnect with my community either through visiting or finding opportunities to stay connected to the political movement in Arizona.

I was woefully unprepared for the roller-coaster ride I was embarking on when I stepped onto Yale's campus on August 17, 2019. I came from a state that regularly ranks 50th in public education. The classes I took my first semester were, on paper, interesting, but they were a struggle. I remember sobbing to my Latinx peer mentor when I dropped my first economics class because I felt like I had failed. It turned out, however, that my struggles were primarily due to not having taken calculus in school, which was a prerequisite for the class, although that was not mentioned.

The remainder of my college experience was a mixed bag with an anticlimactic ending, as I like to tell people. I turned in my 120-page senior thesis while sitting at a kitchen table, and I genuinely forgot to attend my last class ever (still got an A though). I graduated in 2021 during a global pandemic that meant my family saw me graduate on a computer screen, and I had none of the traditional senior week activities. However, even prior to the pandemic, almost every semester I contemplated whether I should keep going, whether I would be better off transferring to a different university, or whether I should just take a leave of absence. If you are ever thinking about the latter, do it. One of my biggest regrets is not listening to my body begging me to take a break.

For many FGLI students, the prevailing belief is that attending college, particularly an Ivy League one, will be the key to success. We are told that when we get to these institutions, we can dust off our hands, sit back, and be anxiety-free about careers and goals. We are led to believe that the schools we attend, and their name, will take care of us and make life easier. However, they do not. The harsh reality is that the competitiveness of the application process never goes away. During the normal school year, students need to apply for internships by December. By junior year, students should be president of a student organization (if not two). By the following semester, students should have their major and its requirements figured out. All of this is stacked on top of the already demanding responsibilities of staying connected to our families, dealing with mental health challenges, and taking care of ourselves.

CONTRIBUTORS TO MY SUCCESS

For most of us, doing any of the above is a difficult feat, but at institutions like Yale you are expected to do all three. So how does a student manage these responsibilities and become a "successful" student? Every quarter or fiscal year, businesses and campaigns conduct something called "organizational strategic planning," in which they set targets, goals, and expectations for a certain period of time. Adopting this framework, I challenged myself at the beginning of every semester to do my own version of this strategic planning. In the week or two prior to the start of the school year, I sat at a coffee shop downtown and planned out my vision for the next semester—including personal goals, application deadlines, and classes and assignments. This plan was not meant to be set in stone, but I wanted it to serve as a guide for what I could expect. I turned all of it into a master spreadsheet I used to answer a few main questions:

- What do I want to achieve by the end of the semester?
- What are my personal priorities, my school's priorities, and my professional and career priorities?
- What commitments have I already made this semester, and what goals from last semester do I need to revisit and keep working toward?

After this reflective exercise, I asked more concrete questions:

- What are my academic deadlines (class registration, major exams, and assignments due)?
- What are my personal priorities (therapy appointments, tournament dates, travel plans back home)?
- What are my professional priorities (connect with a couple alumni in nonprofits, internship deadlines)?

Once these dates were set, I then started filling in my everyday responsibilities, such as classes, work, and study blocks.

The last part of this exercise involved self-reflection on the previous semester and my core values. For me, it was always helpful to revisit my priorities and my successes and failures of the semester prior. This last part may seem simple, but I always approached it with a heavy heart. I learned over the years that during this self-reflection, it is important to give myself grace and treat myself with kindness. Even as a working professional, it is still *very* difficult to do in practice, and so readers should not feel discouraged if they cannot do this exercise on their own. I worked through many of these exercises with my therapist.

I always kept these reflections in my Google Sheet to revisit them throughout and at the end of the semester. When I began doing this exercise in my sophomore year, it marked the beginning of feeling like I was not drowning or getting out of bed to just survive. It was the beginning of feeling like the thousands of students who surrounded me were equals and that I too was capable of being successful in this elite institution.

ROLE OF FAMILY

Despite the distance, my family would come to offer insights that my deans, professors, and even friends could not provide. The most important of these was to ground myself in my core values, the lessons instilled by my family and my political family throughout my upbringing and professional work. My values include a strong belief in mentorship, reflection, self-care, exploration, and empathy; they came to mind in every conversation I had with my mother and mentors.

Institutions like Yale have a central vision of how to best prepare their students for "global leadership." They strive to make communities abstract, replicate privilege and class structures, and offer students a "global lens" in ways that perpetuate colonial frameworks. Those students whose values are not aligned with this vision often have a difficult time being "successful" students—myself being one of them. My family taught me to be critical, to root my work in individuals' lives, and to approach my work empathetically and holistically. They define *actual* success by these metrics. In my conversations with my parents, where I told them almost everything that occurred my freshman year, they reminded me of these values and empowered me to build systems and practices that made the rest of my time in college more manageable.

TIPS AND ADVICE

I was a queer, Latino, FGLI student, and while there were communities on campus around these identities, I was still unpacking all three (particularly the first) at the same time. Early in my first semester, I experienced a traumatic event that also uniquely shaped my college experience. Without going into specifics about the event, my biggest piece of advice is this: Do not be afraid to ask for help when you need it. It may be from a therapist, peer tutor, Title IX office, or professor. The important thing is to ask for help. Those with my triple whammy of identities (immigrant family, low-income, Latino) traditionally keep our heads down, as we have been ingrained with the idea that asking for help is a weakness. Our job as FGLI students is to unpack and completely reverse that notion. Particularly at an Ivy, you cannot get by without getting help along the way. Even if you do not need the help, still seek it out and find it. Treat therapy appointments as simple doctor's appointments to make sure you are okay, or go to office hours once a month for a short check-in with your professor.

Most importantly, lean on your community for balance. Do not feel discouraged by the dissenters or oppressive structures you will meet along the way. Your ability to build your community is extraordinarily beautiful and will come in handy as an undergrad. They will provide you with the one thing that will motivate your perseverance: hope. Facemasks and wine night, performing in my *folklorico* group, quarantining with my best friends, birthdays, late-night study groups, which we would deliriously suffer through until 1:45 a.m.—these are the moments worth living for. It is this chosen family that will stick with you for the rest of your life. Finally, because the editor has told me I have reached my page limit, here are some additional pieces of advice that I think are important:

- When choosing a college, attend *all* of the admitted student days you possibly can, no matter what other commitments you may have. You will be spending the next 4 years there, and you deserve to give yourself a few days to soak it all in. You will meet friends who will be instrumental to your first semester, and you will learn about the resources available to make your first year a little less rocky.
- If you're presented with the type of opportunity that I declined (a program for first-generation students to prepare for college the summer before), take it! Do those hiking programs (if you are into that) or any other preorientation program that is offered; it will absolutely prove to be helpful in the first few months.
- Try to stay away from trauma bonding over experiences and identities. What I mean by this is that if you step back and recognize that you do not have much in common with someone besides a shared experience, you are probably trauma bonding. Trust me, it's not healthy for you or for them, and it is not sustainable in the long run.
- Do not stay in spaces or with friends solely out of convenience or because you have invested X amount of time so you might as well keep going with it. Explore new opportunities and people. You will be happier because of it.
- Go to your teaching assistants' office hours. They are usually cool people you can befriend to learn more about academia (and they also grade your assignments).
- Before making a big decision, get at least five differing perspectives on the issue at hand. Then make a choice. One individual may not have your best interest in mind, so be sure to get a diversity of perspectives.
- Make a playlist on Spotify for each semester. I have a really bad memory, and music helps me position myself if I need to. (Plus it is a really cool archive.)
- Do not date in college if you can help it. It is so much more fun just vibing with your friends.
- Study abroad (if you have the privilege to).
- Spend your summers doing what is grounding to you, and do not feel pressured into getting an internship or taking a summer class.
- Connect with alumni from your school. They are always willing to provide a helping hand.
- Never change yourself for convenience or mold yourself in a way your past self would not recognize.

Most importantly of all, know that you will be fine. However, if you ever need a little extra coaching to get you to the finish line, shoot me an email at henryrosas01@gmail.com and I will see how I can help!

Critical Self-Reflection 3

Adam J. Rodríguez

College exposes us to a new culture and environment, which requires both internal and external adjustments. In my clinical practice, some of the most frequent struggles that first-generation students express are anxiety, grief, confusion, and a sense of overwhelm associated with upward mobility. These struggles are connected to what it means to be bicultural, simultaneously inhabiting two different cultures. One culture is the one you grew up in, which includes the music you listened to, the food you ate, the holidays you celebrated, the people surrounding you, and the languages spoken. It also includes values, traditions, norms, and ways of interacting with others. The new group, associated with college and beyond, will have its own traditions, values, and beliefs. These two cultures will not always align with one another. Upward mobility can be isolating and lonely because you are being introduced to and adjusting to a new set of expectations and customs, which can often produce feelings that you do not fully belong to either group. This transition often involves a shifting sense of selfhood. You may feel like the person you are becoming is different from who you once were. It is helpful to reflect on and name how you think and feel about yourself in the midst of this transition and what it feels like to inhabit these spaces and code-switch between them. The adjustment to the new expectations can create an internal tension, which may result in feelings of loss, guilt, sadness, pain, and often shame.

We can experience a sense of shame because our allegiances to our primary cultural group may conflict with those of our new one; this may cause both internal and external tension. The inherent conflicts we encounter may produce a feeling that there is something wrong with us or that we are in some way betraying our roots. Shame is a feeling about who you are as a person. It is different from guilt, in that guilt is about something you have done wrong. In shame, it can feel like *you* are wrong. Your loyalties and sense of self come under question, not only from outside influences, like family, friends, and faculty, but internally as well, as you question yourself and your values. The ability to develop a fuller awareness of this conflict, including the accompanying emotional experiences, familial and cultural obligations from both ends, and tremendous discomfort that can exist when we occupy a liminal space inhabiting both cultures while simultaneously fully inhabiting neither, is essential for navigating the losses and potential shame associated with this transition. The questions in this section are designed to help develop that awareness.

TWO PRIMARY QUESTIONS

1. As you read through these stories, what came up for you?
2. Having read this group of stories, what advice would past, present, and future you give to yourself?

As you consider these two questions, remember the notion of play and exploration. These questions are designed to help you know yourself better and more fully. Greater self-awareness will assist you in gaining a deeper sense of your emotional states. In this section, several authors described their experiences with depression, anxiety, guilt, and shame, among other emotions. These feelings are polythetical, meaning they manifest differently from person to person. What "depression" is like for you will be different from what it is like for another person. Through the practice of self-reflection, we develop greater awareness not only of what we are feeling but also of the many different dimensions and aspects of it. It is the difference between being able to say merely that you are depressed and being able to say that you have a hard time getting out of bed, that your loneliness feels as though you are standing alone near an abyss, that you feel hopeless and powerless to make changes, and that you fear that you yourself are worthless. You may recognize other dimensions or aspects of depression, including that you have lost interest in activities that are normally appealing to you or that you carry a heavy sadness that feels like a lead weight, making it difficult to breathe at times. Often, when emotional pain begins, you may only have a general sense that something is bothering you but little understanding of what exactly it is. Introspection, reflection, and talking with others are ways to give fuller expression to those feelings so that rather than only being able to say that you are, for example, prone to anxiety, you learn how anxiety manifests for *you*. What does it look like, feel like? What part of your body does it occur in? What thoughts does it produce? Playing with these questions helps you better understand *what it is* that leads you to feel anxious, what may lead to anxiety of one sort versus another, or what may lead to less or more intense anxiety. You may feel a natural inclination to avoid thinking about these feelings. This only temporarily pushes them away. They will return—often more powerfully. The exploration of our emotional life is incredibly important. With your increased understanding and awareness, you greatly improve the chances that you will know when you need help and feel more able to reach out for it.

FURTHER DISCUSSION QUESTIONS

What follows are groups of questions. I am not presenting a specific question that warrants a specific answer. Rather, each item below represents a general domain with multiple questions that may stimulate thoughts, ideas, values, or feelings, which you can begin to elaborate on. You will have in your mind the stories that you have read, and they will help inform how you think about these questions. What is important here is curiosity and exploration.

1. What does emotional health mean to you? What do you require to feel emotionally well, sturdy, and stable? What provides you with a sense of satisfaction, joy, and pleasure? How do you identify those things? What about the things that bring pain, distress, and sadness? Note that feelings may be painful, but they are not inherently bad. Being aware of them helps equip you to better tolerate them, feel less overwhelmed by them, and feel able to reach out for help when they do occur.
2. What does it mean to you to feel "worthy"? You may experience moments of feeling that you do not belong. The authors of this book are confidently assuring you that you are very much worthy. What can you point to that indicates that you are worthy? What does it mean to you to be worthy? What does it look like? What kinds of things happen that seem to attack that sense of worthiness?
3. How do you see yourself in the new environment versus how you thought of yourself before college or once you got to college? Since entering college, what has changed about how you see yourself and what has that meant to you? Is there loss associated with that?
4. Do feelings of shame or guilt appear? Can you identify which? Can you identify what contributes to those feelings? What external factors are leading to you feeling this way?

I return frequently to Ogden's (2005) article "What I Would Not Part With." In the article, the psychoanalyst Thomas Ogden describes "those ways of being and ways of seeing that characterize the distinctive manner in which each of us practices psychoanalysis" (p. 8) and attempts to convey "the values that lie at the core of the way" (p. 8) he practices as a therapist. Assessing traits (aspects of our being or personality that are so essential that they cannot be lost) that are fundamental to who we are helps us to gain insight into how we perform and the extent to which we are comfortable in a variety of roles. In that spirit, I offer a final set of questions:

5. What would you not part with? As you navigate through college, you will be compelled to change parts of yourself, bring parts of yourself more forward or place them more in the back. You will be constantly negotiating selfhood, and you may find that it shifts over time. You have many roles, including student, friend, child, sibling. Consider the characteristics that are deeply important to you and that you would not part with. Different characteristics will likely appear more prominently for different roles. Can you identify some of those qualities? Can you further identify those that feel indispensable and critical to your sense of self? Can you name what you would not part with?

CHAPTER 32   DISCUSSION

Adam J. Rodríguez

> We only need to dig a little deeper to see that in almost all stories of upward mobility, structural forces have conspired to make an individual's success more or less likely.
>
> —Jennifer M. Morton, *Moving Up Without Losing Your Way: The Ethical Costs of Upward Mobility*

First-generation students are not a monolith. Although we are often discussed and researched as if we are one large, homogeneous group, we are actually incredibly diverse. You will share some characteristics with other first-generation students, but not all. First-generation college students vary in terms of socioeconomic status and background, race and ethnicity, gender identity, sexual orientation, religious background, and more. Not only do we represent a broad cross-section of individuals, but the intersection of the varied parts of our identities intensifies our differences and complexity. I use the term "identities" rather than "identity" to capture how our own subjectivity is intrapersonally diverse. We are diverse within ourselves. We all contain multitudes, presenting different parts of self in different contexts and at different times. These different parts of self interact with one another in a complex manner, revealing individuals with unique needs and experiences.

Research in the social sciences relies on descriptive statistics as a way to categorize and understand differences among groups of people. The most simplistic understanding of this model can be reduced to the following idea: $X\%$ of Y type of people do some particular thing $Z\%$ of the time. The introduction to this book is filled with references to this type of research. The data from these types of studies provide valuable information, and we should continue to expand this type of research. However, it is equally important to hear about individuals' personal stories and experiences. It is important to remember that an attribute that can aptly describe a certain percentage of first-generation students is not going to be applicable to *all* first-generation students. The students who are left behind may wind up being those whose identities intersect at multiple marginalized points. Our stories, then, are incredibly important, because faculty and staff develop strategies to support first-generation students based on a "a particular approach [that] has shown its superiority based on statistical averages, [but] the person in front of you is not a statistical average" (McWilliams, 2021, p. 185). As we develop our research, we must be mindful to include a variety of models that consider first-generation students as diverse rather than homogenous. We must grow our body of knowledge with both quantitative research *and* personal stories.

The stories contained in this book reveal how the intersections of various parts of our identities help shape our experiences as first-generation students. We exhibit many differences, and those differences are important. They help inform us of the parts of college we may find challenging, and for which we require support, and those we may thrive in. Our stories give depth, breadth, dimension, and humanity to research. They give a personal face to the reality of how a lack of academic preparation affects a first-generation student, how persistent financial hardships create limitations and stresses, how loneliness and isolation affect college performance and mental health, and how our tremendous work ethic and persistence manifests and propels us to succeed despite our challenges. Without exception, each writer showed they were hard-working, bright, and talented as they found ways to move forward despite obstacles; you have those qualities too. In this chapter, I analyze, synthesize, and review the stories from our contributors. I discuss the stories in sections based on the format the authors used to tell their stories: Applying to and Preparing for College, Experiences in College, Contributors to Success, and Role of Family. I will review tips and advice separately in the next chapter.

APPLYING TO AND PREPARING FOR COLLEGE

For many continuing-generation students, going to college is a near certainty. The same cannot be said for first-generation students. Many potential first-generation students wrestle, sometimes very early on, with the question of whether it is even possible to go to college. Some, like T. Mark, Ivonne, and Raquel, knew from early on that they wanted to go to college. Others, like Kevin, Jenny, and Lynn, had much more doubt and sometimes a sense that, as Jenny noted, a college education may be "way out of reach." Many contributors had some awareness that college offered a potential path to improve some aspects of their lives.

One of the greatest and most consistent challenges the contributors to this book faced was, as Jenny highlights, that they "did not know the steps to get to college." Continuing-generation students often receive support from family and school that help guide them toward resources and can sometimes provide additional extracurricular resources, such as tutoring, SAT/ACT preparation courses, and financial support. The contributors to this book frequently described being on their own to figure out the complicated process of getting into and paying for college. Note the frequent comments by authors about that confusion. David Hernández remarked that he "did not know anyone who applied to college"; Clifton said, "What I was making it to, I had no idea"; and Desireé added, "I realized I had been navigating the process blindly without including my parents." The first-gens in this book rarely knew what path to take and often could not, even if they thought to and wanted to, include their parents, because their parents were not available or did not have the experience to help. They had to figure out the process on their own, which means that sometimes they made costly mistakes.

One of the greatest challenges these authors faced was navigating the financial aspect of the college application process. This part of the process was convoluted and cumbersome, which is especially disadvantageous to those most in need of financial support. In addition, many encountered horrible aspects of the process. Some experienced outright discrimination by guidance counselors. When Stephen requested help with submitting his application, he was shocked to hear the counselor reply, "People like you don't go to college." Adj had to figure out for herself how to complete forms that required an address at a time when her family was experiencing homelessness, and others recognized that colleges would reward them for "selling" their trauma." Adj stated, "In every encounter, no matter the outcome, I always walked in with a tightness in my chest at the prospect of having to tell strangers the innermost trauma of my life in order to be offered support."

For many writers, a variety of nonprofit organizations played a role in helping them prepare for, apply to, and get into college. These organizations, with some requiring more from students than others, provided support, answered questions, gathered information about schools, and helped students improve test scores, prepare essays, and enhance applications. They helped illuminate the path.

Rarely did these authors have a touching or heartwarming experience to share about preparing for college, being accepted, or undergoing the transition to college. Notice how this part of each chapter was brief compared to the process of applying to and getting into college. *Getting into college was the hard part.* The preparation for and transition to college frequently included missed opportunities. Henry noted the importance of an orientation that he chose to skip but wished he had not. Others described lonely trips on their own, with, once again, little help from parents. Kevin wrote that "it was typical of incoming students to come to orientation with their families, but that was far from my experience."

The themes of isolation, loneliness, financial hardships, and first-gens' enormous work ethic appear throughout this section of the narratives. The application process was a dizzying experience of denied opportunities, worry and self-doubt, reliving past traumas, and anxiety over money. Rather than experiencing the application process as an idyllic time of hopes and imagining one's future, more times than not, these first-gens found themselves managing immense confusion while trying to overcome financial limitations and feelings of personal insecurity. Their accounts make it abundantly clear that the application process needs to be made more accessible to first-generation and low-income students.

It was remarkable how hard everyone had to work. Adj reflected that "the need to fight for access and resources would become a recurring theme in [her] college experiences." David Hernández noted that "the application process was an isolating experience." Clifton acknowledged that he did not always know the path forward but that "either way [he] was going to work hard." Many of the hurdles and challenges our first-gens were forced to overcome were directly connected to the ways in which the process is catered to continuing-generation students. Applying to college is a big moment in a young person's life. It will likely be a stressful process for anyone, but it is one that also could be exciting. First-generation students appear to have less space to experience the more minor stresses of going to college (e.g., What sort of friends will I make? Will I like my professors?) or even the excitement (e.g., Which clubs might I join? What will I study?) because of the enormity of the structural barricades they must overcome.

EXPERIENCES IN COLLEGE

"Culture shock" is how most of our writers described it. Author after author wrote about coming onto campus and entering a bewildering environment they were not prepared for. Anthony captured this sentiment well as he described what it was like to be dropped off at school: "This specific moment was filled with fear and, worst of all, the unknown." Shortly after arriving on campus and beginning their courses, these writers recounted feeling anxious, isolated, sad, and lonely. They feared they did not belong and that they were an imposter, and they immediately noticed how they were different from the other students. It is true that many continuing-generation students arrive on campus and also feel overwhelmed, but they are equipped with many more resources, both on a material and an experiential level, to help them through those challenges. For first-generation students, these feelings often last longer. Sonja captured the bewilderment of many students as she pointed out the "many systems, policies, and ways of being that [she] did not understand or know how to navigate." Some contributors who participated in college preparatory programs received a lot of information about college beforehand, but then found, as Jeremy did, that "actually experiencing [college life] firsthand was a totally different reality."

Most of the writers described difficulties in their early adjustment. This is a critical time for first-generation students. First-generation students are adjusting to a markedly new and radically different environment, facing different and often higher academic standards than what they have been accustomed to. Many have to work and struggle financially while feeling "different" and not only alone but very much on their own. T. Mark noted that "it was difficult, confusing, and . . . tough to navigate." Whether they were struggling with academic problems, social limitations, or psychological distress, many of these writers found themselves not performing well academically after the first term, and sometimes beyond. Some failed courses or earned far worse grades than what they were accustomed to or expected. This early struggle can heighten feelings of insecurity and fears of not belonging. Ulises stated, "To be perfectly honest, I did not feel at home until my fourth semester of college." If many first-generation students enter college with fears of being an imposter, early academic challenges can feel like they confirm those fears.

Working part-time or full-time hours, raising children, helping support parents or siblings, and worrying about money were frequent experiences for our first-gens. These obligations often pulled students away from campus and other students. Henry highlighted the impact of these responsibilities when he noted that "first-generation, low-income (FGLI) identity can, and unfortunately most likely will, induce feelings of loneliness and helplessness." The theme of feeling different and alone was echoed by many authors. Kamina said, "No services existed for students like me, working 40 hours a week, living from paycheck to paycheck with a small family," while Maria described her envy of "peers who did not have to work and would talk about their fantastic spring break trips and summer travels." Kevin stated that he was "always thinking about money." Further still, Anthony reflected on the difference between himself and his classmates when he found himself "working more at [his] jobs than having fun . . . or living the 'college life' like all [his] floormates or classmates were doing."

Work and other responsibilities pulled students away, but even when on campus our first-gens felt other differences between themselves and their more privileged peers. For Sean, being a first-generation student meant that "feeling behind was as natural as breathing." He said, "I began to realize more and more that not only were there issues with diversity, equity, and inclusion but that the system itself was not meant for someone like me—a Black, first-generation student." David Hernández described feeling neglected and invisible. Contributors experienced racism, classism, and other forms of discrimination from faculty and staff. Those same authors overcame those experiences and found faculty or staff who believed in them and supported them. We often fail to consider how profoundly corrosive, toxic, and traumatizing it is for anyone to have to absorb and then overcome discrimination.

But we persist. We can conclude from the accounts of our authors that first-gens encounter bumpy starts. First-generation students are in a brand-new culture without a road map and without family available to offer emotional or material support. Working part time or full time, usually off campus, some are also raising children. We help take care of parents or siblings and face a host of challenges, and we find ways to move forward. We start to build connections. We meet people, join clubs, talk to advisors, meet with professors. We start to learn the lay of the land and to figure out what is expected of us. Our stories show how first-gens begin to prove that we were never, ever imposters. None of us are. We always deserved to be there. It was just that college life was not designed with our needs in mind. In hindsight, the amount of outreach and proactive work by the colleges to help support us was woefully inadequate, and so we did it on our own. Once we found ways to build community and seek the help we needed, things began to change for us.

Some people found that smaller, intimate classes helped them thrive. Others loved larger lecture hall courses. Some of our first-gens became so overextended socially that it was detrimental to their success. Others were so isolated that it was harmful. Some were tripped up by campus jargon, and some took full advantage of campus resources in academic tutoring, leadership roles, internships, or studying abroad. We can see the interacting dynamics of the multiple aspects of college life. Some of our writers discovered their academic success was dependent on social success, whereas others did fine academically but felt isolated and alone and needed to build community. Others faced psychological challenges that made the academic and social parts of college harrowing. There is no one answer. Adjusting will involve making mistakes, having awkward moments, correcting course, and more.

CONTRIBUTORS TO SUCCESS

If there is one consistent theme that has emerged in this book, it is the importance of finding one's community and asking for help. You cannot do it alone, nor should you try to. Our first-gens often succeeded by seeking out and getting help. However, following their example is no doubt challenging. Community and help usually do not fall into your lap. You have to seek it, reach out for it, and cultivate it. (Meanwhile, colleges need to do much more to proactively reach out, which we will cover in a later chapter.) These authors made their own way using a variety of means, and their experiences got markedly better in two enormously important ways: (a) by building community and (b) by seeking and receiving support. Much of what makes it difficult to survive in college as a first-generation college student is not having advice, mentorship, and support from others. The contributors to this book, when reflecting on what led them to be successful in college, clearly identified the importance of community support.

They built community through family, roommates, friends, peers, romantic partners, work, or frequently by getting involved in campus organizations and activities. Anthony had an experience that many others shared in recognizing the importance of finding his "home away from home." Many students recounted finding a community they could relate to along racial or ethnic lines or some other part of their identity essential to their college experience. It relieved them of the sense of being different and alone. Trish thrived because of the community that surrounded her and celebrated her at her historically Black university. Students at predominantly white institutions often had to search for that community, but once they found it, they characterized it as transformative. TRIO and other student services programs were a tremendous help to many. Some took longer to build community than others, but community played a critical role in the success of probably every author in this book, myself included. Community provided academic, social, and psychological support. It decreased feelings of loneliness and helped to engender a sense of belonging, support, and purpose. Having a sense of belonging offers us a feeling of home and comfort.

Emilee highlighted the "strength" it took to "ask for help." She reframed the act of getting help—from considering it a weakness to considering it a strength. Some, like Raquel and Henry, were bravely open about the help that psychotherapy was able to provide. Valuable help also came from peer mentors, academic advisors, resident hall assistants, office staff, clubs, and, very commonly, professors. Many of our first-gens found a professor they could connect with and build a relationship. Adj mentioned that she "met with professors in informal settings, not to talk about [her] academic success but to learn about who they were as people." Professors can sometimes be intimidating. It is true that there are some who do not want to extend themselves to students. I do not believe this is true of most of them, however. Remember, at our core, most professors are huge nerds who are deeply passionate about our areas of study. We love to engage in conversations about the field, and sometimes things beyond it, with passionate and interested students. Yes, you may get burned by an overworked and overstressed professor who is curt, unhelpful, or worse, but as hard as it is, I encourage you to persist. And if you happen to be fortunate to find a first-generation professor, remember, we "get it" in a different way and may be even more inclined to offer help.

There was another force that frequently appeared in the narratives. You can call it grit, stick-to-itiveness, internal drive and motivation, or "eyes on the prize." Sean expressed this drive when he said, "Everything I went through would ultimately be worth it in the end." He further wrote, "I was representing something larger than myself; I was representing a legacy." This drive may contain a fear of failure, which so many individuals attempting upward mobility experience. This level of determination and perseverance is likely to be fueled by an internal pressure to overcome internal and external barriers. This type of pressure creates drive, ambition, determination, focus, and a strong work ethic. Such pressure fueled by fears can also produce anxiety, depression, loneliness, excessive self-doubt, and a constant feeling of burden. From these accounts, it is apparent than first-gens can lighten their load and find greater balance through seeking out support and community; doing so will ensure that the pressure does not become unmanageable or debilitating.

A few other factors emerged, including the reality that sometimes, as hard as it is, changing schools provides a new perspective and a fresh start. Some authors were transformed by a course or by discovering a new purpose or area of interest. Others relied on their organizational skills and built structures for themselves that they felt they could rely on.

ROLE OF FAMILY

These writers' accounts regarding the role of their family varied. Some families were supportive, encouraging, and excited for their child to be going to college. For others, their lack of understanding of college culture was so profound that it created an emotional and physical distance. For yet others, their families were so busy with work and other obligations that even if they wanted to be engaged and participate, they could not. For some, family was not available due to death or strained relationships. Finally, in some cases, the author's separation from their family was a good thing, helping them leave an abusive or deeply problematic home life.

In most of the narratives, family was not able to offer material support, direct advice or guidance, connections, or help with building a network. Quite often, parents could not understand what their children were going through. Trish stated that she did not hear from her parents during her time in college—not because they did not care, but "because they simply did not know how to support [her]." Many authors described feeling encumbered and isolated by the crushing weight of their family's expectations. Ivonne said that her family was incredibly supportive and knew that they would listen to her if she wanted to talk to them but that "talking to them about [her] struggles at the time would have made [them] . . . feel 10 times heavier." She said that "it would have made [her] failure real."

As first-generation students already have to manage so much, it appears that we cannot also be the liaison for our families to build connections to the university or college. In a later chapter, I discuss the importance of colleges and universities more proactively including families by inviting them to new student orientations. Institutions can do much more to help bridge the gap between first-generation families and students. In those instances when family can participate and be involved, campuses should invite their engagement and help make it possible.

THE COSTS OF UPWARD MOBILITY

College can be an exciting time of development. Growth, however, is a challenging process that involves establishing new ways of being while modifying or shedding old ones. Although it is exciting, it can also be painful. First-generation students are blazing a trail of upward mobility, which our society encourages and tells us that we should aspire to. Many contributors had this value in mind when choosing to attend college. Upward mobility, however, like any developmental change, is complicated and contains both rewarding and painful elements. Morton (2021) wrote that "transcending the circumstances of one's birth comes with a heavy cost felt across many aspects of our lives that we value—relationships with family and friends, our connection to our communities, and our sense of identity" (p. 125). We strive to improve our lives through school and education, but "the process of upward mobility requires far more than perseverance: it also requires brutal decisions and painful sacrifices, threatens [your] relationships with those who matter most to [you], and destabilizes [your] sense of identity and belonging" (p. 125).

Being upwardly mobile involves contradictions and distinctions. Our old lives do not always mesh well with our new ones. We are often confronted with very difficult choices and irreconcilable situations. The accounts of our contributors stress the importance of community and seeking help, which means that friends, peers, mentors, professors, advisors, and family will offer their advice and make recommendations along the way, but you will have to sort through a lot of decisions. Do you prioritize friends, family, or schoolwork? How much time do you devote to social endeavors, to family, to studying? What is important and what is not? Navigating upward mobility means taking in the advice and information you get from a variety of sources and making decisions that you feel are right for you. First, try and take in information only from people who have your interests at heart more than their own. Second, note that not everybody has the whole picture in mind when they offer you advice. Your family may not understand school demands. Your friends may not appreciate family expectations. Professors and staff may not appreciate the perspective of family or friends, and they likely will not appreciate external demands such as work. That does not mean their advice is invalid; it just means that their input is only part of the puzzle. It is important to remember that not every decision will be clear, easy, or painless. Remember that regardless of the dilemma some of your decisions may pose, there is a reason you are at college and that you belong there. Sometimes you will make the wrong decision. We all do that. It is also important to note that some decisions on the path of upward mobility will have painful consequences with no clear or easy resolution. These are the moments in which we will rely on the help and support of others around us.

CONCLUSION

The interplay of the social, the academic, and the psychological consistently emerged in the narratives included in this book. We must abandon an outdated mentality about college and academics overall; the journey is not simply and reductively about studying, grades, and tests, which we then connect with our intellect. College is a dynamic culture involving a complex interaction of unique academic expectations, social forces, and psychological dimensions.

In the introduction, I compared going to college as a first-generation student to traveling to a different country. Imagine if, while you were in a foreign country, you never asked for directions, never asked someone to explain what they meant when they said a word or used a phrase you did not understand, never met people to hang out with, and simply walked around town for a bit every day by yourself before returning to your room to sleep. Included in so many of the stories in this book is the importance of reaching out and building a community of support. In her chapter, Sonja Ardoin, like so many of our authors, wrote about how she attributes much of her success in college to building relationships with faculty, getting involved in some campus activity or organization, and finding or building a community. Imagine now traveling to that same foreign country not completely on your own but instead surrounded by people who have been there before or arrived before you did. They have built relationships with people staying at or running your hotel or the people who run the local café or work at the museum. These people help you translate terms and landmarks, help you understand what to expect, and introduce you to others who can help you. They help you feel more comfortable. Then, perhaps you start working a few hours at that café, or teaching English to locals, or participating in any number of other activities. When you find yourself unsure of something or start along the wrong path, there is somebody there to offer their perspective and wisdom. Your experience of traveling in that country would be deeply enriched.

It is likely that you will need to work harder at first. You might have to work harder to make up for the disparities in the academic pipeline. That does not mean, however, that you cannot catch up. You can. But it will be hard at first. It will take extra time, effort, and perseverance. It may even be lonely and isolating. But you can make up the difference. That is important to understand. The next chapter is dedicated to tips and advice. Thus far, you have seen the context for these tips, which give them greater depth and dimension than they would have in isolation. On their own, the tips are helpful. Within the context of the narratives of our first-gens, we can see what led them to value these pieces of advice.

CHAPTER 33   TIPS AND ADVICE FOR FIRST-GENERATION COLLEGE STUDENTS AND THEIR FAMILIES

Adam J. Rodríguez

> Asking questions is not a sign of weakness, but rather, a way of getting what you need.
>
> —Anthony A. Jack, *The Privileged Poor: How Elite Colleges Are Failing Disadvantaged Students*

During my undergraduate and graduate school years, I usually sat at the back of the class. (I often still do this at conferences.) I rarely asked questions or spoke. (Again, this still frequently occurs at conferences.) I recall receiving my final paper back from Dr. Jerry Downing, the professor for my third-year graduate school course History and Systems. Although I do not remember exactly what he wrote on my paper, it was full of compliments, including a remark that he had no idea what a "brooding intellect" was silently sitting at the back of the class. We wound up building a relationship. We would meet over coffee and discuss a wide variety of topics (which he kindly initiated), in a manner that felt like we were peers. I revealed to him that I understood that what he saw in class was a quiet kid at the back of the room, but what he was not aware of was the often crippling self-doubt I felt, the fear that I did not belong at school and would be "found out," and reverberations from the years of growing up in a Catholic school where the nuns would hit me if I spoke in class. I grew up lacking confidence in my academic abilities and in a setting in which discipline, quietness, and obedience were rewarded.

First-generation students often enter college with less experience in and reinforcement for vocally carving our paths. We frequently come from cultures in which obedience is prized and the idea of building relationships with teachers can be seen as "kissing ass" or "brown-nosing." Sometimes we are told that we must earn things on our own and are even discouraged from getting help. Lareau (2003), in her book *Unequal Childhoods: Class, Race, and Family Life*, proposes that working-class and poor families raise their children in ways that are different from middle- and upper-class families. She calls these forms of parenting that working-class and poor families adopt the "accomplishment of natural growth." This form of child-rearing involves parents being directive with children, with children initiating their own play, having long periods of free time, and having frequent or daily interactions with extended family, in the context of very clear separation between adults and children. Middle- and upper-class families, by comparison, create more structured activities for their children and have many more discussions between parents and children; these discussions are often focused on explicit mutual understandings of thoughts, feelings, and opinions. This form of parenting is described as "concerted cultivation." Children raised in this manner are much more accustomed to offering their perspective and feeling they are entitled to having their needs met, and they are more comfortable interacting with adults as if they are equals. In contrast, in the accomplishment of natural growth style of parenting, "the cultural logic of child rearing at home is out of sync with the standards of institutions. As a result, while children whose parents adopt strategies of concerted cultivation appear to gain a sense of entitlement" (p. 3), the children raised by poor and working-class families "appear to gain an emerging sense of distance, distrust, and constraint in their institutional experiences" (p. 3).

We are not accustomed to reaching out for help because often we have not been raised in a manner that encourages it. As first-generation students, we enter into a culture at college that encourages and rewards reaching out but does not make this value clear. Even when this value is apparent, we still must overcome a lifetime of experiences that may have punished us for reaching out. Colleges and universities do not explicitly state it, but

> relationships [are] a gateway for securing support for and achieving success in future endeavors. Developing rapport with key faculty and administrators [is] the road not just to assignment extensions, but also to letters of recommendation, on-campus jobs, and off-campus internships. And these connections also [mean] so much more: having a faculty member or dean in your corner often mean[s] getting the benefit of the doubt when in a bind; or the single in the dorm with the nice windows; or introductions to corporate recruiters and help with negotiating job offers. (Jack, 2019, p. 82)

Overwhelmingly, the first-generation contributors to this book discovered how important it was to reach out, form relationships, ask for help, and make and build networks. College is a social endeavor that promotes individualism and neoliberal ideals. The structure of the institution rewards those who build relationships with peers, faculty, and staff to a degree that makes these relationships *essential* for college success.

Table 33.1 presents the tips and advice from the preceding chapters. Strikingly, the tips and advice generally fell into three distinct categories: community and support, personal/aspirational, and academic support. These categories somewhat mirror the sections the chapters have been divided into, demonstrating the importance of each of these areas for college success. The number-one piece of advice, appearing most frequently among contributors, is "ask questions." This advice falls under all three categories, as it was given in some form by nearly half of the contributors and alluded to by most others. The authors in this book encourage you to ask everyone questions:

professors inside and outside of class, other faculty, staff, family, and friends. Do not remain silent. As a professor, I *adore* questions. When presenting, at specific junctures I will pause and say, "Someone ask me a question before I continue," and I will not move on until someone asks a question. Remember, I am a psychologist—I can sit in silence for a very, very long time! I never say, "Do you have any questions?" because I know that people do. Of course, there will be and should be questions, and faculty and staff should work to open up spaces to solicit them.

TABLE 33.1. Tips and Advice

Community and Support	Personal/Aspirational	Academic Support
	Number one: Ask questions	
Get involved on campus	Be self-reflective	Make connections with primary advisor
Get involved with campus organizations that match your interests/identities	Be gentle, kind, and forgiving with yourself	Make connections with financial aid office
Build a personal support system	Allow yourself to be vulnerable	Make connections with career services
Live on campus	Be careful with trauma bonding	Make connections with alumni
Know that you are not alone	Don't compare yourself to others	Locate classrooms early
Find ways to travel	Be persistent/persevere	Read a lot
Participate in study abroad	Use psychotherapy services	Set goals in high school
Make connections with other first-gens (including faculty and staff)	Don't get discouraged by standardized tests	Apply to scholarships, not just for first year but every year
Try to find a mentor	Being first-gen is a positive!	Visit writing center early
	Have fun	Make connections with professors
	College can be a place to find yourself	Visit office hours
	It's okay to be scared or embarrassed	Learn what works for you
	Never suffer in silence	
	Learn to accept failure, rejection, and criticism with grace	
	Maintain desire and curiosity	
	Remember that change is constant	
	Know that you belong!	
	Be yourself, and be proud of who you are	
	Be mindful of when you may be wasting your time or the time of others	

The tips and advice that fall under the categories of "community and support" and "academic support" are mostly about reaching out to others, getting help, building community, and asking questions. I found the personal/aspirational section the most moving. The contributors to this book are expressing their belief in you and love for you. We all know the challenges that we faced in college and wish that things could have been just a little bit easier for us. We believe in you, but we also want you to believe in yourself. We want you to know that you are worthy, that you belong, that you are good enough. When you encounter problems, we want you to persevere and work hard, but we also want you to know that you can overcome them and that they are not your fault. We are a community, and we are here for you. Many of the authors in this book included their contact information in the Contributors section at the end of the book, myself included. We want you to reach out to us. We welcome it.

COLLEGE COUNSELING SERVICES

College is a difficult and stressful time. Students face the stressors of rigorous academics, separation and individuation from family, experimentation with alcohol and other drugs, challenging relationships, discrimination, and sometimes even assault or abuse. Mental health services are an essential college service. Many, if not most, college campuses offer some kind of mental health service. Some offer crisis intervention or facilitate a consultation with a psychiatrist for medications, whereas others offer ongoing psychotherapy. Some colleges do not offer psychotherapy or allow a very limited number of sessions but have a referral network to help you find therapists in the community who accept the university's health insurance plan. Unfortunately, psychotherapy, like other college services, is underutilized by first-generation students, BIPOC students, and students from low-income backgrounds.

College is often an excellent time to be in therapy not only because of the many challenges you are facing but also because it is one of the few times when it is so accessible. I strongly encourage you to utilize therapy while in school. Therapy can help you sort through the most challenging dilemmas. Seek it out early, before things become too difficult or painful. There are, unfortunately, many communities that still have antiquated ideas about therapy. You or your family may hold the belief that therapy is only for people with severe mental illness. In fact, therapists work with people experiencing a range of issues and levels of distress, but we also work with people who simply want to understand themselves and their relationships better. You may also face the difficulty of making time for therapy when a therapist is available. Your school likely provides some support in finding a therapist, but it can still be difficult. Another very significant problem may be finding a culturally sophisticated therapist.

Remember that therapy is a relationship. Research consistently supports the fact that the relationship between you and your therapist is the most important factor in effective therapy. In other words, the rapport and connection you have with your therapist is the most vital component of therapy. Because most therapists are white, come from middle- and upper-class backgrounds, and were more than likely not a first-generation student themselves, they may have a hard time appreciating your experience. It is not necessary, however, to narrow the field to only first-generation therapists. A good therapist works to get to know you and help you, even if they do not share your experiences or background. They will listen attentively and work with you to try to understand who you are and what is troubling you. They work to know you in depth; so if you say you are experiencing depression, anxiety, stress, racism, sexism, classism, panic, self-doubt, or anything else, they will strive to understand what that means to you and what shape it takes for you. Therapists aim to work collaboratively with you to discover more about you than may seem obvious on the surface. Sometimes, this means they will challenge you or confront you, but they will do so in a compassionate way that is focused on your growth and self-improvement. Therapy is also a way to get at what will truly work for you; a therapist is someone who can have the whole picture in mind.

A good therapist will work with you to help you better understand yourself without placing their values or needs on you. This point is important to remember because you will likely be culturally different, in some important way, from your therapist. When some aspect of therapy does not feel right, whether it is because you feel the therapist does not understand you or does not support you, I encourage you to say that, directly, to your therapist. In some ways, this is an important litmus test. A therapist who responds defensively or by placing blame wholly onto you is not going to be helpful to you. A good therapist will respond by being thoughtful, curious, open, and nondefensive about your concern. They will want to understand it better and to examine themselves critically to see how they contributed to the problem. That does not necessarily mean they will agree with you, but they will openly and actively work to understand your concern and what it means to your work together, as well as what to do about it. If you feel that your therapist cannot do this, you can fire them at any time. That is always your right. You cannot do therapy wrong. It is not possible.

Finally, you may not have health insurance or you may have inadequate health insurance; your insurance may not sufficiently cover psychotherapy services or you may not be able to afford copayments for sessions. Some communities offer community mental health services at very low rates or free of charge. These clinics, however, tend to have long waitlists and be understaffed and underfunded, and they may not be conveniently located near campus. The troubling reality is that for many in the United States, quality mental health services are exceptionally difficult or impossible to find. Some therapists in the community may do pro bono (free) work. These limitations make it even more important for colleges to offer ongoing psychotherapy services directly on campus.

ADVICE FOR PARENTS

A close friend of mine was surprised to hear I had purchased special gifts for my wife and parents as I got close to my doctoral graduation. She noted, "But you're the one graduating!" Yes, but I felt as though I was graduating not only because of my abilities but also because of the work, inspiration, sacrifices, and support of the people close to me. We do not do this alone. Reflecting this sentiment, Sonja titled the portion of her chapter discussing the role of her family "It's Not My Degree, It's Ours." My family made tremendous sacrifices to ensure that I would have a better life than them. It was not my degree; it was ours.

There are some ways in which my education created a gap between me and my parents. They are both incredibly intelligent, but they did not have the opportunity to get the education they worked to provide to me. Parents of first-generation students, it is okay to acknowledge you cannot fully comprehend all aspects of what your children experience and learn. However, be supportive in the ways that you can. They are on a journey of new discovery. You can assist them along the way.

If you have come this far and read the stories in this book, you have a much deeper appreciation for the experiences of first-generation students. Read through the glossary at the end of this book to better familiarize yourself with the terms and concepts unique to college life, but also maintain it as a resource for when your child contacts you with a question or update. Help your children find ways to make connections at college to get the support they need. Encourage them to meet with their professors, academic advisors, and financial aid officers, and to join organizations at school. Be sure they attend new student orientations, and if you are able, attend along with them. These orientations are an excellent opportunity for you to learn about college life as much for you as for your children. Help them connect with their school's TRIO program or any other resources available for first-generation students. Reach out to the college's student support department yourself, and ask for information that would be helpful to parents of first-generation students. Ask your children about what they are learning, what is exciting, what is challenging, what is different from what they expected. Provide a space for them to be excited about new ideas and concepts they have been exposed to, as well as a space to express their frustrations and disappointments.

It is also important to keep in mind that college is a new part of their life, which you will not have access to or appreciate in the same way they do. It will involve a kind of separation between them and you. Be mindful to celebrate that with them and be aware that it could produce feelings of guilt within them. They may feel they are abandoning the family or not doing enough to help. Their separation, however, is precisely what you worked so hard and made so many sacrifices for. They can achieve this separation and complete this part of their journey because of what you have done to get them there. They may need to dedicate time and energy to school when you would hope they would be able to dedicate that time to you. Your child is growing, but just as when they first learned to talk and walk, it means they are increasingly becoming their own person. This is both wonderful and sad. This is what it means to be a parent.

CONCLUSION

A theme throughout our stories is perseverance. When faced with massive obstacles, hardships, and discrimination, our first-gens persevered. They continued to claw and fight for what they desired. It is an aspect of upward mobility that is celebrated, but it should not have to be so hard. Perseverance can be good; however, we can also make it so people have less to fight through. We can make education what we wished it would be: demanding but supportive. Sometimes we are forced to persevere through troubling and problematic issues. Other times we must persevere simply because the task itself is inherently challenging.

I will share a brief story to illustrate this point and to pull back the curtain on how challenging some parts of academic life and success are. The original idea for this book emerged in 2014. I initially tried to find coeditors, but each person who was interested was not able to commit to the project for various reasons. Many good people were interested and offered support and guidance, but they could not join the project more intimately. Therefore, I started this process with rejection. I sent my original proposal to some publishers in 2017 and was confronted with the reality that it was a weak book proposal. Again, I encountered rejection, mainly because my work was underdeveloped. I read a lot more and worked to revise the proposal. I strategized to determine which publishers might offer the best fit. I sent letters of interest to 51 publishers (mostly university presses). Fifty rejected me. One publisher, however, loved my proposal and concept and worked closely with me to develop the project. To find the contributors, I searched tirelessly for first-generation graduates. I wound up sending 87 invitations to individuals, nearly all of whom were interested, but only 31 of whom were able to commit to the project. I faced a lot of rejection, over and over and over. Sometimes it was because my work was not yet good enough, sometimes because a publisher may have mistakenly chose to pass on it, and sometimes it was simply because the project was not the right fit. There were many reasons for the rejection. The process to produce the book you are reading was messy and extensive, and it involved a ton of rejection. Further, the sections of this book that I wrote underwent extensive edits and revisions. This is the behind-the-scenes part professionals often do not reveal to students and younger people. The point is, though, that success often comes from persistence and the support of others. For perhaps every success in my life that I currently enjoy, I had to endure repeated rejection before succeeding.

Throughout the stories contained in this book, you read about many challenges as well as many strengths that helped first-gens to overcome those challenges. We should acknowledge the challenges you will face. We cannot ignore them because they are painful. We must also celebrate the perseverance, work ethic, and strengths we possess. From these stories, I can conclude that our models of first-generation students should neither be primarily deficit-based nor strength-based. In both of these models, the emphasis is still on *you* as the first-generation student as the focus of the hardship. I am proposing a model that acknowledges and respects the challenges that first-generation students face and the strengths we possess while simultaneously emphasizing the external mechanisms that create the challenges and necessitate the utilization of our strengths to persevere to achieve academic success. In this model, we acknowledge that there are steps you can take as a first-generation student to improve your experience. However, we must pay sufficient attention to institutional and systemic problems in need of redress to contextualize why first-generation students have struggles. In the final chapter, we turn our attention to those systemic problems and the work that is necessary to change them.

CHAPTER 34   CREATING EQUITY AND JUSTICE: RECOMMENDATIONS FOR COLLEGES, FACULTY, AND STAFF

Adam J. Rodríguez

> Admitting students and giving them financial aid is not enough to make an inclusive campus.
>
> —Anthony A. Jack, *The Privileged Poor: How Elite Colleges Are Failing Disadvantaged Students*

The authors of this book bravely and beautifully shared their experiences, giving a face to the growing body of research on first-generation students. They help us appreciate the stories behind the reports of lower academic performance and higher attrition rates. These stories illuminate the ways in which we—faculty, staff, and institutions—are failing first-generation students. Institutions are called on to shift their focus away from an emphasis on helping first-generation students be more like continuing-generation students and toward creating a system in which universities are enriched by the wisdom and experience of first-generation students while promoting a generative culture for those students.

This support to first-gens must be multidimensional and multilevel, both inside and outside of the classroom and campus. Providing the mechanisms of such support will involve a deeply honest confrontation with the systems and structures within the institution that frequently are so ingrained they are invisible and that cater to a population of continuing-generation students, who are often white and from the middle and upper classes. These structures include tacit standards and expectations for students, as well as an individualistic mentality that places the emphasis on students to proactively seek out what they feel they need, often in competition with their peers. For first-generation students, this environment is a confusing quagmire of nonsensical jargon, intimidating professors, overwhelming responsibilities, unwritten rules, and stressful academics, all of which promote a feeling that they do not belong.

The good news is that, due to an increase in research about the lives of first-generation students, we know a tremendous amount about how to do this. As you read the research presented below, hold in mind the stories from the voices in this book. Recall the struggles to belong and to be accepted, the discrimination and rejection they faced, the confusion and steep learning curve, and the sense of overwhelm. Also hold in mind the striving, the yearning, and the success. The stories here are just a select few, and they only represent those who overcame the odds. There are countless others who did not and should have. These recommendations, at their core, move us toward creating environments of greater equity and social justice.

LAYING THE GROUNDWORK

Universities should train faculty and staff on theoretical models that address inequities and injustices and their impacts. Weber (2021) identified several areas of study undertaken at her institution, Pine Manor College, to meet the university's goal of better serving its student body, which overwhelmingly consists of first-generation, low-income, and/or students of color. These areas of study focus on racial and social equity, trauma-informed approaches, and restorative justice. Resources (including those from Weber) include articles and texts on validation theory (Rendón & Muñoz, 2011), work on communities of cultural wealth (Yosso, 2005, 2006), critical race theory (Harris, 1993; Ladson-Billings, 1998, 2021; Solórzano & Yosso, 2001), queer theory (Brim, 2020), postmodern feminism (Butler, 2006), sense of belonging (O'Keeffe, 2013), wealth inequality (Lareau, 2003), effects of transgenerational trauma (Schwab, 2010), restorative justice (Karp, 2014), college inequality (Gutiérrez y Muhs et al., 2012; Jack, 2019; Rivera, 2015; Tough, 2019), and first-generation student experiences (Heinz Housel, 2019; Longwell-Grice & Longwell-Grice, 2021). Such a theoretical background plays an essential role in laying the foundation for thinking about structural "change to meet student needs rather than forcing students to change to meet institutional norms" (Marshall, 2021, p. 278). It is a process that will be continuously challenging, for a variety of reasons, not the least of which is that it involves examining all aspects of institutional culture *"to assess all of the tasks we perform each day and ask ourselves whether these are helping our students or hurting them"* (Jack, 2019, p. 190; emphasis added).

Theoretical training is the didactic component of change. The experiential component is essential and deserves equal, if not greater, attention. The latter type of change requires active, ongoing, intentional internal efforts and self-reflection by faculty and staff. Faculty and staff are called on to abandon the myth of pedagogic and institutional neutrality in postsecondary education. College is influenced not only by sociocultural injustices and inequities but also by systems that actively maintain inequality. Questioning the basic tenets of how we interact with students requires humility and a willingness to engage in open self-criticism and examination of our assumptions, beliefs, and values, both conscious and unconscious; these are internal influences that impact decisions, pedagogies, standards, and practices. To do this work, we must position ourselves to consider multiple perspectives, to acknowledge our fallibility and limitations, and to be willing to consider overdetermined and complicated dynamics with an open perspective that seeks to hold personal biases at bay as much as possible. It is often true that if the emotional response to introspection creates some discomfort, then there is something internal going on that is worthy of our attention and reflection. Of course, we will not always meet that standard, but openness and receptivity to introspection is prized above all else in examining the forces that uphold and maintain systemic imbalances.

As campuses become increasingly diverse and rates of first-generation students increase, we will not always understand our students or appreciate their needs. One of the most popular terms in the academic and nonacademic lexicon regarding diversity and inclusion training is "competence." Competence is an admirable thing. It is good to be competent. However, mere "competence" is largely didactic and should be the bare minimum that we expect when working with people from differing backgrounds. Multicultural competence training done well will help build greater knowledge and awareness of the needs of large groups of individuals. When done poorly, however, competence training can be reductive, objectifying and essentializing groups of people, broadening asymmetry while denying mutuality.

First-generation students are a heterogeneous group whose identities have many intersecting parts. Such complexity requires that we be more than merely "competent": We must strive to also be "radically open" (Hart, 2017) to people from other cultures. Being radically open involves having an open, self-reflective, and curious stance dedicated to "learning how to become *increasingly undefended* around matters of diversity and otherness such that you can be open: open to the other person who will be, in some significant ways, most certainly different from you" (Hart, 2017, p. 13; emphasis added). When engaged with someone whose perspectives and experiences you do not share, being radically open involves the *"repeated, deliberate abandonment of presumptions, about both self and other while simultaneously maintaining a disposition of curiosity"* (Hart, 2017, p. 13; emphasis added). The task of stepping away from expertise and positioning oneself as both curious and willing to learn necessitates being open to discovering our own biases and limitations. Such a stance is contrary to the position we often maintain as educators, in which we are looked to for our expertise, knowledge, information, and competence. Adopting such a position is often terribly uncomfortable. The stories in this book reveal the necessity of approaching each student with radical openness, as there is often a tremendous amount going on behind the scenes that we do not have access to and that we often cannot relate to.

The act of listening is a far more complex endeavor than it may appear. Truly listening to another, on a deeper level, involves paying attention to more than the manifest content of what a student is talking about. Listening to possible latent meanings, noticing body language, considering the process of the conversation and not only its content, and taking note of what feelings arise within us are functions of listening in depth. Although faculty and staff should not be expected to listen to their students with the depth that a psychologist listens to a patient, we can, however, shift the manner in which we listen to our students; we can listen with greater depth, increased awareness, and radical openness. In this way, we can help create relationships and promote students' proactive engagement. I contend that listening to students in depth saves time. You are more likely to avoid misunderstandings and repeated requests and more likely to identify problems early. It is also aligned with a student-oriented stance.

These two elements—providing didactic training in theoretical models related to social justice and equity and developing a radically open, student-centered stance—lay the groundwork for shifting the college and university atmosphere to one that is more welcoming and useful to first-generation students. The changes that are necessary to support first-generation and low-income students need to occur at the institutional level, within the classroom, and also on a state and federal level. I first discuss changes to institutional services, which directly affect the experience of first-generation college students. These services include early intervention programs, the admissions process, financial aid assistance, tutoring services, residence hall life, academic advising, mentorship programs, mental health counseling and psychotherapy, and increased representation of first-generation, low-income, and BIPOC in faculty and staff, especially in leadership positions. Common to each recommendation is the emphasis on the institution *proactively* reaching out to and establishing relationships with first-generation students.

INSTITUTIONAL CHANGES

Early Intervention

Early intervention is critical. Information is critical. At an early age, continuing-generation students receive information about college, along with resources, financial stability, access to quality education, and reinforcement of the importance of education. They also inherit cultural capital from their parents, which helps them be more successful than their first-generation peers. Recall the accounts of our first-generation student contributors who repeatedly underwent early adjustment and transition challenges. They were in the midst of culture shock. That shock is understandable given the very fact they are first-generation students. What is less obvious, however, is that their culture shock "depends less on class differences than it does on exposure to and knowledge of the norms" of college (Jack, 2019, p. 76). Early intervention works to catch first-generation students before they fall and establishes a sturdy support that will reduce the chance of them falling in the future.

Early intervention should begin with first identifying who is first-gen in your current student body and matriculating cohort. If your school is not tracking this information, you cannot know who to support. Many first-generation students are not even aware they are first-generation students. Begin by establishing the definition. The definition should be based on what best serves students and provides the access they need, not as a "proxy for 'diverse' students without attention to implications of race, social class, and poverty" (Jehangir & Collins, 2021, p. 304). University faculty and staff must organize to establish the definition, the methods for identifying first-generation students, and the methods for outreach. After this step, a first-generation web presence can be established with information, including campus dictionaries; first-generation stories from students, alumni, faculty, staff, and leadership; ways to get involved on campus; and campus resources, including financial aid, academic support, student services, mentorship programs, and community resources.

College access programs played a central role in the journey to completing college for many of the authors of this book. Those programs helped open doors, improve applications, and familiarize them with what to expect at college. The programs were pivotal but not sufficient. Even with this level of support, these students faced major adjustments in their transition to college. Colleges and universities can do a much better job at assisting them in this process. Prior to matriculation, colleges and universities can invest in welcome packets of information, in multiple languages, and new student orientations designed for first-generation students. *Welcome packets must include information for both student and parent.* These packets should describe "what college life is like and what the college sees as the most successful strategies for navigating it" (Jack, 2019, p. 129). They should underscore the importance of new student orientation programs and mentorship programs and include a dictionary of college terms, a detailed explanation of campus services, and an outline of how to prepare for the transition to college.

New student orientations, likewise, should include invitations for parents. These are opportunities to orient the student to campus and campus services and begin establishing mentorship and advising relationships. They are also powerful opportunities to increase parents' awareness of college and cultural capital. First-generation students will need a lot of information, but information dumping on overwhelmed young students is not helpful. Focus instead on creating personal, meaningful relationships. Listen to them and solicit their stories. These are opportunities for the institution to provide a lot of information, but they are also opportunities for students to learn experientially about building relationships, asking questions, and connecting with faculty, staff, and peers. In this way, you are teaching first-generation students that faculty and staff are accessible and invested in them. You are "breaking the ice" for students who may be intimidated and overwhelmed, and who do not understand what types of relationships they are expected to cultivate.

Finally, always keep in mind that some students are coming from situations in which income is limited, family is unavailable or absent, or other stressors or limitations may be present. If you genuinely want to work toward helping students succeed, you must recognize that some students will have limitations in participating in some programs, including orientation. It is important to be sensitive to, and flexible regarding, the diverse situations and needs of your incoming students. Support for them may take the form of providing housing, food, transportation, or other resources. This level of support may come with a financial cost, but investments in supporting students early will pay off for the student and for the university in the long run.

Admissions Process

The current structure of the traditional admissions process favors affluent and continuing-generation students (Jack, 2019; Tough, 2019). Several schools have begun to move away from standardized tests, and even more have been forced to do so due to the COVID-19 pandemic. Jon Boeckenstedt, vice provost at Oregon State University, stated that "if colleges and universities are serious about enrolling more first-generation students, low-income students, or students of color . . . they need to take a serious look at the weight of tests in the admissions process" (Tough, 2019, p. 171). In Dr. Boeckenstedt's blog, at jonboeckenstedt.net, he extensively discusses the limitations and problems of standardized tests. However, even if one steadfastly believes in them (change is difficult for many) as predictors of success, the stories of these first-generation students who were successful in spite of them need to be considered, especially in light of these students' increased potential for success if changes to the structures of colleges, big and small, could be made to better support first-generation students, low-income students, and students of color.

Standardized tests favor affluent and continuing-generation students, who also receive much more support with their admissions essays and other parts of their application. First-generation students, as represented in Sean and Adj's stories among others, have become aware of the currency established by selling their trauma, colloquially termed "trauma porn." Many students are aware that discussing traumatic events from their past is looked on favorably by admissions offices. This grotesque exercise aligns well with the desire among some privileged individuals to hear a heartwarming redemption story where they can position themselves as hero and savior. One should not have to sell one's history of poverty, or story of abuse or loss, to make it into college. There are real people, young people, at the heart of those stories. Not only is sharing trauma under coercive conditions exploitive and harmful; it also makes real people into caricatures, reducing their humanity. Institutions must stop the practice of encouraging, tacitly or otherwise, students to discuss their trauma. Admissions offices should train staff to be aware of the harmful impact of rewarding applicants who sell their trauma. Colleges and universities can post statements on their applications and website that explicitly tell students to be careful and cautious about discussing traumatic or emotionally challenging parts of their lives while making clear that all students have the right to protect any part of their history. Active, clear statements by colleges and universities, supported through staff training, can help break this harmful trend.

Financial Aid Assistance

As we read in the stories contained in this book, finances were a major factor in applying to and attending college for many first-generation students. Colleges can make a concerted effort to attract first-generation students with more approachable explanations of finances (not only for the first year but over 4 or more years to graduation) to assist first-generation students in their decision making. This level of support can and should begin with the application process and continue through students' tenure on campus. R. Longwell-Grice and Hoffman (2021) discuss the sobering reality that, although it is necessary for first-generation students to receive good information about financial aid, many students "regularly express feelings of disappointment with the level of financial support they receive from their college or university" (p. 176). This disappointment "stems from a simple lack of proactive practices on the part of financial aid offices" (p. 176). First-generation students frequently are not fully aware of the different financial aid options and full range of resources available to them;

they are unfamiliar with FAFSA and the process of applying for financial aid and do not understand the terms and conditions of financial aid. Further, they may not know the college culture well enough to anticipate what they will or will not need from a financial perspective. First-generation students may not have parental support to help guide them in making major decisions about money and college. Financial aid offices need to proactively reach out to students early and often to explain the vocabulary associated with financial aid and the options available to them. They should maintain regular communication with first-generation students to check in on them beyond the first term. Although financial aid offices need to be sure they are imparting information clearly and consistently, they must go further in checking in with students to ensure they understand the information.

Tutoring Services

Tutoring services greatly benefit first-generation students, given that they frequently enter college with lower academic readiness than their continuing-generation peers. Early outreach for first-generation students that makes tutoring accessible and comprehensible can help students develop better study habits, overcome gaps in academic experience, and "combat previous negative learning experiences with positive ones [so that they are more likely] to find confidence, purpose, and enjoyment in what they are studying" (Longwell-Grice, 2021, p. 178). Because we have seen how busy and overwhelmed first-generation students are when they enter college, it is important to take proactive steps to encourage and normalize tutoring both to the student and their parents. Outreach for these services can begin in welcome packets and new student orientations prior to matriculation and be reinforced by first-year instructors.

Residence Halls

Many of the contributors identified the importance of living on campus and being involved in campus life. Living in a residence hall is especially beneficial to first-generation students. Benefits include social engagement, organic peer mentorship, academic support, decreased isolation, and a sense of community. College administrators and residence hall staff play an important role in acclimating first-generation students to campus life and are encouraged to "get to know their students early, especially at-risk subgroups like first-generation students, and to connect with them individually and through intentional programs in the first weeks of the new academic year" (Gallagher, 2021, p. 232). Sensitivity and awareness training is needed so they will know how to approach first-generation and at-risk students in an open and collaborative manner. They will also play an important role in helping to integrate first-generation and continuing-generation students into one living environment, which may be a new experience for both groups. The integration of these two groups is important, as simply clustering first-generation students together in one residence can be detrimental (Gallagher, 2021). Although both groups benefit from such integration, prejudices and discriminatory attitudes based on class and race/ethnicity may emerge.

Academic Advising

As mentioned before, the needs of first-generation students are probably more acute during their first term and first year than at any other time. Academic advising can be extremely helpful in supporting their success during this time because first-generation students are likely to be inundated with new terms, under enormous stress regarding managing school and outside commitments, and unclear on various academic options. First-generation students "may not know how to ask the right questions or even what the right questions are." This means that advisors should adopt a different approach than merely "assum[ing] that students come from a place of knowledge regarding academic coursework, student support services, and other aspects of college life" (Swecker & Fifolt, 2021, p. 240). Although first-generation students often are not aware of how to approach advising, they are a heterogenous group with diverse needs, and so the importance they "attach to different advising functions" must be considered in the context of background characteristics, such as "gender, ethnicity, financial need, age/cohort, class level, and enrollment status" (Smith & Allen, 2006, p. 63).

Given the importance of advising for first-generation student success and retention, recommendations include extending office hours to help accommodate students with nontraditional schedules, especially if work or family is involved, and demonstrating subject-matter knowledge (Kalinsowski Ohrt, 2016). Increasing the number of available advisors is also warranted, as well as including training and professional development that will help prepare advisors to work with first-generation students. For example, advisors will be most effective in working with first-generation students by utilizing a direct, caring, and proactive approach associated with *proactive advising*. Finally, targeting outreach to first-generation students while creating the time and space necessary for advisors to work closely with first-generation students and increasing the frequency of advising sessions will improve the chances that first-generation students will succeed in the college environment (Swecker et al., 2013). Swecker et al. (2013) found that "for every meeting with an advisor the odds that a student is retained increase[d] by 13%" (p. 49). Advising plays a central role in helping first-generation students understand what is expected of them and how to navigate their coursework. It can also provide the necessary understanding of course requirements and managing course loads, which allows first-generation students to better integrate dimensions of their personal lives, such as work and family, with academics.

Mentorship Programs

Mentorship plays an important role in improving first-generation student success, including both faculty/staff and peer mentorship. With mentorship, first-generation students are better able to successfully navigate campus life, manage academic expectations, and develop a sense of belonging (Moffat, 2021). An institution that is interested in providing effective mentorship will need to create structures dedicated to this purpose, including providing the personnel, time, and training of faculty and staff who will develop these relationships. Peer mentors serve an additional important role. They possess the knowledge, skills, and experience to help guide their mentees. Also, their similar backgrounds and common experiences help them appreciate the social and psychological demands their mentees face (Plaskett et al., 2018). The additional benefit of peer mentorship is to the mentors themselves. Being a mentor promotes the development of not only the mentee but the mentor as well. The mentorship position provides valuable leadership experience, instills a confidence and sense of purpose, and helps create meaningful connections.

Counseling/Mental Health Services

Student mental health services are an essential component of first-generation student success; however, several barriers to utilizing therapy services remain, including stigma, lack of awareness, accessibility, and time commitments. If your institution has limited services on campus, a directory of community-based clinicians can be established that students can use to find a therapist in their community who accepts their insurance, offers reduced rates, or has specialties in areas needed by students. Recommendations to improve utilization of services include training of mental health service staff and active outreach catered to first-generation students and their needs.

Considering that first-gens often lack familiarity with therapy styles and purposes, outreach efforts should include providing students with information about the types of services offered. The outreach should be inviting and detail *how* therapy services can benefit first-generation students. These areas include addressing isolation, loneliness, depression, and anxiety; acclimating to college and campus life; navigating academic and personal issues; addressing concerns about substance use; and developing relationships with peers, faculty, and staff. Other areas include managing coursework, as well as matters related to family of origin, upbringing, and culture.

An important consideration in establishing counseling centers or referral databases is that the field of psychotherapy continues to be largely inhabited by white clinicians or trainees from middle-class or above backgrounds, many of whom may have a difficult time appreciating the unique needs of first-generation students, low-income students, and students of color. Outreach should emphasize an attunement to broad cultural perspectives. Counseling centers should be "just as well equipped to help a student through the loss of a grandparent as to aid a student whose cousin was caught in the crossfire between two rival gangs" (Jack, 2019, p. 187). They must also be able to work with "poor students from rural backgrounds as they contend with loss from a farming or mining accident, black lung disease, or the growing opioid epidemic" (Jack, 2019, 187). Providing effective services for first-generation students requires ongoing training that focuses on diversity, including race, ethnicity, gender, sexual orientation, religion, socioeconomic status and background, first-generation status, and factors associated with being a nontraditional student. This training should also emphasize the dynamics of upward mobility. An excellent resource for such training is Morton's (2019) *Moving Up Without Losing Your Way: The Ethical Costs of Upward Mobility*. To illustrate the importance of cultural awareness related to first-generation students, I will share a brief clinical vignette. Although this vignette is directly related to therapy services, the themes of openness and receptivity to students' needs are applicable to advising, tutoring, mentoring, and other student services.

I worked briefly with a first-generation, queer Muslim woman in her third year of college, whom I will call Nasrin. Nasrin had created two compartmentalized lives: one on campus in which she adorned herself with multiple (clip-on) piercings, wore hair extensions of vibrant colors, and maintained a relationship with a queer white woman. Every Friday morning, after her classes, she removed her piercings and extensions, changed into more traditional attire, and drove 2 hours to her family home, where she helped take care of her younger sister and helped with household chores in her multigeneration household. Nasrin was confronting a crisis of identity navigating these dual parts of herself. Her identity dilemma was typical for first-generation students, yet I have seen many such cases handled poorly by well-intentioned therapists. Therapists are often biased by their own cultural values and inclined to celebrate the patient's campus life (which is in alignment with Western and postsecondary education ideals) while devaluing their home life. Viewing the former part of the patient's personality as their *true self*, they passively or actively encourage the patient to psychically separate from their family of origin. For Nasrin, such emotional separation would have denied the reality that she loved and cherished both parts of herself and had a difficult time reconciling the duality.

Clinically, it was important to work with Nasrin in a manner that helped her see how each part of herself was important to her and how each felt irreconcilable with the other. Her angst did not derive from the fact that she had at least two dimensions to her selfhood. She was actually quite comfortable with that. She felt that her clip-on piercings and hair extensions were lovely and creative solutions to this bind! Her angst, rather, derived from the fact that she felt that one side could never accept the other: Her family could not accept her progressive and queer lifestyle on campus, and her girlfriend and friends could not accept her family's values. However, each part of her life was deeply important to her. Many first-generation students face a similar struggle between family values and traditions that do not align with the values espoused on a college campus or embodied by their peers. The role of a therapist is not to encourage the patient to choose one over the other; all people contain multitudes. Rather, the role of a therapist is first to *understand what is actually troubling the patient* and not project our own values onto their situation. We are then positioned to help the patient confront these seemingly incompatible parts of their life and the tensions that come with possessing multitudes. Taking this stance involves helping a patient come to terms with their duality and sometimes mourning the loss of the potential for integration (when integration is not possible). There is a price to upward mobility that can be excruciatingly painful. Not every situation provides a neat and tidy resolution. Some involve loss and heartbreak.

Increased Representation

Shortly after I completed my doctorate, I began a private practice, and because I adore teaching, I looked for opportunities to teach. I applied to dozens of jobs and wound up earning a tenure-track position at a small, private liberal arts college in the peninsula in Northern California. This was despite having no idea what a "job talk" (a fundamental part of nearly every faculty interview) was.[1] Because my department chair was open to a nontraditional applicant, I was hired. After I obtained the position, the department chair took me under her wing and began to mentor me in teaching, classroom dynamics, campus politics, and carving a path to earning tenure. (This likely would not have occurred at a larger college.) Her judgment turned out to be astute. I was a talented, effective, productive, hard-working, and beloved faculty member who made significant contributions to the university.

Beyond the fact that I was a very strong faculty member, I brought an additional benefit to the program. I was told by students on occasions too numerous to count that I was the first Latinx professor they had ever had. I was told by some that I was the first teacher who was a person of color that they had ever had. I was told by even more students that I was the first first-generation teacher that they had ever had. The representation that I created was important to the students. It created a connection between us that helped them imagine what they could achieve. It is worth noting that I taught in the graduate program in clinical psychology, which means that I was teaching students in their mid-20s and beyond. This means that in over 17 years of education, many of my students had never had a first-generation teacher or teacher of color.

If schools genuinely want to improve first-generation student success, they must hire more diverse faculty and staff and put them in leadership positions. (I am frequently invited to join diversity committees of local organizations; however, I am rarely invited to join leadership committees or curriculum committees.) In addition, schools must make a focused and concerted effort to hire first-generation faculty and staff, faculty and staff from low-income backgrounds, and BIPOC faculty and staff. In 2018, the overwhelming majority (75%) of U.S. full-time faculty were white (non-Hispanic), with only 6% identifying as Black/African American, 6% Latinx, 12% Asian American/Pacific Islander, and 1% American Indian/Alaska Native or of two or more races (National Center for Education Statistics, 2020). According to the same survey data, the faculty who are promoted to full professor, the position with the highest wage and often the most influence and power, are 80% white. The majority of first-generation students are being taught by people who do not look like them or come from similar backgrounds. Representation is staggeringly low. Once onboard, institutions must also ensure these faculty and staff meet with success by providing attentive and personal mentoring. They will require tremendous support as they withstand racism, sexism, and classism in a wide variety of forms from peers and students on campus.

Although these recommendations require institutional support, which at its core translates to money and time, we cannot simply stack additional duties onto

---

1. I recall asking a member of the search committee what a "job talk" was and receiving a response of, "Oh, you know, just talk about your research interests," with no other instruction. Too embarrassed to ask further, I left it at that. Just before the job talk started, one audience member noticed how I was preparing and remarked, "Oh, you're not using PowerPoint. That's brave!" I was trained as a clinician, not as an academic; I had no idea what a job talk should look like or that most folx used PowerPoint, so I just "winged it." It was yet another experience, among dozens if not hundreds to that point, of not being well versed in the expectations of academia, with others assuming that I understood what something meant.

overburdened faculty; instead, we must carefully examine and reconfigure our expectations for faculty and staff.

There remains one critical recommendation for institutions. Our national investment in higher education has shifted over the decades, with the state providing much less of the operating budget of public universities and colleges now than in the past: from 75% to around 50% currently (Goldrick-Rab, 2017, p. 39). Tough (2019) adds,

> Until relatively recently, public higher education in the United States was cheap, if not free. In Europe and Canada and many other developed nations, it remains that way. In reality, it is the last few decades in the United States that stand out as an anomaly—a brief, disastrous experiment in introducing free-market capitalism into a public service that has a huge impact on a young person's future earning power. (p. 342)

Simultaneous with the decrease in state funding, over these same decades, college enrollment by people of color, people from low-income communities, and first-generation students has exploded. I strongly suspect that the increase in diversity on campus and the decrease in state funding are connected. An investment in education, on the state level and by the institution itself, is an investment in our communities. A well-educated public is an overall healthier public. The issue of financing education needs to be much more prominently advocated for. We must implore our university presidents and leaders to use their power to raise this issue and identify opportunities to make the funding of education, from pre-K to college, a national priority. These are equity and social justice issues.

These changes affect one another, with each expanding on and supporting the other, shifting the college environment from one that feels unwelcoming and confusing to one in which students receive the information they need, feel like they belong and are supported, and are connected to the resources they need. Together these changes will create a much stronger scaffolding of student support and significantly improve onboarding for students. Before their first class, students would have a better idea of what to expect and have better knowledge about where to get support when they need it. Changes within the classroom and in the traditional professor-student relationship can work in conjunction with institutional changes to create a much stronger student body—academically, socially, and psychologically. In the next section, I discuss the importance of changing syllabi, reducing jargon, normalizing adjustment difficulties, and providing extra tutoring, smaller classes, and more engaged faculty.

CLASSROOM LEVEL

Working toward the goal of transforming university structures involves making changes to courses and the classroom. Strategies for improving the classroom experience for first-generation students, such as those offered by Nunn (2019), center on greater transparency about pedagogy, increased communication to students about expectations and the purposes of assignments and other classroom tasks, affirming speech, proactive faculty engagement, additional classroom supports, and earlier and more frequent check-ins on performance. These strategies emerged from attending "to the wider set of educational histories, adult responsibilities, and cultural sensibilities of our entire student body, rather than the narrower set of lived experiences that many of us imagine that a 'typical college student' has had" (p. 5). As they currently stand, many of our classroom practices carry implicit assumptions that the student is academically prepared for the course, is aware of the available resources, is nearly fully conversant in college jargon, and will proactively seek out help, when and if they need it. That is to say, the implicit assumption is that students are continuing-generation students.

Recently, a story was circulated in social media about a professor who hid in his syllabus instructions to find and claim $50, no strings attached. There was no puzzle; the instructions were clearly laid out in the syllabus. All a student had to do to find and keep the money was thoroughly read the entire syllabus. Of course, by the end of the term, the $50 was unclaimed, presumably demonstrating a broader truth that students do not read the syllabus. Students do not read the syllabus. We all know this. However, this is not because students are "lazy" or "irresponsible." Syllabi are often convoluted, dense, unapproachable documents where a lot of relevant and helpful information is obfuscated by pages of jargon, learning outcomes, school policies, and other information students are unlikely to read. Syllabi are designed for deans, department chairs, and provosts, but not for students. The story from social media is a prime example of an opportunity for self-reflection. If most students, let alone all of them, are not meeting a professor's expectation, the problem is with the expectation, not the students. As educators, we can become so ensconced in the cocoon of our habits and traditions that we fail to see when they do not serve students.

The syllabus represents the introduction to the course, classroom, and instructor. It creates a first impression while supplying nearly all the essential information for a course. One place to begin making the classroom a more welcoming environment is rethinking what message we send with the syllabus and what we hope students will get from it. As instructors, we want students to have the relevant information for class. It makes their lives, and ours, easier. The syllabus can be an excellent opportunity to rethink tradition and how we communicate with students. You can still produce the conventional syllabus that satisfies campus requirements. As a supplement, offer a more accessible and intelligible document in which you break down the most salient points in clear, universal language and terms. Some faculty have begun implementing an infographic syllabus, which is a one-page, poster-style image, containing the information most relevant and necessary for students in a clear, approachable format. Infographic syllabi are more dynamic than traditional text-based syllabi, and they are more easily and readily accessed as a resource document. Students do not need to navigate through pages and pages of what seems to them to be useless information to find what they need. When introducing your syllabus, be thoughtful and intentional about how you discuss course requirements. Our own deep entrenchment in the culture of academia makes it difficult to always identify when we are using language that seems intelligible and obvious to us but is actually distancing and confusing to an uninitiated student. See Figures 34.1 and 34.2 as examples provided to me by Kim Fleming of Monmouth University, who uses an infographic syllabus in her classes.

CINE-105: Film Appreciation
T 1:30pm - 4:15pm

with Professor Fleming

What you'll learn

This course will take you on a journey into the world of filmmaking. We will touch down on the basics of film as a medium both technically and theoretically. By the end of the semester you will understand and appreciate the impact of this great medium.

What to expect

Each unit we cover we will watch at least one full length film (sometimes more). We will then discuss that content in class during our lectures. You will follow up with a critical analysis of that unit through the lens of the film(s) screened in class. Each unit will also have a coordinating (online) quiz to explore course concepts and vocabulary.

What you need

If you love a text book (or e-book) option the suggested text for the class is: Barsam and Monahan, *Looking at Movies*.

However, there is an open access text available for you (which means a free online text, which an option to download as a pdf). *Link is posted to Canvas.*

How you will earn your grade

This semester you have an opportunity to earn up to 225 points. Earned points and coordinating letter grades can be found in the full syllabus available on Canvas.

Each student is granted two personal leave credits during the semester. I understand we are still very much in a health crisis, these policies are ultimately flexible.

What does class participation mean? For me, it's a combination of: preparation, focus, and asking questions. Mostly, to your own benefit.

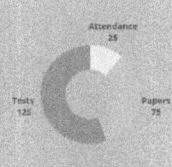

Attendance 25
Tests 125
Papers 75

How to contact me

- message me on Canvas
- email:
- call:
- Office hours: email to set up an appointment

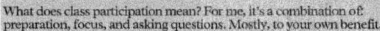

Never hesitate to reach out with questions you have. I will get back to you as soon as I can, typically within 24 hours.

I am here to support you. If anything is keeping you from doing your best work in our class please let me know.

Important final note: Remember, we are still very much in the middle of a pandemic. Things can and will be changing day by day. We are all just doing the best we can, myself included. You and your family can, and should, always come first. In any case, I am here for you. Don't hesitate to reach out if you need anything.

FIGURE 34.1. Example of a Syllabus Infographic
Note. Infographic courtesy of Kim Fleming. Printed with permission.

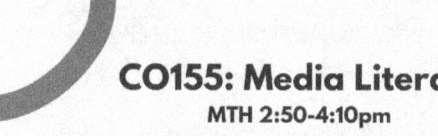

FIGURE 34.2. Example of a Syllabus Infographic
Note. Infographic courtesy of Kim Fleming. Printed with permission.

Reducing jargon involves increasing our self-awareness of when we are using jargon, understanding what we are trying to communicate with the jargon, and shifting to universal language or providing a definition when we use jargon (Ardoin, 2021). Over time, because of our familiarity with the culture of academia and its usefulness in quickly communicating with peers, we unknowingly absorb and integrate more and more jargon. First-generation students do not have this same experience in academia and cannot, and should not, be expected to be familiar with the terms that we take for granted. Explain fundamental aspects of the class clearly, using common language. Do not simply say *when* office hours are; explain *what* office hours are and why they are important. If you are going to refer to the department chair, define what a "chair" is and what role they play. It is worth sharing that when I began college, I did not know what a department was, which college or school my department was part of, let alone what the functions of a dean, provost, or president were. Believe it or not, I learned those facts after I became a tenure-track assistant professor.

Normalizing Adjustment Difficulties

There is an unfortunate cultural norm that encourages us not to share the difficult things we may be experiencing. We know that many students will struggle to adjust to life at college. In her chapter, Ivonne Martinez spoke about her first day in class. It was a class that she was looking forward to and excited to attend. Her professor introduced a complicated topic, and she quickly felt confused. She said, "I looked around the room to try and find another student who looked as lost as I was, but at that moment, I felt as though I was the only one who was not understanding. . . . Not only did I feel like I did not belong in the class, I also felt as if I did not belong at the school." Her professor, Uri Treisman, who had a working-class background as well, made it a point to normalize the sense of overwhelm that Ivonne was experiencing. He would tell his class that struggling was normal and that everyone experiences it and, further, that feeling stressed by this sense of overwhelm is normal. As a consequence of this level of overwhelm, students may even begin to feel they do not belong. He would assure students that the stress is actually an indication that one is learning (Tough, 2019). First-generation students often come from high schools that do not have the same level of rigor as the college they attend. Arriving on campus, it is easy to look around and believe that everyone else in class understands what is going on, that everyone else in class feels comfortable, and that you are the only one feeling like you are under water.

Faculty can make focused efforts, especially in first-year and first-term courses, to explicitly discuss how difficult and different everything can feel when students enter college. They can introduce the reality that struggling is normal and can actually be productive in its own way. Naming the struggle helps students feel less alone and normalizes the reality that everyone will struggle. This kind of opening can be supplemented with explicit discussions about how to get support, including tutoring, writing centers, student support services, study groups, and, most notably, office hours. Sharing that support services include available accommodations for students with differing needs is also important. Normalizing the experience and offering strategies to combat it validates and empowers students. The next part is critical. Treisman understood that "simply *saying* a lot of warm and encouraging things to new students wasn't enough, on its own, to persuade them that they belonged and that they could succeed at advanced work. He had to *show* them it was true" (Tough, 2019, p. 271).

David Laude and the Texas Interdisciplinary Plan

The state of Texas has, since 1998, guaranteed admission to its public universities to any student graduating in the top 10% of their high school. Because of the disparity in how well different high schools prepare students for college success, students with a wide range of academic skills were entering Texas public universities at the same time. David Laude, professor of chemistry at University of Texas at Austin, taught the chemistry department's large freshman survey course and served an administrative role at the university, where he was tasked with improving the overall graduation rate of its students. As a result, Laude was in an excellent position to understand what was contributing to student attrition rates. His analysis and experience revealed to him that students were dropping out not because they did not have the potential to succeed but because "the University of Texas was not prepared to help them succeed" (Tough, 2019, p. 211). Rather than focus on those few students on the margins, he decided to tackle the problem more holistically.

Laude used his freshman chemistry course to implement new strategies for student success. He first identified enrolled students with "adversity indicators" (e.g., low SAT scores, low family income, less-educated parents; Tough, 2019). In addition to the standard section of his chemistry course, he offered a smaller section to those students he identified as being at risk. The smaller section had far fewer students and offered additional, supplemental instruction by peer mentors and faculty advisors—importantly, with identical curriculum as the standard section. With the extra support, students who were less academically prepared for the class were provided the tools necessary to learn the same material. He discovered that both groups, on average, performed equally well in the class. Laude tested the model across other universities and areas of study and each time met with similar success. He stated that if universities "do this right," over the period in which students are between 18 and 22 years of age, they "can arrest the damage that . . . [18] years of mediocre academic preparation has done to a student" (Tough, 2019, p. 217). He concluded, "If you can put somebody in the right place, in the right environment, with the right support structures, you can do wonders" (Tough, 2019, p. 217). The support structures were clear: "small classes, peer mentoring, extra tutoring help, and engaged advisers" (Tough, 2019, p. 215).

Consider how these factors align with first-generation students' needs. Many are coming to their first classes with less academic preparation and fewer social supports but with the talent and work ethic to succeed. They do not always fit well into the traditional college course format. Smaller classes, peer mentoring, extra tutoring help, and engaged advisors help build community and connections and provide the additional support that students who are behind can benefit from.

Providing necessary supports to first-generation students who are transitioning to college and their families will create a dramatically different first-generation student experience. This system would include sending students important information earlier, involving family and parents; providing clearer explanations of financial aid and costs; proactively working to engage students and get them involved in college life, making student services accessible, proactively building and cultivating faculty and staff relationships with students, providing smaller classes with more comprehensible information, and providing more intensive tutoring and mentoring support. In addition, such a system will provide outreach to make students better aware of services, such as mental health counseling, and encourage more active engagement on campus. If these supports were in place, all colleges and universities would see increased retention and improved academic performance and would benefit from the abilities, talents, and valuable perspectives that first-generation students bring with them. These changes are long past due.

CONCLUSION

The national conversation about first-generation students appears to be expanding. When I began this book, in 2014, not much information or research about first-generation students was available. Thankfully, this is changing. The experiences of first-generation students are receiving increased attention from scholars, the term itself is becoming more commonplace and broadly understood, and it appears that college programs are dedicating more resources to first-generation students. The stories in this book are a necessary part of the discussion, bringing real voices to this broad category we call first-generation college students. They highlight several central ideas for our consideration.

First, as we have consistently seen, first-generation students come from a wide variety of backgrounds and have diverse needs. Although some research models will necessarily consider first-generation students as a homogenous group, the studies that utilize those models have important limitations. First-generation students must be thought of as a diverse group, with a recognition of and focus on the intersection of the various aspects of their identities, lives, and experiences, which means that personal narrative should figure prominently in our body of research.

Second, our research oscillates between a deficit-based model and a strength-based model. The deficit-based model was the main model for many years before the recent shift to a strength-based model. Neither is complete nor fully acknowledges systemic problems. Whether we utilize a deficit-based model or a strength-based model, the emphasis has generally been focused on making first-generation students more like continuing-generation students. However, first-generation students bring significant strengths and fresh perspectives to college. Our research must also critically examine what needs to change on campus.

Glossary of Select College Terms

Academic Advisor: On campus, an academic advisor provides intensive advising support through regular contact with students. Advisors help students explore and consider their academic interests, identify resources for additional information and support, develop plans of study appropriate for their educational goals, and determine sequencing of classes, including consideration of prerequisites, corequisites, and managing course loads. Academic advisors can also provide appropriate referrals for other campus services, including academic, personal, and career counseling, financial aid, and tutoring. Academic advisors help students plan which classes to take, and when, based on an understanding of the students' goals and the departments' requirements.

Academic Calendar: Provides essential dates for the academic year (generally August/September through May/June), including the academic year start and end dates, dates for finals week, and campus holidays and events. The academic calendar also typically contains the cancel, withdrawal, and drop deadlines for courses.

ACT: Stands for American College Testing. One of two primary standardized tests used for college admissions (the other being the SAT).

Add/Drop: Refers to enrolling or unenrolling from a course. The academic calendar contains the deadlines to add or drop a class. Dropping a course (prior to the deadline) means that it will not be included on the student's transcript, and it may include financial reimbursement for partial or full tuition for that course. It is important for students to be familiar with the dates and deadlines for adding or dropping a class and to be aware of the financial implications of doing so.

Adjunct Professor/Lecturer: Adjunct professors/lecturers are temporary teachers who work on a contractual basis. Adjunct professors/lecturers are not part of the core faculty for a department and may teach at multiple institutions.

Admissions Office: Officers who works in the admissions office provide information about the school to prospective students. They also review incoming and transfer student applications to determine acceptance or rejection.

Advanced Placement (AP): College-level courses that are taught in high school. Students may take AP exams in high school, which may mean receiving credit for college introductory courses.

Auditing a Course: Refers to attending a class without receiving credit for it. It may be done to explore potential interest in a field of study or out of general interest. Auditing policies vary from campus to campus.

AVID: Stands for Advancement Via Individual Determination. This is an in-school college preparatory program that provides support to students in grades 7 to 12. The program is designed to help prepare students for college eligibility and success.

Campus: Refers to the grounds and buildings encompassing a college, university, or school.

Career Services: The Career Services department provides resources and assistance in supporting career and employment goals. Services can include major and career advising, aptitude assessments, mock interviews, workshops, graduate school planning, résumé support, and job/internship referrals.

Cohort: Generally, "cohort" refers to multiple people treated together as a group. In college, it can refer to the total number of students admitted in a year, or smaller groups, as in majors, departments, or other areas of study.

College Catalog: The college catalog provides comprehensive information about programs, courses, services, student rights, and the organizational structure of a college or university.

College versus University: Terms may be used interchangeably, but "college" often refers to a smaller institution that emphasizes undergraduate education. Universities are typically larger institutions that offer a variety of both undergraduate and graduate programs. The term "college" may also be used within a university to describe areas of study. For example, a university may contain a College of Liberal Arts, College of Natural Sciences, or College of Education.

Commencement: Annual ceremony celebrating and honoring students who have just graduated (or will soon graduate).

Continuing-Generation Student: A student who has at least one parent who completed a college degree.

Corequisite/Prerequisite: "Corequisite" refers to a course (or other requirement) that must be taken simultaneously with another. For example, a chemistry course may include both a lecture and lab section that must be taken the same term. "Prerequisite" refers to a course (or other requirement) that a student must have taken prior to enrolling in a specific course or program. Note that some *courses* have prerequisites (e.g., in order to take Spanish 201, you must have completed Spanish 101 or take a test confirming adequate knowledge), but, additionally, some *programs* have prerequisites (e.g., in order to apply to and begin the graduate program in clinical psychology, you must have completed an introduction to psychology, abnormal psychology, and statistics course during undergraduate study).

Course Load: Refers to the total number of courses a student is taking at one time.

Credit/No-Credit: A credit (CR) course means that credit is earned for the class, but a grade is not given, and the course does not affect GPA. A no-credit (NC) course means that credit has not been earned for a class, which indicates that the class has been failed, but it will not affect GPA. Colleges and universities differ on their policies of when a class may be taken credit/no-credit and how often one may do so. Credit/no-credit may also be referred to as pass/fail.

CSS Profile: Stands for college scholarship profile. CSS is an online application created and maintained by the United States–based College Board, which allows college students to apply for nonfederal financial aid.

Curriculum: Curriculum is a set of courses that are required to complete an area of specialization. "Curriculum" can also refer to a set of courses that make up a given area or specialty of study.

Dean: Deans are responsible for the educational, budgetary, and administrative affairs related to an area of a college or university. A dean is a senior administrator who generally was a tenured professor but whose role is more administrative than instructional. Deans report to provosts.

Dean of Students: A dean of students works as a voice and advocate for students and is focused on ensuring the overall welfare and success of students. The dean of students can assist students with multiple aspects of student life, including health services, financial assistance, academic difficulties, and personal challenges, and helps to ensure that all students have access to the resources they require. A dean of students has many additional responsibilities but is primarily concerned with providing direct support to students.

Dean's List: Scholarly award for students who demonstrate academic excellence, as measured by GPA.

Degrees: A college degree demonstrates completion of all the requirements for a particular program. Degrees vary in length, requirements, and outcomes. An associate's degree is an undergraduate degree generally requiring 2 years of full-time study. A bachelor's degree is an undergraduate degree, which generally requires 4 years of full-time study. A master's degree is a graduate degree, which generally requires 1 to 3 years of study, and a doctorate degree is a graduate degree that can require over 4 years of full-time study. The most common bachelor's degrees offered in the United States are bachelor of arts (BA), bachelor of science (BS), and bachelor of fine arts (BFA).

Department Chair: A faculty member in an academic department who manages the department. The primary role of a department chair is to examine the operations of the department as a whole and manage other faculty in the department.

Dormitories/Resident Halls: On- or off-campus buildings, owned and operated by the school, used for the housing of college students.

Education (Study) Abroad: Opportunity to take courses, study, and/or perform research in a foreign country. Student will usually receive credit for coursework undertaken while away. Students live in residence halls, apartments, or with a local family during their stay while attending courses (or performing research) at a local university.

Electives/Elective Credits: Electives are courses that count toward graduation and completion of a degree but are not requirements for a student's particular area of study.

FAFSA: Stands for Free Application for Federal Student Aid. Prospective and current students complete this form to determine eligibility for student financial aid. A FAFSA must be completed *every year* a student is in college and attempting to receive financial aid. The FAFSA may be completed online at fafsa.gov, or to obtain a PDF of the form, call 1-800-433-3243.

FERPA: Stands for Family Educational Rights and Privacy Act. FERPA is a U.S. federal law that governs access to education records. Signed into law in 1974, FERPA protects the privacy of education/student records and establishes the rights and procedures for parents to access or amend their child's records.

Financial Aid Office: The financial aid office provides assistance and guidance with different types of funding to cover the costs of college, including tuition, fees, books, supplies, residence, meal plans, and other college expenses.

First-Generation Student: A student who does not have a parent who has completed a college degree.

Fraternities and Sororities: Fraternities and sororities are social organizations at colleges or universities. Students generally apply for membership during undergraduate studies. Scope of activities vary from group to group but can include philanthropy and volunteerism, social events, and the creation of networking opportunities.

Freshman: Generally refers to a first-year undergraduate student. More formally, this designation refers to the number of credits completed, which can vary from college to college.

Full Time: In college, usually refers to a schedule of 12 or more semester or quarter credits/hours.

General Education Course: Refers to a standard set of courses, in addition to major requirements, which all students are required to take. The goal of general education courses is to ensure that all graduates have a common set of coursework designed around the university's educational goals.

Grade Point Average (GPA): A single cumulative number that represents academic performance. Letter grades are assigned a numerical value (i.e., A = 4 points; B = 3 points, C = 2 points, D = 1 point, F = 0 points), which are weighted, based on number of credit hours, and averaged. Different scales are sometimes used, but the 0.0–4.0 scale is the most common.

Graduate Student: A student who has completed a graduate degree and is pursuing a post-graduate degree. Examples include master's degree, doctorate (PhD, EdD, PsyD), medical doctor (MD), and juris doctorate (JD).

Historically Black College and University (HBCU): Refers to a college or university that was originally founded to educate students of African American descent.

Incomplete Grade: Nonpunitive grade given only near the end of a term and only if a student is passing a course and has a justifiable reason for not being able to complete the course. Credit is not earned for the course and a grade is not registered until the student later "completes" the course requirements based on their agreement with the instructor.

In-State/Out-of-State: Refers to students' residency. An in-state resident lives and pays taxes in the same state as the college/university. An out-of-state resident lives and pays taxes in a different state than the college/university. Colleges and universities commonly charge a different tuition rate for in-state and out-of-state residents.

International Student Advisor: Provides specialized support to international students, including academic and immigration advising services, career counseling, new student orientation, advising regarding F-1 visas, work permits, reinstatement, reduced course load requirements, change of status, medical leave, and economic hardship employment authorization. Also supports international students experiencing cross-cultural, family, personal, or economic crisis and provides assistance in accessing community services and resources.

Junior: Generally refers to a third-year undergraduate student. More formally, this designation refers to the number of credits completed, which can vary from college to college.

Learning Outcomes: Learning outcomes define the knowledge, skills, or information that an instructor or department intends to impart to students. Course learning outcomes (CLOs) are specific to a course. Program learning outcomes (PLOs) are specific to a department, major, or other broader area of study.

Liberal Arts: Generally refers to subjects or courses in fields that aim to provide general knowledge and comprise the arts, humanities, natural sciences, and social sciences.

Librarian: An academic librarian assists students, faculty, and staff to help research topics related to coursework and teach students how to access information. They also assist faculty and staff in locating resources related to their research projects or studies. Some campuses have multiple libraries, and librarians may specialize in a particular subject. Academic librarians are an often underutilized resource for students who seek to find and acquire information.

Major/Minor: A major is a specific subject that students specialize in. Typically, between a third and a half of courses students take in college will be in their major or related to it. Students can have multiple majors, depending on the institution. Students who complete a degree may refer to having completed their bachelor's *in* that field. For example, a student who majors in business may say that they have a bachelor's *in business* upon completion of their degree. A minor is a secondary area of specialization, in addition to a major, which usually requires fewer courses than a major. Students who complete their degree with a minor may add this language to their degree. A student who majored in business and minored in sociology may state that they have a bachelor's degree *in business with a minor in sociology*.

Matriculation: A matriculated student is admitted, registered for classes, and in good academic standing at college or university.

Office Hours: Office hours are a designated time in which faculty can meet with students. Reasons to attend office hours include asking questions about the course, such as about content, the syllabus, assignments, readings, and due dates; getting study ideas; preparing for an upcoming assignment; reviewing a graded paper or exam; discussing grades; working through practice problems; engaging in general discussion; and asking questions about professional development or career opportunities. Office hours are a primary opportunity for students to have their questions answered and to build relationships with professors.

Ombudsman/Ombudsperson: A member of the college staff who provides information about policies, procedures, rules, and formal or administrative options for addressing concerns within an institution.

Orientation: Orientation is a period before courses begin when new students can learn how things work at their school, meet other students, meet faculty and staff, become familiar with campus services, and familiarize themselves with campus locations.

Part Time: In college, usually refers to a schedule of fewer than 12 semester or quarter credits/hours.

Pell Grants: A Pell grant is a subsidy the U.S. government provides for students who need it to pay for college. Federal Pell grants are generally limited to undergraduate students with demonstrated financial need. Eligibility is determined by first completing a FAFSA. Go to benefits.gov/benefit/417.

Plagiarism: Presenting someone else's work, words, ideas, images, or sounds as your own. Intentional plagiarism occurs when a student knowingly tries to pass off work that they did not produce as if it were their own. Accidental plagiarism can occur when a student does not know how to properly cite the work of another. Well-intentioned students can still commit accidental plagiarism and may still face consequences from the school. Colleges and universities generally use online services that analyze content to determine if it has been plagiarized. Students can consult with a variety of sources for help learning how to properly cite works, including their professor/instructor, a tutor or academic support center, or, most notably, the library. Academic librarians are an excellent resource for helping students better understand how to properly cite other works in their own.

Postsecondary: Refers to education obtained after high school. In the United States, education is generally divided into primary (elementary or middle school; pre-K to grade 5), middle school (grades 6–8), secondary (high school; grades 9–12), and postsecondary (college, university, trade school).

President: A college president is an administrative role responsible for planning and directing all policies, objectives, and initiatives for a single institution.

Private/Public College: Public colleges and universities are institutions that are mainly funded by state governments. Private colleges and universities are institutions that rely more heavily on student tuition, alumni donations, and endowments.

Probation (or Academic Probation): Students are placed onto academic probation if their GPA drops below a certain number, usually 2.0, but this number can vary. Students will be placed back into "good standing" when their cumulative, or total, GPA reaches 2.0 or above. Being placed on probation can affect registration, participation in sports or other activities, or other campus services. Academic probation may affect Pell grants and scholarships.

Professor: Professors are scholars who are experts in their field and teachers of the highest rank. Generally, they have a PhD or other doctorate and perform various functions on campus, including teaching, research, committee involvement, and supervising graduate students. An assistant professor is the entry rank for professors. An associate professor is a midlevel professor. After approximately 6 years, an assistant professor may apply for promotion to full professor. Full professors are senior-level faculty who generally have leadership roles in their department and may serve as department chair.

Provost: Senior academic official/administrator who works with deans, department chairs, and faculty to oversee the quality of academic programs.

Registrar's Office: Registrars register students, record grades, prepare student transcripts, evaluate academic records, assess and collect tuition and fees, plan and implement commencement, oversee the preparation of college catalogs and schedules of classes, and analyze enrollment and demographic statistics.

Registration: Registration is the process of enrolling, or signing up, for courses for a term. Registration dates may be detailed in the academic calendar. Unpaid balances, unprocessed or incomplete financial aid awards, missing prerequisites, and class size can all affect registration.

Resource Centers: Individual colleges and universities possess a variety of resource centers for students. Resource centers are designed to provide an open, safe space on campus where students can access resources and services. These may include primarily academic services, like writing centers, academic advising, career and professional development, international student services, and more. They may include personal/social resources as well, including resources for women, multicultural students, LGBTQIA+ students, veterans, families (for students who are parents), and others.

SAT: Stands for Scholastic Aptitude Test. One of two primary standardized tests used for college admissions (the other being the ACT).

Senior: Generally refers to a fourth- or final-year undergraduate student. More formally, this designation refers to the number of credits completed, which can vary from college to college.

Sophomore: Generally refers to a second-year undergraduate student. More formally, this designation refers to the number of credits completed, which can vary from college to college.

Student Handbook: The student handbook contains information about university policies, support services, student rights and responsibilities, academic policies, campus life, student code of conduct, and other information about resources and navigating the college experience.

Student Senate: The student senate is dedicated to making the college experience better for students and ensuring student voices are heard. The size of the student senate varies from institution to institution. Student senates represent the student voice of the college or university. The senate acts as a body of influence and advocacy, addressing the concerns of the student body and bringing concerns to the attention of the university.

Subsidized versus Unsubsidized Loans: With subsidized loans, the U.S. Department of Education pays all interest accrued while the student is in school, for the 6-month grace period after graduation, and during deferment. With unsubsidized loans, students must pay interest while in school or have the accrued interest added to the principal loan balance.

Syllabus: A document, usually given to students before a class begins or on the first day of class, that communicates information about a specific course and defines expectations, learning outcomes, responsibilities, grading assignments, required texts, instructor information, and other important information.

Tenure: In relation to college, refers to a benefit that certain full-time faculty can earn. To *earn* tenure is essentially to be granted lifetime job security at an institution. In theory, tenure works to guarantee professors academic freedom and freedom of speech by protecting them from being fired no matter how controversial or nontraditional their research, publications, or ideas may be.

Terms: The length of time that a standard course lasts. A semester generally lasts 15 weeks, a quarter generally lasts 10 weeks, and a trimester generally lasts 12–13 weeks. In an academic calendar, there is generally a fall, spring, and summer semester; fall, winter, spring, and summer quarter; or fall, winter, and spring trimester. Each college or university adopts their own system. Students should be aware that if transferring from one school to another, each with a different system, credits must be converted from one system to another.

Thesis: A thesis is an extensively researched and lengthy paper that poses a research question and persuasively responds to that question. Students work closely with a primary advisor and committee of experts (generally made up of university faculty) to complete the thesis paper. Schools vary on thesis requirements.

Title IX: Title IX refers to a federal civil rights law, enacted in 1972, that prohibits discrimination on the basis of sex or gender in education programs and activities. Examples of the types of discrimination covered under Title IX include sexual harassment, failure to provide equal athletic opportunities, sex- or gender-based discrimination in a university department/school, and discrimination based on pregnancy.

Traditional versus Nontraditional Student: A traditional student is a student who began and continued in college immediately following completion of high school. A nontraditional student is generally considered an undergraduate student 24 years and older who enrolled in college 1 or more years after completing high school or who attends college on a part-time basis.

Transcript: A transcript is an official document that provides an inventory of courses taken, dates attended, major(s) declared, and grades earned by a student during their time at a college. Often, unofficial transcripts are free and can be readily printed or downloaded. Official transcripts must be ordered from the Registrar's Office, usually require that you pay a fee, and are considered "sealed." Official transcripts may be required for graduate school admissions.

Transfer: A transfer student is a student who has college experience prior to the college they are moving or applying to. This can include community colleges and traditional 4-year colleges.

TRIO: Federal TRIO programs provide outreach and student services programs designed to identify and provide services for individuals from disadvantaged backgrounds. Programs include services for low-income and first-generation students among others. Go to their website for more: https://www2.ed.gov/about/offices/list/ope/trio/index.html.

Tuition: Tuition is the price for courses. Along with tuition, colleges generally charge fees. Other expenses include room/board, meal plans, books, supplies, technologies, transportation, and personal expenses.

Waitlist: A waitlist can refer to being in line for a chance to attend a college or an individual course. In reference to applying to college, getting onto a waitlist means that a student meets criteria for acceptance at a college, however, the admissions office has not yet accepted them. This generally means that the school has already accepted the number of students that they can admit, but if some of those accepted students choose not to enroll in that school, openings emerge and an applicant on the waitlist can be offered admission. A waitlist for a course means that the class has enrolled the maximum number of students and cannot accept more. A student may be able to move from the waitlist and register for the class based on the professor/instructor/chair's permission.

Withdrawal: Withdrawing from a college course means that the student removes themself from the course *after* the add/drop deadline has passed. Credit will not be earned for the class, and it will not impact GPA. The class will show as "withdrawn" on the transcript. Students should work with faculty, staff, and advisors to determine whether withdrawing from a class, accepting an incomplete for a class, or some other designation is the best choice for them.

Work-study program: Work-study is a federal program that assists students with the costs of college. Students earn money to pay for school through part-time on- or off-campus jobs. Not every school participates in the federal work-study program. Eligibility is granted by first completing the FAFSA.

Appendix: Resources

NATIONAL ORGANIZATIONS

TRIO: https://www2.ed.gov/about/offices/list/ope/trio/index.html
Center for First-Generation Student Success: https://firstgen.naspa.org
Free Application for Federal Student Aid: https://studentaid.gov/h/apply-for-aid/fafsa
FirstGenCollege Consulting: https://myfirstgencollege.com
First Generation College Student Summit: https://classism.org

BOOKS

At the Intersection: Understanding and Supporting First-Generation Students by Robert Longwell-Grice and Hope Longwell-Grice
The Inequality Machine: How College Divides Us by Paul Tough
The Privileged Poor: How Elite Colleges Are Failing Disadvantaged Students by Anthony Abraham Jack
Moving Up Without Losing Your Way: The Ethical Costs of Upward Mobility by Jennifer M. Morton
Pedigree: How Elite Students Get Elite Jobs by Lauren A. Rivera
Paying the Price: College Costs, Financial Aid, and the Betrayal of the American Dream by Sara Goldrick-Rab
The First-Generation Student Experience: Implications for Campus Practice, and Strategies for Improving Persistence and Success by Jeff Davis
33 Simple Strategies for Faculty: A Week-by-Week Resource for Teaching First-Year and First-Generation Students by Lisa M. Nunn
First-Generation College Students: Understanding and Improving the Experience from Recruitment to Commencement by Lee Ward, Michael J. Siegel, and Zebulun Davenport
College Aspirations and Access in Working-Class, Rural Communities: The Mixed Signals, Challenges, and New Language First-Generation Students Encounter by Sonja Ardoin

References

Allan, B.A., Garriott, P.O., & Keene, C.N. (2016). Outcomes of social class and classism in first- and continuing-generation college students. *Journal of Counseling Psychology, 63*(4), 487–496.

Ardoin, S. (2021). How institutional jargon creates in-groups and out-groups in higher education. In R. Longwell-Grice & H. Longwell-Grice (Eds.), *At the intersection: Understanding and supporting first-generation students* (pp. 196–200). Stylus.

Atherton, M.C. (2014). Academic preparedness of first-generation college students: Different perspectives. *Journal of College Student Development, 55*(8), 824–829.

Barkai, A., & Hauser, S. (2008). Psychoanalytic and development perspectives on narratives of self-reflection in resilient adolescent explorations and new contributions. *Annual of Psychoanalysis, 36*, 115–129.

Barry, L.M., Hudley, C., Kelly, M., & Su-Je, C. (2009). Differences in self-reported disclosure of college experiences by first-generation college student status. *Adolescence, 44*(173), 55–68.

Brim, M. (2020). *Poor queer studies: Confronting elitism in the university.* Duke University Press.

Brown, O.G., Hinton, K.G, & Howard-Hamilton, M.F. (2007). *Unleashing suppressed voices on college campuses: Diversity issues in higher education.* Peter Lang.

Butler, J. (2006). *Gender trouble: Feminism and the subversion of identity.* Routledge.

Cataldi, E.F., Bennett, C.T., & Chen, X. (2018). *First-generation students: College access, persistence, and post bachelor's outcomes* (Stats in Brief, NCES 2018–421). National Center for Education Statistics. https://nces.ed.gov/pubs2018/2018421.pdf

Collins, P. (1998). *Fighting words: Black women and the search for justice.* University of Minnesota Press.

Covarrubias, R., & Fryberg, S.A. (2015). Movin' on up (to college): First-generation college students' experiences with family achievement guilt. *Cultural Diversity & Ethnic Minority Psychology, 21*(3), 420–429.

Covarrubias, R., Valle, I., Laiduc, G., & Azmitia, M. (2018). "You never become fully independent": Family roles and independence in first-generation college students. *Journal of Adolescent Research, 34*, 381–410.

Davis, J. (2010). *The first-generation student experience: Implications for campus practice, and strategies for improving persistence and success.* Stylus.

DeAngelo, L., Franke, R., Hurtado, S. Pryor, J.H., & Tran, S. (2011). *Completing college: Assessing graduation rates at four-year institutions.* Higher Education Research Institute, UCLA.

Frankl, V. E. (1997). *Man's search for meaning.* Washington Square Press.

Gallagher, P.J. (2021). Learning where they live: First-generation college students in the residence halls. In R. Longwell-Grice and H. Longwell-Grice (Eds.), *At the intersection: Understanding and supporting first-generation students* (pp. 225–237). Stylus.

Golrick-Rab, S. (2017). *Paying the price: College costs, financial aid, and the betrayal of the American dream.* University of Chicago Press.

Goward, S.L. (2018). First-generation student status is not enough: How acknowledging students with working-class identities can help us better serve students. *About Campus: Enriching the Student Learning Experience, 23*(4), 19–26.

Gutiérrez y Muhs, G., Niemann, Y.F., González, C.G., & Harris, A.P. (2012). *Presumed incompetent: The intersections of race and class for women in academia.* The University Press of Colorado.

Harris, A.P., & González, C.G. (2012). Introduction. In G. Gutiérrez y Muhs, Y.F. Niemann, C.G González., & A.P. Harris (Eds.), *Presumed incompetent: The intersections of race and class for women in academia* (pp. 1–14). The University Press of Colorado.

Harris, C. (1993). Whiteness as property. *Harvard Law Review, 106*(8), 1707–1791.

Hart, A. (2017). From multicultural competence to radical openness: A psychoanalytic engagement of otherness. *The American Psychoanalyst, 51*(1), 12–27.

Heinz Housel, T. (2019). *First-generation college student experiences of intersecting marginalities.* Peter Lang.

Hertel, J.B. (2002). College student generational status: Similarities, differences, and factors in college adjustment. *The Psychological Record, 52*, 3–18.

Ishitani, T.T. (2003). A longitudinal approach to assessing attrition behavior among first-generation students: Time-varying effects of pre-college characteristics. *Research in Higher Education, 44*, 433–449.

Ishitani, T.T. (2006). Studying attrition and degree completion behavior among first-generation college students in the United States. *The Journal of Higher Education, 77*(5), 860–886.

Jack, A. A. (2019). *The privileged poor: How elite colleges are failing disadvantaged students.* Harvard University Press.

Jehangir, R., & Collins, K. (2021). Narratives and counternarratives of the first-generation moniker. In R. Longwell-Grice and H. Longwell-Grice (Eds.), *At the intersection: Understanding and supporting first-generation students* (pp. 301–312). Stylus.

Jenkins, S.R., Belanger, A., Londoño, M., Boals, A., & Durón, K.M. (2011). First-generation undergraduate students' social support, depression, and life satisfaction. *Journal of College Counseling, 16*, 129–142.

Kalinsowski Ohrt, E. (2016). Proactive advising with first-generation students: Suggestions for practice. *The Mentor: An Academic Advising Journal, 18*: https://doi.org/10.26209/mj1861250

Karp, D.R. (2014). *The little book of restorative justice for colleges and universities: Repairing harm and rebuilding trust in response to student misconduct.* Good Books.

Ladson-Billings, G. (1998). Just what is critical race theory and what's it doing in a nice field like education? *International Journal of Qualitative Studies in Education, 11*(1), 7–24.

Ladson-Billings, G. (2021). *Critical race theory in education: A scholar's journey.* Teachers College Press.

Lareau, A. (2003). *Unequal childhoods: Class, race, and family life.* University of California Press.

Longwell-Grice, R. (2021). A review of the data. In R. Longwell-Grice & H. Longwell-Grice (Eds.), *At the intersection: Understanding and supporting first-generation students* (pp. 13–24). Stylus.

Longwell-Grice, R., & Hoffman, M. (2021). And the research says . . . : Program supports across the spectrum. In R. Longwell-Grice & H. Longwell-Grice (Eds.), *At the intersection: Understanding and supporting first-generation students* (pp. 175–183). Stylus.

Longwell-Grice, R., & Longwell-Grice, H. (Eds.) (2021). *At the intersection: Understanding and supporting first-generation students.* Stylus.

Marshall, A. (2021). First-gen graduate students claiming the label. In R. Longwell-Grice & H. Longwell-Grice (Eds.), *At the intersection: Understanding and supporting first-generation students* (pp. 276–281). Stylus.

Massey, D.S., Charles, C.Z., Lundy, G.F., & Fischer, M.J. (2003). *The source of the river: The social origins of freshmen at America's selective colleges and universities.* Princeton University Press.

McWilliams, N. (2021). *Psychoanalytic supervision.* Guilford Press.

Moffat, K. (2021). They're here. Now, what can we do to keep them? In R. Longwell-Grice & H. Longwell-Grice (Eds.), *At the intersection: Understanding and supporting first-generation students* (pp. 260–265). Stylus.

Morton, J.M. (2021). *Moving up without losing your way: The ethical costs of upward mobility.* Princeton University Press.

National Center for Education Statistics. (2020). *Fast facts, race/ethnicity of college faculty.* https://nces.ed.gov/fastfacts/display.asp?id=61

Nichols, L. (2020). *The journey before us: First-generation pathways from middle school to college.* Rutgers University Press.

Nunez, A., & Cucarro-Alamin, S. (1998). *First-generation students: Undergraduates whose parents never enrolled in postsecondary education* (Statistical Analysis Report No. NCES 98082). National Center for Education Statistics. https://nces.ed.gov/pubs98/98082.pdf

Nunn, L.M. (2019). *33 simple strategies for faculty: A week-by-week resource for teaching first-year and first-generation students.* Rutgers University Press.

Obama, M. (2018). *Becoming.* Crown.

Ogden, T.O. (2005). What I would not part with. *FortDa, 11B,* 8–17.

O'Keeffe, P. (2013). A sense of belonging: Improving student retention. *College Student Journal, 74*(4), 605–613.

Pascarella, E.T., Peierson, C.T., Wolniak, G.C., & Terenzini, P.T. (2004). First-generation college students: Additional evidence on college experiences and outcomes. *The Journal of Higher Education, 75*(3), 249–285.

Plaskett, S., Bali, D., Nakkula, M.J., & Harris, J. (2018). Peer mentoring to support first-generation low-income college students. *Phi Delta Kappan, 99*(7), 47–51.

Public School Review (2021). *Average Public School Student Size.* https://www.publicschoolreview.com/average-school-size-stats/national-data

Raque-Bogdan, T.L., & Lucas, M.S. (2016). Career aspirations and the first generation student: Unraveling the layers with social cognitive career theory. *Journal of College Student Development, 57*(3), 248–262.

Redford, J., & Hoyer, K.M. (2017). *First-generation and continuing-generation college students: A comparison of high school and postsecondary experiences* (NCES 2018–009). National Center for Education Statistics. https://nces.ed.gov/pubs2018/2018009.pdf

Rendón Linares, L.I., & Muñoz, S.M. (2011). Revisiting validation theory: Theoretical foundations, applications, and extensions. *Enrollment Management Journal, 22,* Summer.

Rivera, L.A. (2015). *Pedigree: How elite students get elite jobs.* Princeton University Press.

Ross, L.C. (2016). *Blackballed: The black and white politics of race on America's campuses.* St. Martin's Press.

Saenz, V.B., Hurtado, S., Barrera, D., Wolf, D., & Yeung, F. (2007). *First in my family: A profile of first-generation college students at four-year institutions since 1971.* Los Angeles: Foundation for Independent Higher Education.

Schwab, G. (2010). *Haunting legacies: Violent histories and transgenerationl trauma.* Columbia University Press.

Sennett, R., & Cobb, J. (1993). *The hidden injuries of class.* W.W. Norton & Company.

Smith, C.L., & Allen, J.M. (2006). Essential functions of academic advising: What students want and get. *NACADA Journal, 26*(1), 56–66.

Solórzano, D.G., & Yosso, T.J. (2001). Critical race and LatCrit theory and method: Counter-storytelling. *International Journal of Qualitative Studies in Education, 14*(4), 471–495.

Stebleton, M.J., Soria, K.M., & Huesman, R.L. (2014). First-generation students' sense of belonging, mental health, and use of counseling services at public research universities. *Journal of College Counseling, 17*(1), 3–10.

Stern, G.M. (2021). *15 tips for minority students to get accepted into elite universities.* Hispanic Outlook on Education Magazine. https://www.hispanicoutlook.com/articles/15-tips-minority-students

Swecker, H.K., & Fifolt, M. (2021). Advice for advisers. In R. Longwell-Grice & H. Longwell-Grice (Eds.), *At the intersection: Understanding and supporting first-generation students* (pp. 238–243). Stylus.

Swecker, H.K., Fifolt, M., & Searby, L. (2013). Academic advising and first-generation college students: A quantitative study on student retention. *NACADA Journal, 33*(1), 46–53.

Tough, P. (2019). *The inequality machine: How college divides us.* Mariner Books.

Urban Dictionary (2010). *Trish.* https://www.urbandictionary.com/define.php?term=Trish

U.S. Citizenship and Immigration Services. (n.d.). Consideration of deferred action for childhood arrivals (DACA). https://www.uscis.gov/DACA

U.S. Department of Education. (2012). *National Center for Education Statistics, Education longitudinal study of 2002 (ELS:2002), Third follow-up.*

U.S. Department of Education. (2014). *Profile of undergraduate students: 2011–12*. https://nces.ed.gov/pubs2015/2015167.pdf

Vasquez-Salgado, Y., Greenfield, P.M., & Burgos-Cienfuegos, R. (2015). Exploring home-school value conflicts: Implications for academic achievement and well-being among Latino first-generation college students. *Journal of Adolescent Research, 30*, 271–305.

VIP Scholars. (2021). *UCLA's vice-provost's initiative for pre-college scholars*. UCLA Undergraduate Education: Academic Advancement Program. https://www.aap.ucla.edu/units/vip-scholars/#welcome

Ward, L., Siegel, M.J., & Davenport, Z. (2012). *First generation college students: Understanding and improving the experience from recruitment to commencement*. John Wiley & Sons.

Warnock, D.M., & Hurst, A.L. (2016). "The poor kids' table": Organizing around an invisible and stigmatized identity in flux. *Journal of Diversity in Higher Education, 9*(3), 261–276.

Weber, S. (2021). How a college rebuilt itself by centering first-generation college students. In R. Longwell-Grice & H. Longwell-Grice (Eds.), *At the intersection: Understanding and supporting first-generation students* (pp. 294–299). Stylus.

Yosso, T.J. (2005). Whose culture has capital? A critical race theory discussion of community cultural wealth. *Race Ethnicity and Education, 8*(1), 69–91.

Yosso, T.J. (2006). *Critical race counterstories along the Chicana/Chicano educational pipeline*. Routledge.

Index

Academic Advancement Program, 29
academic advisors, 121–22, 197, 199, 237
academics: first-generation students' experiences in, 12; GPA challenges in, 28–30, 51; preparation lacking for, 10; programs for, 191–92; student services for, 162; success achieved in, 30–31
acceptance letter, for college, 22
ACT scores, 17
admissions tour guide, 53
advanced placement (AP), 27, 184
Advancement Via Individual Determination (AVID), 98–100, 121
adversity indicators, 246
advice: from Ardoin, 129–30; from Clark, 164–65; from Cortez, 197–98; from Edwards, 31; from Erb, 55–56; for first-generation students, 225; from Harris, P., 92; from Hernández, 96–97; from Hill, 203–4; from Hughes, G. B., 107–8; from Ibarra, 209–10; from Inez, 139; from Jones, 171; from Lieurance, 101–2; from Luna, 48–49; from Marshall, 187–88; from Martinez, 38; from Menjívar, 158–59; from Montoya, 112–13; from Morales, 150–51; from Nguyen, 176–77; for parents, 227–28; from Pepin, 70–71; from Richardson, K., 134–35; from Richardson, S., 182; from Santaniello, 66; from Santa-Ramirez, 77–78; from Shambry, 192–93; from Stewart, 118–19; from Vargas, 24–25; from Vega, 42–43; from Winston, 60–61; from Wright, K., 124
advisor's office, 115
advocate, finding an, 118
AFDC. See Aid to Families with Dependent Children
affirmative action, 46
African American Experiences, 90
Aid to Families with Dependent Children (AFDC), 94
anxiety, 84, 238
AP. See advanced placement

application process, 115, 184; confusion caused by, 216; financial aid in, 206, 235–36; guidance counselor and, 195; stress from, 200; of students, 9, 94
Ardoin, Sonja, 222; advice from, 129–30; college experiences of, 127–28; college preparation of, 126–27; college success contributions for, 128–29; families' role in college of, 129; as teacher, 125
Arizona Ivy League Project, 206
Arizona State University (ASU), 44, 46
asking for help: in colleges/universities, 224; first-generation students, 38, 48, 78, 119, 124, 129–30, 204, 219; in higher education, 96; questions for, 107; resources and, 171; students, 102
Assefa (college sophomore), 18
ASU. See Arizona State University
attitude problem, 64
Avery Point library, 69
AVID. See Advancement Via Individual Determination

bachelor's degree, 132
being yourself, 96, 112, 182
belonging, in college, 101
Bennett, C. T., 15n4
biases, students facing, 6–7
biology major, 57–58, 174
Biology Scholars Program, 174
Black, Indigenous, and people of color (BIPOC), 73
Black professors, 75
Black students, 27
Boeckenstedt, Jon, 234–35
Bourdieu, Pierre, 4
Bricketto, Matthew, 76
brooding intellect, 223
Brown, Timothy, 75
Brunson, Delores, 104, 106
built-up triple, in dormitory, 51
business cards, 135

265

CAC. *See* Central Arizona College
California State University (CSU), 147–48, 161–62
camp counselor, 99
career goals: during college, 38; first-generation students pursuing, 177; goal-setting of, 134; higher education with enjoyment of, 66; of Marshall, 183; mentorship influencing, 53; opportunities, 198; research-intensive programs for, 29; STEM courses in, 28–29
Carter, Diane, 104, 106
Cataldi, E. F., 15n4
CCP. *See* Community College of Philadelphia
Central Arizona College (CAC), 45
Check Us Out Day, 77
cheerleaders, families as, 129
Chen, X., 15n4
Christianity, 123
church community, 54
Clark, Kallie, 160; advice from, 164–65; college experiences of, 161–62; college preparation of, 161; college success contributions for, 162–63; families' role in college of, 163–64
classism, 3, 5–6, 187, 227
classrooms, 46, 95, 121–22, 241–45
clinical psychology, 3–4
Cobb, J., 64
code-switching, 188
college campus: classroom seating on, 95, 121–22; community feeling on, 149–50, 171; diversity on, 84; first-generation students' contributions to, 56; meal plan at, 60; student involvement on, 122–23, 182; students visiting, 40
College Career Center, 27
college courses, 173
college degrees, 1; bachelors, 132; parents instilling desire for, 26; requirements for, 5, 52; as worth attaining, 21
college experiences: of Ardoin, 127–28; of Clark, 161–62; of Cortez, 196; of Edwards, 28–30; of Erb, 51–55; of Harris, P., 89–90; of Hernández, 94–95; of Hill, 200–202; of Hughes, G. B., 105–6; of Ibarra, 207–8; of Inez, 137–38; involvement in, 102, 182; of Jones, 168–69; of Lieurance, 99–100; of Luna, 45–47; of Marshall, 184–85; of Martinez, 34–37; of Menjívar, 154–56; of Montoya, 110–11; of Morales, 148–49; of Nguyen, 174–75; of Pepin, 68–69; of Richardson, K., 132–33; of Richardson, S., 179–80; of Santaniello, 63–65; of Santa-Ramirez, 74–76; of Shambry, 190–91; of Stewart, 115–17; of Vargas, 22–23; of Vega, 40–41; of Winston, 58–59; of Wright, K., 121–23
college graduates, success of, 195
college preparations: of Ardoin, 126–27; of Clark, 161; of Cortez, 194–95; of Edwards, 27–28; of Erb, 50–51; of first-generation students, 215–17; of Harris, P., 88–89; of Hernández, 93–94; of Hill, 199–200; of Hughes, G. B., 104–5; of Ibarra, 205–6; of Inez, 136–37; of Jones, 167–68; of Lieurance, 98–99; of Luna, 44–45; of Marshall, 184; of Martinez, 33–34; of Menjívar, 153–54; of Montoya, 109–10; of Morales, 147–48; of Nguyen, 172–74; of Pepin, 67–68; of Richardson, K., 131–32; of Richardson, S., 178–79; of Santaniello, 62–63; of Santa-Ramirez, 73–74; of Shambry, 190; of Stewart, 114–15; student information on, 43; of Vargas, 21–22; of Vega, 40; of Winston, 57–58; of Wright, K., 120–21
colleges/universities: acceptance letter for, 22; administration's oppressive models in, 8; admissions process of, 234–35; application process of, 115; asking for help in, 224; belonging in, 101; Black students' enrollment in, 27; book listing, 110; campus meal plan at, 60; career goals while at, 38; class size in, 46; compatibility in, 97; counseling services in, 226–27; cultural capital of, 4–7; discrimination at, 94–95; expenses for, 116–17; failure acceptance at, 175–76; first-generation students' transition to, 246–47; GPAs for, 136–37; happiness from, 139; inequities and injustices in, 231; information on, 167–68; isolation feeling in, 84, 132; medium and large, 5; motivation to go to, 189–90; norms and standards of, 5–6; oppressive models of, 8; orientation sessions of, 121; preparatory academy for, 120; preparatory programs for, 178–79; problem solutions in, 140–41; professional networking in, 83–84; resources available from, 118, 216–17; semester planning for, 208; shopping period for, 158; social aspects of, 12–13; strength-based perspective of, 3–4; struggles at, 174–75; support services of, 245–46; system failing students of, 15; transitioning to, 127; transportation at, 52; types of, 167; unprepared for, 207; upward mobility costs and, 221. *See also* higher education
college tuition: financial aid for, 15–16; parents and, 52; Pell grant for, 53, 187; resident assistant paying for, 52–53; scholarships for, 41

communications, 18, 108, 176–77
community: church, 54; college, 13, 115–16, 201; college campus with feeling of, 149–50, 171; mental health services in, 227; service, 91; students building, 219; students missing feeling of, 23
Community College of Philadelphia, 74
compatibility, 97
competence, 232
computer science, 69
concerted cultivation, 224
confusion, application process, 216
Congreso de Latinos Unidos, 73–74
continuing-generation students, 3; guidance received by, 9; standardized tests favoring, 234–35
corporate scholarships, 51
Cortez, Raquel Gutierrez: advice from, 197–98; college experiences of, 196; college preparation of, 194–95; college success contributions for, 196–97; families' role in college of, 197
Coser, Lewis A., 64
counseling services, 226–27, 238–39
coursework, 18, 100
COVID-19 pandemic, 103, 234
critical race theory, 73
CSS Profile, 187
CSU. *See* California State University
cultural capital, 4–7, 78, 211, 221, 245–46
culture shock, 217–18, 221, 233
curiosity, 213
Cynn, Christine, 106

DACA. *See* Deferred Action for Childhood Arrivals
Davis, J., 2
debt, from student loans, 196, 198
decision-making process, 40
Deferred Action for Childhood Arrivals (DACA), 152–57
depression, 84; from financial stress, 168–69; GPAs influenced by, 154–55; guidance counselor and, 169; loneliness causing, 212; mental health services for, 212, 238; undiagnosed, 154
DeVestern, Diane, 76
didactic training, 233
discrimination: in college, 94–95; fears of, 33; of marginalized groups, 175; prejudices and, 236
diversity, 84, 240
dormitory: built-up triple in, 51; moving into, 200–201; residence hall and, 122, 236; roommate assignment in, 58, 90

Downing, Jerry, 223
Dress for Success Wednesdays, 91
Drexel University, 133

early intervention, 233–34
Educational Opportunity Fund (EOF), 191–92
Edwards, Jeremy, 26; advice from, 31; college experiences of, 28–30; college preparation by, 27–28; scholarships received by, 27; success contributions for, 30
emotional support, 70
emotions, 80
encouragement, 38, 42, 112, 156, 191
engineering studies, 175
English as a Second Language (ESL), 172–73
English major, 116, 180
EOF. *See* Educational Opportunity Fund
Erb, Maria Dykema: advice from, 55–56; college experiences of, 51–55; college preparations by, 50–51; college success contributions for, 53; as undergraduate student, 50
ESL. *See* English as a Second Language
essay writing, 162
ethnic minorities, 2–3
Everglades National Park, 58
exam anxiety, 36
expenses, for college, 116–17
exploration, 213
extracurricular activities, 34, 123

faculty, 245–46
failure acceptance, 175–76
families: Ardoin's college success role of, 129; as cheerleaders, 129; Clark's college success role of, 163–64; Cortez's college success for of, 197; financial aid and limitations of, 110; first-generation students' college success of, 220; hardships of, 48; Harris, P., college success role of, 91–92; Hill's college success role of, 203; Hughes, G. B., college success role of, 106–7; Ibarra's college success role of, 209; Inez's college success role of, 138–39; Jones's college success role of, 170–71; Lieurance's college success role of, 101; Luna's college success role of, 48; Marshall's college success role of, 186–87; Martinez's college success role of, 37; Menjívar's college success role of, 157–58; Montoya's college success role of, 112; Morales's college success role of, 150; Nguyen's college success role of, 176; Pepin's college success role of, 70; Richardson, K., college success role of, 134; Richardson, S., college success role of,

181–82; Santaniello's college success role of, 66; Santa-Ramirez's college success role of, 77; Shambry's college success role of, 192; Stewart's college success role of, 118; student success role of, 9–10, 37, 54–55; value of, 23–24; Vargas's college success role of, 24; Vega's college success role of, 42; Winston's college success role of, 60; working-class, 3; Wright, K., college success role of, 123–24. *See also* parents

family values, 239

fears, of first-generation students, 164–65

feelings, from experiences, 79–80

FGLI. *See* first-generation/low-income students

financial aid, 46; in application process, 206, 235–36; applying for, 94; assistance with, 235–36; for college tuition, 15–16; families' limitations and, 110; forms, 115; guidance counselor questions for, 133–34; immigration status influencing, 153; scholarships and, 52, 195, 200; SSSP advice on, 169; student loans and, 195, 198; through VIPS, 27–28; workshop, 120–21; work-study funding in, 59

financial hardships, 10

financial stress, 66, 168–69

financial support, 96

First Cats program, 39

first-generation/low-income (FGLI) students, 206–7, 217, 240

first-generation students: academic advising for, 237; academic experiences of, 12; admissions process for, 234–35; advice for, 225; asking for help, 38, 48, 78, 119, 124, 129–30, 204, 219; campus community contributions of, 56; campus meal plan for, 60; career path pursued by, 177; challenges facing, 1–2; college campus contributions of, 56; college preparations of, 215–17; college success contributors for, 218–20; college transition of, 246–47; competence of, 232; as contributors, 8–10; cultural capital of, 4–7; defining, 2–4; disadvantages of, 9; diversity and, 240; early intervention for, 233–34; experiences of, 2; families' role in college of, 220; family values struggles of, 239; fears of, 164–65; guidance counselors for, 173–74; inequities faced by, 17–18, 134; institutional services to, 232–33; isolation of, 16, 43; mental health services for, 238–39; mentoring for, 25, 237–38; models of, 229; networks needed by, 31; new culture experienced by, 217–18, 221; numbers decreasing of, 15n4; outsider feeling of, 7; as overwhelmed, 13; parental support for, 236; performance of, 4; personal essays from, 7; pre-SAT for, 173; religious parents of, 55; self-identity for, 24–25, 219; self-reflection by, 14; social aspects of, 12–13; standardized test results of, 17–18; strengths of, 14–16; struggles of, 211; success contributions for, 218–20; themes interconnecting, 10–12, *11–12*; tutoring services benefiting, 236; welcome packets of, 234; work ethic of, 10; work schedule flexibility for, 47

Fleming, Kim, 242

foreign country, 222

Foster, Gaines, 127

framing, 188

Frankl, Viktor, 63–64

Franklin Learning Center High School, 73

freshman year, 41

Friar Foundations, 179, 181

friendships, 23–24, 46–47, 83, 143, 162

full-time jobs, 64–65, 196

Gaining Early Awareness and Readiness for Undergraduate Programs (GearUp), 98

Gans, Herbert J., 64

Gay, Georgia, 88–89

GearUp. *See* Gaining Early Awareness and Readiness for Undergraduate Programs

geology class, 46

global leadership, 209

goals. *See* career goals

Gonzalez, C. G., 5

GPAs: academic challenges influencing, 28–30, 51; for college, 136–37; depression influencing, 154–55; high school, 161; of high school students, 17–18; requirements for, 45–46; for scholarships, 126, 128, 198; semester, 64; student scores for, 111

graduate-level courses, 39, 192

graduate programs, 76

graduation, high school, 199–200

Green, Jack J., 106

guidance counselors, 57, 110; application process and, 195; continuing-generation students receiving, 9; depression and, 169; financial aid questions for, 133–34; for first-generation students, 173–74; minorities experience of, 181; relationships, 156; weaknesses identified with, 196

Hail Mary, 154

handwriting ritual, 118

happiness, from college, 139

hardships, of families, 48
Harris, A. P., 5
Harris, Patricia, 87; advice from, 92; college experiences of, 89–90; college preparation of, 88–89; college success contribution for, 90–91; families' role in college of, 91–92
HBCU. *See* historically Black college and universities
health insurance, 227
Health Policy Studies, 160
Hernández, David, 215–16, 218; advice from, 96–97; college experiences of, 94–95; college preparation of, 93–94; college success contributions for, 95–96; families' role in college for, 96
HESA. *See* higher education and student affairs
The Hidden Injuries of Class (Sennett and Cobb), 64
higher education: access to, 15; ask for help in, 96; career enjoyment from, 66; importance of, 34; national investment in, 241; parental gap from, 228; pride in, 130; school loans for, 15–16; skepticism of, 94; social mobility from, 88–89; structural inequities in, 30; student recruitment for, 126–27; systemic issues in, 27; systemic underfunding of, 205–6; undergraduate, 50, 111, 133, 137–38, 184–85
higher education and student affairs (HESA), 72–73, 77–78
high school: counselors, 137; GPAs, 161; graduation, 199–200; public, 5
high school students: GPAs of, 17–18; scholarship information for, 43; at SLU, 58; work ethic developed by, 69
Hill, Karen: advice from, 203–4; college experiences of, 200–202; college preparations of, 199–200; college success contributions for, 202–3; families' role in college of, 203
historically Black college and universities (HBCU), 87–88
Hoffman, M., 235
HOPE Scholarship, 89
hospitality management, 50
Hotel Administration Department, 51
Howard, Angela, 76
Hughes, Gary C., 106
Hughes, Glynis Boyd: advice from, 107–8; college experiences of, 105–6; college preparation of, 104–5; college success contributions for, 106; families' role in college for, 106–7; poverty experienced by, 103–4

Ibarra, Henry Rosas: advice from, 209–10; college experiences of, 207–8; college preparation of, 205–6; college success contributions for, 208–9; families' role in college of, 209
identity, crisis of, 24–25, 123, 239
immigration, 152–55
imposter syndrome, 39; Inez with feelings of, 138; Lieurance experiencing, 99, 105; Marshall with feelings of, 185; Martinez with feelings of, 38; students experiencing, 56; Vargas experiencing, 22–23; Wright, K., experiencing, 121
The Inequality Machine (Tough), 143
inequities: in college, 231; first-generation students facing, 17–18, 134; in higher education, 30
Inez, Emilee Claire: advice from, 139; college experiences of, 137–38; college preparation of, 136–37; college success contributions for, 138; families' role in college of, 138–39; imposter syndrome feelings of, 138
information: agent of, 80; on colleges, 167–68; from questions, 80–81; seminar, 6–7; for students, 43; welcome packets of, 234
insecurities, of students, 35
institutional services, 232–33
intellect, brooding, 223
internet search, 43
introspection, 14
investments, in higher education, 241
Isaiah (college student), 144
isolation: college feeling of, 84, 132; of first-generation students, 16, 43; loneliness and, 216; mental health services for, 238

Jack, A. A., 83, 223, 230
job talk, 240n1
Jones, Dawna, 166; advice from, 171; college experiences of, 168–69; college preparation of, 167–68; college success contributions for, 169–70; families' role in college of, 170–71
The Journey before us (Nichols), 9n3

Kaplan prep, 173
Kharem, Audrey, 169

Lambda Alpha Upsilon Fraternity (LAU), 75
Lareau, A., 223
large-sized colleges, 5
LASA. *See* Latin American Student Association
LASO. *See* Latin American Student Organization
Latin American Student Association (LASA), 23

Latin American Student Organization (LASO), 74–75
LAU. *See* Lambda Alpha Upsilon Fraternity
Laude, David, 246–47
leadership, 42
learning process, 95, 125
Lechner, Andrew, 59–60
Legacy of Leadership Award, 77
legal studies program, 131
Legette, Karima, 42
letters of recommendation, 60
Lewis & Clark College, 1
LGBTQ women, 239
liberal arts college, 117, 183, 185
Lieurance, Jenny: advice from, 101–2; college experiences of, 99–100; college preparations of, 98–99; college success contributions for, 100; families' role in college of, 101; imposter syndrome experienced by, 99, 105
Limbo (Lubrano), 50
listening, to students, 232
living situation, 41
loneliness, 42–43; depression caused by, 212; isolation and, 216; mental health services for, 238
Longwell-Grice, R., 3, 235
Louisiana State University (LSU), 126
low-income backgrounds, 41, 181
LSU. *See* Louisiana State University
Lubrano, Alfred, 50
Luna, Yvonne M.: advice from, 48–49; college experiences of, 45–47; college preparation by, 44–45; college success contributions for, 47; families' role in college success of, 48

Mangum, Bryant, 106
Man's Search for Meaning (Frankl), 63–64
marginalized groups, 16, 84, 175
Marshall, Adj: advice from, 187–88; career path of, 183; college experiences of, 184–85; college preparation of, 184; college success contributions for, 186; families' role in college of, 186–87; imposter syndrome feelings of, 185
Martinez, Ivonne: advice from, 38; college experiences of, 34–37; college preparations by, 33–34; exam anxiety of, 36; families' role in college success of, 37; imposter syndrome feelings of, 38; success contributions for, 37
Mary Lou Williams Center for Black Culture, 166
Mas Flow Dance Team, 75
master's program, 133
McKinney, Marion, 76

McNair Scholars program, 42
meal plan, 60
medium-sized colleges, 5
Menjívar, Mayra González: advice from, 158–59; college experiences of, 154–56; college preparation of, 153–54; college success contributions for, 156–57; DACA and, 152; families' role in college of, 157–58
mental health, 144–45; community services for, 227; depression in, 212, 238; psychotherapy for, 196–97, 219, 226; services for, 238–39
mentoring: career goals influenced by, 53; emotional support and, 70; for first-generation students, 25, 237–38; through McNair Scholars program, 42; for students, 56, 149; VIPS providing, 27–28
Mickens, Kendrick, 76
microaggressions, 144
Miller, Amy, 74
Miller, Zell, 89
minorities, 2–3, 21, 41, 181, 197
Minority Hoteliers Conference, 55
Montoya, T. Mark: advice from, 112–13; college experiences of, 110–11; college preparations of, 109–10; college success contributions for, 111–12; families' role in college of, 112
Morales, Ulises: advice from, 150–51; college experiences of, 148–49; college preparation of, 147–48; college success contributions for, 149–50; families' role in college for, 150
Morton, Jennifer M., 214, 221, 238
motivation, for college, 189–90
Moving Up Without Losing Your Way (Morton), 214, 238
multicultural affairs, 55

National Society of Black Engineers (NSBE), 29
Natural History of the Vertebrates, 58
NAU. *See* Northern Arizona University
neoliberal ideology, 5
networking: business cards for, 135; colleges/universities with professional, 83–84; first-generation students needing, 31; student government committees for, 128; for support, 176–77
never give up, 38
New Mexico State University, 110
New York City police, 62
New York University (NYU), 153, 155–57
Nguyen, Mytien: advice from, 176–77; college experiences of, 174–75; college preparation of, 172–74; college success contributions for, 175–76; families' role in college of, 176

Nichols, L., 9n3
nontraditional students, 201
Northern Arizona University (NAU), 44, 121
NSBE. *See* National Society of Black Engineers
Nunn, L. M., 10, 241
NYU. *See* New York University

Office of Residence Life (reslife), 122
office space, of professors, 101–2
Ogden, Thomas, 213
one-on-one meetings, 35
opportunities, 108
oppressive models, 8
organizational strategic planning, 208
orientation sessions, 121
outsider within, 7

paralegal program, 45
Parent Plus loan, 195
parents: advice for, 227–28; college degree desire instilled by, 26; college tuition and, 52; first-generation students supported by, 236; first-generation students with religious, 55; higher education causing gap with, 228; student support from, 54; supportive, 138–39
patience, 38
PC. *See* Phoenix College
peer mentors, 237–38
Pell grant, 53, 187
Pennsylvania State University (PSU), 168
Pepin, Lynn: advice from, 70–71; college experiences of, 68–69; college preparation by, 67–68; college success contributions of, 69; families' role in college of, 70
perseverance, 48, 228–29
personal essays, 7
personal lives, 33
person of color, 240
PhD dissertations, 29
PhD programs, 30, 119, 172
Phoenix College (PC), 45–46
Pine Manor College, 231
political consulting firm, 206
political science class, 46
postsecondary education, 1–2, 5
poverty, 103–4
PowerPoint, 240n1
practicum, 6
prejudices, 236
preparatory academy, 120
preparatory programs, 178–79
prerequisite courses, of students, 28
pride, in higher education, 130
private education, 195

The Privileged Poor (Jack), 230
proactive advising, 237
problem solutions, 140–41
professors: Black, 75; office space of, 101–2; one-on-one meetings with, 35; person of color and, 240; students impacted by, 44, 157; student support from, 47; teaching process of, 35
Providence College, 179
PSAT scores, 184
PSU. *See* Pennsylvania State University
psychological history, 144–45
psychology: clinical, 3–4; degree, 1; program, 39; student experiences and, 13; student's history of, 144–45
psychotherapy, 196–97, 213, 219, 226–27
public high schools, 5
Public Loan Forgiveness Program, 198

questions, information from, 80–81

racial minorities, 3
racism, 3, 5–6, 62, 74, 172, 218
realism, 203
rejection, 108, 229
relationships: guidance counselor, 156; networking for, 83–84; psychotherapist, 226–27; questions about, 141
religious identity, 54
representation, 239–40
research-intensive programs, 29
residence hall, 77, 122, 236
Residence Hall Association, 23
resident assistant, 52–53
reslife. *See* Office of Residence Life
resources: asking for help and, 171; colleges with available, 118, 216–17; finding, 182
Reynolds Community College, 104
Rhode Island College, 178
Richardson, Kamina P.: advice from, 134–35; college experiences of, 132–33; college preparation of, 131–32; college success contributions for, 133–34; families' role in college of, 134
Richardson, Sean: advice from, 182; college experiences of, 179–80; college preparation of, 178–79; college success contributions for, 180–81; families' role in college of, 181–82
Ronald E. McNair Post-Baccalaureate Achievement Program, 29
roommate assignment, 58, 90

Sacramento State University, 161
Saint Louis University (SLU), 57–58
San Francisco State University (SFSU), 1, 13

Santaniello, Mike: advice from, 66; college experiences of, 63–65; college preparation by, 62–63; college success contributions for, 65–66; families' role in college success of, 66

Santa-Ramirez, Stephen, 25; advice from, 77–78; college experiences of, 74–76; college preparations by, 73–74; college success contributions for, 76–77; families' role in college success of, 77; HESA experiences of, 72–73

SAT scores, 17, 34, 161, 173

Savannah State University (SSU), 87, 90–91

scholarships, 27, 73; applying for, 200; for college tuition, 41; corporate, 51; financial aid and, 52, 195, 200; finding out about, 134; GPAs for, 126, 128, 198; high school students with information on, 43; for UConn, 68; workshops for, 198

School of The Art Institute, 160

self-awareness, 80, 191, 212, 227

self-criticism, 231

self-development, 185

self-doubt, 116

self-esteem, 118

self-identity, 24–25, 219

self-preservation, 70–71, 78, 176

self-reflection, 14, 208

semester planning, 208

Sennett, R., 64

sexism, 5–6, 62, 227, 240

SFSU. *See* San Francisco State University

Shambry, Clifton E.: advice from, 192–93; college experiences of, 190–91; college motivation of, 189–90; college preparations of, 190; college success contributions for, 191–92; families' role in college of, 192

shame, 211

Sharpe, Shannon, 92

shopping period, for colleges, 158

SLU. *See* Saint Louis University

Smith, R. Dale, 106

social justice, 12–13, 233

social media, 242

social mobility, 88–89

social sciences, 214

social studies teacher, 63

social work, 105

sociology major, 28, 44, 62

sophomore year, 29

Spencer, Andrew, 106

SSS. *See* Student Support Services

SSSP. *See* Student Support Services Program

SSU. *See* Savannah State University

standardized tests, 17–18, 119, 234–35

Stannard-Friel, Don, 197

State University of New York (SUNY), 40

STEM courses, 28–29, 37

Stewart, Joyce: advice from, 118–19; college experiences of, 115–17; college preparation of, 114–15; college success contributions for, 117–18; families' role in college of, 118; self-doubt of, 116

Strategies for Success, 112

strength-based perspective, 3–4

stress, from application process, 200

structural inequities, 30

student government committees, 128

student loans, 41; debt from, 196, 198; financial aid and, 195, 198; for higher education, 15–16

student ministry organizations, 55

students: academic services for, 162; asking for help, 102; biases faced by, 6–7; Black, 27; campuses visited by, 40; college applications of, 9, 94; college campus involvement of, 122–23, 182; college preparation information for, 43; community building by, 219; community feeling missed by, 23; continuing-generation, 3, 9, 234–35; engagement of, 166; faculty and struggles of, 245–46; families' role in success of, 9–10, 37, 54–55; FGLI, 206–7, 217, 240; full-time jobs of, 64–65; GPA scores of, 111; higher education recruiting, 126–27; high school, 17–18, 43, 58, 69; imposter syndrome experienced by, 56; insecurities of, 35; listening to, 232; from low-income backgrounds, 41; mentorships for, 56, 149; nontraditional, 201; parents supporting, 54; prerequisite courses of, 28; professors impacting, 44, 157; professors supporting, 47; psychological experiences of, 13; psychological history of, 144–45; self-preservation by, 70–71; study strategies of, 51; support system needed by, 37; system failing, 15; writing skills of, 18. *See also* first-generation students

Student Support Services (SSS), 123, 201–2

Student Support Services Program (SSSP), 169

study groups, 36, 47

studying abroad, 55–56, 186

study strategies, 51

success: academics with achieving, 30–31; Ardoin getting contributions for, 128–29; Clark getting contributions for, 162–63; college graduates having, 195; Cortez getting contributions for, 196–97; Edwards getting contributions for, 30; Erb getting

contributions for, 53; families' role in college, 9–10, 37, 54–55; first-generation students getting contributors for, 218–20; Harris, P., getting contribution for, 90–91; Hernández getting contributions for, 95–96; Hill getting contributions for, 202–3; Hughes, G. B., getting contributions for, 106; Ibarra getting contributions for, 208–9; Inez getting contributions for, 138; Jones getting contributions for, 169–70; Lieurance getting contributions for, 100; Luna getting contributions for, 47; Marshall getting contributions for, 186; Martinez getting contributions for, 37; Menjívar getting contributions for, 156–57; Montoya getting contributions for, 111–12; Morales getting contributions for, 149–50; Nguyen getting contributions for, 175–76; Pepin getting contributions for, 69; Richardson, K., getting contributions for, 133–34; Richardson, S., getting contributions for, 180–81; Santaniello getting contributions for, 65–66; Santa-Ramirez getting contributions for, 76–77; Shambry getting contributions for, 191–92; Stewart getting contributions for, 117–18; Vargas getting contributions for, 23–24; Vega getting contributions for, 41–42; Winston getting contributions for, 59–60; Wright, K., getting contributions for, 123
SUCCESS acronym, 112
SUNY. *See* State University of New York
support network, 176–77
support services, 245–46
support system, 37, 101
Suttles, Gerald, 64
Swecker, H. K., 237
syllabus, 242, 243–44
systemic issues, 27

Taylor, Toni, 53
teachers, 125, 160
teaching assistants, 210
teaching process, 35
Texas Interdisciplinary Plan, 246–47
theoretical training, 231–33
13-week plan, 29
Thrive Center, 39
time management, 59
top 10% law, 34
Tough, Paul, 143
transportation, 52, 115
trauma bonding, 210
trauma porn, 235

traveling, 60–61, 222
Treisman, Phillip Uri, 34–36, 245
TRIO group, 98, 149, 201–2, 228
Trump, Donald, 155
tutoring services, 236

UC. *See* University of California
UCLA. *See* University of California, Los Angeles
UConn. *See* University of Connecticut
underfunding, of higher education, 205–6
undergraduate education, 50, 111, 133, 137–38, 184–85
undiagnosed depression, 154
Unequal Childhoods (Lareau), 223
UNH. *See* University of New Hampshire
United States Citizenship and Immigration Services, 152
University of Arizona, 39
University of California (UC), 13
University of California, Los Angeles (UCLA), 27, 29
University of Connecticut (UConn), 67–68
University of New Hampshire (UNH), 51, 55
University of North Carolina, 87
University of Southern California (USC), 200
University of Texas, Austin, 37
University of Vermont, 53, 173–74
University of Wyoming (UW), 114, 136
unpaid internship, 6
Upward Bound, 178–79, 181
upward mobility, 211, 221, 228–29
urban dictionary, 87
USC. *See* University of Southern California
UW. *See* University of Wyoming

Vargas, Anthony: acceptance letter received by, 22; advice from, 24–25; college experiences of, 22–23; college preparation by, 21–22; college success contributions for, 23–24; families' role in college success of, 24; imposter syndrome experiences of, 22–23
VCU. *See* Virginia Commonwealth University
Vega, Desireé: advice from, 42–43; college experiences of, 40–41; college preparation by, 40; college success contributions for, 41–42; families' role in college success of, 42; graduate-level courses of, 39
Vice Provost Initiative for Pre-College Scholars (VIPS), 27–28
Virginia Commonwealth University (VCU), 103, 105
vulnerability, 49

Washburn University, 98
Washington Heights Expeditionary Learning School (WHEELS), 21
WCU. *See* West Chester University of Pennsylvania
Weber, S., 231
welcome packets, 234
welfare, 94
West Chester University of Pennsylvania (WCU), 74–75
"What I Would Not Part With" (Ogden), 213
WHEELS. *See* Washington Heights Expeditionary Learning School
White, Meg, 163
Winston, David: advice from, 60–61; college experiences of, 58–59; college preparation by, 57–58; college success contributions for, 59–60; families' role in college success of, 60
Winterer, Erica, 35–36
work ethic, 10, 69
working-class families, 3
work schedule, 47
work-study programs, 53, 59
Wright, Kevin: advice from, 124; college experiences of, 121–23; college preparation of, 120–21; college success contributions for, 123; families' role in college of, 123–24; imposter syndrome experienced by, 121
Wright, Richard, 91
writing skills, 18

Yale School of Medicine, 172
Yale University, 206–9

About the Contributors

Sonja Ardoin, PhD, is a learner, educator, facilitator, and author. Proud of her rural hometown of Vidrine, Louisiana, her working-class Cajun roots, and her first-generation college student-to-PhD journey, Sonja holds degrees from Louisiana State University, Florida State, and North Carolina State. She considers herself a scholar-practitioner of higher education; she served as an administrator for 10 years before shifting to the faculty in 2015. Sonja studies social class identity, college access and success for rural and first-generation college students, student and women's leadership, and career preparation and pathways in higher education and student affairs. Sonja has published four books and numerous book chapters and journal articles. She stays engaged in the broader field through the American College Personnel Association, the Association of Fraternal Leadership and Values, the Association for the Study of Higher Education, the Center for First-Generation Student Success, the National Association of Student Personnel Administrators, and several journal editorial boards. She enjoys books, traveling, music, sports, laughing, and spending time with her husband and pup. Learn more about Sonja's work at www.sonjaardoin.com.

Glynis Boyd Hughes is a recent MEd graduate of Merrimack College and delights in using her social justice–based education daily. She is currently a grant writer and storyteller for Ahsek Innovation. She is finding that meaningful work and purpose can go hand in hand. She is actively involved in community work in her hometown of Richmond, Virginia, and hopes her efforts will encourage others to find their place in "being the change they wish to see." Glynis is a fan of all things purple, puppies, and listening to elders tell their life stories. She welcomes hearing from students and can be reached at glynisboydhughes@gmail.com.

Kallie Clark, PhD, is a researcher with University of California San Francisco's Philip R. Lee Institute for Health Policy Studies. Kallie's research focuses on evaluating interventions aimed at reducing disparities in education, health, and basic needs such as food and housing. Kallie's research has been featured in numerous news outlets such as the *New York Times*, *Forbes*, the *Washington Post*, and *Inside Higher Ed*. Kallie lives in Sacramento, California, with her wife and two children.

Maria Dykema Erb, MEd, is the inaugural director of the Newbury Center, which was established to foster the success of first-generation undergraduate, graduate, and professional students at Boston University. Prior to joining Boston University, Maria had a 3-decade career in higher education and student affairs at the University of Vermont, Elon University, and Duke University. Most recently, she served as co-director of diversity and student success in the graduate school at the University of North Carolina at Chapel Hill, where she established multiple diversity and inclusion initiatives at the graduate education level, including the Carolina Grad Student F1RSTS for first-generation graduate and professional students. As a proud first-generation graduate, she has a BS from the University of New Hampshire and an MEd in interdisciplinary studies from the University of Vermont. Email Maria at mariadykemerb@gmail.com.

Jeremy Edwards, PhD, is a lecturer for the Program in Writing and Rhetoric at Stanford University. He earned his MA and PhD in education from University of California Santa Barbara with an emphasis in human development and cultural studies and his BA in psychology at University of California, Los Angeles. Dr. Edwards's research centers on the Black experience in areas of higher education. Through a critical race lens, his work examines higher education practices and policies that impact Black student experiences and identifies relationships between Black students and university spaces. As an education instructor and researcher at the university level, his work fights for more inclusivity in course curriculum and campus-wide support networks.

Mayra González Menjívar is a communications professional who has worked in the education advocacy field for 3 years. She has written talking points and speeches for a former secretary of education from the Obama administration. She has also written and talked about her journey as a DACA recipient in op-eds, interviews, and speeches. She and her parents immigrated to the United States from El Salvador in 2001, when she was just 4 years old. She was raised on the east end of Long Island and currently resides in Brooklyn, New York. She holds a BS in media, culture, and communications from New York University.

Raquel Gutierrez Cortez, MSMFT, MSCP, has dedicated her career to assisting neurodiverse individuals grow to their full potential. Previously, she was a clinician in substance abuse treatment and a service coordinator at San Andreas Regional Center in Northern California. She is currently a stay-at-home mom while developing a startup consulting agency serving individuals with neuro and developmental differences.

Patricia Harris earned a bachelor's degree in sociology from Savannah State University and obtained a master's degree in counseling from Argosy University. She is currently pursuing a doctorate degree in higher education management from the University of Georgia, where she studied comparative higher education in both Europe and China. In 2019, she completed the Women in Education program at Harvard University. Patricia has close to 20 years of experience in higher education. She currently serves as the senior director of recruitment for education, operations, and initiatives in the Office for Diversity and Inclusion at the University of North Carolina at Chapel Hill. Patricia is the owner and principal consultant for IKnowHigherEdu, LLC, an educational consulting company that specializes in helping first-generation students and families navigate through the college admission process. Throughout her career, she has been committed to equity, college access, and improving outcomes for students from historically underrepresented populations. Connect with Patricia on LinkedIn: https://www.linkedin.com/in/patriciaharrisiknowhigheredu.

David Hernández, PhD, grew up in Southern California, first in Cudahy and then in Whittier. He was raised with two brothers, mostly by a single mother with a large extended family nearby. He applied to one university and was accepted. He majored in business economics only to, years later, obtain a PhD in ethnic studies. He is now a tenured professor at Mount Holyoke College. Email David at dhernand@mtholyoke.edu.

Karen Hill (she/her) received an AA in general studies and an AS in respiratory care from El Camino College. She also received a BA in psychology from California State University, Dominguez Hills. Karen will earn an MS in counseling with an option in student development in higher education from California State University, Long Beach in May 2022. Her educational journey has been very nonlinear. It took her three universities, half a dozen community colleges, and 26 years to earn her BA degree. Now she advocates for and supports college students in higher education. She recently took a leap of faith and left her full-time position at a 4-year university to gain more experience in the California Community College system. Karen hopes to help more students with multiple marginalized identities achieve their dream of earning a college degree. You can contact her on LinkedIn (www.linkedin.com/in/karen-hill-nufp) if you have any questions.

Dawna Jones is the director of the Mary Lou Williams Center for Black Culture at Duke University. Dawna has worked in higher education student affairs for nearly 15 years. She has worked in crisis and case management, housing and residential life, and multicultural and first-generation student support and engagement. Dawna is passionate about college access, civic engagement, and leadership development. Dawna holds degrees in sociology (BA), higher education management (MEd), and social work (MSW).

Emilee Claire Inez is a recent first-generation graduate from the University of Wyoming, where she studied animal and veterinary sciences concentrated in communication and food animal production. She grew up on the beaches of Southern California but since then has fallen in love with the mountains of Wyoming, where she lives today. Coming to college without a clue of what she wanted to do or who she was as a person was a daunting endeavor. Through the support and guidance of peers, mentors, and campus resources, she was able to find success in the unknown collegiate terrain. Emilee is now an admissions representative for University of Wyoming and is always looking for ways to help all students better navigate their college searches and experiences.

Jenny Lieurance is originally from Emporia, Kansas. She has one brother, one sister, and seven nieces and nephews. In May 2018, she received her BA in communication studies with a minor in poverty studies from Washburn University. Continuing her education, she received an MEd in higher education student affairs from the University of South Carolina in May 2020. Jenny uses her values of family, education, empathy, and social justice constantly in her daily life. She is currently the first-generation recruitment and retention specialist within the Center for Student Success and Retention at Washburn University. Jenny knows that a college education holds power—not only in the life of the student but in that of the student's family as well. In her free time, she loves spending time with her loved ones, swimming, playing card games, and traveling to new places to make new memories.

Yvonne M. Luna is a professor of sociology and associate vice provost for curriculum and assessment at Northern Arizona University and served as the chair of the Department of Sociology from 2016 to 2021. She is a 2018 graduate of the Harvard Management Development Program and recipient of the Outstanding Latino/a Faculty for Teaching and Service in Higher Education, an award of the Pete C. Garcia, Victoria Foundation. Yvonne is dedicated to student success and earned the 2019 College of Social and Behavioral Sciences' Teaching Innovation Award. Her recent publications center on teaching and learning and Deferred Action for Childhood Arrivals (DACA). Learn more about Yvonne at www.linkedin.com/in/yvonne-m-luna.

Adj Marshall is an equity, diversity, and inclusion trainer, writer, and advocate for socioeconomic equity with a focus on cross-class communication. Her work has been published in the collections *Teaching Economic Inequality and Capitalism in Contemporary America* and *At the Intersection: Understanding and Supporting First-Generation Students*. In 2012, Adj founded the First Gen Summit, the oldest cross-campus gathering of first-generation low-income college students, which she continues to lead today. Her experience growing up as a member of a chronically poor, and often homeless, single-parent family is what led her to this work. Adj earned her BA while supporting her brothers' pursuits of associate degrees. She holds her first MA in public humanities and cultural heritage from Brown University and her second in intercultural leadership and management from the School for International Training.

Ivonne Martinez was born in Piedras Negrad, Coahuila, Mexico. She immigrated to the United States with her family when she was 6 years old, where she was raised in San Antonio, Texas. Ivonne is a first-generation Latina working toward her master's degree in data science at Harvard University and is expected to graduate in May 2023. She is an advocate for Latinx in STEM as well as women in STEM. Ivonne hopes to be able to inspire many people like herself and help them accomplish their dreams. Email Ivonne at ivonneam0925@gmail.com or visit her on LinkedIn at www.linkedin.com/in/ivonneam.

T. Mark Montoya, PhD, is director and associate professor of ethnic studies at Northern Arizona University. A first-generation college student, Montoya attended New Mexico State University, where he received a BA in history and an MA in government. He moved to Arizona to pursue a PhD in political science at Northern Arizona University, which he completed with distinction in 2009. Montoya's scholarship centers broadly on the U.S.-Mexico borderlands, borderlands pedagogy, citizenship, ethnic studies, DACA, hip-hop, and first-generation student experiences. At Northern Arizona University, he is most involved with the First-Generation Learning Community, the Teaching Academy, and the Commission on Ethnic Diversity. Montoya also serves as president of the Association for Borderlands Studies and chair of the Northern Arizona Dream Fund. He is also on the editorial board of the *Journal of First-Generation Student Success* and is a CatalystFIRST speaker of the National Association of Student Personnel Administrators Center for First-Generation Student Success. Montoya's awards include the Northern Arizona University President's Distinguished Teaching Fellow (2022–2026 term), the "Government Department Star" of the College of Arts and Sciences at New Mexico State University (2020), the Victoria Foundation's Outstanding Latinx Faculty Service/Teaching in Arizona Higher Education Award (2019), the Northern Arizona University College of Social and Behavioral Sciences Teacher of the Year (2015), the Northern Arizona University Outstanding Advocate Award for First-Generation College Students (2013), and the Northern Arizona University President's Award for Ethnic Diversity (2012). He is most grateful for his partner, Katy, and to their dog, Maya. Online, he can be found by searching his full name and @TMarkM.

Ulises Morales, most commonly known as Uli, is a first-generation college graduate from Redwood City, California. He graduated in the spring of 2021 from California State University Monterey Bay with a bachelor's degree in business administration. His experiences in college led him to connect with a community of first-generation college students, and he discovered how to utilize his passions for the benefit of his community. He is currently an executive assistant and was working as a music marketing intern for Slay Sonics, bridging the gap between independent artists and new audiences. With a deep admiration for creative expression, he writes poetry and utilizes his abilities to uplift as many voices as he can. Visit Uli on Instagram at @ulitunes or email him at umorales@csumb.edu.

Mytien Nguyen is an MD/PhD candidate at Yale School of Medicine. She is a biracial Black-Vietnamese immigrant and a first-generation and low-income college student. She attended Burlington High School in Burlington, Vermont, then studied biological sciences and biological engineering at Cornell University. Since matriculating at Yale School of Medicine, Mytien has been deeply involved in advocating for visibility and access of first-generation and low-income students in medicine, founding the National First-Generation and/or Low-Income in Medicine Association (FGLIMed, fglimed.org). She is also an advocate for health equity and diversity in the physician workforce. Email Mytien at mtn29@cornell.edu.

Yolanda Norman, EdD, currently serves as CEO of FirstGenCollege Consulting. As a low-income, first-generation college student-athlete when she entered college, Dr. Norman often questioned her own journey toward a college education and daily fought the negative thoughts telling her she did not belong. Today she spends her time on campus and within the community championing strategies focused on successful student development, working nationally with organizations to help students aspire to and persist toward college graduation, and engaging with first-generation college graduate professionals helping to build strong leadership. Dr. Norman holds a doctor of education from the University of St. Thomas, a bachelor of science in journalism, a master of science in sports management and administration, and a master of education in counseling and college student personnel from the University of Southern Mississippi. Learn more about her work at MyFirstgenCollege.com and stay engaged with her online at @FirstGenCollege.

Lynn Pepin, BSE, is a computer scientist and current third-year PhD student with the University of Connecticut in Storrs. They grew up in New London County, Connecticut. Their early childhood interest in game development led them to pursue computer-aided drafting at Grasso Technical High School (2010–2014), then computer science and engineering at University of Connecticut (2014–2018). They love to learn, to teach and tutor on subjects in which they are knowledgeable, and are passionate about progressive movements and social justice activism.

Kamina Richardson, MSOD, was born and raised in Philadelphia. She studied business at Peirce College and organizational development and leadership at the Philadelphia College of Osteopathic Medicine under the psychology department. She proceeded to work in academia, providing students and faculty members with experiential learning methods, academic advising, and career counseling. She is passionate about life learning and is an autodidact who believes in learning everything about many subjects. With encouragement from friends, family, and colleagues, Kamina started a blog in 2015 that focuses on wealth inequality, American history, African American culture, discrimination, mental health, and poverty traps in this country. In her free time, she mentors high school students and consults on organizational behavior and diagnosing company concerns to presidents and executives in small companies. Kamina makes sure you are held accountable through quality learning, training, and emotional intelligence. She is currently the Legal Studies Department's assistant program director/prelaw advisor for the Fox School of Business at Temple University. As a prelaw advisor, she promotes leadership and networking while building a professional brand for law school or law-related careers. She can be reached at tulegalstudies@temple.edu.

Sean Richardson is from Pawtucket, Rhode Island, and graduated from Providence College in 2020, studying sociology and public and community service. He was involved in student government, residence life, and multicultural programming. He is currently a master's candidate in higher education at Boston College and is hoping to work in first-generation student support upon graduation. Email Sean at rich.sj8@gmail.com.

Adam J. Rodríguez, PsyD, is a first-generation college graduate and psychoanalytic psychologist in private practice. His pursuit of a college degree took him 15 years, spanning four community colleges, including Diablo Valley College in Pleasant Hill, California; two 4-year universities, including San Francisco State University, where he completed his bachelor's degree at the age of 32; and 4 years of graduate school at the Wright Institute in Berkeley, California, where he earned an MA and PsyD. In his practice and scholarly work, Dr. Rodríguez is interested in the study of first-generation college students, multiracial identities, the intersection of race/ethnicity and class, and the connections between music and clinical work. He is a board member of Psychotherapy Action Network, an organization that advocates for therapies of depth, insight, and relationship. Dr Rodríguez plays bass, loves the ocean and is probably getting another tattoo of a sea creature, and spends as much time with his son as his son will allow. As Common spoke, "Through eight-tracks, wax, CDs and tapes, I am music."

Henry Rosas Ibarra is a proud born and raised Arizonan and the son of immigrants from Durango, Mexico. He earned a bachelor's degree in ethnicity, race, and migration at Yale University. During his undergraduate career, he worked extensively to build programming for fellow first-generation and Latino students. Outside of this work, he danced with Yale's Baile Folklorico team for 3 years. Motivated by his upbringing under Arizona's immigration law SB 1070, he volunteered for his first political campaign at 14 and has since been passionately committed to improving Latino representation in politics and policy spaces. He currently works for Iconico Campaigns, a political consulting firm in Phoenix. Before joining Iconico, he served as a staff assistant for Congressman Ruben Gallego and was a Líderes Avanzando fellow with UnidosUS.

Mike Santaniello, PhD, is currently an adjunct professor of sociology at Adelphi University. He was a full-time professor for 25 years. He has been a college professor since 1985 and an adjunct professor at Adelphi since 1987. Dr. Mike was the first person in his extended family to attend college, earning a bachelor's degree in sociology at State University of New York at Stony Brook, two master's degrees in sociology at Columbia University, and a PhD in sociology, also at Columbia. Dr. Mike has studied working-class college students extensively, publishing his doctoral dissertation, *Beating the Odds: College Attenders and Nonattenders from the Working Class*, in 1995. More recently, Dr. Mike published *College Bound and Moving Up: Why Your Children Must Attend College, and How You Could Help*. He says that helping working students succeed against the odds is his life's work.

Stephen Santa-Ramirez, PhD, (he/him), says that his personal and professional experiences in higher education have played formative roles in developing his research agenda, which broadly investigates the ideological, historical, and structural inequalities that impact racially minoritized and migrant communities. Drawing on critical scholars who advance the lives and knowledge of minoritized and economically neglected communities—in addition to his own identities as a scholar-practitioner-advocate, first-generation collegian, and sexual nonmajority person of color—his scholarship aims to ensure liberation, inform theory, and create equitable higher education policies and practices.

Clifton E. Shambry Jr. is a first-generation, limited-income college graduate, raised on the East Coast. He attended 13 different schools in five states and the District of Columbia, spending most of his years in New Jersey. Clifton enjoys playing card and board games (especially spades), singing at church, and finding spots to sit, relax, read, and enjoy the outdoors. Clifton looks to work with folks to see how they are including social identities and how they shape one's life journey. Clifton's experiences have included academic enrichment, multicultural affairs, student engagement, student organization and leadership development, and career services with a focus on using design thinking to design one's life. He is an educator and advocate for affinity space, mentoring, and equitable experiences for all. If Clifton could tell his college self anything, he'd say be bold, be curious, and be you to the fullest.

Joyce Stewart has been a writing teacher for many years. She served as the director of first-year composition for 5 years at the University of Wyoming. Since 2003, she has taught in the Bridge program, a learning community for students admitted to the university with support. She is currently seeking her doctoral degree in education in curriculum and instruction with an emphasis on literacy education. Her research interests include multisensory multimodal composition and British girl comics.

Anthony Vargas, (he/him), is a student affairs professional currently fulfilling his duties as a full-time residence hall director at the University at Buffalo, located in New York. Vargas is in his final year of the higher education and student affairs master's program at the University at Buffalo. Vargas is a 4-year veteran of the United States Marine Corps Reserves, as well as an avid swimmer who has swam for over a decade, including internationally. Born to two immigrant parents from the Dominican Republic, he was born and raised in a very populated Latinx neighborhood located in Upper Manhattan, known as Washington Heights. Vargas loves to dance, listen to music, and watch his favorite movie: *In The Heights*. He can be reached at ajvargas@buffalo.edu.

Desireé Vega, PhD, is an associate professor in the School Psychology program at the University of Arizona. She completed her BA in psychology at State University of New York Binghamton University and her MA and PhD in school psychology at The Ohio State University. Dr. Vega worked as a school psychologist for the Omaha Public Schools district for 3 years prior to beginning her faculty career at Texas State University. Her research, teaching, and service intersect to focus on advancing the academic outcomes of culturally and linguistically minoritized students and preparing future school psychologists and researchers to engage in advocacy and implement culturally responsive practices. Dr. Vega's research focuses on three main areas: identifying best practices in the training of bilingual school psychologists; preparing culturally competent school psychologists; and advancing the educational success of African American, Latinx, and emergent bilingual youth. In 2021, she was awarded the Excellence in Graduate Teaching and Mentoring Award from the Graduate College at the University of Arizona and the New Leader Award from The Ohio State University. Dr. Vega was also named an Emerging Scholar by Diverse: Issues in Higher Education in 2017 and a Hispanic Serving Institution Fellow in 2019.

David Winston, MD, PhD, has been a forensic pathologist for 25 years. He is currently employed at the Pima County Office of the Medical Examiner in Tucson, Arizona. Dr. Winston's main responsibilities are to determine the cause and manner of death for persons whose death falls under the jurisdiction of the medical examiner as outlined by the Arizona Revised Statutes. Other duties include discussing autopsy findings with family members; meeting with attorneys and law enforcement regarding criminal and civil proceedings associated with these deaths; testifying in court; and teaching undergraduate, graduate, and medical students as well as pathology residents and forensic pathology fellows. In his spare time, he has collaborated with a colleague publishing a novel, *Crossing the Line*, under the pseudonym of A. L. Gomortis, which is available for download in many e-book stores. A second novel is forthcoming.

Kevin Wright, PhD, currently serves as a senior equity facilitator/consultant for the Center for Equity and Inclusion. Kevin is responsible for raising consciousness, building skills, and developing strategies to socialize and operationalize equity efforts throughout organizations. Wright's commitment to racial justice, equity, and inclusion is rooted in his approach with shifting cultures and processes one system at a time to advocate for individuals with historically marginalized identities. Feel free to connect with Dr. Wright at kevinwright2092@gmail.com or follow him on Twitter at @k_wright92.

www.ingramcontent.com/pod-product-compliance
Lightning Source LLC
Chambersburg PA
CBHW060231240426

43671CB00016B/2905